EU NEIGHBOURHOOD LAW

Brexit and the rekindling of the European Union enlargement talks require a reappraisal of the law of the EU's proximity policies. In that light, this book turns *Wider Europe* into an analytical concept to capture the legal and political facets of the extension of the EU's legal space in the Union's neighbourhood.

The book follows three lines of inquiry. Firstly, it reflects on the similarities and differences between internal and external integration, drawing a distinction between EU membership law and EU neighbourhood law. Secondly, it unravels the techniques for the extension of the EU's legal space across different partnerships in the Union's neighbourhood. Thirdly, it sheds light on the political covenants underlying the variety of institutional arrangements of the extended EU's legal space.

The book discusses how EU neighbourhood law entails a reconfiguration of how sovereignty is exercised both in the EU and in third countries participating in *Wider Europe*.

Volume 125 in the Series Modern Studies in European Law

Modern Studies in European Law

Recent titles in this series:

Exporting the European Convention on Human Rights
Maria-Louiza Deftou

Judicial Authority in EU Internal Market Law: Implications for the Balance of Competences and Powers
Vilija Velyvyte

The Changing European Union: A Critical View on the Role of Law and the Courts
Edited by Tamara Capeta, Iris Goldner Lang and Tamara Perisin

The Structural Transformation of European Private Law: A Critique of Juridical Hermeneutic
Leone Niglia

The Future of EU Constitutionalism
Edited by Matej Avbelj

The Changing Role of Citizens in EU Democratic Governance
Edited by Davor Jancic

The EU and the Baltic Sea Area
Edited by Allan Rosas and Henrik Ringbom

The Evolving Governance of EU Competition Law in a Time of Disruptions: A Constitutional Perspective
Edited by Carlo Maria Colombo, Kathryn Wright and Mariolina Eliantonio

The European Integrated Border Management: Frontex, Human Rights, and International Responsibility
Giulia Raimondo

Private Autonomy in EU Internal Market Law: Parameters of its Protection and Limitation
Rufat Babayev

Free Movement and Welfare Access in the European Union: Re-Balancing Conflicting Interests in Citizenship Jurisprudence
Victoria Hooton

EU Trade and Investment Treaty-Making Post-Lisbon: Moving Beyond Mixity
Gesa Kübek

The Normative Foundations for EU Criminal Justice: Powers, Limits and Justifications
Jacob Öberg

EU Neighbourhood Law: *Wider Europe* and the Extended EU's Legal Space
Alessandro Petti

For the complete list of titles in this series
see www.bloomsbury.com/uk/series/modern-studies-in-european-law/

EU Neighbourhood Law

Wider Europe *and the Extended EU's Legal Space*

Alessandro Petti

•HART•
OXFORD • LONDON • NEW YORK • NEW DELHI • SYDNEY

HART PUBLISHING

Bloomsbury Publishing Plc

Kemp House, Chawley Park, Cumnor Hill, Oxford, OX2 9PH, UK

1385 Broadway, New York, NY 10018, USA

Bloomsbury Publishing Ireland Limited, 29 Earlsfort Terrace, Dublin 2, D02 AY28, Ireland

HART PUBLISHING, the Hart/Stag logo, BLOOMSBURY and the Diana logo are trademarks of Bloomsbury Publishing Plc

First published in Great Britain 2024

A catalogue record for this book is available from the British Library.

A catalogue record for this book is available from the Library of Congress.

ISBN: HB: 978-1-50996-665-3
ePDF: 978-1-50996-667-7
ePub: 978-1-50996-666-0

Typeset by Compuscript Ltd, Shannon

For product safety related questions contact productsafety@bloomsbury.com

To find out more about our authors and books visit www.hartpublishing.co.uk. Here you will find extracts, author information, details of forthcoming events and the option to sign up for our newsletters.

ACKNOWLEDGEMENTS

This book is the product of an intellectual journey undertaken in several places with scholars and practitioners of different disciplines. It brings together a variety of research interests pursued along this journey: those on EU external relations law, on the law of the EU's proximity policies, and on the geographic and conceptual borderlands of Europe. The book originates from my doctoral thesis carried out at the Sciences Po law school in Paris, where I had the opportunity to grow within a stimulating and dynamic academic environment. Fruitful exchanges with colleagues and fulfilling teaching experiences have been crucial for the development this work. At the EUI, the Max Weber Programme has been a superb platform for turning the PhD thesis into a book. The nurturing and supportive context of the Centre for European Law at the University of Oslo has hosted the crucial stages of the writing of this work.[1]

The journey has been enriching and rewarding especially for the people I was fortunate enough to encounter. I wish to thank the members of my PhD panel for the enriching discussion ensuing from the defence. My profound gratitude goes to my supervisor, Loïc Azoulai, an inspiring *maestro*, whose thoughtful comments have led me to appreciate a broader conception of the law, making its study more enjoyable and challenging. My passion for EU external relations law has been fostered by the inspiring works, comments and mentoring of Marise Cremona, who has accompanied me with her extraordinary expertise during different stages of this project. A special acknowledgment goes to Giacinto della Cananea, who is a kind mentor and generous source of knowledge and guidance. I wish to thank Cécile Rapoport for her insightful observations and remarks on my thesis. I am particularly grateful to Christophe Hillion for the interest he demonstrated in this work. As a colleague in Oslo, his expertise and foresight continue to trigger inspiring ideas on the developments of the *Wider Europe*.

I am in debt to Joanne Scott for her unparalleled guidance and advice during my stay at the visiting period at the EUI during the PhD and then as a mentor during my Max Weber fellowship. I am sincerely grateful to Tarjei Bekkedal and colleagues of the LEVEL project in Oslo for the fruitful discussions that have enriched my understanding and my perspective on EEA law. I thank them for the generous support and encouragement in the final stages of the completion of this book. I am also grateful to Jean Bernard Auby, Gordon Antony, Bruno

[1] In the framework of the LEVEL project funded by the Research Council of Norway (Project n 325328).

de Witte, Pascal McDougall, Fernanda Nicola, Luigi Pedreschi, and Niamh Nic Shuibhne, for helpful comments and provoking questions on different parts of my work.

I wish also to thank the many academics who have helped and inspired me in the course of the first enriching experiences of this journey through their support and valuable advice in Naples, Pavia, Konstanz, the EUI and the College of Europe. Among these, I wish to thank Gia Caglioti, Andrea Graziosi, Sieglinde Gstöhl, Erwan Lannon, Enrico Letta, Dirk Leuffen, Imola Streho and Jacques Ziller. My gratitude also goes to the officials of the European Commission and the EEAS, particularly of the DG NEAR B.3 unit for exposing me to the gateways of *Wider Europe*.

TABLE OF CONTENTS

PART II
WIDER EUROPE AND MULTILATERAL REGIMES:
THE POLES OF THE EU NEIGHBOURHOOD LAW CONTINUUM

PART III
WIDER EUROPE THROUGH BILATERAL PARTNERSHIPS

ABBREVIATIONS

AA	Association Agreement
ACAA	Agreement on Conformity Assessment and Acceptance of Industrial Products
AFSJ	Area of Freedom, Security and Justice
AG	Advocate General
AP	Action Plan
AU	African Union
CETA	Canada-European Union Comprehensive Economic and Trade Agreement
CoE	Council of Europe
CFI	Court of First Instance (EU)
CFSP	Common Foreign and Security Policy
CJEU	Court of Justice of the European Union (General Court + European Court of Justice)
DCFTA	Deep and Comprehensive Free Trade Area/Agreement
DSM	Dispute Settlement Mechanism
EA	Europe Agreement
EASA	European Union Aviation Safety Agency
EC	European Community
ECAA	European Common Aviation Area
ECFR	European Union Charter of Fundamental Rights
ECHR	European Convention on Human Rights and Fundamental Freedoms
ECJ	European Court of Justice
ECtHR	European Court of Human Rights
EEA	European Economic Area

EEAS	European External Action Service
EEC	European Economic Community
EFTA	European Free Trade Association
EMAA	Euro-Mediterranean Association Agreement
EnCT	Energy Community Treaty
ENI	European Neighbourhood Instrument
ENPI	European Neighbourhood and Partnership Instrument
ENP	European Neighbourhood Policy
EU	European Union
EU HR for CFSP	European Union High Representative for the Common Foreign and Security Policy
EUCFR	European Union Charter of Fundamental Rights
EuroMed	Euro-Mediterranean
FMPA	Free Movement of Persons Agreement (EU–Switzerland)
FRONTEX	European Border and Coast Guard Agency
FTA	Free Trade Area
GAMM	Global Approach to Migration and Mobility (EU)
GATS	General Agreement on Trade in Services
GATT	General Agreement on Tariffs and Trade
GC	General Court of the European Union
InstA	EU-Switzerland Draft Institutional Agreement
MENA	Middle East and North Africa
MP	Mobility Partnership
MRA	Mutual Recognition Agreements
NDICI	Neighbourhood, Development and International Cooperation Instrument
NGO	Non-Governmental Organisations
OECD	Organisation for Economic Co-operation and Development
PCA	Partnership and Cooperation Agreement

PINI	Protocol on Ireland and Northern Ireland (EU–UK Withdrawal Agreement)
PNCR	Plan Nationale Convergence Réglementaire (Morocco)
RSA	Réussir le Statut Avancé (Moroccan Programme linked to the Advanced Status)
SAA	Stabilisation and Association Agreement
SADR	Sahrawi Arab Democratic Republic
SAP	Stabilisation and Association Process
SCA	Surveillance and Court Agreement
SES	Single European Sky
SNIA	Stratégie Nationale d'Immigration et d'Asile (Morocco)
TCA	Trade and Cooperation Agreement (EU–UK)
TCT	Transport Community Treaty
UN	United Nations
UNCRC	UN Convention on the Rights of the Child
UNGA	United Nations General Assembly
UNHRC	United Nations Human Rights Council
USMCA	United States of America, the United Mexican States and Canada Agreement
VCDL	1961 Vienna Convention on Diplomatic Relations
VCLT	1969 Vienna Convention on the Law of Treaties
WA	Withdrawal Agreement (EU–UK)
WTO	World Trade Organization

1

Introduction

Europe is confronted with two intertwined challenges. One pertains to the meaning and confines of the European Union membership. The other relates to the ambitions of an enhanced geopolitical role for the Union.[1] These challenges and transformations are not entirely new: the confines of EU membership have been interlinked with the EU's geopolitical role since the Union's enlargements at the start of the new millennium. In those times, the *Wider Europe* formula was used to delineate the new proximity policies of the Union. The ambition was that of creating a legal and diplomatic space predicated on the extension of the EU model in its neighbourhood. Recent events are pointing towards a reconfiguration of this space. *Brexit* and the set of new legal relations between the EU and the UK challenge the paradigms of gravitation around the EU legal order governed by the *Wider Europe* legal frameworks. Moreover, while bringing to the fore the geopolitical tenor of the extension of the EU's legal space, the Russian military aggression in Ukraine is eliciting a twofold change in the *Wider Europe* design. On the one hand, it is giving new impetus to the enlargement of the Union to the East.[2] On the other hand, it is forcing the EU to confront the prospects that the confines of its (extended) legal space would be in part decided by war.

This book discloses the practices and the significance of the *Wider Europe* design. It argues that the ensuing extension of the EU's legal space amounts to a *lato sensu* reconfiguration of the Union's borders through law and diplomacy. In the context of a quintessentially legal project like the EU, thinking of geopolitics requires reflecting on the role of law in shaping the relation between spaces, power, sovereignty and governance. The central questions that arise are: how does law structure the relations between the EU and third countries in the EU's geographical proximity? What is the nature of this EU neighbourhood law? What does this regional law reveal about the of EU law and on the posture of the Union as a regional legal actor? Why and in which ways the extension of the EU's legal space is contested?

To answer these questions, the book turns *Wider Europe* into an analytical concept to expound the interplay between law, diplomacy and geopolitics in the

[1] Ursula von der Leyen, 'Speech in the European Parliament Plenary Session by the President Elect of the European Commission', ec.europa.eu/info/sites/info/files/president-elect-speech-original_1.pdf; see also Josep Borrell, 'Embracing Europe's Power' (Project Syndicate, 8 February 2020).

[2] Roman Petrov and Christophe Hillion, 'Guest Editorial: "Accession through War" – Ukraine's Road to the EU' (2022) 59 *Common Market Law Review* 1289. See also European Commission, '2023 Communication on EU Enlargement Policy', COM(2023) 690 final.

EU's relations with its neighbours. By doing so, the book offers a novel theoretical and analytical framework to capture the entirety of the EU's proximity policies characterising in the extension of the EU's legal space.

The narrative develops along three related lines of inquiry. The first sheds light on the similarities and differences between EU internal and external integration. The first line of inquiry thus pertains to the legal understanding of the dynamics of inclusion and exclusion inherent to *Wider Europe*. By appreciating the demarcation and complex relations between what is internal and external to EU law, the book draws a distinction between EU membership law and EU neighbourhood law. It discusses the role of the principle of autonomy in avoiding that the extension of the EU's legal space affects the distinctive characteristics of EU membership law. The second line of inquiry pertains to the techniques used for extending the EU's legal space. These techniques of EU neighbourhood law govern the scope and the intensity of third country gravitation around the EU's legal order. The extension of the EU's legal space does not only take the form of legally binding institutional arrangements but also of more elusive processes of third country socialisation in *Wider Europe*. The foregoing lines of inquiry are strictly related to the third, which brings to the fore the different political covenants underlying legal relations in *Wider Europe*. Political covenants nurture the interplay between politics, sovereignty and law. The study of this interplay requires a twofold engagement. First, it calls for a reflection on the distinctive political covenant of EU membership law. Secondly, it entails examining differences across political covenants of EU neighbourhood law by unravelling their varying relationships with EU membership law, their sources, and the techniques they mobilise. In that light, the study of techniques of EU neighbourhood law enables us to comprehend the reconfiguration of sovereignty exercise in *Wider Europe*. Such a reconfiguration derives both from the extension of the EU's claims to authority in the extended EU's legal space and from the political, economic and legal relations reflecting and nurturing interdependences in the EU's proximity. Crucially, although *Wider Europe* is characterised by a marked asymmetry in favour of the EU, the reconfiguration of sovereignty exercise in the extended EU's legal space does not only affect third countries but also the Union.

Part one of the book is devoted to turning *Wider Europe* into an analytical concept. Chapter two unravels the interplay of law and geopolitics and the paradigms of inclusion and exclusion in the EU's neighbourhood. By reflecting on the sources of *Wider Europe*, its constitutional foundations, and the pre-existing web of legal arrangements vehiculating the extension of the EU's legal space, the second chapter emancipates *Wider Europe* from the European Neighbourhood Policy. Against this backdrop, it discusses how *Wider Europe* as an analytical concept captures the old and new proximity policies providing for the extension (or retrenchment) of the EU's legal space. Chapter three further contributes to this analytical and conceptual development. By disclosing different manifestations of the principle of autonomy of EU law in the extended EU's legal space, the chapter unravels the demarcation and the complex relationship between what is internal and external to the EU legal order. It is argued that the *Wider Europe* formula evoking the Union surrounded by a ring of friends with whom to 'share everything but the institutions', epitomises the dynamics of inclusion and exclusion in the extended EU's legal space. The preclusion of sharing institutions precisely derives from the principle of autonomy of EU law. In that light, chapter three explains the novel semantic and methodological choices of the book against the background of the existing literature on internal and external integration. The notions of *renvois* and mechanisms of organisational interaction with EU law are introduced to account for the patterns of third country gravitation around the EU legal order. Finally, the chapter discusses the distinctiveness of the EU membership political covenant compared to the covenants of EU neighbourhood law.

Part two of the book examines the multilateral institutional arrangements of EU neighbourhood law and their role in shaping the EU neighbourhood law continuum. Chapter four reviews the EEA Agreement as a major source of the *Wider Europe* design and reflects on its two-pillar (EU and EEA EFTA States) configuration. It explains why in the EEA, and more broadly in the special relationship between the EU and Iceland and Norway, the demarcation between EU membership law and EU neighbourhood law is thinner. The chapter offers a first overview of the EU neighbourhood law continuum by reviewing the extension of a piece of EU social security legislation in different regimes of EU neighbourhood law. It also offers a reflection on the evolution of the political covenant underlying the special relations between the EU, Iceland and Norway. Chapter five examines the functional dimensions of *Wider Europe* through multilateral regimes extending portions of the EU *acquis*. The European Common Aviation Area (ECAA) Agreement is investigated as the major paradigm of a one-pillar model of EU neighbourhood law, also inspiring the Transport Community Treaty (TCT). The peculiarity of the ECAA's techniques of extension of the EU's legal space entailing an extraterritorial extension of the powers of the EU institutions beyond membership is also discussed. The variety of institutional arrangements in EU aviation law in the EU's proximity is considered as an additional exemplification of the EU neighbourhood law continuum. The chapter also examines the Energy Community Treaty (EnCT), with a focus on the absence of mechanisms of organisational interaction with the EU legal order. Part two thus enriches the understanding of the variety of institutional arrangements of EU neighbourhood and the underlying political covenants.

Part three discusses some of the key bilateral partnerships of EU neighbourhood law. These partnerships bring to the fore the legal and political challenges currently characterising *Wider Europe*. Chapter six is devoted to studying the extension of the EU's legal space in Ukraine. It proffers a characterisation of Ukraine as a conceptual and legal borderland between *Wider Europe* and the *Russkiy mir*. It examines Ukraine's frontrunner status in the ENP against the backdrop of its initial tightrope walking between Brussels and the Kremlin, leading to a convoluted process for the signature of the new generation EU–Ukraine Association Agreement. It discusses the 'European Choice' of Ukraine, prevailing in the context of the Maidan protests in Kyiv in 2013 and the ensuing signature of the Association Agreement with the EU. The far-reaching techniques of extension of the EU's legal space enshrined in the EU–Ukraine Association Agreement are examined as paradigmatic arrangements of EU neighbourhood law.

Chapter seven addresses the reconfiguration in *Wider Europe* brought about by the *Brexit* process. The UK's withdrawal has not only reconfigured the confines of EU membership, but has also questioned the paradigms of gravitation around the EU legal order inherent to *Wider Europe*. Notwithstanding that, the chapter posits that *Wider Europe* paradigms inform both processes of extension and retrenchment of the EU's legal space. In fact, one could not think of a better application of the *Wider Europe* formula of 'everything but institutions' than the operation of the EU–UK Withdrawal Agreement. In that light, the chapter reviews the Protocol on Ireland and Northern Ireland as recently amended by the *Windsor Framework*. The chapter discusses how the UK's withdrawal has led to a rethinking of the balance between the benefits and obligations in its bilateral relations, especially those with Switzerland. The chapter then evaluates how *Brexit* has affected the political covenants of EU neighbourhood law.

The analysis of the bilateral partnerships in *Wider Europe* concludes with the study of the Moroccan case in chapter eight. Morocco was considered a front-runner of the ENP and was the first country mentioned in Prodi's *Wider Europe* speech. By reflecting on the EU's partnership with Morocco, the chapter appreciates the more legally elusive techniques of extension of the EU's legal space stemming from processes of neighbouring country socialisation. The study of the EU–Moroccan partnership reveals the operation of patterns of inclusion and exclusion in *Wider Europe*. Inclusion is governed by a dense web of legal relations ensuing from soft law instruments and technical assistance programmes managed through EU funds whereby Morocco commits to internalising norms and practices of EU law. Rather paradoxically, exclusion is also channelled through processes of (inclusive) socialisation. In this respect, the chapter investigates how the extension of the EU's legal space may take the form of externalisation of EU border controls. Cooperation in of the migration domain illustrates how neighbouring countries weaponise the EU's dependence on them with regard to migration control in order to obtain material and geopolitical incentives. Furthermore, the chapter discusses the judicial-political saga on the controversial application of the EU–Morocco Agreements to the contested territory of Western Sahara unraveling Morocco's geopolitical positioning. The chapter concludes with a consideration of how the elusive techniques of *Wider Europe* are an expression of an equally elusive political covenant of EU neighbourhood law.

Part three of the book attempts to disclose and make sense of the patterns of gravitation and contestation of EU neighbourhood law. Chapter nine provides an assessment of the repertoires of techniques of the EU's legal space. It reviews the variety of institutional arrangements in *Wider Europe* while reflecting on the *scope* and *intensity* of gravitation around the EU legal order. It evaluates how different combinations of techniques of EU neighbourhood law calibrate proximity to the EU legal order. The chapter devotes special attention to the enforcement mechanisms of extended EU law that are expression of different reconfiguration of sovereignty within *Wider Europe*. The chapter also examines the motives of contestation of EU neighbourhood law, including the EU partners' wish to recur to more canonical forms of international law in the convoluted moments of their relationship with the EU. The conclusion summarises the main findings of the book. It reflects on the interaction of the three lines of inquiry with a particular focus on the political covenants of EU neighbourhood law and the sources of legitimacy of the extension of the EU's claims to authority beyond its borders. It appraises the nature of EU neighbourhood law as a distinctive type of regional law as governing the often-undefined interregnum between *friendship* and *membership*. In that light, the conclusions recast the themes and the lines of inquiry of the book in a reflexive way and call attention to the new challenges arising from the interregnum between *friendship* and *membership* in *Wider Europe*.

PART I

Turning *Wider Europe* into an Analytical Concept

2

Wider Europe as an Analytical Concept: The Interplay of Law and Geopolitics

I. Introduction

This chapter establishes the foundations for turning *Wider Europe* from a policy formula into an analytical concept with a view to capturing a variety of old and new relationships forged by the EU in its neighbourhood. Construed as an analytical concept, *Wider Europe* brings to the fore the interplay of law and geopolitics characterising the extension of the EU's legal space. While acknowledging its intimate connection with the European Neighbourhood Policy (ENP), this chapter emancipates *Wider Europe* from this specific policy initiative in four steps.

First, it assesses the context in which *Wider Europe* originated as a proximity policy. In times of *enlargement fatigue*, the EU policy-makers sketched out a cooperation platform for its new neighbours predicated on the passage form *membership* to *friendship*. Building on the enlargement experience, the EU intended to base its new proximity relations on the extension of its laws in the attempt to achieve similar outcomes in terms of security and stability (section II). Secondly, the chapter identifies the constitutional foundations of *Wider Europe* discussing the EU's constitutional mandate to extend its legal space (section III). Thirdly, it reviews the mosaic of legal arrangements pre-existing the launch ENP and premised on a more or less explicit extension of the EU's *acquis*. These Agreements, including the Ankara Agreement, the Euro-Mediterranean Agreements with the southern neighbours, and the Partnership and Cooperation Agreements with the eastern partners, nourished the legal and political infrastructure of *Wider Europe* (section IV). Finally, the turning of *Wider Europe* into an analytical concept is further developed through a reflection on the geopolitical rationales of the extension of the EU's legal space (section V).

II. The Inception of *Wider Europe*: From Membership to Friendship

The geopolitical tool of EU membership changed the political and legal landscape of Europe. Especially in the context of the new enlargements of 2004–07, the reconfiguration of the European political geography elicited the need to devise different forms of association with new neighbouring states distinct from membership. This was already clear in 1993 when the landmark European Council meeting in Copenhagen not only set the criteria for membership but also referred to the limits of the enlargement experience.[1]

In the wake of the ensuing *enlargement fatigue*, the EU institutions progressively started to devise ways for adapting to the new EU membership confines while continuing to build on the positive motives that had inspired the EU's enlargement. In 2002, the then President of the Commission, Romano Prodi, delivered a speech eloquently entitled 'A Wider Europe – A Proximity Policy as the key to stability'. Prodi recognised that the enlarged EU would have a new role as a global actor and would be concerned with ensuring stability and prosperity in the region. He identified the necessity of 'projecting stability beyond the current candidate countries, which [were] already sharing in our prosperity'.[2]

The geopolitical challenges of the post-enlargement period were addressed by the EU with an attempt to upgrade its toolbox aimed at safeguarding the stability and the security of its new borders. In Prodi's words, this would include a 'substantive and workable concept of proximity' predicated upon stimuli for reforms targeting countries not necessarily enjoying membership prospects. Having clarified that 'accession [was] not the only game in town',[3] the ENP would borrow the conditionality methodology of the enlargement policy.[4] Enlargement would thus be a major source for the realisation of *Wider Europe*. Within a single methodological framework, the new European Neighbourhood Policy would encompass relations with a diverse set of countries driven by different aspirations. Prodi maintained that this new proximity policy would result in 'a "ring of friends" surrounding the Union and its closest European neighbours, from Morocco to Russia and the Black Sea'.[5] The challenges coming from enlargement would be addressed with an extension and consolidation of the legal paradigms that were already characterising the EU's proximity relations.

The legal and the political meaning of the passage from *membership* to *friendship* in the EU's proximity was largely left undefined. In Prodi's speech, the offer would consist of something 'more than partnership and less than membership' and would result in the creation of a 'Common European Economic Space' where the EU could 'ultimately share everything but institutions'.[6] The underlying rationale would be the attempt to project the internal market as a source of stability and prosperity in the EU neighbourhood. Several passages of the *Wider Europe*

[1] European Council, Conclusions of the Presidency, Copenhagen 21–22 June 1993, 13.

[2] Romano Prodi, European Commission 'A Wider Europe – A Proximity Policy as the Key to Stability', Speech/02/619, 2.

[3] ibid 4.

[4] On enlargement and conditionality see Marise Cremona, 'Accession to the European Union: Membership Conditionality and Accession Criteria', 25 *Polish Yearbook of International Law* 219.

[5] Prodi (n 2) 4.

[6] ibid 6.

Communication following Prodi's speech referred to an 'enlarged area of political stability and functioning rule of law'[7] and 'an area of shared prosperity and values based on deeper economic integration'.[8] In that light, the European Economic Area would hence constitute a paradigm for the novel orientations of the EU proximity policies.

By identifying the EEA as a major source of the *Wider Europe* design, the EU stressed the role of law in shaping its neighbourhood. The long-term goal of the new policy would be to move

> towards an arrangement whereby the Union's relations with neighbouring countries ultimately resemble the close political and economic links … enjoyed with the European Economic Area. This [would imply] the partners taking on considerably deeper and broader obligations, specifically when it comes to aligning with Community legislation.[9]

The development of the EU neighbourhood relations premised on the extension of EU law reflected the understanding of the EU as a quintessentially legal project. In Prodi's own words, the underlying motive of *Wider Europe* was to 'extend to this neighbouring region a set of principles, values and standards, which define the *very essence* of the European Union'.[10] The single market and the EU *acquis* would be a driver for change also beyond EU membership. The relevant Communication affirmed that 'all the neighbouring countries should be offered the prospect of a stake in the EU's internal market and further integration and liberalisation to promote the free movement of persons, goods, services and capital'.[11] It went on to state that 'if a country has reached this level, it has come as close to the Union as it can be without being a member'.[12] Not dissimilarly from what had happened in the EU, trade would be a stabiliser and a driver for further cooperation.

The construction of a *Wider Europe* had geopolitical motives. The enlargement *fatigue* required the Union to come to terms with the geographic limits of its integration experience. To be sure, in those times, the notion of *enlargement fatigue* evoked a recognition of the limits of the EU's absorption capacity more than the limits of the alleged universality of its model. Yet, it urged the EU to reflect on its territorial extension, on the confines of its membership, and on a new engagement with the neighbourhood driven by the necessity to enhance the security of its new borders. The geopolitical motives of *Wider Europe* can also be inferred from the policy climate preceding Prodi's speech. As early as in August 2002, Commissioner Christopehr Patten and EU High Representative Javier Solana had issued a joint document also entitled *Wider Europe*. It read that 'stability, prosperity, shared values and the rule of law along our borders are all fundamental for our

[7] European Commission, 'Wider Europe – Neighbourhood: A New Framework for Relations with Our Eastern and Southern Neighbours', COM(2003) 104 final, 3.

[8] ibid 9.

[9] ibid 15.

[10] ibid (emphasis added).

[11] ibid 10.

[12] ibid.

own security. Failure in any of these areas will lead to increased risks of negative spill-over on the Union.'[13] Enlargement of the Union would entail a reconfiguration of its security needs and an increased engagement with its new neighbours. Some commentators have convincingly argued that the ENP could be understood as 'a regional implementation of the European Security Strategy'.[14] As a matter of fact, the European Security Strategy recognised that:

> The integration of acceding states increases our security but also brings the EU closer to troubled areas. Our task is to promote *a ring of well governed countries* to the East of the European Union and on the borders of the Mediterranean with whom we can enjoy close and cooperative relations.[15]

Notwithstanding these evident geopolitical motives characterising *Wider Europe*, the EU refrained from speaking the language of power inherent in geopolitics.[16]Although framed in terms of good governance, the challenges faced by the Union were geopolitical in nature and concerned the limits of its experience, its engagement with its new borders and issues of security and stability.

III. The Constitutional Foundations of *Wider Europe* as an Analytical Concept

The extension beyond membership of the EU model based on law is mandated by the provisions of the EU Treaties. Several TEU articles can be construed as the constitutional foundations of *Wider Europe*. In particular, Article 21 TEU mandates that the Union's action on the international scene 'shall be guided by the principles which have inspired its own creation, development and enlargement, and which it seeks to advance in the wider world'. Similarly, Article 3(5) TEU mentions that 'in its relations with the wider world, the Union shall uphold and promote its values and interests and contribute to the protection of its citizens'. In that light, openness and extension of its model should run in parallel to a form of closure of 'protection' especially of its citizens. Moreover, EU values and interests have been considered as inextricably linked.[17] The 2016 EU Global Strategy particularly brought to the

[13] Joint letter by EU Commissioner Chris Patten and the EU High Representative for CFSP on *Wider Europe*, 7 August 2002 (emphasis added), web.archive.org/web/20041023063525/http:/www.europa.eu.int/comm/world/enp/pdf/_0130163334_001_en.pdf.

[14] Marise Cremona and Christophe Hillion, 'L'Union Fait La Force? Potential and Limitations of the European Neighbourhood Policy as an Integrated EU Foreign and Security Policy', EUI Working Paper Law No 2006/36.

[15] Council of the EU, *European Security Strategy, A Secure Europe in a Better World*, Brussels, 12 December 2003.

[16] See Luuk van Middelaar, *Le réveil géopolitique de l'Europe* (Paris, Collège de France, 2022).

[17] Marise Cremona, 'Extending the Reach of EU Law: The EU as an International Legal Actor' in Marise Cremona and Joanne Scott, *EU Law Beyond EU Borders: The Extraterritorial Reach of EU Law* (Oxford University Press, 2019) 69.

fore the relationship between values and interests, characterising EU values as the 'vital interests underpinning [the EU's] external action'.[18]

The extension of the EU legal model also informs the EU constitutional provisions covering the Union neighbourhood. Often referred to as the 'neighbourhood clause', Article 8 TEU is placed under the title of the common provisions of the EU encompassing the EU's foundational values and constitutional principles. It is not located in the part of the TEU devoted to external action. This position in the Treaty framework suggests the overarching scope of the provision, 'in the sense of holding both internal and external dimensions'.[19] The Article thus complements the broader 'external action mandate'[20] of the EU's constitutional provisions. It reads:

1. The Union shall develop a special relationship with neighbouring countries, aiming to establish an area of prosperity and good neighbourliness, founded on the values of the Union and characterised by close and peaceful relations based on cooperation.
2. For the purposes of paragraph 1, the Union may conclude specific agreements with the countries concerned. These agreements may contain reciprocal rights and obligations as well as the possibility of undertaking activities jointly. Their implementation shall be the subject of periodic consultation.

Although seldomly used in practice,[21] this clause has attracted scholarly attention for its normative implications. Hillion has highlighted the constitutional 'transformative mandate' bestowed upon the EU when interacting with neighbourhood states.[22] Hanf has contended that the neighbourhood clause enshrined in Article 8 TEU amounts to '"constitutionalising" the concept of "integration without membership"'.[23] However, Article 8 TEU is hardly ever used for concluding international agreements in the EU neighbourhood.

The reasons for the scarce use of Article 8 TEU are manifold. First, its similarity with Article 217 TFEU should be noted. Article 217 TFEU provides the substantive legal basis for association agreements that may ultimately render Article 8 TEU redundant. Indeed, both articles appear to codify the *Demirel* findings according to which association agreements create 'special, privileged links with a non-member

[18] European Union, 'Shared Vision, Common Action: A Stronger Europe: A Global Strategy for the European Union's Foreign and Security Policy' (June 2016) 13.

[19] Christophe Hillion, 'Anatomy of EU Norm Export towards the Neighbourhood: The Impact of Article 8 TEU' in Peter van Elsuwege and Roman Petrov (eds), *Legislative approximation and application of EU law in the Eastern neighbourhood of the European Union : towards a common regulatory space?* (Routledge, 2014) 16.

[20] Christophe Hillion and Vincent Delhomme, 'EU Enlargement, Extra-Territorial Application of EU Law and the International Dimension' in Inge Govaere and Sacha Garben (eds), *The interface between EU and international law: contemporary reflections* (Hart Publishing, 2019).

[21] European Commission, 'EU Relations with the Principality of Andorra, the Principality of Monaco and the Republic of San Marino Options for Closer Integration with the EU', COM(2012) 680 final.

[22] Christophe Hillion, 'The Neighbourhood Competence under Article 8 TEU' (2013) *Notre Europe Policy Paper* 7.

[23] Dominik Hanf, 'The ENP in the Light of the New "Neighbourhood Clause" (Article 8 TEU)' (2011) *College of Europe Research Paper in Law* 4.

country which must, at least to a certain extent, take part in the community system'.[24] In addition, Article 8 TEU is rather silent on the procedural dimension of neighbourhood agreements and would hardly be used on a standalone legal basis.[25] Perhaps more importantly, the 'neighbourhood' label is not favoured by European countries that have membership aspirations.[26] In the case of Ukraine, Article 217 TFEU was preferred: in contrast to 'neighbourhood', 'association' might be understood as entailing a '(long-term) membership perspective'.[27] Notwithstanding this, the mandate enshrined in Article 8 TEU has informed the EU's policy-making. As a matter of fact, the 2011 ENP Communication considered Article 8 TEU as a basis for 'deeper economic integration' with neighbouring countries: it amounted to 'sharing with [the EU's] neighbours the experiences of European integration and progressively involving them into EU policies'.[28] Besides, although the neighbourhood clause was not mentioned in the 2015 ENP review, nor in the Communication on a renewed partnership with the Southern Neighbourhood in 2021,[29] it is significant that the first Article of the EU–UK Trade and Cooperation Agreement partly replicates the wording of Article 8 TEU.[30]

The *Wider Europe* design and the launch of the new proximity policy thus run in parallel to a process of constitutionalisation characterising the early 2000s, of which the current Treaty of Lisbon is a product. Key defining elements of the constitutional identity of the EU as a global actor were identified by Cremona in a fortunate contribution in 2004. Some of these elements addressed in particular the Union's engagement in its proximity. This is the case, for instance, of the EU's role as a 'stabilizer' and as 'a magnet and a neighbour'.[31]

[24] Case 12/86, *Demirel* EU:C:1987:400 [9].

[25] Peter van Elsuwege and Roman Petrov, 'Article 8 TEU: Towards a New Generation of Agreements with the Neighbouring Countries of the European Union?' (2011) 36 *European Law Review* 688, 697.

[26] Christophe Hillion, 'Mapping-Out the New Contractual Relations between the European Union and Its Neighbours; Learning from the EU–Ukraine Enhanced Agreement' (2007) 12 *European Foreign Affairs Review*, fn 3.

[27] Guillaume Van der Loo, *The EU–Ukraine Association Agreement and Deep and Comprehensive Free Trade Area : A New Legal Instrument for EU Integration without Membership* (Brill Nijhoff, 2016) 173.

[28] European Commission and EU High Representative for CFSP, 'A New Response to a Changing Neighbourhood', COM(2011) 303 final, 28.

[29] A problematic aspect of Art 8 TEU is that it mandates to develop a special relationship based 'on the values of the Union'. In this respect, the 2015 ENP Review was less ambitious than the 2011 ENP Communication: the emphasis was on 'universal values', not on the values of the Union. In the 2021 Communication targeting southern neighbours (targeting largely the same countries as the 2011 Communication), the focus shifted to 'shared values'. Not surprisingly, instead, the 2023 Enlargement Communication (targeting also countries formerly in the Eastern dimension of the ENP) strongly refers to EU values. See respectively European Commission and EU High Representative for CFSP, 'Review of the European Neighbourhood Policy', JOIN(2015) 50 final, 'Renewed partnership with the Southern Neighbourhood' JOIN(2021) 2 final, and European Commission, '2023 Communication on EU Enlargement Policy', COM(2023) 690 final.

[30] EU–UK Trade and Cooperation Agreement [2021] OJ 149/10. See further ch 6. Significantly, Art 1 does not mention values.

[31] Marise Cremona, 'The Union as a Global Actor: Roles, Models and Identity' (2004) 41 *Common Market Law Review* 553.

IV. *Wider Europe* and the Mosaic of Legal Arrangements Pre-existing the ENP

The 'substantive and workable concept of proximity' mentioned in the *Wider Europe* speech was far from being a rupture with the past. The ENP itself was conceived on the experience of pre-existing agreement that the EU had concluded in its proximity, including the EEA Agreement. The EEA is premised upon the extension of the EU *acquis*. Its preamble can be construed as echoing and reinforcing some of the constitutional rationales underpinning Article 8 TEU. The EEA Agreement refers to the 'privileged relationship' between the EU and the EFTA states 'based on proximity, long-standing common values and European identity'.[32] The preamble also refers to the objective of extending the EU internal market providing for the 'fullest possible realization of the free movement of goods, persons, services and capital within the whole European Economic Area'.[33] The text of the Agreement itself recognises that EEA rules may be 'identical in substance to the corresponding provisions of EU law'.[34] A different paradigm underlies the EU's relations with Switzerland, a prominent EFTA State, whose government had actively participated in the negotiation of the EEA Agreement.[35] Differently from Iceland, Norway and Lichtenstein, however, Switzerland did not join the EEA: following the result of a referendum held on 6 December 1992, it rejected EEA membership. EU–Swiss relations then continued to develop on a bilateral basis, with a set of agreements enriching that establishing a Free Trade Area dating back to 1972. A relevant Commission Communication of 1993, at the basis of the bilateral path of EU–Swiss relations, clarified that 'Any agreement would need to deal satisfactorily with the [EU] acquis and the need for Switzerland to accept the discipline involved'.[36]

The role of the EU as a model and a magnet also underpinned of other arrangements antecedent to the launch of *Wider Europe*. Still today, the legal fabric of the EU's relations with the southern neighbourhood is largely governed by the Euro Mediterranean Association Agreements adopted in the framework of the Barcelona Process in 1995.[37] These Agreements were concluded with Morocco, Tunisia, Jordan, Israel, Algeria, Egypt, Lebanon and the Palestinian Authority.[38]

[32] Agreement on the European Economic Area [1994] OJ L1/3, Recital 2.

[33] ibid recital 5.

[34] ibid, art 4.

[35] Philippe G Nell, *Suisse-Communauté européenne – au coeur des négociations sur l'Espace économique européen* (Economica, 2012).

[36] European Commission, 'Future Relations with Switzerland', COM(93) 486 final 3.

[37] See further ch 7.

[38] EuroMed Agreement with Tunisia, [1998] OJ L97/2; EuroMed Agreement with Morocco, [2000] OJ L70/2; EuroMed Agreement with Israel [2000] OJ L147/3; EuroMed Agreement with Jordan, [2002] OJ L129/3; EuroMed Agreement with Egypt, [2004] OJ L304/39; EuroMed with Algeria, [2005] OJ L 265/2; EuroMed Agreement with the PLO, [1997] OJ L187/3, EuroMed Agreement with Lebanon [2006] OJ L143/2.

They aimed at fostering a political dialogue between the EU and its Member States on the one hand, and the Southern Mediterranean countries on the other. The Euro Mediterranean (Euro-Med) Agreements provided for the progressive establishment of free-trade areas and included provisions on the free movement of persons and cultural dialogue. The Agreements include clauses on legislative approximation amounting to best endeavours commitments of legislative convergence. Albeit differently worded, these provisions were predicated on the gravitation of third countries' legal systems around the EU legal order, a paradigm that was further developed with the ENP.[39]

The landscape of bilateral agreements concluded by the EU in the East before the launch of the ENP is more composite. Partnership and Cooperation Agreements (PCA) were concluded with the Newly Independent States following the dissolution of the USSR. These Agreements were in place with Ukraine, Moldova, Armenia and Azerbaijan.[40] Like the Euro Mediterranean Agreements, they were intended to foster political dialogue and enhance trade relations in line with WTO rules. Legislative approximation was a clear objective of the Agreements: this would foster gravitation around the EU legal order.

The *Wider Europe* rationales in the framework of the PCAs were evident both in the legislative approximation clauses and provisions on EU technical assistance.[41] The Agreements with Ukraine, Georgia and Moldova have been replaced with a new generation of association agreements concluded within the framework of the Eastern Partnership, the Eastern regional dimension of the ENP, starting from 2014. Especially in light of their Deep and Comprehensive Free Trade Area (DCFTA) chapters, these Agreements are far-reaching in terms of legislative approximation and incorporation of EU *acquis* into the third countries' legal orders. They also embed ENP conditionality in a hard law framework.[42] With the former eastern partners of the ENP, the confines between friendship and membership in *Wider Europe* have become increasingly blurred especially after the Commission recommended the granting of candidate status to Georgia and to open EU accession negotiations with Ukraine and Moldova in November 2023.[43]

[39] The wording of the approximation clauses varies in language. Art 52 of the Agreement with Morocco: 'Cooperation shall be aimed at helping Morocco to bring its legislation closer to that of the Community in the areas covered by this Agreement'. Art 49 of the Agreement with Lebanon (and similarly Art 55 of Agreement with Israel): 'The Parties shall use their best endeavours to approximate their respective laws in order to facilitate the implementation of this Agreement'. The latter would suggest a bi-directional approximation. The practice, however, is that of a unidirectional approximation of the third countries law to those of the EU.

[40] EU–Ukraine PCA, [1998] OJ L49/3; EU–Georgia PCA, [1999] OJ L205/3; EU–Moldova PCA [1998] OJ L 181/3; EU–Armenia PCA, [1999] OJ L239/3; EU–Azerbaijan PCA, [1999] OJ L246/3.

[41] See EU– Georgia PCA (n 39), Art 43(1) and (3) respectively.

[42] See further ch 6 of this work.

[43] See European Commission, COM(2023) 690 final (n 29). A recommendation that was endorsed by the Council and the European Council in December 2023. See respectively Council of the EU, Conclusions, 16707/23, Brussels 12 December 2023 and European Council, Conclusions, CO EUR 16, Brussels 14–15 December 2023. This followed the granting of the status of candidate to membership to Ukraine and Moldova in June 2022. See European Council, Conclusions, Brussels, 24 June 2022,

In the original design, Russia was intended to be included in the *Wider Europe* project. The EU–Russia PCA envisioned the creation of 'an appropriate framework for the gradual integration between Russia and a wider area of cooperation in Europe'.[44] Article 55(1) of the EU–Russia PCA establishes that 'Russia shall endeavour to ensure that its legislation will be gradually made *compatible* with that of the [Union] in a defined range of subject areas'.[45] Although the Agreement envisaged the establishment of a free-trade area and cooperation in other sectors, Russia has been reluctant to take part in the *Wider Europe* project. In fact, the Kremlin did not welcome its initial inclusion among potential ENP countries.[46] As one commentator put it, Russian thinking qualified EU engagement in the proximity 'as an attempt to engender hegemonic control'.[47] It decided to embark upon a cooperation based on 'common spaces' which would suggest greater equality among the partners.[48]

The compatibility commitments were indeed thought to be unidirectional as the EU–Russia PCA did not feature any corresponding provisions addressed to the EU regarding commitments to adapt to Russian legislation.[49] Yet, the institutional set-up of the common spaces would have left margins for a joint and more equal participation of the Partners with respect to the canonical ENP framework.[50] This was particularly the case of the establishment of the High Level Working Group, pursuant to Article 93 EU–Russia PCA, with a view to defining the concept of Common European Economic Space (CEES) and other spaces of cooperation and preside over their 'gradual development' in the framework of the PCA.[51] As highlighted by Hillion, while the ENP would be managed primarily by the services of the Commission and of the HR for the CFSP, the 'common spaces' would not be solely the product of EU institutions' thinking and management. The Member States would play a crucial role in the running of the High Level Working Group.[52]

EUCO 24/22. The Conclusions clarified that the European Council would be 'ready to grant the status of candidate country to Georgia once the priorities specified in the Commission's opinion on Georgia's membership application have been addressed'. See also European Commission, 'Opinion on Georgia's application for membership of the European Union', Brussels, 17 June 2022, COM(2022)405 final.

[44] EU–Russia PCA [1997] OJ L 327/3, Art 1.

[45] ibid, Art 55(2) emphasis added.

[46] Nikolay Kaveshnikov and Olga Potemkina, 'EU and Russia in Search of Strategic Partnership' in Francesco Maiani, Roman Petrov and Ekaterina Mouliarova, *European Integration Without EU Membership: Models, Experiences, Perspectives*, EUI Working Paper MWP 2009/10, 48. See further discussion in ch 6 of this work, section III.

[47] Nathalie Tocci, 'Can the EU Promote Democracy and Human Rights Trough the ENP? The Case for Refocusing on the Rule of Law' in Marise Cremona and Gabriella Meloni, *The European Neighbourhood Policy: A Framework for Modernisation?*, EUI Working Paper LAW No 2007/21, 30.

[48] Christophe Hillion, 'The Evolving System of European Union External Relations as Evidenced in the EU Partnership with Russia and Ukraine' (PhD thesis, University of Leiden, 2005) 210 ff.

[49] As Hillion (n 48) points out, 'Nowhere is it envisaged in the Agreement that the EU should do the same with respect to Russia's legislation', 210–16.

[50] ibid 214.

[51] EU–Russia Summit, Joint Statement, St. Petersburg, 31 May 2003, 9937/03 (Presse 154), www.consilium.europa.eu/uedocs/cms_data/docs/pressdata/en/er/75969.pdf.

[52] Hillion (n 48) 210–16.

The EU–Russia partnership would result 'in a privileged relationship commensurate with their proximity … focusing on regulatory and legislative convergence and trade and investment facilitation'.[53]

The composite framework of EU relations with Eastern European countries was enriched by Europe Agreements (EAs). These agreements, which are no longer in force, also predated the ENP. Premised upon the gravitation of signatory countries around the EU legal order, they were concluded in the 1990s with central and Eastern European states, which all eventually became members of the EU.[54] More convoluted is the role of the Stabilisation and Association Agreements (SAAs) between the EU and Western Balkan countries.[55] Although subsequent to the EAs, the SAAs largely share with the former the content and the scope of the approximation. Significantly, the SAAs include in their preamble the recognition of the EU's partner countries' status as a potential candidate to EU membership.[56] Drafted along the lines of the Europe Agreements, SAAs were tailored on the perceptions of the EU on the different needs of the Western Balkan countries.[57] Approximation commitments to the EU *acquis* were in fact slightly differentiated in their wording across the SAAs.[58]

The SAAs were accompanied by the Stabilisation and Association Process (SAP), which started in 1999. The main aim of the process was to assist the Western Balkan countries in the fulfilment of the Copenhagen criteria for membership.[59] The Process borrowed the methodology of conditionality and soft law instruments that had characterised the pre-accession strategy of the Central and Eastern European states.[60] The EU formally recognised the potential candidate status of the Western Balkan Countries in 2003, at the EU–Western Balkan Summit in Thessaloniki.[61] Croatia, one of the Western Balkans targeted by the SAAs, joined the EU,[62] while the other remain in the pre-accession process. Notwithstanding

[53] EU/Russia High Level Group, 'Report on the Common European Economic Space'. Submitted to the EU/Russia Summit 11 November 2002, en.kremlin.ru/supplement/3541/print.

[54] Hillion, (n 48) 33 ff.

[55] Now they include the EU Agreements with Albania [2009] OJ L107/166, with Bosnia and Herzegovina [2015] OJ L164/2, with Macedonia [2004] OJ L84/13, with Montenegro [2010] OJ L108/3, with Serbia, [2013] OJ L278/16 and with Kosovo [2016] OJ L/71/3.

[56] See for instance the recitals of the EU– Albania SAA: 'recalling the European Union's readiness to integrate to the fullest possible extent Albania into the political and economic mainstream of Europe and its status as a potential candidate for European Union membership on the basis of the Treaty on European Union and fulfilment of the criteria defined by the European Council in June 1993, subject to the successful implementation of this Agreement, notably regarding regional cooperation.'

[57] David Phinnemore, 'Stabilisation and Association Agreements: Europe Agreements for the Western Balkans?' (2003) 8 *European Foreign Affairs Review* 90.

[58] Adam Łazowski and Steven Blockmans, 'Between Dream and Reality, Challenges to the Legal Rapprochement of the Western Balkans' in Roman Petrov and Peter Van Elsuwege, *Legislative Approximation and Application of EU Law in the Eastern Neighbourhood of the European Union: Towards a Common Regulatory Space?* (Taylor and Francis, 2014) 112.

[59] Ilaria Vianello, 'EU External Action and the Administrative Rule of Law: A Long-Overdue Encounter' (PhD Thesis, European University Institute, 2016) 13.

[60] ibid 19.

[61] EU–Western Balkans Summit, 'Declaration', Thessaloniki, 21 June 2003, 10229/03 (Presse 163).

[62] See Accession Treaty of the Republic of Croatia to the European Union, [2012] OJ L112/10.

the different outcomes of the SAAs Agreements, their underlying motive was to 'integrate to the fully possible extent [the targeted countries] into the *political and economic mainstream of Europe*' in light of their status as 'potential candidate[s] to EU membership'.[63] In the more recent enlargement momentum in 2022–23, Bosnia and Herzegovina was granted candidate status to EU membership.[64]

Turkey occupies a special place in the landscape of the EU proximity policies entailing a gravitation around the EU legal order. Its relations with the EU are governed by the oldest Association Agreement still in force and dating back to 1963 (the Ankara Agreement). Also for Turkey, the original conception of the Association Agreement was that of a '*genuine pre-accession*' Agreement.[65] Several integration elements characterised the arrangement. The objective of the establishment of a customs union with the EU was achieved with Decision 1/95 of the Association Council of the Ankara Agreement.[66] The Agreement thus features a strong 'integration dimension'.[67] Article 9 provides for non-discrimination on grounds of nationality that 'shall be prohibited in accordance with the principle laid down in [Article 18 TFEU]'.[68] Various rights concerning free movement of workers were established through decisions of the Association Council,[69] which articulated the patterns of approximation to EU law. While since 1999 Turkey has benefited from having the status of a candidate country, the accession negotiations started in 2005 were characterised by many challenges.[70] Cooperation has been far from linear, and the pre-accession process has delivered only limited results.[71] As Ott put it, the oldest EU Association Agreement currently in place 'is characterised by incremental changes but also political set-backs and standstill'.[72] In its protracted 'journey into the unknown',[73] Turkey's membership prospects appear distant.[74] Accession negotiations with Turkey have been at a standstill

[63] See last recitals of the preamble of SAAs, emphasis added.

[64] European Council, Conclusions, Brussels, 15 December 2022, EUCO 34/22.

[65] Marc Maresceau, 'Turkey: A Candidate State Destined to Join the Union' in Niamh Nic Shuibhne and Laurence W Gormley, *From Single Market to Economic Union: Essays in Memory of John A. Usher* (Oxford University Press, 2012) 318.

[66] Decision No 1/95 of the EC–Turkey Association Council on implementing the final phase of the Customs Union, [1996] OJ L 35/1; [2014] OJ L13/74.

[67] Maresceau (n 65).

[68] EU–Turkey Association Agreement, [1963] OJ L361/29, Art 9.

[69] Steve Peers, 'Living in Sin: Legal Integration Under the EC–Turkey Customs Union' (1996) 7 *European Journal of International Law* 411.

[70] European Commission, 'Enlargement Strategy and Main Challenges 2008–2009', COM(2008) 674 Final, 3: 'The pace of accession negotiations with Turkey reflects the pace of reform as well as the country's fulfilment of the relevant conditions. Turkey now needs to renew its political reform effort'.

[71] European Court of Auditors, 'Special Report: EU Pre-Accession Assistance to Turkey: Only Limited Results so Far (Pursuant to Article 287(4) TFEU)', Luxembourg 2018.

[72] Andrea Ott, 'The EU–Turkey Association and Other EU Parallel Legal Orders in the European Legal Space' (2015) 42 *Legal Issues of Economic Integration*.

[73] Nathalie Tocci, 'Turkey and the European Union, A Journey in the Unknown', Center on the United States and Europe, Brookings 2014.

[74] While a recent Commission Communication endeavoured, more or less inconsequentially, to 'reinvigorat[e] the accession process' for the Western Balkans, similar initiatives were not taken for Turkey. See, European Commission, 'Enhancing the accession process – A credible EU perspective for the Western Balkans' COM(2020) 57 final, Brussels, 5 February 2020.

since 2018.[75] In the 2023, the Commission maintained that 'Türkiye has not reversed the negative trend of moving away from the European Union, with serious backsliding in a number of key areas'.[76]

Wider Europe as a policy design was then launched in the consolidation of an ecosystem of pre-existing arrangements in the EU's proximity providing for the extension of the EU *acquis*. More recently, *Wider Europe* as a policy design has been reviewed in the guise of the European Political Community.[77] Differently from the original *Wider Europe* design, where the EU *acquis* and legal mechanisms were placed at the forefront, the European Political Community is intended to be 'a platform for political coordination of European countries'.[78] Indeed, while the overall objectives remain those of achieving 'security, stability and prosperity',[79] the European Political Community appears more oriented towards high-level discussions on the strategic orientation of the continent rather than on the granular extension of the EU *acquis*. The European Council Conclusions on the European Political Community are limited to briefly mentioning that the new political framework 'will not replace existing EU policies and instruments, notably enlargement'. At present the European Political Community appears to be a rather inconsequential attempt to revive *Wider Europe*. Irrespective of the future of the European Political Community, the topicality of studying *Wider Europe* today arises principally form the challenges posed by *Brexit* and the new enlargement momentum at the East of the Union.

V. The Union's *Limes*: The Geopolitical Foundations of Inclusion and Exclusion in *Wider Europe*

The common threads of the arrangements nurturing the *Wider Europe* design are captured by the 'everything but institutions' formula. The formula encapsulates the endeavour to extend the EU's legal space without extending the EU's membership and institutional confines. The ensuing dynamics of inclusion and exclusion inherent in *Wider Europe* reflect the dynamics of openness and closure animating the EU itself.

In the conceptualisation of the Union, Weiler had identified a tension between the 'community' and 'unity' visions. The 'community vision' is 'premised on recognizing … the reality of *interdependence* … and on counterpoising to the exclusivist ethos of statal autonomy a notion of a *community* of states and peoples sharing values and aspirations'.[80] The 'unity vision' relates to the traditional model

[75] See Council of the EU, Conclusions, Brussels, 26 June 2018, 10555/18.

[76] European Commission, COM(2023) 690 final (n 29), 7. These areas include fundamental rights, rule of law, deficiencies in the judicial system, the moving away from market-oriented policies, and the lack the refrain from aligning with EU restrictive measures against Russia. These areas are mentioned in detail in European Commission, 'Türkiye 2023 Report', SWD(2023) 696 final.

[77] European Council Conclusions, Brussels, 24 June 2022, EUCO 24/22.

[78] ibid, 1.

[79] Prodi (n 2) 5; Commission (n 7).

[80] Joseph HH Weiler, 'The Transformation of Europe' (1991) 100 *The Yale Law Journal* 2403, 2478–79.

of statal intercourse premised on full 'sovereignty', 'autonomy', 'independence'.[81] The reflection on borders and boundaries is central to this moral quest to imagine a political association developing beyond statal paradigms with a view to governing emerging and increasingly interdependent polities. In political theory, functionalism has been at the centre of the conceptualisation of the EU's openness: a functional system would bypass the vexed question of boundaries.[82] For Mitrany, 'while a federal system is bound to be closed and exclusive; a functional system is naturally open, as changes in membership can be absorbed without doing violence to policy and administration'.[83]

The tension between openness and closure could be read in the broader framework on the tensions between the *ethos* and *telos* of the Union. The former is predicated on an open functional system envisioned with a view to preventing the abuses of closed states. The latter is epitomised in Article 1(2) TEU and refers to the 'process of creating an ever-closer Union among the peoples of Europe'. Such a *telos* appears to entail a demarcation between members and non-members.[84] The tension between openness and flexibility, and unity and autonomy, has been key to the development of the Union. It acquires a particular meaning in the context of the different forms of association between the Union and non-member countries in the EU's proximity relations. In the early days of the Union (then Community), this tension was evident in the relations that the EU would entertain with the OEEC countries (now OECD) that were not willing to become member of the Communities. In this context, the EU drafted a memorandum on the European Economic Association. Earlier versions of the document praised the flexibility that association could bring in granting third countries wide discretion to choose which provisions of the Treaty of Rome to adopt while retaining their full individuality on the political plane.[85] However, in subsequent iterations of the memorandum, the Commission appeared antagonistic to forms of associations which did not explicitly lead to full membership: these associations were considered as being predisposed to limit the EU's freedom of action and the process of evolution towards a more complete union.[86]

When translated into the external domain, the tension between openness and closure informing the Union's internal development would inevitably involve

[81] ibid.

[82] Lucian M Ashworth, *A History of International Thought : From the Origins of the Modern State to Academic International Relations* (Routledge, 2014) fns 176–77.

[83] David Mitrany, 'The Prospect of Integration: Federal or Functional' (1965) 4 *Journal of Common Market Studies* 119, 141.

[84] Pre-Brexit, the European Council, however, clarified that: 'the concept of ever closer union allows for different paths of integration for different countries, allowing those that want to deepen integration to move ahead, while respecting the wish of those who do not want to deepen any further'; European Council, Conclusions, Brussels, 27 June 2014, EUCO 79/14.

[85] Mitrany (n 83) 141; see also European Commission – Working Document, 'First Memorandum from the Commission of the European Economic Community to the Council of Ministers of the Community (Pursuant to the Decision of the Council of 3 December 1958), Concerning the Problems Raised by the Establishment of a European Economic, Association', 26 February 1959.

[86] Miriam Camps and Royal Institute of International Affairs, *What Kind of Europe? : The Community since De Gaulle's Veto* (Oxford University Press, 1965) 65.

the EU's engagement with its external borders. In the external domain, borders could not be easily bypassed. The EU's engagement with geopolitics in the wake of the enlargement occurred in the EU's own tenuous and rather ambiguous terms. The language and the logic of power were distant from the *Wider Europe* narrative. Power relations were largely cast in terms of extension of a legal and economic project. In the words of van Middelaar, the enlargement itself was experienced as 'an expansion of a civilisational and economic project, not as an extension of power against opponents'.[87] Although driven by the acknowledgment of the transformative and geographical limits of the EU's experience, the *Wider Europe* design was imbued with universalist ambitions and territorial ambiguity, premises which contrast with canonical geopolitical thinking. Prodi's intimations of a *Wider Europe* extending 'from Morocco to Russia' harboured a universalist and utopian conception of *Europe* manifested in the indefinite character of its frontiers.[88]

In this sense, Hans Lindhal posits that 'Europe is, properly speaking, a *utopia*: it is nowhere and "no-when"'.[89] *Europe* features several times in the TFEU preamble. More than as a geographical location, *Europe* denotes a 'normative unity' of which the EU funding states are self-proclaimed representatives.[90] The idea of European unity is in itself plural as exemplified by the *peoples* of *Europe*. Yet, this notion of *Europe* presupposes an already existing unity, and hence closure, at the time of the establishment of the Treaty. In Lindahl's words, the Union boundaries are derived 'from a closure lost in an irretrievable, undatable past'.[91] In this understanding, *Europe* and its boundaries emerge with a representation which is given concreteness through a legal expression of the union's territorial unity in the notions of 'internal market' and the 'area of freedom security and justice'.[92]

In spite of the rather inadvertent and ambiguous attitude *vis à vis* geopolitics, the 'everything but institutions formula' encapsulated a renewed engagement with borders by the Union entailing forms of inclusion and exclusion. Internally, as described by Foucher, the European project is one where

> existing borders must be made tension-free through mutual understanding and economic and political interdependence; frontiers must be downgraded in association

[87] van Middelaar (n 16) 11–32, para 18 (my translation).

[88] The very idea of a pan-Europa, conceived by Coudenhove-Kalergi, a frontrunning thinker of European integration, was often associated with utopianism. For a discussion on pan-Europa and Geopolitics Benjamin James Thorpe, 'The Time and Space of Richard Coudenhove-Kalergi's Pan-Europe, 1923–1939' (University of Nottingham, 2018). See also Lucio Caracciolo, *La pace è finita. Così ricomincia la storia in Europa* (Feltrinelli, 2022).

[89] Hans K Lindahl, 'Finding a Place for Freedom, Security and Justice: The European Union's Claim to Territorial Unity' (2004) 29 *European Law Review* 461, 479.

[90] Hans Lindahl, 'Sovereignty and Representation in the European Union' in Neil Walker (ed), *Sovereignty in Transition* (Hart Publishing, 2003) 102–03.

[91] Lindahl (n 89) 477.

[92] ibid.

with a strategy of cross-border cooperation and by encouraging the movement of people, cultural goods and assets.[93]

This internal paradigm is partially replicated externally on the basis of the universal and utopian conception of Europe.

The extension of EU functional boundaries beyond membership nuances the meaning of borders and engenders hybrid spaces or borderlands.[94] The exercise in reconfiguration of its borders undertaken by the EU via extending its laws, norms and values is not dissimilar to the historical experiences of empires of the past. As Hassner put it, from the 'Roman *limes* to the Austro-Hungarian *confines or Grenze or Krajinas*, all empires have known … peripheral zones where settler-soldiers served as ever-embattled buffers for the imperial centre.'[95] In that understanding, the EU enlargement itself has been identified as a process typical of empires to deal with borders.[96] In Catherine the Great's terms, defending one's borders would entail extending them.[97]

The Union's functional (and utopian) identity may be construed as premised on theoretically indefinite borders. An analogy could be made also with the Roman empire and the *pax Romana* which, according to Plinius, was without frontiers (*sine finibus*).[98] The politics of the Roman *limes*, which in contrast to confines was established unilaterally,[99] is thus not dissimilar from the rationales of the EU's proximity policies. In that regard, in a study on the political genealogy of spatial disposition in ancient times, Dario Gentili reflects on the differences between borders (*finis*) and boundaries/frontiers (*limes*): 'while the *finis* is related to the city, the *limes* is related to the empire'.[100] The engagement with borders of imperial powers (as Ancient Rome) is also premised by a 'de-bordering in order to expand'.[101] In ancient times as today, frontiers can be intended as political institutions with 'an ambivalent nature: engendering tensions and contrasts as

[93] Michel Foucher, 'The Geopolitics of European Frontier' in Eberhard Bort and Malcolm Anderson (eds), *The frontiers of Europe* (Pinter, 1998) 237.

[94] Raffaella Del Sarto, 'Borderlands: The Middle East and North Africa as the EU's Southern Buffer Zone' in Dimitar Bechev and Nicolaidis Kalypso (eds), *Mediterranean Frontiers: Borders, Conflict and Memory in a Transnational World* (IB Tauris, 2010) 151–52.

[95] Pierre Hassner, 'Fixed Borders or Moving Borderlands? A New Type of Border for a New Type of Entity' in Jan Zielonka (ed), *Europe unbound: enlarging and reshaping the boundaries of the European Union* (Routledge, 2002) 39.

[96] Jan Zielonka, *Europe as Empire* (Oxford University Press, 2006); Fabrizio Tassinari, *Why Europe Fears Its Neighbors* (ABC-CLIO, LLC, 2009) 17.

[97] Robert Cooper, *The Breaking of Nations : Order and Chaos in the Twenty-First Century* (Atlantic Books, 2003) 78.

[98] Aldo Schiavone, 'Limes, La Politica Dei Confini Dell'impero Romano' in *Frontiere : politiche e mitologie dei confini europei* (Istituto Italiano di Scienze Umane, 2003) 2.

[99] Manlio Graziano, *Frontiere* (Il Mulino, 2017) 7.

[100] Dario Gentili, 'Hic Sunt Leones. Border/Frontier. The Political Genealogy of a Spatial Disposition' in Wolfgang Müller Funk, *Borders of Europe* (Istituto Italiano di Studi Germanici, 2021) 112. See also van Middelaar (n 11) 11–32.

[101] Gentili (n 100) 113.

well as relations and contacts'.[102] *Wider Europe* is about the open and peaceful development of an outside space that would be complementary to the Union's borders following its enlargement in the 2000s. The *Wider Europe* design could be thus associated with the establishment of the Union's *limes*, creating contact and contrasts in an often asymmetrical manner. In this respect, Foucher has noted:

> The Roman *limes* was not a continuous closed wall. It was essentially a strategy aiming both at containing unwelcomed migrants and at organizing trade with Romanised peoples and to bring them into a sustained peaceful relationship with the Empire. To the extent that a comparison is possible, the interaction between Europe as an organised union and its southern flank, from Morocco to Turkey, is similar to a '*limes*-style' strategy, where the border is closed to migrations and citizenship but open to trade, ideas and languages, in an asymmetrical relationship which remains a permanent source of tension.[103]

The geopolitical motives of *Wider Europe* can be inferred by considering its relations with power, geography and narrative.[104] In that regard, the significance of law in the *Wider Europe* is paramount especially in light of the utopian character of *Europe* and the role of law as a key source of EU power.[105] Law thus plays a crucial part in the EU encounter with geopolitics. The language of power typical of geopolitics is translated into, often asymmetric, legal techniques for extending the EU *acquis*. The EU's engagement with geography and territory is largely intangible: it is about the creation of a legal space more than a bounded place.[106] The narrative of the *Wider Europe* design is certainly EU-centric, predicated on the transformative successes of the Union and of its enlargement. The narrative of the 'ring of friends' with whom to share everything but institutions evoke on the one hand a hub-and-spoke arrangement[107] where the EU models and practices derive from the centre that remains in charge of the (institutional) decision-making. Yet, *Wider Europe* primarily signals the desire to extend beyond EU membership a set of legal relations and practices often construed as venues for sustainable modernisation and peaceful interactions among political entities.

[102] Giovanna Daverio Rocchi, 'Il Concetto Di Frontiera Nella Grecia Antica' in Marta Sordi, *Il confine nel mondo classico* (Vita e Pensiero, 1987) 25–31. See also Mireille Rosello and Stephen Wolfe, 'Introduction' in Johan Schimanski and Stephen Wolfe, *Border aesthetics : concepts and intersections* (Berghahn Books, 2017) 11, here the authors construe borders (or in the present chapter's reflection 'frontiers') as 'liminal zones that not only separate but also connect'.

[103] Foucher (n 93) 236.

[104] The articulation of geopolitics in power, territory, and narrative is borrowed from van Middelaar (n 13).

[105] For a discussion on the role of law as a key source of EU power see Marise Cremona and Joanne Scott, 'Introduction', *EU Law Beyond EU Borders: The Extraterritorial Reach of EU Law* (Oxford University Press, 2019); Anu Bradford, *The Brussels Effect : How the European Union Rules the World* (Oxford University Press, 2020).

[106] cf Lindahl (n 89).

[107] To be sure the EU proximity policies have also a regional integration dimension. This has taken the form of various regional initiatives as the Barcelona Process and the Union for the Mediterranean in the south and the Eastern Partnership in the east. Attempts of regional integration have also underpinned the EU policies towards the Western Balkans. The Stabilisation and Association Process indeed included regional integration as an element of conditionality (see the preamble of the SAAs Agreements). *cf* Marise Cremona, 'The ENP and Multilateralism in Sara Poli' (ed) Cremona in Sara Poli, *The European Neighbourhood Policy – Values and Principles* (Routledge, 2016).

VI. Conclusions

This chapter has initiated the endeavour of turning *Wider Europe* into an analytical concept. As a policy initiative, *Wider Europe* originated in the early 2000s following the EU enlargements and the acknowledgment of the exhaustion of the Union's capacity of absorbing new members. The EU attempted to engage with its new neighbours by developing a new concept of proximity entailing a passage from *membership* to *friendship*. The main sources of this concept would be the enlargement policy, with its conditionality methodology, and the EEA model, with the extension of the EU *acquis* beyond membership. By discussing the constitutional foundations of the extension of the EU's legal space and examining the composite mosaic of pre-existing legal arrangements, the chapter has emancipated *Wider Europe* from a single proximity policy. The potential of *Wider Europe* to capture a variety of EU proximity policies clearly emerges from the geopolitical motives underlying the extension of the EU's legal space. The 'everything but institutions' formula in *Wider Europe* is the expression of complex dynamics of inclusion and exclusion which, although largely inadvertently, evoke a *lato sensu* reconfiguration of the Union's borders. It amounts to the extension of the Union's limes.

3

The Relationship between EU Membership Law and EU Neighbourhood Law

I. Introduction

This chapter engages with the legal facets of the *Wider Europe* 'everything but institutions' formula. It discloses how the principle of autonomy of EU law governs the dynamics of inclusion and exclusion in the extended EU's legal space. The chapter starts by examining the role of the principle of autonomy of EU law in articulating and defending the distinctive political covenant of EU membership law (section II). The specific characteristics of EU integration are assessed in light of the scholarly developments from Pescatore's *The Law of Integration* to Cappelletti, Seccombe and Weiler's *Integration through law* (section III). The methodological shifts informing these developments bring to the fore the importance of reflecting on three dimensions of EU law relevant to *Wider Europe:* the pre-normative phase of the law; the post-normative of the law; and the notion of EU citizenship. These three dimensions are used as prisms to investigate the complex relations between EU membership and EU neighbourhood law (section III.A–C). The distinctive character of EU membership law as compared to arrangements extending the EU's legal space lead us to interrogate the categories of 'EU integration without membership' and 'external differentiated integration' developed by the EU legal scholarship (section IV). On the methodological plane, the theoretical corpus of Santi Romano's *The Legal Order* is mobilised to investigate the interactions between legal systems in their relationships of relevance or irrelevance, superiority and dependence while accounting for the various types of *renvois* (section IV.A). The chapter then discloses how the extension of the EU's legal space also occurs through more legally elusive phenomena of third country socialisation in *Wider Europe* (section IV.B). The chapter concludes with a reflection on the political covenants of EU membership and EU neighbourhood law (section V).

II. The Principle of Autonomy: Safeguarding EU Membership Law and its Political Covenant

The legal facets of the dynamics of inclusion and exclusion inherent to the *Wider Europe* design are governed by the principle of autonomy of EU law. By identifying the unique features of the political and sovereignty covenant of EU law, the Court of Justice has progressively delineated the distinctive character of the EU integration experience. In *Van Gend en Loos*, the Court famously qualified the EU as 'a new legal order of international law[1] for the benefit of which states have limited their sovereign rights, albeit within limited fields, and the subject of which comprise not only Member States but also their nationals'. It went on to emphasise 'the establishment of institutions endowed with sovereign rights, the exercise of which affects Member States and also their citizens'. It noted how 'the nationals of the states brought together in the [Union] are called together to cooperate in the functioning of this [Union] through the intermediary of the European Parliament'. In the Court's view, the (EU funding) Treaty 'is more than an agreement which merely creates mutual obligations between the contracting states', and this is confirmed by the preamble 'which refers not only to governments but to peoples'.[2]

International cooperation among the Member States of the EU has engendered a reconfiguration in their exercise of sovereignty and in their relationship with their nationals. This distinctive political covenant of EU membership law is not replicated in *Wider Europe*. In fact, the participation in the EU institutional machinery is not contemplated in international arrangements concluded by the EU in its neighbourhood. Interestingly, in a subsequent and equally famous pronouncement of the Court, *Costa v ENEL*, the upholding of the distinctiveness of EU membership law has run in parallel with the development of the principle of autonomy. Indeed, the Court spelled out the sovereignty arrangement underlying the EU by stating that the EU legal order contains 'its *own* institutions' and 'real powers stemming from a limitation of sovereignty or a *transfer of powers* from the States to the Community'. Moreover, in the French version of the case, EU law was characterised as '*issue d'une source autonome*' with a view to marking EU law primacy over conflicting national laws.[3]

The legal scholarship has endeavoured to further articulate the political covenant of EU membership law. In his work on the *Law of Integration*, Pescatore highlighted how international relations based on a conception of sovereignty as 'indivisible, unassailable and absolute' would render 'Relationships forged in such

[1] Case 26-62 *Van Gend and Loos*, EU:C:1963:1, in the french version: 'un nouvel ordre juridique de droit international'.

[2] ibid.

[3] In the English version the adjective *autonome* was translated with 'independent' (emphasis added). A similar translation was used within the context of EU primacy over national law in Case 11–70 *Internationale Handelsgesellschaft*, EU:C:1970:114 [3].

conditions[...] inevitably weak and unstable'. But this conception of sovereignty is an '*a priori* assumption'. The EU (then the European Community) instead was 'built upon a refashioning of sovereignties' which would 'permit variations, from the point of view of structure and relationship, far more diverse than those possible under the international law of cooperation'. Pescatore continued by noting how 'Such a refashioning depends on the nature of the prerogatives surrendered, on the methods of organising them in the context of a new complex with the residual sovereignty of the states'.[4]

The protection of the distinctiveness of the EU legal order and its underlying political covenant is governed by the principle of autonomy. The principle has been developed by the Court of Justice especially in its opinions delivered pursuant to (now) Article 218(11) TFEU on the compatibility of international agreements concluded in the EU's neighbourhood with EU law. In *Opinion 1/76*, the Court was asked to deliver an opinion on a draft agreement establishing a European laying-up fund for inland waterway vessels in European rivers including the Rhine and Moselle. Switzerland would be party to the proposed Convention together with the Union and some of its Member States. For the Commission, the arrangement was controversial as it envisaged for the EU 'a certain delegation of powers of decision and judicial powers to bodies which are independent of the common institutions.'[5]

The Court considered that the provisions of the envisaged Convention would 'call into question the power of the institutions of the [Union] and, moreover, alter in a manner inconsistent with the Treaty the relationship between Member States within the EU.'[6] The management of the envisioned fund would lead to a 'substitution in the structure of the organs of the Funds, of several Member States in place of the EU and its institution' in a field covered by EU rules.[7] This substitution was problematic in light of some Member States' exclusion from the fund, and because the decision-making procedures and concepts of EU law would risk being altered: the scope of the proposed convention covered matters where EU legislation had been adopted.[8] The Court stressed how that 'far from restricting itself to the solution of problems resulting from' requirements of the EU international cooperation, the envisaged Convention would constitute 'both a surrender of the *autonomy* of action[9] of the [EU] in its external relations and a change in the internal constitution of the [EU] by the alteration of essential elements of the [Union] structure as regards both the position of the institutions and the position of the

[4] Pierre Pescatore, *The Law of Integration: emergence of a new phenomenon in international relations, based on the experience of the European Communities* (Sijthoff, 1974) 30–31.

[5] *Opinion 1/76*, EU:C:1977:63.

[6] ibid [10].

[7] ibid [11].

[8] ibid [11].

[9] My translation from French: 'autonomie d'action'. In the English version 'independence of action' was used; (emphasis added).

Member States *vis-à-vis* one another.'[10] In other words, the envisaged Convention would challenge the Union's membership covenant by altering the equilibria of the exercise of sovereign powers within the EU. Such a challenge would arise from the fact that EU institutions would have transferred 'to non-[EU] organisms powers or part of the powers granted by the Treaty'.[11]

The Court's pronouncement aimed at safeguarding the distinctiveness of the EU legal order and particularly its decision-making autonomy from influences that may arise from mechanisms of international law. The findings in *Opinion 1/76* were subsequently developed in other Court's pronouncements on draft international agreements providing for the extension of the EU's legal space. *Opinion 1/91* addressed the compatibility with EU law of the establishment of the European Economic Area. The Court noted that the objective of this arrangement was that of ensuring legal homogeneity throughout the EEA. Such an aim was to be achieved inter alia by means of replicating EU rules through the EEA regime. Moreover, Article 6 of the envisaged agreement required the EEA Court therein established to interpret EEA provisions corresponding to the EU Treaties in conformity with the case law of the Court of Justice delivered prior to the signature of the agreement. The CJEU found that this was not sufficient to guarantee homogeneity not only because of the temporal limitation of the requirement, but also because conformity with the interpretation did not include the essential principles of EU law, such as primacy and direct effect.[12] *Opinion 1/91* on the establishment of the EEA thus intimates a demarcation between the EU legal order and the international legal regimes replicating EU law provisions.

A key passage of the *Opinion* clarified the different nature between EU membership law and the law of the extension of the EU's legal space in light of the different underlying political covenants. Differently from Union membership law, in fact, the

> EEA [was] to be established on the basis of an international treaty which, essentially, merely creates rights and obligations as between the Contracting Parties and provides for no transfer of sovereign rights to the inter-governmental institutions which it sets up.[13]

This is in stark contrast with the Court's findings in *Van Gend en Loos*.[14] The correspondence between rights and obligations hinted to by the Court in *Opinion 1/91* (and further developed in Recital 4 of the EEA Agreement) is crucial in the governance of international agreements concluded in the EU's neighbourhood. This is stressed in Article 8(2) TEU and has informed the negotiating stance of

[10] *Opinion 1/76* (n 5) [12].
[11] ibid [15].
[12] *Opinion 1/91* EU:C:1991:490 [26]–[27].
[13] ibid [20].
[14] Here the Court famously stated that the EEC Treaty 'is more than an agreement which merely creates mutual obligations between the contracting states. This view is confirmed by the preamble to the Treaty which refers not only to governments but to people', *cf van Gend and Loos* (n 1).

the EU political institutions in the context of *Brexit*.[15] Prior to delivering *Opinion 1/91*, the Court had already elucidated the difference of the EU legal order from international law arrangements stressing that 'the [EU] Treaty is not limited to creating reciprocal obligations between the different natural and legal persons to whom it is applicable',[16] and is not based on reciprocity.[17]

An additional and problematic aspect found by the ECJ with respect to autonomy of the EU was that the envisaged EEA Court would have had 'organic links' with the Court of Justice. In other words, judges from the Court of Justice would also have to sit on the EEA Court. The ECJ thus highlighted the different aims and contexts characterising the EEA and the EU legal order, with the latter being described as broader in scope and more ambitious than the former. As a result,

> depending on whether they are sitting on the Court of Justice or on the EEA Court, the judges of the Court of Justice who are members of the EEA Court [would] have had to apply and interpret the same provisions but using different approaches, methods and concepts in order to take into account the nature of each treaty and of its particular objectives.[18]

The extension of the EU institutional structure alongside the extension of EU's legal space would ultimately undermine the specific political covenant underlying the EU legal order, premised upon a transfer of sovereign powers from the Member States to the EU institutions.

A subsequent version of the EEA Agreement was then considered compatible with Union law by the Court of Justice in *Opinion 1/92*.[19] The new Agreement was still premised upon the replication of EU law within the EEA regime. Yet, it did not envisage an extension of the EU institutional structure. A separate institutional framework was set up for the EEA EFTA States. The CJEU case law remained the authoritative source of interpretation on the provisions of the extended EU law and a role for the CJEU was also envisaged in the Agreement's dispute settlement mechanisms.[20] In that light, the new version of the EEA Agreement invites us to qualify the 'everything but institutions' formula. In fact, the use of the EU institutions outside the EU Treaty framework is not entirely precluded. It is the extension of the EU's institutional structure beyond EU membership to be ruled out: by including non-members, the extended institutional structure would be liable to undermine the distinctiveness of the political covenant of EU membership law.

[15] See for instance European Commission, 'Remarks by Michel Barnier following Round 3 of negotiations for a new partnership between the European Union and the United Kingdom', Brussels, 15 May 2020, SPEECH/20/895. This especially concerned the UK's request to maintain some benefits of the EU single market without the corresponding obligations.
[16] Joined Cases 90 and 91/63, *Commission v Luxembourg and Belgium* EU:C:1964:80.
[17] Case 325/82, *Commission v Germany* EU:C:1984:60 [11].
[18] *Opinion 1/91* (n 12) [51].
[19] *Opinion 1/92*, EU:C:1992:189.
[20] See further ch 4 of this work.

The criteria for the use of EU institutions outside the EU Treaty framework in arrangements extending the EU's legal space have been articulated principally in *Opinion 1/00* on the establishment of the European Common Aviation Area (ECAA).[21] Here, the Court developed the principle of autonomy 'as a clearly defined external relations law principle'.[22] It established two criteria for the use of EU institutions outside the EU Treaty framework to be compatible with the principle of autonomy. First, the essential character of the powers of the EU and its institutions as conceived in the Treaty should remain unaltered.[23] Secondly, the procedures for ensuring uniform interpretation of the rules of the Agreement and for resolving disputes would not have the effect of binding the EU and its institutions to a particular interpretation of EU law contained in the Agreement.[24] The Court delineated the conditions under which EU institutions could carry out tasks similar to those provided by the Treaties beyond EU membership law.[25] It mandated, however, that EU institutions shall not be altered in function and composition. Besides, the principle of autonomy of EU law would require that the mechanisms for the extension of the EU's legal space would not affect the autonomous interpretation of the provisions of EU law among EU members.

The case law examined above brings to the fore a distinction between EU membership law and international agreements extending the EU's *acquis* in the neighbourhood. As aptly noted by Öberg, the Court has proved more willing to sacrifice the homogeneity of the extended EU legal space than to undermine the autonomy of EU membership law.[26] The principle of autonomy serves thus to protect the distinctiveness of EU membership law from mechanisms of international law liable to jeopardise the essential characteristics of the EU legal order[27] and of its underlying political covenant.

The separation of EU membership law from international law mechanisms was notably developed in the controversial *Opinion 2/13* where the Court of Justice sanctioned the incompatibility of EU law with the second draft agreement on the EU accession to the European Convention of Human Rights (ECHR).[28] Here, the

[21] See further ch 5 of this work.

[22] Rass Holdgaard, *External Relations Law of the European Community: Legal Reasoning and Legal Discourses* (Kluwer Law International, 2008) 85.

[23] *Opinion 1/00*, EU:C:2002:231 [12].

[24] ibid [27]. See also Fernando Castillo de la Torre, 'Opinion 1/00 proposed agreement on the establishment of a European Common Aviation Area' (2002) 39 *Common Market Law Review* 1373. This was also firmly upheld in the subsequent case law. See *Opinion 1/09*, EU:C:2011:123 [78].

[25] See also Case C-370/12 *Pringle v Ireland* EU:C:2012:756. For a problematisation see Alessandro Petti, 'EMU *Inter-se Agreements: EMU inter-se agreements: a laboratory for thinking about associative institutionalism*, 2015, EUI, LAW, LLM Thesis.

[26] Marja-Liisa Öberg, 'Autonomy of the EU Legal Order: A Concept in Need of Revision?' (2020) 26 *European Public Law* 705, 727.

[27] See further Cristina Contartese, 'The Autonomy of the EU Legal Order in the ECJ's External Relations Case Law: From the "essential" to the "Specific Characteristics" of the Union and Back Again' (2017) 54 *Common Market Law Review* 1627.

[28] For the first rejection, see *Opinion 2/94*, EU:C:1996:140.

'essential characteristics' of EU membership law, and the underlying political covenant, were powerfully depicted as

> a structured network of principles, rules and mutually interdependent legal relations linking the EU and its Member States, and its Member States with each other, which are now engaged … in a 'process of creating an ever closer union among the peoples of Europe'.[29]

Moreover, the draft agreement failed to take into consideration the fact that

> the Member States, have, by reason of their membership of the EU, accepted that the relations between them as regards the matters covered by the transfer of powers from the Member States to the EU are governed by EU law to the exclusion, if EU law so requires, of any other law.[30]

The draft agreement on accession to the ECHR did not sufficiently protect the distinctiveness of EU law from international law mechanisms, especially from those of a judicial nature.[31] In fact, the subsequent instances whereby the Court declared the compatibility of EU law with international law dispute settlements were characterised by an adequate separation between EU law and the international law arrangement entered into by the EU.[32] The contours of the principle of autonomy of EU law from international law have been further spelled out in the context of *Brexit* in the *Wightman* case.[33] More recently, in the cases concerning the challenges by Hungary and Poland of the Conditionality Regulation,[34] the Court has made it clear that the special political covenant of EU membership, based on the values of the Union and safeguarded by the principle of autonomy, shall sustain legal relations within the Union in all phases of EU membership.[35]

The preservation of the specific characteristics of the EU legal order is articulated in different facets. In this regard, Cécile Rapoport highlights three components of the principle of autonomy: the structural, the institutional and the material.[36] The structural dimension[37] pertains to the preservation of the set of relations among the EU and its Member States in sustaining the EU

[29] *Opinion 2/13*, EU:C:2014:2454 [167].

[30] ibid [193].

[31] ibid [253].

[32] *Opinion 1/17*, EU:C:2019:341; This separation is emphasised by Cécile Rapoport, 'Balancing on a Tightrope: Opinion 1/17 and the ECJ's Narrow and Tortuous Path for Compatibility of the EU's Investment Court System (ICS)' (2020) 57 *Common Market Law Review* 1725.

[33] Case C-621/18, *Wightman*, EU:C:2018:999 [45].

[34] Regulation (EU) on a general regime of conditionality for the protection of the Union budget, [2020] OJ L 433I/1.

[35] Case C-156/21 *Hungary v Parliament and Council*, EU:C:2022:97 [125]–[126]; Case C-157/21 *Poland v Parliament and Council*, EU:C:2022:98 [143]–[144].

[36] Cécile Rapoport, 'Autonomy of the EU Legal Order and International Agreements Extending the Acquis: Opinion 1/00 (European Common Aviation Area)' in Graham Butler and Ramses A Wessel, *EU External Relations Law: The Cases in Context* (Hart Publishing, 2022).

[37] Inspired by the analysis in Marise Cremona, 'Structural Principles and Their Role in EU External Relations Law' in Marise Cremona (ed), *Structural principles in EU external relations law* (Hart Publishing, 2018).

legal order.[38] This component is particularly significant in mixed agreements where the Union is a party alongside its Member State to the relevant international instrument. Autonomy thus protects the specific characteristics of EU law from international law mechanisms.[39] In *Opinion 1/00* the institutional dimension featured prominently. The institutional component pertains to the preservation of the essential characters of the powers of EU institutions, especially when these powers extend extraterritorially.[40] Finally, the material component is concerned with the safeguard of 'the canons of interpretation of [EU] law'[41] and is connected to the authoritative role of the case law of the CJEU in agreements which extend the EU's legal space.[42]

A closer look at the principle of autonomy and its institutional dimension unravels the legal facet of the 'everything but institutions' formula. The principle of autonomy indeed presides over the dynamics of inclusion and exclusion inherent to the extension of the EU's legal space. While inclusion is predicated on a 'set of principles, values and standards which define the very essence of the European Union' to be 'extended' to the neighbouring region,[43] a primary form of exclusion appears in the guise of neighbouring country preclusion from taking part in the decision-making and institutional set-up of the Union. Exclusion is aimed at safeguarding the decision-making autonomy of the Union as an essential dimension of EU membership law.

III. The Demarcation and Complex Relationship between EU Membership Law and the Law of the Extension of the EU's Legal Space

The requirements of the principle of autonomy intimate a demarcation between the EU internal and external experiences. As highlighted by Cremona, 'the EU as an integration project has an external as well as an internal quality',[44] and EU law defines 'the boundary between internal and external'.[45] This boundary is governed by the principle of autonomy of EU law. In order to expound the demarcation and complex relationship between the internal and external, this

[38] See Rapoport (n 36) 426.
[39] *Opinion 2/13* (n 29); *Opinion 1/17* (n 32); *Opinion 1/09* (n 24).
[40] Rapoport (n 36).
[41] *Opinion 1/00* (n 23) [5].
[42] Rapoport (n 36).
[43] Romano Prodi, European Commission 'A Wider Europe – A Proximity Policy as the Key to Stability', Speech/02/619.
[44] This is also captured in Art 21(1) TEU: 'The Union's action on the international scene shall be guided by the principles which have inspired its own creation, development and enlargement'.
[45] Marise Cremona, 'Extending the Reach of EU Law: The EU as an International Legal Actor' in Marise Cremona and Joanne Scott, *EU Law Beyond EU Borders: The Extraterritorial Reach of EU Law* (Oxford University Press, 2019) 66.

section relies on the methodological shift characterising the developments in the EU legal scholarship from Pescatore's *The Law of Integration* (LoI)[46] to the Cappelletti, Seccombe and Weiler *Integration through Law* (ItL).[47] The developments mainly revolved around a move from law to governance in the study of the EU legal experience.[48] The ensuing metodological shift entails the consideration of three dimensions of EU law: the pre-normative; the post-normative phases of the law;[49] and the specificities of EU citizenship law.[50] These scholarly developments are utilised as prisms to appreciate the different nature of EU membership law and EU neighbourhood law in light of the principle of autonomy.

A. The Pre-normative Phase of the Law: The Exclusion from the EU Institutions

The dynamics of exclusion inherent to *Wider Europe* emerge in the pre-normative phase. EU neighbouring countries participating in the extended EU legal space are excluded from the EU institutions and the relevant decision-making process. In other words, the difference between EU membership law and the law extending the EU's legal space is due to the fact that only EU members are empowered to make EU law. Consequently, countries participating in *Wider Europe* are largely rule-takers.

Even in the most developed forms of the extension of the EU's legal space, non-EU members are allowed to take part *only* in the decision-shaping phase of the laws that they ultimately are going to adopt.[51] The generally limited degree of joint ownership of the extended EU legal space appears to confirm that its construction is more concerned with the preservation of the autonomy of the EU than with the homogeneity of the wider European legal space.[52]

Outside the status of membership, no participation is envisaged in the decision-making process of (extended) EU law. At best, only participation in the decision-shaping of the law is envisaged. In the cases of the most developed partnerships in the EU, as in the EEA arrangement, participation in the decision-shaping may entail an obligation from the Commission to seek advice from the non-EU states' experts 'in the same way' as it seeks advice from the experts of the

[46] Pescatore (n 4).

[47] Mauro Cappelletti, Monica Seccombe and Joseph H Weiler, *Integration through Law: A Political, Legal and Economic Overview* (De Gruyter, 1985).

[48] On this and more in general on the relationship between the *Law of Integration* project and the *Integration through Law* see Loïc Azoulai, 'Integration through Law and Us' (2016) 14 *International Journal of Constitutional Law* 449.

[49] Cappelletti, Seccombe and Weiler (n 47) 61.

[50] ibid 68. See further Azoulai (n 48).

[51] See EEA Agreement [1994] OJ L1/3, Art 99.

[52] Cécile Rapoport, *Les partenariats entre l'Union européenne et les États tiers européens: étude de la contribution de l'Union européenne à la structuration juridique de l'espace européen* (Bruylant, 2011) 563.

EU states, although this consultation is informal.[53] However, non-EU states have no voting and decision-making powers in the institutions devoted to the crafting of EU law. On a legal plane, the non-EU members do not consent to transfer their sovereignty, a transfer that would give them the right to participate in EU legislative production.[54] This is due to the different political covenant underlying EU membership and the legal arrangements in the EU neighbourhood. Although EU partner countries remain formally sovereign, the nature of the partnership is largely asymmetric as third countries are often required to align their legal systems with EU law.[55] In other words, EU-led international regimes engender claims to authority going beyond the EU's territory. This entails a reconfiguration of the way in which sovereignty is exercised.

Exclusion of third countries from the decision-making and institutional structures of the Union in the pre-normative phase of the law can be construed as an expression of the principle of autonomy of EU law. The 'everything but institution formula' precisely captures the EU's desire to safeguard internal regulatory autonomy and sovereignty shielding it from external influence.

B. The Post-normative Phase: The *Polydor* Principle

The demarcation between the internal and external may be also appreciated in the context of the post-normative phase of the institutional arrangements of *Wider Europe*. The case law on these agreements clarifies that extended EU law does not possess the same nature and qualities of EU law and is not necessarily to be interpreted in the same way as EU law provisions. Borrowing from Cremona's words, the EU law extended to countries in the proximity does not possess the 'infrastructure for the constitutional model of integration'[56] reserved for its members. Consequently, the interpretation of provisions replicating those of EU law may be different from that of EU law proper.

In *Polydor*, the Court inaugurated the copious case law contributing to defining the effects and the nature of extended EU law. The case at issue concerned the provisions of the trade area established between the EEC and Portugal through a bilateral agreement.[57] The Court had to decide on whether Article 23 of the EC-Portugal Agreement could be interpreted in the same way as Article 36 EEC (now Article 36 TFEU). Following the path traced by the Advocate General, the

[53] EEA Agreement (n 51), Art 99(1).

[54] Rapoport (n 52) 557.

[55] ibid. The author notes 's'il reste juridiquement souverain, l'Etat tiers européen entretenant avec l'Union des relations de nature partenariale peut se trouver en position de *suivisme juridique*, lorsqu'il consent à reprendre dans son ordre juridique interne le droit de l'Union.' (Emphasis added).

[56] Marise Cremona, 'Flexible Models: External Policy and the European Economic Community' in Grainne de Búrca and Joanne Scott (eds), *Constitutional Change in the EU: From Uniformity to Flexibility?* (Hart Publishing, 2000) 93.

[57] Case 270/80 *Polydor*, EU:C:1982:43.

Court established that the similarity in wording of the provision of the EEC Treaty and the EEC–Portugal Agreement '[was] not a sufficient reason for transposing to the provisions of the agreement the [Union] case-law' with a view to interpreting the said Agreement.[58] The scope of application of that case law had to be 'determined in light of the [Union's] objectives and activities'.[59] The Court found that the Union's objectives were more ambitious than those of the Agreement at issue as they intended 'to unite national markets into a single market having the characteristics of a domestic market'.[60]

These findings were soon reiterated in *Metalsa*, a case concerning the prohibition of discriminatory measures of a fiscal nature in the context of the EEC–Austria Free Trade Agreement. Building on the considerations made in *Polydor*, the ECJ clarified that, pursuant to the 1969 Vienna Convention on the Law of the Treaties (VCLT),[61] the interpretation of the terms of a treaty shall be informed by the context of the Agreement as well as by its objectives and purposes.[62] The Court thus outlined the contours of the contextual interpretation under international law of agreements replicating substantive provisions of EU law. It established that:

> It is clear … that the extension of the interpretation of a provision in the Treaty to a comparably, similarly or even identically worded provision of an agreement concluded by the Community with a non-member country depends, inter alia, on the aim pursued by each provision in its particular context and that a comparison between the objectives and context of the agreement and those of the Treaty is of considerable importance in that regard.[63]

The *Polydor* findings intimate once again a demarcation between the EU membership law and the law of the extended EU legal space. The distinction is predicated on the different objects and contexts of EU law and the law extending the EU's legal space. The *Polydor* principle had been temporarily dormant in the free movement case law principally concerning the 'Europe Agreements' promoting the association between the EEC and Central and Eastern European Countries that would join the EU in the waves of enlargements of the 2000s. For instance, the *Pokrzeptowicz-Meyer* case concerned the prohibition of discrimination based on nationality with respect to the conditions of employment for Polish workers in EC Member States. Here, the Court established that the equal treatment provision enshrined in the Europe Agreement under scrutiny was of the same tenor as the corresponding EC internal market provision.[64] Similarly, in *Jany*, the Court

[58] ibid [5].

[59] ibid [16].

[60] ibid.

[61] See particularly Vienna Convention on the Law of the Treaties, UN Treaty Series, 23 May 1969, Art 31.

[62] Case C-312/91 Metalsa EU:C:1993:279 [12].

[63] ibid [11].

[64] Case C-162/00 *Pokrzeptowicz-Meyer* EU:C:2002:57 [41]. Here the Court posited a similar interpretation of Art 37(1) of the EC-Poland Europe Agreement [1993] OJ L384/2, and the then Art 48 EC (now Art 45 TFEU).

maintained that the reference to 'economic activities as self-employed persons' referred to in the Association Agreements between the EC and Poland and the Czech Republic had to be interpreted in the same manner as corresponding provisions of EU law.[65]

Remarkably, this line of reasoning also seemed applicable in the context of the EU–Russia Partnership Agreement. In *Simutenkov*, the CJEU found that the provision on non-discrimination on the basis of nationality enshrined Article 23(1) of the Agreement, precluded 'any Member State from discriminating, on grounds of nationality, against Russian workers, vis-à-vis their own nationals, so far as their conditions of employment, remuneration and dismissal are concerned'.[66] The dormant *Polydor* case law was mentioned in *Pokrzeptowicz-Meyer*,[67] but not in *Jany* or *Simutenkov*. These cases promoted the analogous interpretation of agreements which replicated EU law provisions and proper EU law. They may be read in the framework of an incremental jurisprudence whereby such an analogous interpretation was often established in parallel to the direct effect of those provisions.[68] This led some commentators to remark that the *Polydor* jurisprudence was fading especially after *Simutenkov*, and to acknowledge a shift in the Courts' pronouncements from a contextual to a more textual method of interpretation.[69]

The *Simutenkov* case was particularly interesting as the Agreement with Russia was not a *Europe Agreement* but a PCA Agreement. As noted by the Advocate General, the Agreement 'lagg[ed] behind the Europe agreements' both for its substantive content and its institutional provisions.[70] The Court largely followed the Advocate General by underscoring how the scope and objectives of the Partnership Agreement were not intended 'to establish an association with a view to the gradual integration of that non-member country into the [EU] but is designed rather to bring about "the gradual integration between Russia and a wider area of cooperation in Europe"'.[71] This, however, did not discourage the Court from granting direct effect to the PCA non-discrimination provision.[72]

This incremental jurisprudence on direct effect and analogous interpretation of agreements concluded by the EU in its neighbourhood also characterised the association agreements concluded with southern countries. In *Kziber*, the CJEU interpreted the non-discrimination clause enshrined in Article 41(1) of the Cooperation Agreement then in force with Morocco as being directly applicable.[73]

[65] Case C-268/99 *Jany* EU:C:2001:616 [50].
[66] Case C-265/03 *Simutenkov*, EU:C:2005:213 [22].
[67] *Pokrzeptowicz-Meyer* (n 64) [32].
[68] See ibid [30; *Jany* (n 65) [28]; *Simutenkov* (n 66) [26].
[69] Christophe Hillion, 'Case C–265/03, Igor Simutenkov v. Ministerio de Educación y Cultura, Real Federación Española de Fùtbol, [2005] ECR I–2579' (2008) 45 *Common Market Law Review* 828, see also his fn 56.
[70] Case C-265/03 *Simutenkov*, Opinion of Advocate General Stix-Hackl, EU:C:2005:6 [33]–[34].
[71] *Simutenkov* (n 66) [35].
[72] See generally Hillion (n 69) 830.
[73] Case C-18/90 *Kziber*, EU:C:1991:36 [17].

In *Kziber*, the Court established that the direct applicability of the clause applied also in the field of social security. In its reasoning, the Court referred to the criteria spelled out in *Demirel*[74] which would enable the provision of an agreement concluded by the EU to be directly applicable.[75] The Court again upheld its findings irrespective of the fact that the Agreement did not refer to 'Morocco's association with or future accession to' the EU.[76] In fact, the period from the fall of the Berlin Wall to EU enlargement in the 2000s was characterised by a climate of general confidence on the exportability of the EU model.[77]

Such incremental jurisprudence, however, did not challenge the tenets of the *Polydor* principle: contextual interpretation was an integral part of the Court's reasoning. The Court largely based its findings on the observation that the agreements concluded in the eastern neighbourhood were intended 'to create an appropriate framework for the progressive integration [of third countries] into the [EU]'.[78] The context (and the political climate) of the agreement remained fundamental in the interpretation of the provisions of the cooperation agreements in the southern neighbourhood.[79] This incremental jurisprudence, however, would not develop linearly and would undergo a retrenchment in the event of contextual changes preventing analogous interpretation. As occurred in the *Demirel* case, these contextual changes could be geopolitical in nature.[80]

The parallelism of the lines of reasoning on the two separate issues of direct effect and analogous interpretation of the provisions of the EU bilateral agreements to the corresponding provisions of EU law was destined to be contingent. As early as in *Kupferberg*, where the direct effect of bilateral trade agreements was forcefully upheld, the findings on direct effect and on the analogous interpretation of the bilateral Agreement's provisions to those of EU law were developed along two distinct paths. To be sure, both the issue of direct effect and analogous interpretation were analysed in the review of the context of the Agreement. In particular, the Court established that the purpose of and context of the Agreement suggested that some of its provisions were unconditional and sufficiently precise to be granted direct effect. This was the case with regards to the provision of non-discrimination on matters of taxation enshrined in Article 21 of the Agreement.[81] Nevertheless, the article at issue, in light of the different contexts and purposes of the EU–Portugal Agreement and EU law, would not 'be applied by way of simple analogy' in the same manner as the corresponding EC–Portugal Agreement.[82]

[74] Case 12/86 *Demirel*, EU:C:1987:400.
[75] *Kziber* (n 73) [15].
[76] ibid [21].
[77] The policy design of *Wider Europe* resonated with this belief; Prodi (n 43).
[78] Case C-162/00 *Pokrzeptowicz-Meyer* (n 64) [42]; *Simutenkov* (n 66) [27]; *Jany* (n 65) [4].
[79] *Kziber* (n 108) [15] and [23].
[80] On this see Georg Nolte, 'Case 12/86, Meryem Demirel v. Stadt Schwäbisch Gmünd, Judgment of 30 September 1987' (1988) 25 *Common Market Law Review* 403.
[81] Case 104/81 *Kupferberg* EU:C:1982:362 [26].
[82] ibid [30].

The separate tracks for the ascertainment of direct effect and analogous interpretation to the corresponding provisions of EU law would be confirmed in later case law.[83]

The *Polydor* principle made its return into the framework of EU–Swiss relations and in particular in the Bilateral Agreement on the Free Movement of Persons (FMP). In *Grimme*, the Court was asked to determine whether the FMP Agreement could be broadly interpreted as guaranteeing freedom of establishment not only to natural persons but also to legal persons. It relied on the *Polydor* principle to refuse such an interpretation noting how Switzerland had

> refused to subscribe to the project of an economically integrated entity with a single market …. In that context, the interpretation given to the provisions of [Union] law concerning the internal market [could not]be automatically applied by analogy to the interpretation of the [FMP] Agreement, unless there [were] express provisions to that effect laid down by the Agreement itself.[84]

The principle was also applied in the context of the EU–Swiss Air Transport Agreement. The Agreement extends substantive provisions of EU law and the EU institutions reach of powers.[85] In *Switzerland v Commission*, the Court did not uphold an interpretation on the provisions concerning the Air Transport Agreement that precluded discrimination based on nationality[86] as including freedom to provide services. The Court held that the Agreement

> does not contain any specific provision such as to enable the air carriers concerned to benefit from the provisions of European Union law on the freedom to provide services. The interpretation given to those provisions cannot therefore be transposed to that Agreement.[87]

Moreover, in the framework of the EU–Swiss relations, the ECJ stressed that a difference in treatment to third countries is not contrary to EU law: in the Court's words, there is 'no general principle obliging the Union, in its external relations, to accord in all respects equal treatment to different third countries and traders do not in any event have the right to rely on the existence of such a principle'.[88] Arguably, albeit in an indirect manner, the ECJ sanctioned the conformity of EU law of different echelons of gravitation around the EU legal order. The ECJ posited that, 'the Union must, therefore, be in a position to choose its policies and to apply, according to the objectives that it pursues, a distinction between third countries, without being obliged to grant equal treatment to all third countries'.[89]

The *Polydor* principle was also subsequently upheld in the framework of the Ankara Agreement. In *Demirkan*, the Court excluded the interpretation of

[83] Case C-221/11 *Demirkan* EU:C:2013:583 [38] and [62].
[84] Case C-351/08 *Grimme* EU:C:2009:697 [27]–[29].
[85] See further ch 6.
[86] EU–Switzerland Air Transport Agreement, [2002] OJ L114/ 73, Art 3.
[87] Case C-547/10 P *Switzerland v Commission*, EU:C:2013:139 [81]–[83].
[88] Case C-272/15 *Swiss International Air Lines*, EU:C:2016:993 [26].
[89] ibid [24].

Article 41(1) of the Additional Protocol to the Ankara Agreement as conferring upon Turkish nationals the rights to visit a Member State of the Union in order to obtain services.[90] Here, the Court contentiously qualified the *Ankara* Agreement as having a purely economic purpose, adding that the 'Association Agreement and its Additional Protocol are intended essentially to promote the economic development of Turkey'.[91] Against this backdrop, it did not extend to the *Ankara* Agreement the jurisprudence developed internally in *Luisi and Carbone*.[92] Pursuant to this jurisprudence, EU Treaty provisions on freedom to provide services (then Article 59 EEC, now Article 56 TFEU) are interpreted as entailing freedom for recipients of services to go to another Member State with a view to receiving services.[93]

In addition, the 'temporal context' of the Agreement,[94] whereby the Agreement and its Additional Protocol were antecedent to *Luisi and Carbone*, does not seem to be a key factor to preclude the extension of the *Luisi and Carbone* jurisprudence to outside of the membership context. In fact, the right to the passive provision of services was also excluded in the EU–Switzerland FMPA signed after the *Luisi and Carbone* cases.[95]

Demirkan concerned the operation of Article 41(1) of the Additional Protocol, a standstill clause prohibiting any new restrictions in EU–Turkey relations relating to free movement of workers and freedom to provide services. The clause had been successfully invoked in cases involving the provision of services. For instance, *Soysal and Savatli* concerned Turkish workers of a Turkish company active in the international transport of goods. They were employed as drivers of lorries owned by a German company and experienced problems obtaining entry visas. Soysal and Savatli claimed that the visa requirement introduced by Germany in 1980 was an additional restriction subsequent to the entry into force of the standstill provision of the Protocol in 1973. The Court agreed with this interpretation and found that the visa requirement, although introduced pursuant to EU legislation, was incompatible with the Protocol.[96]

The difference in approach between *Demirkan* and *Soysal* may be partly explained in the light of an increased sensitivity to the links between free movement of services and migration policy. As aptly pointed out by de Witte, 'Whereas *Soysal and Savatli* was still inspired by the free movement logic, the Grand Chamber in *Demirkan* was more sensitive to the migration policy implications and took an approach that was less favourable to Turkish nationals'.[97] Significantly, the

[90] *Demirkan* (n 83) [60] and [63].
[91] ibid [51].
[92] Joined cases 286/82 and 26/83 *Luisi and Carbone*, EU:C:1984:35.
[93] Case C-221/11 *Demirkan* (n 83) [60] and [63].
[94] ibid [57].
[95] Case C-70/09 *Hengartner and Gasser*, EU:C:2010:430 [43].
[96] Case C-228/06 *Soysal and Savatli*, EU:C:2009:101.
[97] Bruno De Witte, 'Visa Requirements for Turkish Citizens: Soysal & Savatli and Demirkan' in Graham Butler and Ramses A Wessel (eds), *EU External Relations Law: The Cases in Context* (Hart Publishing, 2022) 585.

justification of the more restrictive approach adopted by the Court in *Demirkan* rested on the different objectives pursued by the EU Treaties and the Ankara Agreement. Indeed, the Court affirmed that the extension of

> the interpretation of a provision in the Treaty to a comparably, similarly or even identically worded provision concluded by the European Union with a non-member State depends on, inter alia, the aim pursued by each provision in its own particular context.[98]

The regressive attitude in the interpretation of the Ankara Agreement with respect to earlier case law[99] has been qualified as 'politically unavoidable and yet legally embarrassing'.[100]

Analogous interpretation with EU law was promoted through the Ankara Agreement in the field of family reunification. In *Genc*, the Court highlighted how Article 12 of the Ankara Agreement envisages 'securing freedom of movement for workers' progressively between Turkey and the EU whilst being guided by the relevant EU primary law provisions.[101] In light of this, and in accordance with 'the exclusively economic aim' of the Ankara Agreement, 'the principles accepted in the context of [relevant EU] provisions *must be extended*, so far as possible, to Turkish nationals who enjoy rights under that Association Agreement'.[102] The closeness of the EU–Turkey Association law to the EU legal order can also be explained by the fact that the Ankara Agreement envisages far-reaching substantive *renvois* to EU law[103] and mechanisms for the CJEU's involvement in dispute settlement.[104] In *Genc*, the Court reviewed the standstill clause provided for in Article 13 of the Association Council Decision 1/80 on free movement of workers. The clause prohibited the imposition of new restrictions among the contracting parties on the condition of access to employment applicable to workers and member of their families.[105] The 2004 Danish law provision restricted visa permits for family members to the extent to which the applicant 'has or has the possibility to establishing such ties with Denmark that there is a basis or successful integration in Denmark'.[106] This was considered as a 'new restriction' within the meaning of Article 13 of the 1/80 Decision, which was not justifiable.[107]

The Court therefore replicated the reasoning developed in *Dogan* where the standstill clause enshrined in Article 41(1) of the Additional Protocol to the Ankara Agreement on freedom of establishment and on freedom to provide

[98] *Demirkan* (n 83) [46]–[48].

[99] Case C-37/98 *Savas*, EU:C:2000:224; Joined cases C-317/01 and C-369/01 *Abatay and Sahin*, EU:C:2003:572; Case C-16/05 *Tum and Dari*, EU:C:2007:530.

[100] Vassilis Hatzopoulos, 'Turkish Service Recipients under the EU–Turkey Association Agreement: *Demirkan*' (2014) 51 *Common Market Law Review* 647, 653.

[101] EU–Turkey Association Agreement, [1963] OJ L361/29, Art 12.

[102] Case C-561/14 *Genc*, EU:C:2016:247 [52], emphasis added.

[103] See EU–Turkey Association Agreement (n 101), Arts 13–14.

[104] ibid Art 25(2).

[105] Decision 1/80 of the EU–Turkey Association Council of 19 September 1980 on the development of Association, not published in the Official Journal.

[106] *Genc* (n 102) [10].

[107] ibid [67].

services was at issue.[108] Also, in this case, the economic purposes of the Ankara Agreement did not hinder the findings of the Court on the unlawfulness of German domestic restrictions to family reunification.[109] This 'new restriction' impinged upon the exercise of freedom of establishment by Turkish nationals.[110]

It is worth stressing that although the *Genc* and *Dogan* case law extended EU law principles on free movement of workers and freedom of establishment to the Ankara regimes, they also circumscribed the range of application of this extension.[111] This finding has been confirmed in subsequent pronouncements and gives a certain margin of discretion to national competent authorities.[112] Ultimately, the case law examined above allows for the interpretation of standstill clauses as relative and subject to derogation, not as an absolute prohibition.[113] More importantly, the extension of analogous interpretation in family reunification cases was strictly connected to the economic aims of the Ankara Agreement. This is in line with the Court's findings in *Demirkan*. In this context, Hailbronner posits that 'there is a fundamental difference between movement for the purpose of engaging in economic activities and the concept of free movement of person as an integral part of Union citizenship'. In fact, 'it is only when the activity in question is the corollary of the exercise of an economic activity that the standstill clause may relate to the conditions of entry and residence of Turkish nationals.'[114]

Similarly to the exclusion of third countries in the pre-normative phase, the *Polydor* case law can be construed as an expression of the principle of autonomy of EU law. The relevant judicial pronouncements intimate a demarcation between what it is internal and external to the EU integration experience in the post-normative phase. As it has been shown, this demarcation is not absolute as the combined interpretation of the wording and context of EU neighbourhood agreements may lead to an interpretation by analogy to EU membership law.

C. The Distinctiveness of EU Citizenship

The case law reviewed above suggests another element of demarcation between the EU internal and external experience connected to the *Polydor* principle, namely Union citizenship. In *Integration through Law*, Union citizenship was portrayed as 'the new dimension of the rule of law in international life' derived from the

[108] Case C-138/13 *Dogan*, EU:C:2014:2066.
[109] ibid [35] and [39].
[110] ibid [36].
[111] *Genc* (n 102) [29]; *Dogan* (n 108) [37].
[112] Case C-123/17 *Yön*, EU:C:2018:632 [84].
[113] Narin Tezcan Idriz, 'Family Reunification under the Standstill Clauses of EU–Turkey Association Law: *Genc*' (2017) 54 *Common Market Law Review* 263 [275]–[276].
[114] Kay Hailbronner, 'The Stand Still Clauses in the Eu-Turkey Association Agreement1 and Their Impact upon Immigration Law in the Eu Member States' in Daniel Thym and Margarite Zoeteweij-Turhan, *Rights of Third-Country Nationals under EU Association Agreements: Degrees of Free Movement and Citizenship* (Brill, 2015) 200.

novel role that individual plays in Union law.[115] Here, 'the rights of citizenship [are released] from the economic considerations attached to freedom of movement in the realm of the internal market'.[116]

The citizenship dimension of EU law is usually absent from the extension of the EU's legal space to non-EU members. The distinctive status of EU citizenship with respect to arrangements extending the EU internal market beyond EU membership can be indeed construed as an expression of the principle of autonomy of EU law. The EU Citizenship Directive[117] is usually not the object of the extension of EU law provided for in association agreements. This consideration also applies to the Ankara Agreement, which is a rather advanced example of extension of the EU's legal space with respect to the provisions on free movement of workers. In fact, the principles pertaining to the guarantees accorded by Union citizenship law in the context of expulsion for wrongful acts were not extended to the Ankara Agreement.[118]

The EU citizenship directive has been incorporated into the EEA Agreement. However, the Parties to the Agreement have inserted a rather nebulous joint declaration with a view to specifying that citizenship remains a notion specific to EU law:

> The concept of Union Citizenship as introduced by the Treaty of Maastricht … has no equivalent in the EEA Agreement. The incorporation of Directive 2004/38/EC into the EEA Agreement shall be without prejudice to the evaluation of the EEA relevance of future EU legislation as well as future case law of the European Court of Justice based on the concept of Union Citizenship. The EEA Agreement does not provide a legal basis for political rights of EEA nationals.[119]

The literature and the practice on the place and the role of EU citizenship law in the EEA remains somewhat undefined and is still under development. The concept of EU citizenship has been referred to as 'a non-entity under EEA law'.[120] In that respect, Tobler has contended that when 'non-economic matters' are at stake, the Court may decide not to interpret EEA law by analogy to EU law, especially as far as social benefits are concerned.[121] The purport of the joint declaration, however,

[115] Cappelletti, Seccombe and Weiler (n 47) 68.

[116] Loïc Azoulai, '"Euro-Bonds" The Ruiz Zambrano Judgment or the Real Invention of EU Citizenship' (2011) 3 *Perspectives on federalism* 35.

[117] Directive 2004/38/EC on the right of citizens of the Union and their family members to move and reside freely within the territory of the Member States, [2004] OJ L 158/77.

[118] Case C-371/08 *Ziebel*, EU:C:2011:809 [73].

[119] Joint Declaration by the Contracting Parties to Decision of the EEA Joint Committee No 158/2007 of 7 December 2007 amending Annex V (Free movement of workers) and Annex VIII (Right of establishment) to the EEA Agreement, incorporating Directive 2004/38/EC of the European Parliament and of the Council into the Agreement, [2008] OJ L 124/20.

[120] Halvard H Fredriksen and Christian NK Franklin, 'Of Pragmatism and Principles: The EEA Agreement 20 Years On' (2015) 52 *Common Market Law Review* 629, 638–39.

[121] Christa Tobler, 'Context-Related Interpretation of Association Agreements. The Polydor Principle in a Comparative Perspective: EEA Law, Ankara Association Law and Market Access Agreements between Switzerland and the EU' in Daniel Thym and Margarite Zoeteweij-Turhan, *Rights of*

shall not be overemphasised in the context of the EEA Agreement. The declaration is unlikely to deprive individuals of 'rights that they have already acquired under the EEA Agreement'[122] prior to their incorporation into the citizenship directive. Moreover, social benefits are governed by the Regulation on social security coordination[123] that is an integral part of EEA law.[124] A different reading suggesting a more complete application of the EU citizenship directive to the EEA has recently been put forward by Advocate General Emiliou in *Nordic Info*.[125] In the implementation of the EEA Agreement, a substantial weight has been attached to the objective of homogeneity and in the principle of equal treatment both in the judicial pronouncements originating from the EU[126] and EFTA pillar.[127] In that light, except for political rights, the EEA free movement rights and the EU citizenship rights may be construed as largely comparable.[128] Yet, the EEA remains a rather unique paradigm in the composite spectrum of arrangements concluded in the EU neighbourhood. As it will be argued further, notwithstanding the narrow gulf between EU citizenship law and free movement law in the EEA, the EEA Agreement is a different regime from EU law, not least because it does not entail a transfer of sovereignty to common institutions.

IV. The Scholarship on External Integration

The reflection on the methodological bases of the *Integration through Law project* has brought to the fore three of the main different features that exist between EU membership law proper and the provisions of EU law that have been extended beyond EU membership. Firstly, in the pre-normative phase of EU law (and extended EU law), EU non-members do not enjoy participation within the EU decision-making process. Secondly, and more significantly, the provisions of international agreements that replicate provisions of EU law are not necessarily interpreted and applied by analogy to EU law. The *Polydor* principle thus points out

Third-Country Nationals under EU Association Agreements: Degrees of Free Movement and Citizenship (Brill, 2015) 122–123; Christa Tobler, 'Free Movement of Persons in the EU v. in the EEA: Of Effect-Related Homogeneity and a Reversed Polydor Principle' (2019) 3 *European Papers* 1429, 1434.

[122] Case E-26/13 [2014], *Gunnarssson*, EFTA Court Report 254 [80].

[123] Regulation (EC) No 883/2004 on the coordination of social security systems (Text with relevance for the EEA and for Switzerland), [2004] OJ L 166/1.

[124] See inter alia EEA Joint Committee, Decision No 76/2011 amending Annex VI (Social security) and Protocol 37 to the EEA Agreement [2011] OJ L 262/33. I am grateful to Øyvind Bø for highlighting this.

[125] Case C-128/22 *Nordic Info*, Opinion of AG Emiliou, EU:C:2023:645 [46]–[47].

[126] Case C-897/19 PPU, *IN v Ruska Federacija* EU:C:2020:262; Case C-431/11 *United Kingdom v Council [EEA]* EU:C:2013:589 [58]–[59].

[127] Case E-28/15 *Jabbi*, [2016] EFTA Court Report 575 [60].

[128] Christian NK Franklin and Halvard H Fredriksen, 'Differentiated Citizenship in the European Economic Area' in Dora Kostakopoulou and Daniel Thym (eds) *Research Handbook on European Union Citizenship Law and Policy* (Edward Elgar Publishing, 2022) 297. On this see a more detailed discussion in ch 4 of this work, especially section IV.

the separation of extended EU law from the originating law in the post-normative phase. Thirdly, EU citizenship law is mostly absent from the experiences of the extension of the EU's legal space. These three dimensions may be construed as expression of the principle of autonomy of EU law, which intimates a demarcation between what it is internal and external to EU membership law.

The foregoing considerations lead us to reflect from a novel perspective on the inspiring literature focusing on the linkage between the internal and external dimensions of the openness of the EU legal order. This reflection of the legal scholarship on this theme originates from an insightful strand of International Relations research, which is also sensitive to the geopolitical motives underlying the extension of EU rules beyond EU borders. In particular, Sandra Lavenex powerfully captures the main tenets of the *Wider Europe* design. She posits that rule extension can be construed as a way to 'increase the efficiency and problem-solving capacity of internal policies' in light of interdependence as well as 'a foreign policy goal geared at stabilising the neighbourhood of the enlarged Union'.[129] She relies on the notion of 'governance' to describe 'the multi-level and multi-actor constellation' resulting in 'a form of political organisation which cannot be adequately described anymore by the concept of externally and internally sovereign state'.[130]

The governance perspective put forward by Lavenex, and subsequently relied upon by de Búrca,[131] refers to 'modes of network governance [providing] for forms of flexible integration for non-member states [based on] regulatory approximation and organisational inclusion of ENP countries'.[132] In her comment on Weiler's 'Transformation of Europe', de Búrca highlights the mission of 'civilising interstatal relations' that was encapsulated in Weiler's 'community vision'. She observes that in the EU, the divide between domestic and foreign policy is increasingly indefinite. She then maintains that:

> [T]he idea of a political system committed to civilising interstatal relations, not only between the member states of the EU amongst themselves, but between the EU and its neighbouring states, between the EU and other regions, and more generally in the EU promotion of processes of global governance, is a vision of community rather than unity.[133]

In other words, the ethical dimension of the EU internal integration experience is projected in its external relations. Against this backdrop, EU external relations

[129] Sandra Lavenex, 'EU External Governance in "Wider Europe"' (2004) 11 *Journal of European Public Policy* 680, 681.

[130] ibid 682.

[131] ibid.

[132] Sandra Lavenex, 'A Governance Perspective on the European Neighbourhood Policy: Integration beyond Conditionality?' (2008) 15 *Journal of European Public Policy* 938, 939. See also Tanja A Börzel and Thomas Risse, 'From Europeanisation to Diffusion: Introduction' (2012) 35 *West European Politics* 1.

[133] Gráinne de Búrca, 'The Transformation of Europe Revisited: Civilising Interstatal Relations' in Miguel Poiares Maduro and Marlene- Wind, *The transformation of Europe: twenty-five years on* (Cambridge University Press, 2017) 117.

legal scholarship associates the international agreements concluded by the EU in its proximity with the internal integration experience. Maresceau introduces the category of 'integration agreements' to describe agreements providing for the incorporation of a part of the EU *acquis* into the domestic legal orders of EU neighbouring countries. They aim for the 'partial integration' of neighbouring countries into the sectoral domains of activities or policies of the Union. He acknowledges different kinds of 'integration agreements' which may vary as a function of their 'objectives, content, and institutional structures'.[134] Along these lines, Rapoport investigates the agreements concluded by the EU with neighbouring non-candidate countries aiming at the permanent incorporation of the EU *acquis*. These are expressively referred to as 'integrated legal spaces', which often envisage mechanisms for ensuring a homogeneous interpretation of the rules thereof included.[135] In this instance, legal alignment to EU law is seen as promoting 'integration into the Union legal system'.[136]

In a similar vein, Łazowski and Van der Loo account for the agreements concluded by the EU in its proximity as promoting forms of 'integration without membership'.[137] Describing the variation among the different types of agreements, Łazowski distinguishes agreements entailing 'the obligation to apply selected pieces of the [EU] *acquis*' thus creating 'a common legal space between the EU and a third country' from cases of mere voluntary approximation.[138] The former typology of agreements, engendering the 'phenomenon of legal integration without membership in the European Union',[139] has inspired Van der Loo in his thorough analysis of the EU–Ukraine Association Agreement and the relevant Deep and Comprehensive Free Trade Area (DCFTA). For Van der Loo, integration without membership agreements are characterised as a '*conditio sine qua non*', namely the 'obligation to apply, implement or incorporate a predetermined selection of the EU *acquis*'.[140]

The research into the internal and external patterns of integration has offered further perceptive IR studies on the nature and the dynamics of differentiation. For instance, Schimmelfennig and Winzen define differentiated integration as comprising the 'entirety of EU legal rules for which territorial validity does not

[134] Marc Maresceau, 'Les Accords d'intégration Dans Les Rélations de Proximité de l'Union Europeénne' in Claude Blumann, *Les frontières de l'Union européenne* (Bruylant, 2013) 153 (my translation).

[135] Rapoport (n 52) 160.

[136] ibid 79 ff (my translation).

[137] Adam Łazowski, 'Enhanced Multilateralism and Enhanced Bilateralism: Integration without Membership in the European Union' (2008) 45 *Common Market Law Review* 1433; Guillaume Van der Loo, *The EU–Ukraine Association Agreement and Deep and Comprehensive Free Trade Area: A New Legal Instrument for EU Integration without Membership* (Brill Nijhoff, 2016).

[138] Lazowski (n 15) 1436. This distinction is present although in slightly different terms also in the works of Rapoport (n 52) and Maresceau (n 134).

[139] Lazowski (n 137) 1436.

[140] Van der Loo (n 137) 28.

coincide with the formal, organisational borders of the EU'.[141] They note how external differentiation arises when 'EU rules are legally valid in at least one non-member state for some time'.[142] Their definition of external differentiated integration is at the basis of Pedreschi and Scott's work, which offers a sound legal understanding on the adoption of EU rules by third countries. They investigate the external dimension of the flexibility and differentiation, which have characterised the constitutional development of the EU integration experience.[143] Their study on external differentiated integration focuses on the process 'through which a third country either adopts EU law or aligns its law with the EU acquis'.[144] Their work represents the first endeavour in the legal scholarship to systematise a rather complex and composite phenomenon into a rigorous theoretical framework.[145] By offering a set of variables to map the mechanisms of external differentiated integration, their study enriches the legal scholarship on integration without membership reviewed above. The variable of *strength* serves to assess the intensity of the obligation to adopt or align with EU law. *Scope* helps to define the range of the EU *acquis* and is used as reference for said obligation. In turn, *substance* serves to indicate the obligations' degree of precision in relation to the adoption or alignment with EU law. *Time* captures the temporal evolution of this obligation in line with the development of EU law. Finally, the variables of *surveillance* and *enforcement* are used to identify the mechanisms for monitoring third countries' alignment with the *acquis* and to issue binding interpretations of EU-derived law.[146]

Significantly, the authors qualify the categorisation of the phenomenon as developing along 'a continuum of activity more than a rigid dichotomy'.[147]

[141] Frank Schimmelfennig and Thomas Winzen, *Ever Looser Union?: Differentiated European Integration* (Oxford University Press 2020) 15. See also Frank Schimmelfennig, 'EU Enlargement and Differentiated Integration: Discrimination or Equal Treatment?' (2014) 21 *Journal of European Public Policy* 681.

[142] Schimmelfennig and Winzen (n 141) 15. For a seminal analytical framework on the links between internal and external differentiated integration see Dirk Leuffen, Berthold Rittberger and Frank Schimmelfennig, *Differentiated Integration: Explaining Variation in the European Union* (Palgrave MacMillan, 2013).

[143] See in this respect the rich scholarship Bruno de Witte, Dominik Hanf and Ellen Vos, *The Many Faces of Differentiation in EU Law* (Intersentia, 2001); Gráinne de Búrca and Joanne Scott, *Constitutional Change in the EU: From Uniformity to Flexibility?* (Hart Publishing, 2000); Bruno de Witte, 'Variable Geometry and Differentiation as Structural Features of the EU Legal Order' in Bruno de Witte, Andrea Ott and Ellen Vos, *Between flexibility and disintegration: the trajectory of differentiation in EU law* (Edward Elgar Publishing, 2017).

[144] Luigi Pedreschi and Joanne Scott, 'External Differentiated Integration: Legal Feasibility and Constitutional Acceptability', EUI Working Paper RSCAS 2020/54, 5.

[145] For the International Relations scholarship see, inter alia, Leuffen, Rittberger and Schimmelfennig (n 143); Frank Schimmelfennig, Dirk Leuffen and Berthold Rittberger, 'The European Union as a System of Differentiated Integration: Interdependence, Politicization and Differentiation' (2015) 22 *Journal of European Public Policy* 764; Sieglinde Gstöhl, 'Models of External Differentiation in the EU's Neighbourhood: An Expanding Economic Community?' (2015) 22 *Journal of European Public Policy* 854.

[146] Pedreschi and Scott (n 144).

[147] ibid 5.

In addition,building on Scott's pioneering works on territorial extension,[148] their study captures 'unilateral external differentiated integration', which 'arises when EU law establishes a framework for assessing whether third country law is sufficiently aligned with that of EU'.[149] The authors remark that several pieces of EU legislation 'promote alignment between EU and third country law' in sectors such as banking and financial regulation, data protection, food safety, aviation security, and climate change, especially when equivalence schemes are in place.[150]

V. The Departure from Integration Categories: Semantic and Methodological Choices

This book enriches the literature on external integration and integration without membership by further reflecting on the interplay between law and diplomacy. Lavenex perceptively captures the geopolitical motives of the *Wider Europe* design and the extension of EU rules.[151] Yet, while the reliance on 'governance' offers precious insights on the use of policy networks by the EU,[152] the notion of 'governance' remains rather nebulous with regard to legal nature, techniques and dynamics characterising the extension of the EU's legal space. In turn, while Pedreschi and Scott's work offers a thorough analytical apparatus for studying the extension of EU rules to third countries, the geopolitical mainspring of the process is not addressed. This work also enriches the analytical study by Öberg on the boundaries of the internal market.[153] It complements her study with a broader spectrum of proximity policies investigated and a reflection on the geopolitical motives and implications on the extension of the EU's legal space.

By turning *Wider Europe* into an analytical concept to capture the interplay of law and diplomacy, this book endeavours to develop a theoretical apparatus accounting for the legal and geopolitical dynamics characterising the extension of the EU's legal space. Taking seriously the geopolitical rationales of *Wider Europe*, and the ensuing paradigms of exclusion, entails a departure from integration categories, which are proper to the internal economic, legal and political experience of the Union. In legal terms, autonomy triggers dynamics of exclusion, protecting what is specific to the EU legal order. Moreover, the distinctive political covenant underlying EU membership law is not replicated in the arrangements presiding over the EU's relations with neighbouring countries.

[148] Joanne Scott, 'Extraterritoriality and Territorial Extension in EU Law' (2014) 61 *The American Journal of Comparative Law* 87; Joanne Scott, 'The new EU "extraterritoriality"' (2014) 51 *Common Market Law Review* 1343.
[149] Pedreschi and Scott (n 144) 41.
[150] ibid.
[151] Lavenex (n 129).
[152] Lavenex (n 132).
[153] Marja-Liisa Öberg, *The Boundaries of the EU Internal Market: Participation without Membership* (Cambridge University Press, 2020).

The departure from integration categories is thus not only a semantic but also a methodological choice. The present work will refer to the phenomenon of extension of the EU *acquis* and legal practices in the EU's neighbourhood as the extension of the EU's legal space. Semantically, this choice arises from policy documents, judicial pronouncements and scholarly reflections. In his *Wider Europe* speech, Prodi mentioned the aim 'to *extend* to this neighbouring region a set of principles, values and standards which define the very essence of the European Union'.[154] Along similar lines, the ensuing Communication depicted the new proximity framework as one intending to '*extend* existing Community policies, programmes and instruments to neighbouring countries'.[155] In the context of the EEA Agreement, the CJEU subsequently recognised in *Ospelt* how 'the internal market established within the European Union [would be] *extended* to the EFTA States'.[156] In the same period as the *Wider Europe* Communication, in *Opinion 1/00* the CJEU qualified the international agreements replicating EU law provisions in legal regimes established by third countries as aiming to '*extend* the [EU] *acquis* to new States, by implementing in a larger geographical area rules which are essentially those of [EU] law'.[157]

In the legal scholarship, the notion of legal space was introduced by Harding to convey a sense of 'the complex, non-hierarchical, overlapping, interlocking and evolutionary character of contemporary legal phenomena'.[158] He regarded the EU Treaties as the core of this space including the EU, the EEA, the Council of Europe and the OCSE. The EU policy documents, the judicial pronouncements, and the scholarly reflection suggest that the EU's engagement in its proximity is not exhausted in the extension of the EU's *acquis*. It includes practices and processes of socialisation as well as the fostering of administrative networks of cooperation. In this work, the 'extension of the EU's legal space' is used interchangeably with 'EU neighbourhood law'. The combined use of these notions offers a fuller account of the interplay between law and geopolitics in the EU's engagement in its proximity. Both '*Wider Europe*' and 'extension of the EU's legal space' rest comfortably with the EU's elusive engagement with geography and territory. '*Wider Europe*' evokes the elusive geographical confines of *Europe*.[159] 'Extension of the EU's legal space'

[154] Prodi (n 43) 5.
[155] European *Commission*, 'Wider Europe – Neighbourhood: A New Framework for Relations with Our Eastern and Southern Neighbours' COM (2003) 104 final, 18 (emphasis added).
[156] Case C-452/01 *Ospelt*, EU:C:2003:493 [29] (emphasis added).
[157] *Opinion 1/00* (n 23) [3] (emphasis added).
[158] Christopher Harding, 'The Identity of European Law: Mapping Out the European Legal Space' (2000) 6 *European Law Journal* 128; see also Rapoport (n 52) and subsequently Armin von Bogdandy, 'European Law Beyond "Ever Closer Union" Repositioning the Concept, Its Thrust and the ECJ's Comparative Methodology] (2016) 22 *European Law Journal* 519; Armin von Bogdandy, 'The Idea of European Public Law Today' in Peter M Huber, Sabino Cassese, Armin von Bogdandy, *The Max Planck Handbooks in European Public Law* (Oxford University Press, 2017); Andrea Ott, 'The Building Blocks and Stumbling Stones of Constructing the European Legal Space' in Wybe T Douma et al. (eds.), *The Evolving Nature of EU External Relations Law* (Springer, 2021) 205.
[159] cf ch 1, section IV.

is largely borrowed from the language of EU institutions and evokes a boundless area governed by law but where the distinction between what is and what is not EU membership law is not immediate. Besides, the very 'European Neighbourhood Policy' label conflates what pertains to the EU and its laws and what does not.

The notion of 'EU neighbourhood law' introduced in this book captures the geographical and geopolitical motives underlying the ENP while suggesting a distinction between what is EU membership law and what is not. Such a notion is therefore methodologically more accurate in light of the demarcation and complex relation between what is internal and external to the EU, between EU membership law and EU neighbourhood law. The cognate notion of 'extension of the EU's legal space is still used in this work for a two-fold reason. First, the notion is deferent to the institutional and judicial language of institutional documents and judicial pronouncements related to the extension of the EU *acquis*. Secondly, the notion helps us describing the circumstance that in *Wider Europe* the more defined institutional arrangement of EU neighbourhood law often coexist with more indefinite forms of socialisation in the extended EU's legal space.

Wider Europe is far from a uniform legal space and includes the law of well-established legal set-ups as the EEA as well as combination of association agreements and technical assistance programmes resulting in less defined forms of extension of EU laws and practices. The value of the category of EU neighbourhood law can be appreciated when considering that the complex phenomenon combining legal and geopolitical motives in the extension of the EU's legal space can be emancipated from a single proximity policy, namely the ENP.[160] Indeed, as will be illustrated in the following chapters, some techniques of the extension of the EU's legal space are employed across different institutional arrangements extending the EU's legal space. EU neighbourhood law originates from international law: the relations between the EU and its neighbours are governed by international law. Yet, EU neighbourhood law is a special type of international law as it vehiculates the extension of the EU's legal space in EU-led international regimes.

On the methodological plane, the departure from integration categories, stemming from the demarcation and complex relationship between EU membership law and EU neighbourhood law, requires investigating the relationship among legal regimes of a different nature. The legal patchwork characterising *Wider Europe* certainly includes some degree of 'integration' *lato sensu*, but the different nature of the legal orders calls for investigating the relationships among different regimes. Two interrelated methodological perspectives will be mobilised for the study of the extension of the EU's legal space. The first pertains to the need to investigate the composite set of relations among them. The second is related to the practices of socialisation in *Wider Europe*, which, although legally elusive, have a major legal significance in shaping the relations between the EU and its neighbouring countries.

[160] See ch 1 of this work.

A. Relations and Asymmetries Among Legal Regimes

A defining feature of EU neighbourhood law is the asymmetry in the relations between the EU and its neighbouring countries. This primarily derives from trade and hence from the greater size of the EU market.[161] It also ensues from the recognition by third countries of the EU's capacity to set the normative standards in several policy and regulatory domains.[162] Asymmetry is reflected in the relationship between legal orders. The understanding of how asymmetry work may require a detachment from the canonical categories of international law. Within the legal scholarship, Sabino Cassese has examined the legal standing of the EU looking at the empires in an historical comparative perspective to explore the analytical value of such a comparison. When it comes to the EU, this approach displays the heuristic potential of overcoming the state-centric 'cultural "dictatorship"' of international law.[163] In the past, Cassese noted, disequilibria and differences among legal orders brought some public powers into the orbit of others.[164]

In order to account for the interactions between legal regimes operated by EU-led international agreements, this work is inspired by the methodological apparatus of 'The Legal Order' by Santi Romano.[165] As noted by Natalino Irti, in the second part of his work, Romano 'ingeniously investigates the relationships between legal systems, that are arranged in relationships of relevance or irrelevance, of superiority or dependence; he deals with the various types of referral [*renvoi*]'.[166] Romano defined the 'relevance' of a legal order to another when 'the existence, the content, or the effectiveness of one legal order is made conditional upon the other legal order on the basis of a legal title'.[167] These are the grounds upon which Romano configured the relationship of independence, subordination, or presupposition of one order to another, also envisaging cases where relevance is unilaterally attributed by an order to another.[168]

In the case of the extension of the EU's legal space, the EU legal order constitutes the originating legal order presupposing EU-derived international law regimes extending the EU's legal space. The relevance of the EU legal order for the latter operates via multiple legal titles. Firstly, the EU legal order is relevant to EU-led international law agreements due its *existence* and for the fact that the EU itself is party to international legal regimes extending the EU's legal space.

[161] Chad Damro, 'Market Power Europe' (2012) 19 *Journal of European Public Policy* 682.

[162] Anu Bradford, *The Brussels Effect: How the European Union Rules the World* (Oxford University Press, 2020).

[163] Sabino Cassese, 'Che Tipo Di Potere Pubblico è l'Unione Europea?' (2002) 31 *Quaderni Fiorentini per la storia del pensiero giuridico moderno* 141, 143.

[164] ibid 142.

[165] Santi Romano, *L'ordinamento Giuridico*, 1st edn (Annali Delle Università Toscane, 1917–18); the edition I refer to is the one published by Quodlibet 2018; for the English version see Santi Romano and Mariano Croce (tr), *The Legal Order* (Taylor & Francis Group, 2017).

[166] Natalino Irti, *Un diritto incalcolabile* (Giappichelli, 2016) 198 (my translation).

[167] Romano (n 165) 126–27 (my translation).

[168] ibid 128.

Secondly, inherently connected to its *existence*, is the *content* of the EU legal order. Indeed, the regimes extending the EU's legal space operate substantive *renvois* (referrals) to EU law in the body of the agreement or in the annexes. The reception of extended EU law into the third country legal order is thus mediated by the international regime and its mechanisms. The mediation also occurs through the joint bodies established by the agreements (usually the joint committees) that update the annexes in line with the development of EU law. Thirdly, in the context of the extension of the EU's legal space, the *effectiveness* of the title of relevance depends on the mechanisms of organisational and procedural interaction among legal systems and the possible involvement of EU institutions in the management and enforcement of the extended of EU legal space. This applies especially to the role of the Court of Justice in the interpretation of extended EU law.

The relevance of the EU legal order for regimes of EU neighbourhood law is not only limited to the content or substance of extended EU law; crucially, it also pertains to the mechanisms of organisational interaction defining the effectiveness of the title of reference. These mechanisms are related to the management and implementation of the EU neighbourhood law agreements. Significantly, mechanisms of organisational interaction may also involve EU institutions; this would amount to an institutional *renvoi*. EU institutions are de facto used as 'organs' by the EU outside its institutional framework. They are employed to carry out specific tasks in the regime which extends the EU's legal space. The notion of 'organisational interaction' in the external sphere is related to but different from the notion that EU institutions are 'organs' lacking genuine autonomy which has been developed to characterise some practices of the EU internal experience. In arrangements of EU neighbourhood law, the ensuing organic vision was one where EU institutions were considered as organs in the hands of EU Member States. This was contraposed to the institutional vision where EU institutions were understood as belonging to an autonomous and independent legal order.[169] In the present work, the mechanisms of organisational interaction are construed as techniques of EU neighbourhood law. They are to be found in the articulation of bilateral and multilateral agreements extending the EU's legal space. Here, the substantive *renvois* to EU law are often accompanied with borrowing of EU institutions to perform tasks in the monitoring, implementation and interpretation of extended EU law. The extension EU institutions' tasks to EU neighbourhood regimes is governed by the requirements of the principle of autonomy of EU law.

Thus, extension of the EU's legal space occurs through a variety of mechanisms providing for the gravitation of EU neighbourhood regimes around the EU legal order. The exercise of legal influence of a legal regime on another is far from new.

[169] Loïc Azoulai, 'The Many Visions of Europe' in Marise Cremona and Anne Thies (eds), *The European Court of Justice and external relations law: constitutional challenges* (Hart Publishing, 2014); Loic Azoulai, 'Appartenir à l'Union européenne' in Christian Mestre (ed), *Europe(s), droit(s) européen(s): une passion d'universitaire: Liber amicorum en l'honneur du professeur Vlad Constantinesco* (Bruylant, 2015).

Influences among legal orders were particularly common in the XVIII century in the territories subject to Roman law before the process of codification. In this respect, Gorla highlighted how gaps in the different legal orders were filled with the recourse to '*lex alius locii*' (the law of another land). This applied especially among lands that were considered to be a 'community', as opposed to a political order, such as countries in which *ius comune* was applied.[170] Among the criteria to choose the law of another land there were the *vicinitas* (proximity) and the particular expertise of the juriconsults of that land in regulating a given domain.[171] Expertise of juriconsults was particularly significant in guaranteeing the '*uniformitas*' of the applied law.

B. Third Country Socialisation in the *Wider Europe* Legal Space

Santi Romano's theoretical framework is most appropriate to map the interrelations between legal regimes when the extension, and the retrenchment, of EU legal space is vehiculated through international law agreements. Yet, the extension of the EU's legal space is not always mediated by agreements of international law. Although not through formal substantive *renvois* to EU law and mechanisms of organisational interaction with the EU, the EU legal order remains relevant for third countries socialised by the EU within the extended EU's legal space. On the substantive plane, the Romano's '*relevance*' can take the form of third countries' legislative mimetic imitation of EU and EU Member States laws. Legislative imitation is often embedded in programmes of convergence to EU law with a view to obtaining a degree of EU market access. This may occur without formal mechanisms of organisational interaction with the EU legal order. Indeed, especially when *renvois* to EU institutions are not contemplated, a thinner degree of *effectiveness* may be envisaged. In these cases, the extension of the EU's legal space may rely on administrative networks of cooperation and EU-led programmes with the employment of EU funds.

The processes of socialisation can be understood as facilitating the extension of the EU's legal space. With a view to better grasping the purport of third country socialisation in *Wider Europe*, it is useful to refer to the literature on processes of socialisation in international law. The relevant studies are regarded as the province of constructivist scholarship.[172] In international relations theory, constructivist scholarship emphasises the relevance of ideational factors in shaping international

[170] Gino Gorla, 'Il Ricorso Alla Legge Di Un Luogo "Vicino" Nell'ambito Del Diritto Comune Europeo', *Diritto Comparato E Diritto Comune Europeo*, vol 21 (Giuffré, 1981) 619.

[171] ibid 633.

[172] Jeffrey T Checkel, 'The Constructivist Turn in International Relations Theory' (1998) 50 *World Politics* 324.

players' patterns of behaviour.[173] Borrowing from the studies of March and Olsen, constructivist theory illustrates that international actors are not only driven by material interests, but also by a 'logic of appropriateness'.[174] By reviewing the international socialisation literature, Schimmelfenning has powerfully summarised that 'social constructivism postulates that identities and interests of international actors are endogenous, that is, constructed through international social interaction and involvement in international institutions'.[175] Schimmelfenning defines international socialisation as 'the process of inducting actors into adopting the constitutive schemata and rules of an international community'.[176]

The emphasis is hence on the process: it remains open the extent to which the socialised actors will ultimately conform with the norms of the community.[177] In this respect, together with ideational aspects, materials factors continue to play a crucial role in the transfer of rules and schemata of an international community. Among the ideational and material mechanisms of socialisation, Schimmelfenning singles out *imitation*, *social learning*, *social influence* and *bargaining*. With the mechanism of *imitation*, 'the community rules are templates that help actors understand and interpret social situations and provide scripts for the roles that "socialisees" are supposed to play'.[178] In *social learning*, the process of 'normative internalisation' occurs insofar as 'community rules are validity claims argumentatively justified by the socialisation agencies in international discourses'.[179] In turn, *social influence* 'is based on the use of social incentives such as image and status'. Finally, in *bargaining*, '"socialisees" are promised material rewards (such as financial aid or military protection) if they adopt community rules'.[180]

In a similar vein, in international law, constructivist scholarship is contributing 'to build a richer understanding of the interplay between material power and interests on the one hand, and identity, culture and norms on the other'.[181] In this respect, Koh focuses on the processes of interactions that engender compliance:

> One or more transnational actors provokes an *interaction* (or series of interactions) with another, which forces an *interpretation* or enunciation of the global norm applicable to the situation. By so doing, the moving party seeks not simply to coerce the other party but to *internalize* the new interpretation of the international norm into the

[173] John G Ruggie, 'What Makes the World Hang Together? Neo-Utilitarianism and the Social Constructivist Challenge' (1998) 52 *International Organization* 855.

[174] James G March and Johan P Olsen, 'The Institutional Dynamics of International Political Orders' (1998) 52 *International Organization* 943, 949.

[175] Frank Schimmelfennig, 'Transnational Socialization Community-Building in an Integrated Europe' in Wolfram Kaiser and Peter Starie, *Transnational European Union: Towards a Common Political Space* (Taylor & Francis, 2005) 62.

[176] ibid 63.

[177] ibid.

[178] ibid 65.

[179] ibid.

[180] ibid.

[181] Jutta Brunnée and Stephen J Toope 'Constructivism and International Law' in Jeffrey L Dunoff and Mark A Pollack (eds), *Interdisciplinary Perspectives on International Law and International Relations: The State of the Art* (Cambridge University Press, 2012) 139.

> other party's internal normative system. ... Such a transnational legal process is normative, dynamic, and constitutive. The transaction generates a legal rule which will guide future transnational interactions between the parties; future transactions will further internalise hose norms; and eventually, repeated participation in the process will help to reconstitute the interests and even the identities of the participants in the process.[182]

The processes of internalisation described by Koh broadly correspond to Schimmelfenning's mechanism of *social learning*. These are complementary to conditionality. In the social constructivist theory of international law, Goodman and Jinks stress the difference between 'coercion' and persuasion' from the mechanism of socialisation they call 'acculturation'. The authors describe 'acculturation' as 'the general process of adopting the beliefs and the behavioural patterns of the surrounding culture'.[183] The process includes 'mimicry, identification, and status maximisation' and thus largely reflect to the notion of imitation put forward by Schimmelfenning.

The interactions promoted by the ENP are a defining feature of EU membership law and of the processes of Europeanisation of the EU Member States.[184] As Börzel and Risse put it, 'the EU can be understood as a gigantic socialisation agency which actively tries to promote rules, norms, practices, and structures of meaning to which Member States are exposed and which they have to incorporate into their domestic structures'.[185] Significantly, these mechanisms are also relevant in the extension of the EU's legal space. In particular, the sites of socialisation in the wider European legal space may be found in EU-led international networks of cooperation in which third countries participate.

As a matter of fact, interactions of the ENP's webs of dependence and interdependence are oriented towards internalising EU law norms into the third countries' domestic jurisdictions. ENP Programmes may result in third countries' mimetic imitation of EU law. In that process, conditionality is a factor of 'persuasion' in the process of EU norm internalisation, but it is not the key motive behind the establishment of privileged partnership in the neighbourhood. As will be shown in the case of Morocco, privileged partnerships continue to operate largely independently from conditionality. The Moroccan case will be also illustrative of the fact that through the process of bargaining, third countries manage to weaponise patterns of dependence and cross dependence both to maximise their status and material incentives for the participation in *Wider Europe*. A narrow understanding of legal analysis is hence not enough to appreciate the different facets of

[182] Harold Hongju Koh, 'Why Do Nations Obey International Law Review Essay' (1996) 106 *Yale Law Journal* 2599, 2646.

[183] Ryan Goodman and Derek Jinks, 'How to Influence States: Socialization and International Human Rights Law' (2004) 54 *Duke Law Journal* 621, 638.

[184] Jeffrey Lewis, 'The Janus Face of Brussels: Socialization and Everyday Decision Making in the European Union' (2005) 59 *International Organization* 937; Lucia Quaglia, Fabrizio De Francesco and Claudio M Radaelli, 'Committee Governance and Socialization in the European Union' (2008) 15 *Journal of European Public Policy* 155.

[185] Börzel and Risse (n 132) 7.

the extension of the EU's legal space. The extension of the EU's legal space is in part a legally elusive phenomenon that requires the examination of policy documents, the operation of administrative networks of transnational corporations and reports of the Commission and the Court of Auditors.

VI. Political Covenants of EU Membership Law and EU Neighbourhood Law

The distinctiveness of the political covenant of the EU and its relationship with the political covenants of EU neighbourhood law can be examined in light of Neil Walker's studies. In today's complex configurations of exercise of public and private powers, the idea of sovereignty as 'an image-based claim to ultimate authority' appears largely inadequate to fully answer empirical and normative questions on 'how we ought to be governed'.[186] This inadequacy derives from the fact that 'While the state remains the focus of political organisation, it is now merely first among equals. In place of a universal and uniform template of sovereign statehood, we have highly differentiated mosaic of legal and political capacities'.[187] The exercise of sovereignty in contemporary settings is not only characterised by a limitation of nation-state sovereign powers but by a roader reconfiguration of the way in which sovereignty is exercised. As Walker forcefully demonstrates, the 'sovereignty surplus' – that is to say the proliferation of claims to final authority – also captures the 'sovereignty's augmented reworkings in existing contexts'.[188] The sections above have illustrated how the claims of newness of the EU legal order and the distinctiveness of its legal-political covenant were fashioned through the sovereignty language both by the Court and influential legal scholars and practitioners like Pescatore. In *Costa v ENEL*, the Court explicitly characterised Union membership as entailing a 'permanent limitation of the sovereign rights'.[189]

The reconfiguration of state powers in the EU thus challenges traditional conceptions developed in the modern French political and legal thinking on the absolute and indivisible nature of sovereignty.[190] Yet, the EU did not produce the demise of sovereignty. Instead, it has reconfigured the way sovereignty is exercised, not least by questioning its unitarian conception, or better, its unitarian representation. This has triggered copious literature on constitutional pluralism in the EU

[186] Neil Walker, 'The Sovereignty Surplus' (2020) 18 *International Journal of Constitutional Law* 370, 381.

[187] ibid 394.

[188] ibid 383.

[189] Case 6-64, *Flaminio Costa v ENEL* EU:C:1964:66.

[190] For a problematisation of this also in light of the Constitution of the French Fifth Republic, see Jacques Ziller, 'Sovereignty in France: Getting Rid of the Mal de Bodin' in Neil Walker, *Sovereignty in transition* (Hart Publishing, 2003).

which makes sense of the 'competing constitutional claims of final authority'[191] primarily among the EU and its Member States. The Union has contributed to the refashioning of sovereignty. The pluralist understanding of sovereignty does not obliterate power and force relations among competing claims to ultimate authority: governance itself ultimately functions in a context of asymmetry of power, when a pole is stronger than the other.[192]

The sovereignty and political covenant underlying Union membership is relational: Member States collectively renounce part of their regulatory independence and autonomy to participate as decision-makers in a larger, and more effective, regulatory project. In Walker's powerful understanding, EU Member States thus benefit from a 'sovereignty surplus'. The exercise of sovereignty in the EU responds to the rationale identified with foresight by Abram and Antonia Chayes in their work on sovereignty. They posit:

> Sovereignty, in the end, is status – the vindication of the state's existence as a member of the international system. In today's setting, the only way most states can realise and express their sovereignty is through participation in the various regimes that regulate and order the international system.[193]

In *Van Gen den Loos* and *Costa v ENEL*, the Court captured a transfer of sovereignty entailing a reconfiguration of its exercise among the EU Member States and their peoples. This reconfiguration would, in turn, enhance the regulatory clout of the Union.[194] In light of the Union's limited capacity to independently raise taxes and spend, its prominent role as a regulator largely defines its identity.[195] Moreover, the sovereignty legal and political covenant of the EU is one that 'has the potential and the vocation to compensate the structural democratic deficits of nation-statehood'.[196] By placing part of the decision-making above domestic national polity, the EU attempts to manage interdependence by equating the object and the subjects of the law.[197] In other words, EU law has the capacity to include

[191] Miguel Poiares Maduro, 'Three Claims of Constitutional Pluralism' in Matej Avbelj and Jan Komárek, *Constitutional pluralism in the European Union and beyond* (Hart Publishing, 2012) 69.

[192] Antonio Negri, 'Sovereignty between Government, Exception and Governance' in Hent Kalmo and Quentin Skinner (eds), *Sovereignty in Fragments: The Past, Present and Future of a Contested Concept* (Cambridge University Press, 2010) 217–19.

[193] Abram Chayes and Antonia Handler Chayes, *The New Sovereignty: Compliance with International Regulatory Agreements* (Harvard University Press, 1995) 27. On the relational Mario Draghi's inaugural speech to the Italian Parliament, affirming in the context of EU membership that: 'Non c'è sovranità nella solitudine' (there is no sovereignty in solitude).

[194] Anu Bradford, *The Brussels Effect: How the European Union Rules the World* (Oxford University Press, 2020).

[195] Giandomenico Majone, 'From the Positive to the Regulatory State: Causes and Consequences of Changes in the Mode of Governance' (1997) 17 *Journal of Public Policy* 139, 150.

[196] Christian Joerges, '"Brother, Can You Paradigm?"' (2014) 12 *International Journal of Constitutional Law* 769, 782.

[197] Joseph Corkin, 'Who, Then, in [European] Law, Is My Neighbour? Limiting the Argument from External Effects' in Samo Bardutzky and Elaine Fahey (eds), *Framing the Subject and Objects of Contemporary EU Law* (Edward Elgar, 2017) 74.

the externalities that domestic national policies would entail on neighbours by scaling up the decision making at the Union level. In this way, the EU citizens and their governments, which are objects of EU law, are also subjects of this law.[198]

The EU political covenant is *not* extended beyond membership. The patterns of exclusion inherent in *Wider Europe* prevent extending the distinctive political covenants of EU membership law through EU neighbourhood law. The 'everything but institution formula' precisely captures the EU's desire to safeguard internal regulatory autonomy and special sovereignty-political arrangement. The preservation of the distinctiveness of the Union political covenant in *Wider Europe* is governed by the principle of autonomy, which may be construed thus as a proxy for sovereignty.[199] In the EU, the congruence between sovereignty and autonomy is apparent, in its twofold legal-political nature, if one thinks that 'the key to sovereignty is the double-claim to ultimate authority' over the boundary between the internal and the external and over the ultimate power to counteract any claim of '"external" encroachment'.[200] Autonomy of EU law thus serves to preserve the distinctive political covenant of EU membership and the ensuing arrangements of sovereignty reconfiguration from the mechanisms of international law (including those of EU neighbourhood law). Given that sovereignty may be construed as the 'relational interface between law and politics',[201] the relationship between EU membership and EU neighbourhood law is often fraught with tensions that ultimately relate to the interface between law and politics.[202] Countries participating in the extended EU's legal space are largely rule takers, EU neighbourhood law thus entails asymmetry in the reconfiguration of sovereignty exercise. In that light, countries that do not wish to gravitate around the EU legal order express political contestation of EU neighbourhood law through a quest for recourse to more symmetric forms of international law.[203]

Certainly the extension of the EU's legal space is partly premised on the dynamics of inclusion in *Wider Europe*. Arguably thus part of the EU membership covenant reverberates in arrangements extending the EU's legal space. As highlighted in the works by Lavenex and de Búrca mentioned above, part of the EU governance mode may be construed as extending beyond membership. The techniques extension of the EU's legal space foster administrative networks of cooperation partly mirroring the relational reconfiguration of sovereignty

[198] ibid; see also Alexander Somek, 'The Argument from Transnational Effects I: Representing Outsiders through Freedom of Movement' (2010) 16 *European Law Journal* 315.

[199] Jan Willem van Rossem, 'The Autonomy of EU Law: More Is Less?' in Ramses A Wessel and Steven Blockmans (eds), *Between Autonomy and Dependence: The EU Legal Order under the Influence of International Organisations* (TMC Asser Press, 2013).

[200] Neil Walker, 'Late Sovereignty in the European Union', *Sovereignty in transition* (Hart Publishing, 2003) 22.

[201] Jens Bartelson, 'The Concept of Sovereignty Revisited' (2006) 17 *European Journal of International Law* 463, 469.

[202] The EU–UK future relations agreement and negotiations are an example of this. See further ch 6.

[203] See further ch 9 of this work.

exercise proper to EU membership law. Indeed, it is at this level of administrative networks of cooperation that the agencies of third countries participate on a more equal footing with 'sister agencies' of EU Member States. This increases the competence of the agencies and fosters 'transnational networks linked to the particular policy field' while developing a 'certain amount of loyalty to a common European administration in their policy area'.[204] Moreover, in the most advanced cases of extension of the EU's legal space, a full market access may be envisaged at the same conditions applying in EU Member States.[205]

VII. Conclusions

The *Wider Europe* 'everything but institutions' formula captures the dynamics of inclusion and exclusion characterising the extension of the EU's legal space. These dynamics are governed by the principle of autonomy of EU law that safeguards the distinctiveness of the political covenant of EU membership law and its specific sovereignty arrangements. In that light the 'everything but institutions' formula can be construed as an expression of the principle of autonomy of EU law and particularly of decision-making autonomy. The chapter has argued that the principle of autonomy of EU law also finds expression in the demarcation between EU membership and EU neighbourhood law originating from the differences in the pre-normative and post-normative phase of the law as well as the specific characteristics of EU citizenship law. The foregoing considerations advise against using integration categories to describe the institutional arrangements extending the EU's legal space. In that light, the semantic choices of this book are also methodological. This book describes the gravitation around the EU's legal order through substantive *renvois* and mechanisms of organisational interaction reflecting the scope and the intensity of such a gravitation. The ensuing analytical apparatus is based on Santi Romano's theoretical *corpus*, which allows us to unravel the patterns of dependence and the ensuing asymmetries in the relations among regimes. The notions of extension of the EU's legal space and EU neighbourhood law are thus mobilised. The combined use of these categories, used interchangeably, serves to account for several factors of the complex relationship between EU membership and EU neighbourhood law. The notion of extension of the EU's legal space reflects the ECJ's characterisation of arrangements extending the EU's *acquis*. Moreover, the notion includes the processes of socialisations that do not result in defined legal orders but in the establishment of a more elusive

[204] Morten Egeberg and Trondal Jarle, 'National Administrative Sovereignty: Under Pressure' in John E Fossum and Erik O Eriksen (eds), *The European Union's non-members: independence under hegemony?* (Routledge, 2015) 183.

[205] This is particularly the case of the EEA and the ECAA Agreements; for a broader discussion see Marja-Liisa Öberg (n 153). See also next chapters of this work.

'legal space' where legal and political dependences and interdependences are at play. Furthermore, the notion of EU neighbourhood law captures the geographical element of the interplay of law and geopolitics particularly occurring in the EU's proximity. The demarcation and complex relationship between EU membership and EU neighbourhood law reflect their different underlying political covenants.

The arrangements of sovereignty reconfiguration entailed in EU membership law are not replicated in *Wider Europe*. Regimes extending the EU's legal space are thus in a relationship of dependence and presupposition with the EU legal order. Third countries gravitating around the EU legal order are largely rule takers. Notwithstanding these asymmetries, the patterns of inclusions of *Wider Europe* arguably allow for an extension of the governance mode beyond membership and third countries participating in the extended EU's legal space may benefit from the relational configuration of sovereignty at play in *Wider Europe*.

PART II

Wider Europe and Multilateral Regimes: The Poles of the EU Neighbourhood Law Continuum

4

The European Economic Area: A Paradigm and a Pole of the EU Neighbourhood Law Continuum

I. Introduction

The European Economic Area (EEA) Agreement stands at the core of the twofold dimension of *Wider Europe* as a policy design and as an analytical concept. Indeed, the EEA has been a source of inspiration and a model for the launch of the ENP as a proximity policy. The Agreement also served as a paradigm for the techniques of extension of the EU's legal space bringing about a *lato sensu* reconfiguration of EU's borders. This chapter starts with a review of the genesis of the EEA characterised by a balancing and recomposition of different forces and interests leading to its two-pillar configuration. These forces and interests include the principle of autonomy of EU law, the willingness to ensuring legal homogeneity in the EEA, and the averseness of EEA EFTA states to relinquish sovereignty to supranational institutions (section II). The chapter then examines the far-reaching techniques of extension of the EU's legal space with a focus on the scope of the substantive *renvois* and the mechanisms of organisational interaction between the EEA regime and the EU legal order (section III). The tension between the principle of autonomy in the EU and homogeneity in the EEA is reconsidered in light of the question of whether the *Polydor* principle applies to EEA law (section IV). To answer this question the chapter mobilises a strand of the EEA case law on the free movement of persons (section IV.A) and reflects on the broader relations between the EU legal order and the EEA regime (section IV.B). Moreover, by examining the practice of extension of an EU Regulation on social security in different arrangements of EU neighbourhood law, the chapter offers a first overview of the EU neighbourhood law continuum. For the scope and intensity of gravitation around the EU's legal order, the EEA can be construed as being the arrangement most proximate to EU law (section V). Finally, the chapter discusses the distinctiveness of the political covenant of the EEA in light of the reconfigurations of sovereignty it entails (section VI).

II. The EEA Agreement: Autonomy and Homogeneity

The EEA Agreement stands as a unique paradigm of extension of the EU's legal space and has profoundly inspired the *Wider Europe* project. The Agreement was signed in 1992 between the European Community, its Member States and EFTA states. Among the (then seven) EFTA members participating in the negotiations, Austria, Finland and Sweden eventually became members of the Union, while Switzerland rejected the possibility of joining of the EEA in a referendum in 1992.[1]

The Agreement establishes a relationship between the EU legal order and the legal system of the participating EFTA states via an EU-led international regime. The EEA Agreement can be construed as the most successful paradigm of extension of the EU's internal market.[2] The closeness of the EEA regime to the EU legal order is a function of the foundations and objectives of the EEA Agreement, identified in the preamble. The 'privileged relationship' between the EU and EFTA states is indeed grounded 'on proximity, long-standing common values and European identity'.[3] The objective is that of creating 'a dynamic and homogeneous European Economic Area, based on common rules and equal conditions of competition, and providing for the adequate means of enforcement including at the judicial level, and achieved on the basis of equality and reciprocity and of an overall balance of benefits, rights and obligations for the Contracting Parties'.[4]

The Agreement covers the free movement of goods, people, services and capital. It sets out common rules on competition and includes the so-called 'horizontal and flanking policies'. These encompass cooperation on social policy,[5] consumer protection[6] and the environment.[7] The substantive scope and institutional structure of the EEA have attracted the attention of legal scholarship studying the EU's proximity policies. Magen characterised the Agreement as 'the most prominent case of *acquis* export outside the enlargement paradigm'.[8] Maresceau depicted it as 'a real intellectual masterpiece of legal thinking on integration'.[9] The Agreement is thus a reference model for alternatives to membership in the proximity.[10] Although the EEA Agreement can be regarded as the archetype of EU neighbourhood law providing for the closest echelons of gravitational intensity

[1] On Switzerland see further ch 6 of this work.

[2] Marise Cremona and Alessandro Petti, 'Extending the Internal Market Through Free Trade Agreements' in Robert Schütze and Takis Tridimas (eds), *Oxford Principles of European Union Law*, vol 2 (Oxford University Press, forthcoming).

[3] EEA Agreement [1994] OJ L1/3 (hereinafter EEA Agreement), recital 2.

[4] ibid recital 4.

[5] ibid pt V, ch I.

[6] ibid pt V, ch II.

[7] ibid pt V, ch III.

[8] Amichai Magen, 'Transformative Engagement through Law: The Acquis Communautaire as an Instrument of EU External Influence' (2007) 9 *European Journal of Law Reform* 361, 377.

[9] Marc Maresceau, 'Integration Oriented Elements in Bilateral Agreements Concluded by the EU with Third States: A Few Examples', speech delivered in Nicosia, 24 June 2010, 3.

[10] Sieglinde Gstöhl, 'The European Economic Area as a "Prototype" for the Integration of EU Neighbours?' in Sieglinde Gstöhl (ed), *Mapping the European Union's Neighbourhood Relations* (Routledge, 2016) 17.

around the EU legal order, its institutional structure has never been replicated in other arrangements of EU neighbourhood law.

The EEA's institutional set-up plays an important role in ensuring homogeneity while safeguarding the distinctive characteristics of the EU legal order. The EEA Agreement is based on a structure consisting of the separate EU and EFTA pillars. The 'relevance' of the EU legal order for the EEA regime is that of a de facto superordination of the latter over the former.[11] The EEA regime is not only dependent upon the *existence* and *content* of EU law, but it is also more dependent on the EU institutional structure than on the EFTA pillar. The two-pillar configuration was envisioned to respond to the CJEU's pronouncements on the draft EEA design. In particular, the EFTA pillar was established to fulfill the requirements of EU autonomy set out it the pronouncements of the Court of Justice on the compatibility of the draft agreement with EU law.[12] The original single-pillar model would have also entailed an extended Council of Ministers with legislative functions and the power to enact laws. The arrangement was dismissed by the EU and was also adversely received by the EFTA States as it would have entailed a transfer of sovereignty which was distant from the wishes of the involved non-EU countries.[13] As indicated by the Commission, in the initial EEA Agreement draft submitted to the CJEU's review:

> The decision-taking procedure provided for in the agreement [would reflect], on the one hand, the interest in extending the [EU] *acquis* and its future development to the EEA whilst safeguarding autonomous decision-taking by the [EU] and, on the other hand, respect for the wishes of the sovereign States which intended neither to transfer powers nor to confer legislative power on the institutions set up by the agreement.[14]

In *Opinion 1/91*, the Court's main concern was the preservation of the autonomy of the EU legal order and of its judicial prerogatives. In particular, the judicial mechanisms were found to be in breach of the principle of the autonomy of EU law. In the draft EEA Agreement, homogeneity was expected to be ensured through a single court composed of judges of both the Court of Justice and EFTA partners, thus creating organic links between the EU legal order and the EFTA regime.[15] The option for a single-pillar model was rejected. The incompatibility of the EEA arrangement with the principle of autonomy of EU law was not found in the existence per se of an external judicial system established by an international agreement.[16] It was ascribed, instead, to the threat that the envisaged court system could pose on 'the ability of the Court of Justice to carry out its functions

[11] See similarly with regard to the judicial structure, Marise Cremona, 'The "Dynamic and Homogenous" EEA: Byzantine Structures and Variable Geometry' (1994) 19 *European Law Review* 508, 517.

[12] *Opinion 1/91* EU:C:1991:490.

[13] Cremona (n 11) 510.

[14] *Opinion 1/91* (n 12) see in particular the summary of the written observations submitted by the Institutions.

[15] ibid, [47].

[16] This was confirmed more recently in *Opinion 1/17*, EU:C:2019:341 [106].

in complete independence'.[17] The *Opinion* led to the overhaul of the draft agreement with the set-up of a two-pillar model to preserve the CJEU's independence (and autonomy).

The new draft of the EEA Agreement based on a two-pillar configuration was found to be compatible with the principle of autonomy of EU law in *Opinion 2/91*. The safeguard of the specific characteristics of EU law was attained primarily through a degree of separation between the institutional structures presiding over the management of the EEA Agreement and those of the Union. Yet, in the new version of the Agreement, when the interaction between the two pillars is envisaged, the EU institutional structure enjoys a de facto superordinate status. The Court found several guarantees for the preservation of the autonomy of the EU legal order. First, the Agreement no longer set up an EEA Court, but a separate EFTA Court with 'no personal or functional links with the Court of Justice'.[18] Secondly, the binding nature of the pronouncements of the Court of Justice was recognised both in possible dispute settlement procedures pursuant to the Agreement[19] and with regard to the powers conferred upon the of the Joint Committee designed to pursue the objective of homogeneity of the EEA.[20] Significantly, moreover, the revised Agreement no longer included 'any provision requiring the Court of Justice to pay due account to decisions of other courts'.[21]

III. The EEA's Far-reaching Techniques of Extension of the EU's Legal Space

The 'dynamic' and 'homogeneous' EEA is articulated through an overarching set of substantive *renvois* and organisational interactions among the EU legal order and the EEA regime. The text of the EEA Agreements itself replicates or largely mirrors provisions of EU law especially on the free movement of goods,[22] persons,[23] services[24] and capital.[25] The same applies to the specific provisions on the right of establishment.[26]

[17] *Opinion 1/91* (n 12) [53].
[18] *Opinion 1/92*, EU:C:1992:189 [13].
[19] ibid [14]–[15].
[20] ibid [22]–[25].
[21] ibid [16].
[22] Customs duties are regulated by Art 10 of the EEA Agreement replicating Art 30 TFEU. Quantitative restrictions on imports are governed by Arts 11,12 and 13 of the EEA Agreement largely replicating the wordings of Arts 34, 35, 36 TFEU.
[23] Free movement of workers is governed by Art 28 EEA Agreement, replicating Art 45 TFEU. See also the correspondences between Art 31 EEA Agreement and Art 49 TFEU and between Art 36 EEA and Art 56 TFEU.
[24] Art 36 EEA Agreement is identical in substance to Art 56 TFEU.
[25] Art 40 EEA Agreement corresponding to former Art 67(1) TEEC, now Art 63 TFEU.
[26] See Arts 31 and 34 EEA Agreement and Arts 49 and 54 TFEU respectively.

Uniformity of interpretation of extended EU law is paramount in the EEA Agreement. Its Article 6 establishes that EEA provisions that are identical in substance to EU law shall be interpreted and applied in conformity with the relevant CJEU's case law prior to the signature of the Agreement. Article 6 can be thus characterised as an interpretative *renvoi* to the CJEU's case law based on the substantive correspondence of the provisions of EEA law to those of EU law. Although Article 6 EEA Agreement envisages that the conformity of interpretation applies only to CJEU rulings antecedent to the signature of the EEA, dynamism in the extension of the EU's legal space is pursued through a twofold arrangement. First, Article 3(2) of the Agreement between the EFTA states on the establishment of a Surveillance Authority and a Court of Justice[27] (SCA) prescribes that the EFTA Surveillance Authority (the homologue of the Commission in the EFTA pillar) and the EFTA Court 'shall pay due account to the principles laid down by the relevant rulings by the [CJEU] given after the signature of the EEA Agreement' for rules that are identical in substance to those of EU law. Second, substantive homogeneity is guaranteed by the activity the EEA Joint Committee, composed of representatives from the Contracting Parties.[28] The Joint Committee not only 'shall keep under constant review the development of the case-law of the Court of Justice … and of the EFTA Court',[29] but it is also responsible for amending the Annexes of the EEA Agreement to reflect the adoption of new EU law.[30] The procedure for amending the annexes may be thus construed as a dynamic substantive *renvoi* predicated on the relevance of EU law for the development of the EEA regime. These mechanisms reinforce the interpretative *renvoi* resulting from Article 6 EEA Agreement.

The dynamic adaptation of the substantive *renvois* that the EEA regime operates to the EU legal order is therefore left to the political decisions of the EEA Joint Committee, which is ultimately a diplomatic body. If no agreement is reached on the amendments of the Annex to the EEA Agreement reflecting the evolution of EU law, Article 102(5) EEA contemplates a partial suspension of the Agreement. Substantive homogeneity between the EU and the EEA legal order thus rests upon mechanisms of organisational interactions between different legal regimes. These also include systems of information exchange between the EU and EFTA Courts.[31] Moreover, organisational interaction is not only based on mirroring the EU's monitoring and surveillance schemes in the EFTA pillar,[32] but may result in institutional *renvois*. This happens if courts of the EEA EFTA States ask the Court of Justice to decide on the interpretation of an EEA rule.[33]

[27] [1994] OJ L 344/3.
[28] Art 93 EEA Agreement.
[29] Art 105(2) EEA Agreement.
[30] Art 102 EEA Agreement.
[31] Arts 106 and 109(2) EEA Agreement.
[32] Art 108 EEA Agreement.
[33] Art 107 EEA Agreement and Protocol 34 for preliminary references of courts of the EEA EFTA States to the CJEU.

In addition to this, in the context of dispute settlement, if a dispute fails to be solved by the EEA Joint Committee and relates to interpretation of EU provisions incorporated in the Agreement, 'the Contracting Parties to the dispute may agree to request the [CJEU] to give a ruling on the interpretation of the relevant rules'.[34] Clearly however, 'EFTA states are highly unlikely to agree to such a request being made'[35] and this procedure has never been triggered.

Organisational mechanisms of information exchange and financial contributions are also envisaged for structural adjustments and to reduce economic and social disparities in the EEA.[36] Moreover, some arrangements are in place for the adaptation of the EU *acquis* for EFTA States.[37] It is worth stressing that the EFTA pillar is not a mere replication of EU structures within the EEA. Indeed, the system of the preliminary rulings is absent in the EFTA since the EFTA Court does not hold the exclusive power of final interpretation of EEA law. In the words of the EFTA Court, this circumstance derives from the fact that 'the depth of integration under the EEA Agreement EFTA advisory opinion system is less far-reaching that under the EU treaties', which in turn may mean that the relationship between the EFTA Court and the national courts of the EFTA States is 'more partner-like'.[38] Furthermore, while the Court of Justice may exercise judicial control over Council decisions on the positions to be taken by the EU in the EEA Joint Committee pursuant to Article 218(9) TFEU, no corresponding power has been accorded to the EFTA Court. Furthermore, recourse to international arbitration mechanisms in the EEA is precluded if the matters of the dispute concern the interpretation of provisions of the Agreement which 'are identical in substance to the corresponding rules of the [EU Treaties]'.[39]

For non-solved disputes concerning the interpretation of (extended) EU law that are not submitted to the CJEU, only safeguards measures[40] or suspension of the Agreement[41] are envisaged. If the dispute is not brought before the EEA Joint Committee, the results can hence be more detrimental to the weaker party to the Agreement suffering from the imbalanced architecture.[42] It is also worth stressing that to safeguard the independence of the CJEU, there is no requirement for the CJEU to take into account the decisions of other courts, nor can a decision of the

[34] Art 111(3) EEA Agreement.

[35] Halvard Haukeland Fredriksen and Christian NK Franklin, 'Of Pragmatism and Principles: The EEA Agreement 20 Years On' (2015) 52 *Common Market Law Review* 629, fn 167.

[36] See Part 3 EEA Agreement and Protocols 38, 38A, 38B and 38C.

[37] See Art 119 EEA Agreement.

[38] Case E-18/11 *Irish Bank* [2012] EFTA Ct Rep 592 [57].

[39] Art 111(4) EEA Agreement.

[40] Arts 113–14 EEA Agreement.

[41] Art 102 EEA Agreement.

[42] Christophe Reymond, 'Institutions, Decision-Making Procedure and Settlement of Disputes in the European Economic Area' (1993) 30 *Common Market Law Review* 449, 467; Marja-Liisa Öberg, *The Boundaries of the EU Internal Market: Participation without Membership* (Cambridge University Press, 2020) 268.

CJEU be superseded by an act of the Joint Committee.[43] Significantly, only the Court of Justice holds the power of judicial review of the internal market *acquis*.[44]

The foregoing arrangements thus 'accord a *de facto* pre-eminence of the judicial structure of the Court of Justice without making this explicit'.[45] It has been convincingly argued that the homogeneity of the EEA Agreement was preserved not only by letting the CJEU's interpretations prevail, but also through the 'voluntary compliance' of the national courts of the EFTA States in order to ensure alignment with CJEU's case law.[46] This often occurred at the expenses of *travaux préparatoires* of the relevant EEA EFTA States' legislation.[47] The de facto superordination of the EU legal order into the two-pillar arrangement emerges from the substantive and institutional *renvois* to EU law exemplifying the fact that in Romano's terms, the EEA regime presupposes the EU legal order. The EEA thus emerges as the archetype of the extension of EU's legal space: the gravitational force exercised by the EU is not limited to the substantive mirroring and *renvois* to EU law but also includes interpretative and institutional *renvois* to the EU legal order.

IV. Does the *Polydor* Principle Apply to EEA Law?

The demarcation between EU law and the EEA regime as originally delineated by the CJEU raises questions on whether the *Polydor* principle applies to EEA law. In *Opinion 1/91*, the Court reaffirmed that 'the fact that the provisions of the Agreement and the corresponding [EU] provisions are identically worded does not mean that they must necessarily be interpreted identically'.[48] Yet, in the EEA, the counterforce of the *Polydor* jurisprudence intimating a demarcation between EU membership law and EU neighbourhood law is the principle and objective of homogeneity. Homogeneity requires uniformity in the implementation and application of EEA law.[49]

The joint efforts of the CJEU and the EFTA Court have thinned out the possibilities of divergent interpretation of EEA rules. In *L' Oréal*, the EFTA Court recognised that 'differences in *scope* and *purpose* may under specific circumstances lead to a difference in interpretation between EEA law and [EU] law'.[50] The EFTA Court soon after offered reassurances on its commitment to dynamic homogeneity by stating that in 'its interpretation between EEA rules, the Court

[43] Cremona (n 11) 516.

[44] Arts 263–64 TFEU.

[45] Cremona (n 11) 517.

[46] Halvard H Fredriksen, 'The EEA and the Case Law of the CJEU: Incorporation without Participation?' in Erik Oddvar Eriksen and John Erik Fossum (eds), *The European Union's non-members: independence under hegemony?* (Routledge 2015) 110.

[47] ibid.

[48] *Opinion 1/91* (n 12) [14].

[49] Carl Baudenbacher (ed), *The Fundamental Principles of EEA Law* (Springer, 2017).

[50] Joined Cases E-9/07 and E-10/07 *L'Oréal* [2008] EFTA Ct Rep 159 [27] (emphasis added).

has consistently taken into account the relevant rulings of the ECJ given after [the date of signature of the EEA Agreement]'.[51] Deference to the objective of homogeneity has been manifested on several occasions by the Court of Frist Instance that interpreted EEA rules by analogy to the corresponding rules of EU law. In *Opel Austria*, the Court of First Instance ruled on the analogous interpretation of Article 10 EEA on prohibition of customs duties and any measures having an equivalent effect with the corresponding provisions of EU law.[52] It is worth stressing that the interpretation by analogy inaugurated by the CJEU in *Opel Austria* derives from the interpretative *renvoi* to the case law of the CJEU made by Article 6 EEA Agreement. By reviewing the context and the purposes of the Agreement, in *Opel Austria* the Court of First Instance found that 'the EEA Agreement involves a high degree of integration, with objectives which exceed those of a mere free-trade agreement'.[53] Indeed, *Opel Austria* inaugurated a copious CJEU case law confirming the interpretation by analogy of EEA provisions which are 'identical in substance' to provisions of EU law.[54]

In that light, it might be argued that the *Polydor* principle does not apply to EEA law. The above-referred case law on interpretation by analogy substantiated by the objective of homogeneity may point towards this direction. Yet, on the other hand, the *Polydor* principle essentially revolves around interpretative motives of international law. These were not only used by the CJEU in *Opinion 1/91* but were confirmed in the very *Opel Austria* judgment.[55] Here, the analogous interpretation of EEA law to the corresponding provisions of EU law was exactly established on the basis of the context of the EEA Agreement and its objective and purpose.[56]

A. The Free Movement of Persons in the Special Relationship between the EU and the EEA EFTA States

The gulf between free movement of persons law in the EEA and EU citizenship law has narrowed, notwithstanding the absence of the notion of citizenship in

[51] ibid [28]–[29].

[52] Case T-115/94 *Opel Austria* EU:T:1997:3 [110]–[111].

[53] ibid [107].

[54] By way of example, for the interpretation by analogy of Arts 34 and 36 TFEU and Arts 11 and 13 EEA Agreement, see Case C-143/06 *Ludwigs-Apotheke München* EU:C:2007:656 [43]. Note that the Art 6 EEA Agreement's wording of 'identical in substance' is at times rendered in the case law as 'essentially identical' in the English version. In the French version of the judgments, however, the wording adopted mirrors the wording of Art 6 EEA Agreement: 'identiques en substance'. For analogous interpretation of Art 28 EEA Agreement and Art 45 TFEU see inter alia Case C-104/06 *Commission v Sweden* EU:C:2007:40 [32]; Case C-39/10, *Commission v Estonia* EU:C:2012:282 [67]. For the provisions on freedom of establishment see Case C-503/14 *Commission v Portugal* EU:C:2016:979 [92]–[93]. For non discrimination in the domain of free movement of goods see Joined Cases C-204/12 to C-208/12 *Essent Belgium* [72] and [123]. On these issues see the thorough analysis by Halvard H Fredriksen, 'The European Economic Area' in Robert Schütze and Takis Tridimas (eds), *Oxford Principles of European Union Law*, vol 2 (Oxford University Press, forthcoming).

[55] *Opel Austria* (n 52) [116].

[56] ibid [107]–[109].

EEA law. In the EEA Agreement, there are no articles mirroring Articles 20–25 TFEU on EU citizenship. Nevertheless, a lengthy process leading to the incorporation of the EU Citizenship Directive into the Annexes of the EEA Agreement has guaranteed a dynamic *renvoi* to EU citizenship secondary law. As mentioned before,[57] the incorporation of the directive was accompanied with the rather neboulous reservation mentioning that 'the concept of Union citizenship has no equivalent in the EEA Agreement'.[58]

The scepticism surrounding the incorporation of the EU Citizenship Directive into the EEA Agreement principally revolved around the following question, vividly formulated by Franklin and Fredriksen: 'Would acceptance of the directive in its entirety lead to a de facto broadening of the scope of the EEA Agreement, effectively introducing EU citizenship through the back door?'[59] The issue slowed down the incorporation of the Directive into the EEA Agreement but only after years of discussion and the European Commission's recourse to the conciliation procedure under Article 102 EEA.[60]

In the absence of the primary law provisions on citizenship in the EEA law, the EFTA Court's pursuance of the objective of homogeneity has engendered a departure from the methodology of interpretation of the CJEU in cases relating to the free movement of persons. Interestingly, however, such a departure was motivated by the very need of ensuring that the operation of the EEA Agreement would accord the same rights for the nationals of the EEA EFTA States as those accorded to EU citizens. The methodology used by the EFTA Court is that of inflating the interpretation of the EU Citizenship Directive with rights that the CJEU's would infer not from the Directive but from EU primary law (and particularly Article 21 TFEU).

In *O and B*, the CJEU extended the scope of the rights granted by the EU Citizenship Directive as to include derived rights of third country nationals who are family members of a citizen of an EU Member State having resided in a different Member State to that of which he is national. Crucially, these derived rights of third country nationals were extended to circumstances where the said citizen returns to his Member State of origin (with his family members).[61] The derived

[57] See ch 3 of this work.

[58] Joint Declaration by the Contracting Parties to Decision of the EEA Joint Committee No 158/2007 of 7 December 2007 amending Annex V (Free movement of workers) and Annex VIII (Right of establishment) to the EEA Agreement, incorporating Directive 2004/38/EC of the European Parliament and of the Council into the Agreement, [2008] OJ L 124/20. In Case E-15/12 *Wahl v Iceland* [2013] EFTA Ct Rep 534 [74]–[77], the EFTA Court found that the exclusions of the concept of union citizenship and immigration policy from the EEA Agreement established by the Joint declaration 'must be assessed on a case-by-case basis and may vary accordingly'. It also found that the said exclusion had 'no material impact' in the case at issue.

[59] Christian NK Franklin and Halvard H Fredriksen, 'Differentiated Citizenship in the European Economic Area' in Dora Kostakopoulou and Daniel Thym (eds) *Research Handbook on European Union Citizenship Law and Policy* (Edward Elgar Publishing, 2022) 308.

[60] ibid.

[61] Case C-456/12 *O & B*, ECLI:EU:C:2014:135.

rights invoked against a home State of the EU citizen's family members are not guaranteed by the Directive itself. The CJEU ruled on the extension of these rights by applying by analogy the provisions of the Directive to situations of return in the home Member State. The Court established that in these circumstances,

> the conditions for granting a derived right of residence to a third-country national who is a family member of that Union citizen, in the latter's Member State of origin, should not, in principle, be more strict than those provided for by that directive for the grant of a derived right of residence to a third-country national who is a family member of a Union citizen who has exercised his right of freedom of movement by becoming established in a Member State other than the Member State of which he is a national.[62]

Significantly, in the EU, the interpretation by analogy of the Directive's derived rights in situations of return to the home Member State occurred via a mediation of EU primary law provisions, notably Article 21 TFEU.[63] Similar factual circumstances occurred in pleadings before the EFTA Court in *Gunnarsson*, *Jabbi* and *Campbell*. In *Jabbi*, the EFTA Court noticed the widening gap between the EU and the EFTA pillar of the EEA, with the former having been amended multiple times while the text of the EEA Agreement remained 'substantially unchanged'.[64] By reviewing the *O & B* case, the EFTA Court recognised that the CJEU 'reached its conclusions on a legal basis *not* existing in the EEA. … Consequently, an unequal level of protection of the rights to free movement of persons within the EEA could ensue.'[65] The EFTA Court noted how the CJEU had considered the *Singh*[66] and *Eind*[67] cases as relevant for interpreting the rights accorded to the family members of Union citizens upon a return of the home state under Article 21(1) TFEU.[68] The EFTA Court thus relied on this case law to interpret Article 7(1)(b) of the Citizenship Directive with a view to ensuring the same results as those stemming from the ECJ's reliance on Article 21(1) TFEU. The EFTA Court found that:

> A right to move freely from the home EEA State to another EEA State cannot be fully achieved if that person may be deterred from exercising the freedom by obstacles raised by the home State to the right of residence for a spouse.[69]

In that light, the EFTA Court confirmed the extension of the rights accorded by the EU Citizenship Directive also to situations of return to the home state.[70]

Crucially, while the CJEU inferred the extension of these rights from Article 21(1) TFEU, the EFTA Court inflated rights stemming from the EU Citizenship Directive

[62] ibid 61.

[63] The approach has been confirmed inter alia in Case C-133/15 *Chavez-Vilchez* EU:C:2017:354 [54]–[56]; Case C-230/17 *Altiner and Ravn*, EU:C:2018:497 [27].

[64] Case E-28/15 *Jabbi* [2016] EFTA Ct Rep 575 [62].

[65] ibid [66] (emphasis added).

[66] Case C-370/90 *Singh*, EU:C:1992:296.

[67] Case C-291/05 *Eind*, EU:C:2007:771.

[68] *Jabbi* (n 64) [67].

[69] ibid [49].

[70] ibid [82].

in the EEA recurring to a different interpretative toolbox. Although departing from the ECJEU's methodology, the EFTA Court's stance resonated with the underlying motives of the *Polydor* jurisprudence: it relied on the context and the purpose of the EU and the EEA Agreement. With regard to the objectives, it highlighted the need to ascertain whether the objective of 'homogeneity in the EEA [could] be achieved based on an authority included in the EEA Agreement'. It maintained that the ensuing inquiry 'must be based on the EEA Agreement, legal acts incorporated into it and case law'.[71] It referred to the preamble of the EEA Agreement and the objective of maintaining 'a uniform interpretation and application of the EEA Agreement.'[72] Significantly, the EFTA Court put forward that normally the contextual reading of the case law of the CJEU does not pose problems for the EFTA Court, 'because the context is the same'. In the circumstances arising in *Jabbi*, however, the EFTA Court observed that the context was different insofar the CJEU 'partly ruled out the application of the Directive and instead applied the concept of Union citizenship in evolution of the free movement of persons in the EU'.[73]

In *Campbell*, the EFTA Court was slightly more overt in unravelling the implications of the different contexts of the EEA and EU Agreement and the common objective of homogeneity. It posited that 'In the context of EEA law, the fact that no parallel to Article 21 TFEU exists in EEA law entails that the Directive must be interpreted differently in the EEA, in order to realize the objective of the Directive'.[74] The EFTA Court highlighted that its findings in *Jabbi* were based 'on the specific legal context of the EEA Agreement' whereby the interpretation of the Directive 'must take into account the context in which the Directive is situated in EEA law and the manner in which this context differs from the EU pillar'.[75] It went on by saying that 'the legal context remain[ed] unaltered since *Jabbi*, and accordingly, as firmly supported by the ESA and the Commission', it found 'no reason to depart form the understanding of homogeneity and effectiveness expressed in that judgment'.[76]

The EFTA's Court reasoning was thus premised on the objective of homogeneity and the different contexts of the EEA Agreement and the EU legal order. Although such a reasoning was granted the same level of protection of rights to EU and EEA nationals, it was far from being an interpretation by analogy to the EU case law. In that regard, Tobler has perceptively pointed out a 'new, reversed version of the *Polydor* principle: different contexts of the same provision must lead to different interpretations, where that is necessary in order to achieve the same overall result in terms of the level of peoples' protection'.[77] Indeed, the moving away

[71] ibid [68].
[72] ibid [70].
[73] ibid [71].
[74] Case E-4/19 *Campbell*, EFTA Ct Judgment of 13 May 2020 nyr [57].
[75] ibid [56].
[76] ibid [58].
[77] Christa Tobler, 'Free Movement of Persons in the EU v. in the EEA: Of Effect-Related Homogeneity and a Reversed Polydor Principle' in Nathan Cambien, Dimitry Kochenov and Elise Muir (eds), *European Citizenship under Stress* (Brill Nijhoff, 2020) 1448.

from the interpretation by analogy by the EFTA Court was oriented towards achieving in the EFTA pillar the same outcomes or results achieved in the EU pillar.[78]

In the EEA, the inflation of secondary law with content that the CJEU derives from EU primary law is not specific to the citizenship domain. It occurs more generally in areas where there is a lack in the EEA of EU-specific primary law, including the EU Charter of Fundamental Rights (EUCFR). In *Deveci*, the freedom to conduct a business enshrined in Article 16 EUCFR was invoked before the EFTA Court. The EFTA Court insisted on the interpretation of secondary law, and particularly Article 3 of Directive 2001/23/EC on the transfer of undertakings.[79] While substantially following the observations of the Commission that the ECJ in *Alemo-Herron* found that Article 3 of the Directive is to be interpreted in accordance of Article 16 of the Charter,[80] the EFTA Court maintained that it found 'no reason to address the question of Article 16 of the Charter'.[81] It restricted itself to the interpretation of secondary law, while indirectly inflating the interpretation of the Directive with the content of the EU Charter.

On the EU side, deference to homogeneity predicated upon the canons of interpretation by analogy was shown by the CJEU in the *IN* case. In its reasoning, the CJEU emphasised the scope of the 'special relationship' between the EU and the EEA EFTA States. Such a relationship that does not only include the EEA but includes cooperation in the Area of Freedom, Security and Justice (AFSJ), through the Surrender Procedure Agreement[82] and the Schengen acquis Agreement.[83] *IN* concerned an extradition request of IN, a person holding both Russian and Icelandic nationality, from Croatia to Russia. The case revolved around the question of whether the findings of the *Petruhhin* jurisprudence[84] developed in EU membership law could be extended to 'a citizen of the Republic of Iceland with which the European Union maintains particular links'.[85]

The *Petruhhin* case concerned the extradition of an Estonian citizen (Petruhhin) from Latvia. In pursuance to Latvian domestic laws, Petruhhin would not have been extradited to Russia if he had been a Latvian national. The CJEU sanctioned the incompatibility with Union law of 'national rules on extradition … giv[ing] rise to a difference in treatment depending on whether the person concerned is a national of the Member State in question or a national of another Member State'.[86] In particular, the domestic measures under scrutiny were found

[78] Franklin and Fredriksen (n 60).

[79] Council Directive 2001/23/EC on the approximation of the laws of the Member States relating to the safeguarding of employees' rights in the event of transfers of undertakings, businesses or parts of undertakings or businesses [2001] OJ L 82/16.

[80] C-426/11 *Alemo-Herron*, EU:C:2013:521 [31].

[81] Case E-10/14 *Deveci* [2014] EFTA Ct Rep 1364 [63].

[82] [2006] OJ, L 292/2.

[83] [1999] OJ L 176/36.

[84] Case C-182/15, *Petruhhin*, EU:C:2016:630.

[85] Case C-897/19 PPU, *IN v Ruska Federacija* (hereinafter *IN*), EU:C:2020:262 [26].

[86] *Petruhhin* (n 196) [32].

to be a restriction of freedom of movement within the meaning of Article 21 TFEU.[87] In fact, nationals of other Member States, not granted the protection against extradition enjoyed by nationals of the Member State in question, would have seen their freedom of movement within the EU significantly hindered.[88] The CJEU clarified the mechanisms of cooperation entailed in the Framework Decision 2002/584 on the European Arrest Warrant (EAW) for surrendering suspected criminals for the purposes of prosecution among EU Member States.[89] It did so by relying not only on Article 21 but also on Article 18 TFEU on Union citizenship.

The *IN* case was more complex as it concerned a national of Iceland. Here, the notion of EU citizenship and therefore the Article 21 TFEU could not apply. In *IN*, the CJEU reviewed a host of ancillary international agreements composing Iceland's 'special relationship with the European Union, which goes beyond economic and commercial cooperation'.[90] As highlighted by Frederiksen and Hillion, the CJEU decided to interpret these agreements in a holistic fashion, locating the EEA Agreement at the core of the 'special relationship'.[91] The purposes of the EEA define the foundations of the political covenant informing the legal relationship between the EU and EEA participating EFTA States. As a matter of fact, the Court found that IN had

> the status of the national of an EFTA State, which is party to the EEA Agreement [and] that State implements and applies the *Schengen acquis*, renders the situation of that person objectively comparable with that of an EU citizen to whom, in accordance with Article 3(2) TEU, the Union offers an area of freedom, security and justice without internal frontiers, in which the free movement of persons is ensured.[92]

The CJEU thus found that Article 36 EEA on the provision to provide services could be interpreted by analogy to the corresponding EU law provision which also encompassed the freedom for recipients of services to go to another Member State in order to receive services there.[93] The CJEU thus explicitly extended in the EEA framework the passive provisions of services developed in the EU membership jurisprudence[94] and which had not extended to other arrangements of EU neighbourhood law.[95] On this basis, the Court established that an Icelandic national 'who presented himself at the border of a Member State in order to enter its territory and receive services there, falls within the scope of the EEA Agreement

[87] ibid 33.
[88] ibid 132.
[89] ibid 43–50.
[90] *IN* (n 85) [44].
[91] Christophe Hillion and Halvard H Fredriksen, 'A. Court of Justice: The "Special Relationship" between the EU and the EEA EFTA States – Free Movement of EEA Citizens in an Extended Area of Freedom, Security and Justice: Ruska Federacija v. I.N.' (2021) 58 *Common Market Law Review* 860.
[92] *IN* (n 85) [58].
[93] ibid [53].
[94] Joined cases 286/82 and 26/83 *Luisi and Carbone*, EU:C:1984:35.
[95] For Turkey, see most notably Case C-221/11 *Demirkan*, EU:C:2013:583.

and, consequently, of EU law'.[96] In that manner, the CJEU further contributed to decrease the gulf between the free movement rights in the EEA and EU citizenship law. The CJEU's understanding in that case endorses the thesis of this book of an extension of EU legal space arising from the composite interaction of interrelated regimes. The case marked a step forward in the establishment and consolidation of the homogeneous EEA legal space.[97]

B. The *Polydor* Principle in EEA Law: Demarcation, Techniques and Political Covenant

The question of whether the *Polydor* principle applies in the EEA defies simplification. In most cases, the CJEU and the EFTA Court would interpret EEA provisions corresponding to EU law in the same manner. This is done in light of the objective of homogeneity pursued in the EEA and the ensuing requirement of uniform interpretation. The context of the application of the EU and EEA Agreements can be thus considered generally similar. Nevertheless, 'the citizenship gulf' emerging between EEA free movement of persons law and EU citizenship law has led the EFTA Court to inflate EU secondary law, and particularly the Citizenship Directive, with content that the ECJ derived from EU primary citizenship law. This 'EEA secondary law inflation' does not solely pertain to the citizenship domain but has also occurred in the context of the application of the Charter. This rather peculiar stance by the EFTA Court is, in fact, oriented to ensure equal protection of rights in the EU and EFTA pillar of the EEA. Although the 'EEA secondary law inflation' in the EFTA Court jurisprudence entails a departure from the interpretation by analogy with the CJEU case law, it is intended to fully substantiate the objective to maintain 'a uniform interpretation and application' of the EEA Agreement.[98]

In its observations to the *Campbell* case, the Norwegian Government criticised the EFTA Court's approach in *Jabbi*. It maintained that:

> To argue that a less extensive scope and purpose at the level of primary law (the main part of the EEA Agreement) militate in favour of construing secondary law (the Directive) more extensively in the EEA would defy logic. This would not only reintroduce the *Polydor* doctrine into EEA law, but would put that doctrine on its head.[99]

Yet, it is hard to forego the *Polydor* doctrine in the contest of EU neighbourhood law. As put forward in this book the arrangements of EU neighbourhood law can be explained in terms of demarcation, techniques of extension of the EU's legal

[96] *IN* (n 85) [54].
[97] In this sense see also Case C-128/22 *Nordic Info*, Opinion of AG Emiliou, EU:C:2023:645 [46]–[47].
[98] EEA Agreement, recital 15.
[99] See the written observations of the Norwegian government in *Campbell* (n 74), as stated in the Report for the Hearing, para 50, see more broadly paras 47–53.

space and political covenants. The tortuous case law on the 'EU citizenship gulf' in EEA law exemplifies the demarcation and complex relations between the EU legal order and the regimes of EU neighbourhood law. The EEA arrangement is characterised by a robust political covenant founded on common European identity and values and on the pervasive objective (and principle) of homogeneity. This objective has been constantly pursued and nourished both in the EU and the EFTA pillar, albeit with different techniques. The robust political covenant, however, does not obliterate the demarcation between EU law and EEA law. The absence in the EEA context of primary law provisions on citizenship, and the absence of the EUCFR from the primary law of the EEA Agreement (with respect to the EFTA Pillar) are some examples of the demarcation between EU membership law and this special EU neighbourhood law regime.

The analogous interpretation between EU and EEA law does not extend to the entirety of the Agreement or to the distinctive principles characterising EU law. This was spelled out by AG Cosmas who marked the differences between the EU and the EEA legal order. He asserted that some of the 'essential characteristics' of the EU legal order, such as primacy and direct effect, 'do not extend to the legal structure created by the EEA Agreement'. Considerations of a similar nature precluded the extension of the *Francovich* doctrine on state liability to the EEA Agreement.[100] In this respect, although the principle of state liability was introduced into the EEA legal order through the back door by the EFTA Court,[101] the premise of this introduction was different and mirrored the differences between the two legal regimes. In *Sveinbjörnsdóttir*, the Commission and several EFTA States contended that the case law in which the CJEU developed the doctrine of state liability was developed on the basis of principles specific to the EU legal order. In the view of the Commission and of some EFTA states, 'since the case law is largely based on the special characteristics of the [EU] legal order that are not found in the EEA Agreement, this case law is not transferable to the EEA Agreement by virtue of Article 6 EEA'.[102] Among the differences singled out, the absence of the 'transfer of legislative powers, direct effect and primacy of [EU] legislation' in the EEA Agreement were highlighted.[103]

These differences, however, did not preclude the EFTA Court from finding that 'EFTA States must be obliged to provide for compensation for loss and damage caused to an individual by incorrect implementation of a directive'.[104] Such a finding was motivated by the EEA's objectives of uniform interpretation, extended EU law and of 'equal treatment and equal conditions of competition, as well as adequate means of enforcement'.[105] In contrast to the Commission's submission in *Sveinbjörnsdóttir*, the Court of Justice also confirmed the existence in the EEA

[100] C-321/97 *Andersson v Svenska state*, Opinion AG Cosmas, EU:C:1999:9 [49].
[101] Öberg (n 42) 175.
[102] Case E-9/97 *Sveinbjörnsdóttir*, [1998] EFTA Ct Rep 95 [44].
[103] ibid [56]–[57].
[104] ibid [60]–[63].
[105] Especially EEA Agreement, Arts 3 and 108–110.

regime of the principle of state liability stemming from 'the objective of uniform interpretation and application which informs the EEA agreement'.[106]

Analogous interpretation occurs precisely in light of the objectives, the context and the institutional structure established by the EEA Agreement. It is worth stressing again that this does not obliterate what has been defined as the 'ultimately separate nature of the [EU] and the EEA legal orders'.[107] Indeed, the demarcation between EU membership law and EEA law was also established in the recent ECtHR *Konkurrenten.no* pronouncement. Here, the Strasbourg Court did not extend the *Bosphorous* doctrine to the EEA.[108] The doctrine at issue recognised the EU legal order as offering the equivalent protection of fundamental rights to the ECHR.[109] In the proceedings, the Strasbourg Court noticed that in contrast to its findings in *Bosphorous* with respect to the EU, the principles of direct effect and primacy are not applicable to the EEA.[110] This signalled again the different nature of the EU and the EEA regime by precluding the extension of *Bosphorous* case law to the EEA which has been confirmed in subsequent pronouncements.[111]

In that light the question of whether the *Polydor* principle applies to EEA law should be further problematised. Essentially, the *Polydor* principle asserts that provisions of EU neighbourhood law agreements worded identically to those of EU law shall not be necessarily interpreted by analogy with the corresponding provisions of EU law. Due account should also be paid to the context and the objective and purpose of the Agreement. This principle is far from being revolutionary and responds to the canons of interpretations established in Article 31 of the Vienna Convention on the Law of the Treaties. In this broader sense, the *Polydor* principle certainly applies to EEA law. The question of whether the Polydor principle applies to the EEA could thus be more meaningfully reframed. The gist of the question lies in whether EEA law is to be interpreted analogously to EU law 'by default'.[112] Also in this formulation, the question can be answered in the affirmative with respect to EU internal market law. This stems from the very purpose of the EEA and the underlying political covenant intending to extend EU internal market law to the EEA.

[106] Case C-140/97 *Rechberger*, ECLI:EU:C:1999:306 [39].

[107] Cremona (n 11) 512.

[108] ECtHR, decision of 5 November 2019, no 47341/15, *Konkurrenten.no* [45]. See on this issue Halvard H Fredriksen and Stian Ø Johansen, 'The EEA Agreement as a Jack-in-the-Box in the Relationship Between the CJEU and the European Court of Human Rights?' (2020) 5 *European Papers* 707, 710.

[109] ECtHR, judgment of 30 June 2005, no. 45036/98, *Bosphorus* [155].

[110] ECtHR *Konkurrenten.no* (n 108) [43].

[111] ECtHR, judgment of 10 June 2021, no 45487/17, *LO and NFT* (*Holship*) [108]: the ECtHR proceeded 'on the basis that for the purposes of this case the *Bosphorous* presumption does not apply to EEA law'.

[112] See Hillion and Fredriksen (n 92) 866. They argue: 'What the judgment in *I.N.* confirms, is that the ECJ approaches these agreements on the presumption that they indeed do extend the application of EU law to the relevant EEA EFTA States, so that the burden of proof lies with anyone arguing for a different solution in any given case. For the continued success of the EEA, this "default" is important.'

The EEA and the EU relations with the EEA-participating EFTA States thus stand very close to EU membership law. This is due to the far-reaching substantive, institutional and interpretative *renvois* that the constellation of legal agreements governing EU relations with the EEA EFTA States operate to the EU legal order. The closeness of these 'special relationships' to EU membership law, however, does not imply the identity of the political covenants of EU membership law with that of the legal regimes gravitating around EU law. The demarcation between EU membership law and EU neighbourhood law is illustrated inter alia by the absence in the EEA of the essential characteristics of EU law, such as primacy and direct effect and the absence of EFTA countries in the decision-making processes of EU law, and therefore extended EU law. It is also illustrated by the absence of primary law provision on citizenship and by the absence of the EUCFR in the primary law of the EEA Agreement (with regard to the EFTA Pillar).[113]

The foregoing leads to qualify the previous findings on the application of the *Polydor* principle to EEA law. To pursue the overarching objective of homogeneity and to ensure equal protection of rights in the EU and EFTA pillars, interpretation by analogy is not always warranted in light of the different contexts of EU law and the EEA regimes and the relevant constitutional asymmetries. Different techniques may be used for the interpretation and application of the EEA Agreement in its two pillars. An interesting aspect of the tortuous case law examined above is that the EFTA Court with the 'EEA secondary law inflation' has devised original and autonomous techniques of extension of the EU legal space reinforcing the political covenant of the 'special relationship' between EU and EEA EFTA States.

V. The EU Neighbourhood Law Continuum

The different composition of techniques of extension of the EU's legal space result in different echelons gravitational intensity of regimes of EU neighbourhood law around the EU's legal order. The EEA Agreement stands significantly close to the EU legal order in such a continuum. This is due to the replication of EU primary law provisions, the ensuing substantive and interpretative *renvois* to the EU legal order, as well as the mechanisms of organisational interaction, which may result in institutional *renvois*.

Precious elements for characterising this EU neighbourhood law continuum have been offered by a series of pronouncements where the UK opposed the Council. These judgments concerned the amendment of the EU's social security system legislation to be incorporated into different agreements providing for the extension of the EU's legal space. At issue there was the upgrade of the EU renewed regulatory framework for social security brought about by Regulation (EC) 883/2004.[114]

[113] For a problematisation see Tarjei Bekkedal, Christophe Hillion and Alessandro Petti (eds) 'Fundamental Rights Protection in Europe: shedding light on a system of interrelated regimes', (2025) *Maastricht Journal of European and Comparative Law*, (forthcoming).

[114] Regulation (EC) No 883/2004 on the coordination of social security systems, [2004] OJ L 166/1.

Twelve decisions were taken pursuant to Article 218(9) TFEU being used as the procedural legal basis to incorporate this piece of legislation in the relevant association agreements concluded by the EU. The substantive legal basis featuring in the relevant Council Decisions varied in function of the scope and the objective of the different arrangements of EU neighbourhood law.

The incorporation of the Regulation into the EEA Agreement, the EU–Swiss FMPA, and into the EU–Turkey Agreement[115] occurred through the same substantive legal basis featuring in the EU Regulation itself, namely Article 48 TFEU. Instead, for most of other EU association agreements, the substantive legal basis was Article 79(2)b TFEU covering immigration policies in the Area of Freedom, Security and Justice.[116] The use of Article 79(2)b TFEU would be beneficial to the UK in the context of EEA, FMP and Ankara Agreements, as it might have been secured an opt-out pursuant to Protocol No 21 to the TFEU. The UK hence contested the choice of the legal basis in those Council Decisions envisaging Article 48 TFEU.

In the EEA case, the Court found that the Council decision was legitimately adopted on the basis of Article 48 TFEU.[117] It established that

> the contested decision is ... precisely one of the measures by which the law governing the EU internal market is to be extended as far as possible to the EEA, with the result that nationals of the EEA States concerned benefit from the free movement of persons under the same social conditions as EU citizens.[118]

Were the same social conditions not upheld, the 'development of the association and the realisation of the objectives pursued by the EEA' would be undermined.[119] The Court did not reiterate the reasoning on the extension of the internal market to Switzerland. Nevertheless, it sanctioned the appropriateness of Article 48 TFEU as the substantive legal basis for the contested decision in the FMPA.[120] It underscored the objective of ensuring free movement of persons 'on the basis of the rules applying in the [EU]',[121] including on the matter of the social security system, whereby Switzerland is to be equated with the EU.[122]

The examination of the Ankara Agreement brought the Court to different conclusions. Indeed, the CJEU mandated the adoption of a dual legal basis including both Article 217 and Article 48 TFEU.[123] The association legal basis (Article 217 TFEU) was found necessary to complement the internal market legal

[115] In this case with some qualifications, see text to nn 124–28.
[116] This was the case of the Agreements with Morocco, see Council Decision of 21 October 2010 on the position to be taken by the EU within the Association Council of the EU–Morocco EuroMed Agreement with regard to the adoption of provisions on the coordination of social security systems [2010], OJ L 306/1. It was also the case of Tunisia, Algeria, Israel, the Former Yugoslav Republic of Macedonia (FYROM), Croatia, Albania, Montenegro and San Marino.
[117] Case C-431/11 *United Kingdom v Council [EEA]*, EU:C:2013:589 [50]–[61].
[118] ibid [58].
[119] ibid [59].
[120] Case C-656/11 *United Kingdom v Council [Switzerland]*, EU:C:2014:97 [64].
[121] ibid [55].
[122] ibid [58].
[123] Case C-81/13, *United Kingdom v Council [Turkey]*, EU:C:2014:2449.

basis (Article 48 TFEU). The Court contended that the EU–Turkey Agreement and its Additional Protocol[124] aimed to 'secure by progressive stages freedom of movement of workers between them'.[125] However, the progressive establishment of free movement of workers had not been fully completed.[126] The Court also noticed that in contrast to the cases of the EEA and FMPA with Switzerland, the amended Regulation was not incorporated into the EU–Turkey Agreement 'so as to extend to Turkey the rules on coordination of social security systems contained in it'. Besides, the Court established that 'Turkey cannot be equated with a Member State for the purposes of the application of those regulations'.[127]

This set of cases highlights the perception of the Court in locating the agreements extending the EU's legal space differently in the EU neighbourhood law continuum.[128] Indeed, the Court held that Article 48 can be used only in cases where EU and third country workers can be 'placed on the same footing'.[129] This equal standing does not apply to the Ankara Agreement or any other agreement of EU neighbourhood law amended through a Council Decision with Article 79(2)b TFEU as substantive legal basis. The equal standing to the EU was instead the case of the EEA Agreement and the FMPA with Switzerland.[130]

The Court's reasoning and findings on the uses of the appropriate legal basis to extend a piece of EU legislations in arrangements of EU neighbourhood law give an overview of the EU neighbourhood law continuum and of its different echelons of gravitational intensity around the EU's legal order. The choice of Article 48 TFEU in the EEA Agreement and FMPA cases do not alter the different considerations on the ultimately different nature of these arrangements of EU neighbourhood law from EU law. They indicate, however, how the interplay between techniques of extension of the EU's legal space and political covenants is nourished by the foundations and objectives of different agreements of EU neighbourhood law.[131] The different interplay between techniques and political covenants calibrate proximity to the EU legal order.[132]

VI. Political Covenants of EU Neighbourhood Law

Political covenants represent the interaction between sovereignty, politics and law. The demarcation and the complex relationship between EU membership law

[124] Additional Protocol annexed to the EEC–Turkey Agreement [1972] OJ L 293/3.
[125] *United Kingdom v Council [Turkey]* (n 124) [43].
[126] ibid [52].
[127] ibid [58].
[128] See in different terms, Öberg, *The Boundaries of the EU Internal Market* (n 179) 168.
[129] *United Kingdom v Council [EEA]* (n 118) [28]; See similarly *United Kingdom v Council [Switzerland]* (n 120) [58].
[130] As noted by Öberg, this treatment does not extend to the other bilateral agreements concluded with Switzerland: Öberg (n 42) 168.
[131] See also Cremona and Petti (n 2).
[132] See further chapter 9 of this work.

and EU neighbourhood law reflect this interaction. The special political covenant presiding over the relationship between the EU and the EEA EFTA States has evolved with inputs by both sides. The attention has been particularly placed on the reconfigurations of sovereignty exercise that this arrangement of EU neighbourhood law could entail. While the EU has been principally concerned with safeguarding its decision-making and judicial autonomy, the EEA EFTA States have appeared wishing to distantiating themselves from several political dimensions of EU membership.

Most of the original EEA EFTA States have eventually joined the EU, the current EEA EFTA States may be considered as potential candidates for membership pursuant to Article 49 TFEU. The small size of Lichtenstein might pose adaptation challenges to the EU institutional setup in potential membership negotiations and Lichtenstein itself may have problems with regard to the administrative capacity to implement the EU *acquis*.[133] Yet, it is unlikely that any major technical obstacle would raise in the potential negotiations for membership of Norway and Iceland.

The EEA EFTA States' choice not to be part of the EU is political and is inherently related to their reluctance to subscribe to the sovereignty reconfigurations that EU membership law would entail. As pointed out by Bull, in light of the Norwegian regained independence after the unions with Denmark (1380–1814) and with Sweden (1814–1905), 'the promise, now found in the preamble to the [TEU] of an "ever closer union" has always seemed more like a threat'.[134] This political choice of non-membership is strictly related to the legal modes of reconfiguration of sovereignty which EFTA states consider to be less far-reaching under the EEA than under EU law. This particularly regards the nature of EEA law and its difference with respect to EU membership law. As highlighted by Bull, 'the direct effect and primacy of EU law … have always ignited passionate resistance to EU membership in Norway'.[135] Indeed, given that these EU law notions are intimately connected to the reconfiguration of sovereignty, during the EEA negotiations, it was 'of the utmost importance for Norway to avoid as far as possible any form of direct effect and primacy'.[136]

In EEA law the view on the absence of the EU law notions of primacy and direct effect remains predominant.[137] With regard to primacy, in addition to the

[133] See European Commission, 'EU Relations with the Principality of Andorra, the Principality of Monaco and the Republic of San Marino: Options for Closer Integration with the EU', COM(2012) 680, para 5.5.

[134] Henrik Bull, '"Shall Be Made Part of the Internal Legal Order": The Legislative Approaches' in Carl Baudenbacher *et al*, *The EEA and the EFTA Court: decentred integration* (Hart Publishing, 2015) 204. He shows how similar considerations may be extended to Iceland in light of its union with Denmark (205).

[135] ibid 204.

[136] ibid.

[137] Franklin and Fredriksen (n 60) 661; Sven Norberg and Martin Johansson, 'The History of the EEA Agreement and the First Twenty Years of Its Existence' in Carl Baudenbacher, *The Handbook of EEA Law* (Springer, 2016). See also Davíð Þór Björgvinsson, 'Fundamental Rights in EEA Law' in *The EEA and the EFTA Court* (n 134) 265.

clarification that the EEA does not entail transfer of legislative powers, Protocol 35 to the EEA mentions the commitment of EFTA States 'to introduce, if necessary, a statutory provision to the effect that the EEA rules prevail' in cases of 'possible conflicts between implemented EEA rules and other statutory provisions. As noted by Fredriksen and Franklin:

> Protocol 35 only requires primacy for the benefit of implemented EEA rules and only over other statutory provisions (i.e. not over constitutional law). Furthermore, as the legal basis for this "quasi primacy" of EEA law is only a statutory provision, rather than a constitutional one, it does not guarantee against the possibility that the national legislature may later enact a statutory provision setting the primacy provision aside.[138]

The way in which homogeneity has been employed and developed in the implementation of the EEA Agreement as 'a legal principle (not only a political goal)'[139] has reinforced and nourished the political covenant of EEA law. As the previous sections have shown, homogeneity has been often construed as conducive to granting equal rights and obligations in EEA law and EU law, with substantially similar effects of the corresponding provisions. Different interpretation secondary law regarding EU citizenship has been necessary to maintain equal rights and obligations in the EU and EFTA pillars of the EEA. This can be construed as a consequence of a demarcation between the EU legal order and the EEA regime and the ensuing constitutional asymmetries. The distinctiveness of the EU membership law covenant stands in contrast even with the most advanced forms of extension of the EU's legal space. While the recitals of the EEA Agreement read that the establishment of a dynamic and homogeneous EEA shall be achieved through 'an overall balance of benefits, rights and obligations for the Contracting Parties',[140] in *Van Gend en Loos*, the EU Treaty Framework was qualified as being 'more than an agreement which merely creates mutual obligations between the contracting states'. Indeed, it established 'institutions endowed with sovereign rights'.[141]

The EU membership covenant has not resulted in a demise of sovereignty of EU Member States but in a reconfiguration of how sovereignty is exercised. By a similar token, rather new paradigms of sovereignty exercise are inherent to the political covenants of EU neighbourhood law. The *Wider Europe* design is premised on an extension of the EU's claim of authority beyond its membership that result in a *lato sensu* reconfiguration of the EU's borders. For the EEA EFTA States, the tailored participation in the European legal space, consisting in a number of 'opt-outs' in sensitive policy domains including citizenship (to a certain degree), the monetary union, and specific arrangements of the EU internal market, is

[138] Fredriksen and Franklin (n 35) 662.

[139] Finn Arnesen et al, 'Introduction: The EFTA States, the EEA and the Different Views on the Legal Integration of Europe', *Agreement on the European Economic Area: a commentary* (CH Beck, 2018) 6. The scholars vividly maintain that 'Homogeneity is a legal principle (not only a political goal) which applies also to the question of the legal effect of EEA law in the legal order of the Contracting Parties'.

[140] EEA Agreement, recital 4.

[141] Case 26-62 *Van Gend and Loos*, EU:C:1963:1.

counterbalanced by a lack of a genuine participation in the decision-making process of rules they are going to adopt.[142] The absence of a genuine participation in the decision-making of the laws of the extended EU legal space for non-EU members has led EEA scholars to study the patterns of 'independence under hegemony'.[143] As a matter of fact, while non-membership of the EU has been regarded as a way to safeguard sovereignty in key crucial policy areas where domestic preferences appeared to require an independent decision-making,[144] in the vast realms of the EU internal-market, EEA EFTA States are largely rule-takers. Indeed, it has been noted how sovereignty arguments regularly put forward by EEA EFTA States before the EFTA Court have been largely unsuccessful.[145] This appears to invalidate the belief according to which the EEA regime would allow for a wider margin of appreciation compared to EU law.[146]

Notwithstanding the extension of the EU's claims to authority engendered by the patterns of gravitation around the EU's legal order inherent in the *Wider Europe* design, the reconfiguration of sovereignty entailed in the extended EU's legal space have consequences also for the EU side. Hillion has perceptively highlighted how the EEA Agreement and the related agreements presiding over the relationship between the EU and the EEA EFTA States may serve to counteract the rule of law regression in some EU Member States. At least two significant episodes point towards this direction.[147] The first falls within the remit of the Norway/Iceland Surrender Procedure Agreement extending the European Arrest Warrant to the two Nordic countries.[148] Several courts in Norway have manifested reservations concerning their duties of mutual recognition for executing judicial decisions of Polish courts against the backdrop of the backsliding of guarantees for judicial independence in that country.[149] The second pertains to the decision of the EEA EFTA States not to disburse funding for the benefit of Hungary pursuant to the EEA Financial Mechanism. This decision has occurred against the background of the democratic and rule of law regression in Hungary and the harassment of civil society organisations also operating thanks to EEA funds.[150] The foregoing indicates that although

[142] Arnesen et al (n 139) 3.

[143] Erik O Eriksen and John E Fossum, *The European Union's Non-Members: Independence under Hegemony?* (Routledge, 2015).

[144] This is particularly the case for agricultural and fisheries products. See in that regard, Art 8(3)a and Protocol EEA specifying the products covered by the Agreement and the special rules on fisheries to be found in Protocol 9 EEA. See also the special regime for energy as resulting from Annex IV EEA and Art 24 EEA. See further Frederiksen (n 54).

[145] Mads Andenas, 'Sovereignty' in Carl Baudenbacher (ed), *The Fundamental Principles of EEA Law: EEA-ities* (Springer, 2017) 104.

[146] ibid.

[147] See Christophe Hillion, *The EU external action as mandate to uphold the rule of law outside and inside the Union* (2023) 29 *Columbia Journal of European Law* 228, 269 ff.

[148] Council Framework Decision of 13 June 2002 on the European arrest warrant and the surrender procedures between Member States – Statements made by certain Member States on the adoption of the Framework Decision, [2002] OJ L 190/1.

[149] Hillion (n 147) 270.

[150] ibid.

asymmetrically favouring the EU, the political covenants of EU neighbourhood law are bi-directional and affect not only the sovereignty exercise of countries participating in the extended EU's legal space but also of the EU and its Member States. In other words, political covenants of EU neighbourhood law are an expression of the relational dimension of sovereignty exercise in *Wider Europe*.

VII. Conclusions

The design and implementation of the EEA Agreement has been characterised by the rebalancing and cohabitation of different forces and objectives. Arguably, while in the drafting phase of the EEA Agreement the principle of autonomy has prevailed, in the evolution of the special partnership between the EU and the EEA EFTA States, homogeneity acquired a paramount importance for ensuing equivalent rights and obligations across the EEA. The political covenant of the EEA has been nourished by a strong commitment to homogeneity both in the EU and the EFTA pillars, which has ensured a significant intensity of EEA gravitation around the EU legal order. The scope of this gravitation does not only cover the principal domain of the EEA (EU internal market law) but also encompasses domains of the AFSJ in light of the relevant additional agreements forging the special relationship between the EU and the EEA EFTA States. Against this backdrop, the question of whether the Polydor principle applies to EEA law defies easy answers. While it can be maintained that interpretation by analogy of extended EU law is the norm in the EEA, the principle of homogeneity has been construed as not necessarily entailing uniform interpretation. This has happened in the EFTA pillar to respond to the absence of EU citizenship provisions in the EEA primary law. As a matter of fact, the EFTA Court has developed techniques of extension of the EU's legal space to narrow the gulf between EU citizenship law and free movement of persons in the EEA. The EFTA Court has inflated EEA secondary law with content that the CJEU had found to be stemming from EU citizenship primary law (absent from the EEA Agreement). More than uniformity in interpretation, scholars have highlighted the importance of uniformity of results in what has been defined as a reversed Polydor principle. In that light, the proximity to the EU legal order of the regimes governing the special relationship between the EU and Norway and Iceland do not obliterate the demarcation between EU membership and EU neighbourhood law. The political covenant of EU membership is not replicated in the EEA, not least because the EEA EFTA States have chosen not to subscribe to reconfigurations of sovereignty exercise entailed in EU membership law. While the principle of autonomy of EU law makes the EEA EFTA States rule-takers and the two-pillar structure is based on a de facto pre-eminence of the EU pillar, the relevant asymmetries in the reconfigurations of sovereignty entailed in the gravitation around the EU legal order are somewhat counterbalanced.

Indeed, the EEA EFTA States participate in the systems of check and balance of the EEA: they have a say regarding the legal implications of the Rule of Law backsliding in some of the EU countries. Therefore, the reconfiguration of sovereignty entailed in the political covenant of the special relationship between the EU and Norway and Iceland, though asymmetrical, emerges as a bi-directional. Legal relations between the EU and the EEA EFTA States are, although in a tenuous manner, thus liable to affect the reconfiguration of sovereignty of EU countries.

5

Wider Europe Through Functional Regimes

I. Introduction

This chapter explores the extension of the EU's legal space through functional sectoral regimes. By extending provisions and practices of EU law into a larger geographical area, these regimes are part of the *lato sensu* reconfiguration of the EU's borders through law in *Wider Europe*. Civil aviation law occupies a central place in the chapter in light of the significance of the European Common Aviation Area (ECAA) for the institutional arrangements of EU neighbourhood law. The chapter starts with some considerations on the internal and external dynamics of EU aviation law. It discusses the challenges posed by the notions of EU aviation law to the established practices of international law. These challenges stem from the distinctiveness on the basis of the political covenant of EU membership law and the reconfigurations of sovereignty it entails (section II). Next, the chapter examines the ECAA Agreement as a paradigm of *Wider Europe* contributing both to the sectoral development of the ENP and the pre-accession process of the Western Balkans (section III). It reviews *Opinion 1/00* on the establishment of the ECAA reflecting on how the principle of autonomy governs the specificities of the one-pillar structure (section III.A). The techniques of the extension of the EU's legal space in the ECAA, subsequently adopted also in the context of the Transport Community Treaty (TCT) are discussed (section III.B). The chapter illustrates the varying echelons of gravitational intensity around the EU's legal order in EU aviation law through the analysis of different bilateral arrangements of EU neighbourhood law in the aviation domain (section IV). The arrangements scrutinised include those in place with Switzerland (section IV.A), Ukraine (section IV.B), Morocco (section IV.C), and the UK (section IV.D). The chapter subsequently examines the Energy Community Treaty as an additional example of functional development of *Wider Europe* and as a different arrangement of EU neighbourhood law (section V).

II. Internal and External Developments in EU Aviation Law

The complex relationship between the internal and external facets of EU aviation law had been unravelled with the landmark *Open Skies* judgments.[1] In the relevant pronouncements, the CJEU sanctioned the exclusivity of the EU external aviation competences[2] thus triggering a rethink of the external dimensions of EU aviation law. In particular, the Court reviewed the clause on ownership and control of bilateral agreements with the US concluded separately by some EU Member States.[3] These clauses are also referred to as the 'nationality clauses'.[4] While 'perfectly customary in bilateral agreements concluded in the air transport sector',[5] nationality clauses were found to be contrary to EU law. Since they did not safeguard EU carriers' operation within the Single European Sky, they would discriminate against some Member State nationals. They would have precluded EU Member States that were not party to the bilateral agreements from enjoying equal treatment as the Member States that were party to the agreement with the US. Against this backdrop, the *Open Skies* line of cases attracted criticism for the frictions that EU law would pose to consolidated notions of international law. In particular, the Court's extensive interpretation of the right of establishment had been regarded as undermining the sovereignty of Member States.[6]

The canons of international aviation had already been challenged by the Union with its legislative initiatives in aviation policy. The Single European Sky framework was developed in the immediate aftermath of the adoption of the Single European Act in 1986. It consisted of three packages of measures. The first two packages in 1987 and 1990 started liberalising fares and rates. It was with the adoption of the third package in 1992 that the distinctive traits of the Union aviation market emerged.[7] The third package liberalised access to air transport markets in the EU and facilitated cross-border investment by European airlines.[8]

[1] Piet Jan Slot and Jacqueline Dutheil de la Rochère, '(Open Skies Judgments) Judgments of the Full Court of 5 November 2002.' (2003) 40 *Common Market Law Review* 697. The cases are Case C-466/98 *Commission v United Kingdom*, EU:C:2002:624; Case C-467/98 *Commission v Denmark*, EU:C:2002:625; Case C-472/98 *Commission v Luxembourg*, EU:C:2002:629; Case C-475/98 *Commission v Austria*, EU:C:2002:630; Case C-476/98 *Commission v Germany* EU:C:2002:631.

[2] *Commission v Denmark* (n 1) [99]–[104].

[3] See for instance the clause enshrined in the US agreement with Germany mentioned in Case C-476/98, *Commission v Germany* (n 1) [30].

[4] Cases C-466/98, C-468/98, C-469/98, Case C-471/98, C-472/98, C-475/98, C-476/98 *Open Skies*, Opinion of AG Tizzano, EU:C:2002:63 [118].

[5] Case C-467/98 *Commission v Denmark* (n 1) [119].

[6] Henri Wassenbergh, 'The Decision of the ECJ of 5 November 2002 in the "Open Skies" Agreements Cases.' (2003) 28 *Air Space Law* 19, 24.

[7] Council Regulations (EEC) Nos 2407/92, 2408/92 and 2409/92, now replaced by Regulation (EC) No 1008/2008 on common rules for the operation of air services in the Community (Recast), [2008] OJ L 293/3.

[8] European Commission, 'Communication on the consequences of the Court judgments of 5 November 2002 for European air transport policy' COM(2002) 649 final, 2–3.

In the words of the Commission, it 'turned all Community-owned airlines, regardless of the Member State in which they were legally established, into "[EU] air carriers" with equal rights of access to the entire internal market and with equal responsibilities under the law.'[9]

The notion of *EU air carrier* was thus quite revolutionary in EU aviation law. EU air carriers enjoy equal rights to access the EU internal market and to all of the freedoms of the air[10] irrespective of the EU Member State in which they are established. Perhaps more importantly, the notion of EU air carrier challenges the 'substantial ownership and control' provision of the International Air Services Transit Agreement (IASTA). The IASTA provision at issue establishes that:

> [E]ach contracting State reserves the right to withhold or revoke a certificate or permit to an air transport enterprise of another State in any case where it is not satisfied that the substantial ownership and effective control are vested in nationals of a contracting State ...[11]

The above entitlement has been described as a 'natural byproduct of the well-established principle of sovereignty.'[12] By obliterating the distinction between domestic and international air services within the EU, the third package of the Single European Sky thus challenged the canonical nationality clauses on ownership and control.[13] Regulation (EC) No 1008/2008,[14] consolidating the third package, identifies an *EU air carrier* as an undertaking that is owned by more than 50 per cent and effectively controlled[15] by Member States and/or nationals of Member States.[16] In that light, the clause on ownership and control of airline companies also questions the 'nationality rule' with respect to ownership and control: EU Member States are construed as being a single state. The EU clause further challenges the inherent protectionism associated with the nationality rule by setting the threshold of the 'substantial ownership' notion of IASTA to 50 per cent

[9] ibid.

[10] For the definition of the freedoms of the air see ICAO, see www.icao.int/pages/freedomsair.aspx.

[11] International Air Services Transit Agreement, Chicago 7 December 1944, Art 1(5); a similar provision may be found in the International Air Transport Agreement, Havana 19 April 1945, Art 1(6).

[12] Andrea Trimarchi, 'Foreign Investment in National Air Carriers: Political Background, Legal Constraints, and Recent Developments' (2018) 17 *Issues in aviation law and policy* 237, 240.

[13] Kristen Bohmann, 'The Ownership and Control Requirement in U.S. and European Union Air Law and U.S. Maritime Law-Policy; Consideration; Comparison' (2001) 66 *Journal of Air Law and Commerce* 689, 718.

[14] Regulation (EC) No 1008/2008 (n 7).

[15] Differently from the rather vague corresponding IASTA provision, EU law attempts to define the notion of 'effective control' in Regulation (EC) No 1008/2008 (n 7), Art 2(9): '"effective control" means a relationship constituted by rights, contracts or any other means which, either separately or jointly and having regard to the considerations of fact or law involved, confer the possibility of directly or indirectly exercising a decisive influence on an undertaking, in particular by: (a) the right to use all or part of the assets of an undertaking; (b) rights or contracts which confer a decisive influence on the composition, voting or decisions of the bodies of an undertaking or otherwise confer a decisive influence on the running of the business of the undertaking.'

[16] See Regulation (EC) No 1008/2008 (n 7), Art 4.

of shares. Indeed, 'substantial ownership' is interpreted in a more liberal fashion when compared to other regimes in place in other jurisdictions where this threshold is set to a higher level.[17] Subsequent measures on the development of the Single European Sky were taken from 2004 with a view to increase both capacity and efficiency of air transport management. Two packages of norms on the Single European Sky continued to transform the previously fragmented European air space based on standard practices of international law and intergovernmental cooperation.[18]

In the same months of the delivery of the *Open Skies* judgments, a Commission Communication would delineate the steps for the creation of a regional aviation area. Crucially, this would provide for 'the expansion of the internal market' in aviation law 'on the basis of [EU] legislation'. The objective was that in this new area, 'all airlines [would] enjoy the same freedoms … enjoyed by [EU] carriers.'[19] The Commission noted how significant steps had already been taken by extending the internal market to Iceland and Norway. By virtue of the EEA Agreement air carriers from these countries would be included in the category of EU air carriers.[20] Moreover, a bilateral agreement with Switzerland effectively extended the EU internal market.[21]

[17] Note that while the EU poses the limit at 49% to foreign [intended as non-EU] ownership of airlines, the thresholds of foreign voting equity in a national carrier normally allowed in the US and Japan are lower (respectively 25% and 33%). See Sheri Linzell, 'Ownership and Control Restrictions in US Aviation Law' (2010) 35 *Air and Space* Law 379, 384. See also World Economic Forum, 'A New Regulatory Model for Foreign Investment in Airlines' [2016] Industry Agenda, www3.weforum.org/docs/IP/2016/MO/WEF_AT_NewRegulatoryModel.pdf. Especially in developing countries, however, derogations from these rules have started emerging from the 1990s as the need for foreign investment was essential for securing operability of air transport. A number of countries have raised the foreign ownership limit to more than 40%. Singapore is an outstanding exception in so far as it allowed 100% of foreign capital investment in their aviation companies, as it is the case in Hong Kong where the approach is on the principal place of business rather than nationality of the owner. See Isabelle Lelieur, *Law and Policy of Substantial Ownership and Effective Control of Airlines: Prospects for Change* (Routledge, 2003) 52–54 and Trimarchi (n 12) 245.

[18] Single European Sky (SES) I included: Regulation (EC) No 549/2004 laying down the framework for the creation of the single European sky; Regulation (EC) No 550/2004; Regulation (EC) No 550/2004 on the provision of air navigation services in the single European sky (the service provision Regulation); Regulation (EC) No 551/2004 on the organisation and use of the airspace in the single European sky (the airspace Regulation); Regulation (EC) No 552/2004 on the interoperability of the European Air Traffic Management network (the interoperability Regulation); and SES II: Regulation (EC) No 1070/2009 amending Regulations (EC) No 549/2004, (EC) No 550/2004, (EC) No 551/2004 and (EC) No 552/2004 in order to improve the performance and sustainability of the European aviation system.

[19] European Commission, 'Communication on the consequences of the Court judgments of 5 November 2002 for European air transport policy', Brussels, 19 November 2002, COM(2002) 649 final, paras 16–17.

[20] See European Commission, 'Impact of the third package of air transport liberalisation measures', COM(96) 514 Final, 1.

[21] European Commission, 'Communication on the consequences of the Court judgments of 5 November 2002 for European air transport policy' (n 11), para 19.

III. The European Common Aviation Area and the Sectoral Development of *Wider Europe*

The European Common Aviation Area (ECAA) Agreement extended EU internal market law in the aviation domain.[22] The Agreement was intended to establish broader partnerships which were modelled upon the EU's experience in civil aviation. The ECAA also inaugurated the sectoral development of *Wider Europe*.[23] Furthermore, the ECAA Agreement served as a blueprint for the later adoption of the Treaty Establishing the Transport Community (TCT)[24] signed on 12 July 2017 in Trieste, which largely replicates the ECAA architecture and functioning. The geopolitical motives animating the extension of the EU's legal space in the transport sector are the same that inspired the *Wider Europe* design, of which the ECAA and TCT can be intended as sectoral developments. A relevant Commission proposal highlighted how 'regional cooperation within the Western Balkans is a key element for political stability, security, economic prosperity and social development in the region'.[25]

The peculiarity of these functional regimes is that they aim to establish a homogeneous legal space[26] in the extension of the relevant section of EU law. In contrast to the EEA model, however, they are not premised upon a two-pillar institutional structure. They are governed, instead, by a Joint Committee (Regional Steering Committee in the TCT case) and through particular organisational interactions between the ECAA and the TCT regimes and the EU legal order, often resulting in institutional *renvois*. The institutional *renvois* made by these regimes to the EU legal order characterise their one-pillar structure whereby EU neighbourhood law arrangements principally rely on EU institutions.

A. *Opinion 1/00*: The 'Single Pillar' Model

In *Opinion 1/00*, the Court was asked to assess the legality of a draft ECAA Agreement.[27] The *Opinion* set the canons for the sectoral replication of EU

[22] Multilateral Agreement between the European Community and its Member States, Albania, Bosnia and Herzegovina, Bulgaria, Croatia, the former Yugoslav Republic of Macedonia, Iceland, Montenegro, Norway, Romania, Serbia and the United Nations Interim Administration Mission in Kosovo on the establishment of a European Common Aviation Area [2006] OJ L 285/3; hereinafter 'ECAA Agreement'.

[23] Peter Bombay and Máté Gergely, 'The 2006 ECAA Agreement: Centrepiece of the European Community's Aviation Policy Towards Its Neighbours' (2008) 33 *Air and Space Law* 214, 218–19. European Commission, 'A Community Aviation Policy towards Its Neighbours' COM(2004) 74 final.

[24] Treaty Establishing the Transport Community [2017], OJ L 278/3; hereinafter 'TCT'.

[25] European Commission, 'Proposal for a Council Decision on the conclusion, on behalf of the European Union, of the Treaty establishing the Transport Community', COM/2018/532 final.

[26] See ECAA Agreement, Arts 16(3) and 18(7); and TCT, Art 24(7).

[27] *Opinion 1/00* ECAA, EU:C:2002:231.

rules via a multilateral international agreement. The Court's findings were key to understanding how the principle of autonomy would govern the design of EU-led international agreements different from the EEA model. In the compelling words of Castillo de la Torre, *Opinion 1/00* shed light on the limits to the EU '*Integrationsgewalt*, that is, the constitutional substantive limitations to the Community's competence to conclude international agreements creating rule-making or, at least, decision-making structures'.[28] These limits arise from the principle of autonomy of EU law and intimate again a demarcation between EU membership law and EU neighbourhood law.

In this respect, it is worth stressing that the contribution offered by *Opinion 1/00* derives from the fact that the draft agreement submitted to the legality review of the Court of Justice was designed as having a 'one-pillar' structure. In the findings of the Court of Justice, the 'single pillar' foundation of the ECAA is 'a solution which is made possible and necessary by the absence of pre-existing institutional links in the area of air transport'.[29] Notwithstanding the differences in the institutional structure and the scope, the Court noted the similarities with the EEA Agreement with regard to the extension of the *acquis*.[30] The Court maintained that:

> [A]lthough the proposed agreement, unlike the EEA Agreement, is limited to one sector, air transport, its aim, like that of the EEA Agreement, is to extend the *[EU] acquis* to new States, by implementing in a larger geographical area rules which are essentially those of [EU] law.[31]

In the Court's words, the extension of the EU aviation *acquis* in the ECAA would 'bring about the juxtaposition within a single geographical area (that of the ECAA) of *rules of [EU] law and rules replicating them*, which will not be applied or interpreted systematically by the same authorities or bodies'. The Court then underlined how the 'Commission is made responsible for applying a number of rules in that agreement outside the [EU], thereby creating *specific relations* between the [EU] and the States Parties'.[32] The Court clarified the patterns of the extension of the EU's legal space mobilising, inadvertently, the notions employed by Santi Romano. As a matter of fact, the ECJ did not only point out the relevance of the EU's legal order for the ECAA in terms of presupposition and dependence through the replication of EU rules. It also referred to, although in different terms, the organisational interactions operating through institutional *renvois*.

For the Court, the ascertainment of the compatibility of the draft agreement with EU law amounted to assessing whether the agreement included

[28] Fernando Castillo de la Torre, 'Opinion 1/00, *Proposed Agreement on the Establishment of a European Common Aviation Area*' (2002) 39 *Common Market Law Review* 1374.

[29] *ECAA Opinion* (n 27) [7].

[30] Cécile Rapoport, 'Autonomy of the EU Legal Order and International Agreements Extending the Acquis: Opinion 1/00 (European Common Aviation Area)' in Graham Butler and Ramses A Wessel, *EU External Relations Law: The Cases in Context* (Hart Publishing, 2022).

[31] *ECAA Opinion* (n 27) [3].

[32] ibid [10] (emphasis added).

> adequate measures … to guarantee that neither the endeavour to ensure uniform interpretation of those rules nor the *new institutional links* established by the ECAA Agreement between the [Union] and the States Parties affect the autonomy of the Community legal order.[33]

In the forgoing passage, the Court highlighted that ensuring homogeneity of the legal space through uniform interpretation is not coterminous with guaranteeing EU autonomy, as was seemingly maintained by the Commission.[34] Homogeneity or uniform interpretation is not per se safeguarding EU autonomy: EU law and extended EU law are different in nature. As noted by the Council, although equal in wording, the EU rules and those of the ECAA 'belong to different legal orders'.[35] The mechanisms for ensuring homogeneity and uniform application may be liable, especially if they create 'institutional links', to affect the autonomy of EU law.

The ECJ singled out the two criteria to be fulfilled for preservation of EU autonomy in one-pillar arrangements extending the EU's legal space. First, it is required that 'the essential character of the powers of the Community and its institutions as conceived in the Treaty remain unaltered'.[36] Secondly, the arrangements shall ensure

> that the procedures for ensuring uniform interpretation of the rules of the ECAA Agreement and for resolving disputes will not have the effect of binding the Community and its institutions, in the exercise of their internal powers, to a particular interpretation of the rules of Community law referred to in that agreement.[37]

In the ECAA, the Court did not find difficulties in ascertaining that the political institutions' powers remained unaltered. Two factors informed this appraisal. The first was the identical wording of the extended EU rules; the second pertained to the 'single pillar' structure.[38] The single pillar structure would guarantee that the powers of the Commission would be extended to a larger geographical area without altering its composition or functions. Similar considerations applied to the extended powers of the Court of Justice. Moreover, the pronouncement of the CJEU envisioned by the Agreement would be final and binding.[39] Furthermore, and crucially, in the *Opinion*, the Court found that

> the mechanisms ensuring uniform interpretations of the rules of the ECAA Agreement and for resolving disputes [would] not have the effect of binding the Community and its institutions, in the exercise of its internal powers, to a particular interpretation of the rules of the [EU] incorporated in the agreement.[40]

[33] ibid [11] (emphasis added).
[34] ibid I-3507. The Commission maintained that Art 23(1) ECAA preserved 'the autonomy of the Community legal order by requiring the ECAA Agreement to be interpreted in conformity with the decision of the Commission and the ruling of the Court…'.
[35] ibid I-3515.
[36] ibid [12].
[37] ibid [13].
[38] ibid [22].
[39] ibid [23]–[25].
[40] *ECAA Opinion* (n 27) [45].

In Rapoport's powerful reading of *Opinion 1/00*, the ECJ delineated the confines of the extraterritorial extension of the powers of EU institutions. In its institutional dimension, the principle of autonomy amounts to safeguarding the essential nature of the powers of EU institutions.[41] It can be argued thus that when the EU institutions exercise extraterritorial powers, the relevant technique to extend the EU's legal space amounts to institutional *renvois* operated by the EU neighbourhood law regime to the EU legal order. The *Opinion* also shed light on what Rapoport defines as the material dimension of the principle of autonomy[42] with regard to the need to preserve unaltered 'the canons of interpretation of [EU] law'.[43] As Castillo de la Torre puts it, EU law and international law have different genetic codes, 'cloning is allowed only insofar as there are guarantees that the clone will not become the real thing'.[44] The severing of the two regimes guarantees the demarcation between EU membership law and EU neighbourhood law.

B. Techniques for the Extension of the EU's Legal Space in the ECAA and the TCT

The ECAA Agreement has served as a blueprint for paradigms of extension of the EU legal space with a one-pillar structure. The Transport Community Treaty largely replicates the design and functioning of the ECAA Agreement. Both the arrangements provide for the extension of the EU's legal space with substantive *renvois* and mechanisms of organisational interaction between the relevant EU neighbourhood law regimes and the EU legal order.

The substantive *renvois* may be discerned already in the first articles of the Agreements. Article 1 of the ECAA bases the regime on 'free market access, freedom of establishment, equal conditions of competition, and common rules including in the areas of safety, security, air traffic management, social and environment'. The common (EU) rules in these domains are detailed in the Annex I of the Agreement. Similarly, Article 1 of the TCT clarifies the scope of the extension of the EU's legal space. It explicitly mentions the 'integration of transport markets of the [EU neighbours] into the European Union transport market on the basis of the relevant *acquis*'.[45] Especially in the ECAA, the substantive *renvois* do not only relate to the pieces of EU legislation but also to the objectives and principles underpinning the EU's aviation space. The ECAA provisions indeed replicate the motives and rationales of the rights of establishment in EU law.[46] The provisions progressively envisage mutually free market access between EU and non-EU

[41] Rapoport (n 30).
[42] ibid.
[43] *ECAA Opinion* (n 27) [5].
[44] Castillo de la Torre (n 28) 1391.
[45] TCT, Art 1(1).
[46] See ECAA Agreement, Arts 7–10.

ECAA members. In addition, the introduction of the notion of ECAA air carrier is an example of replication of the EEA regime's concepts and notions of EU law.[47]

The ambitious scope and objectives of the Agreement are tempered by safeguard measures. In case of failure of implementation, these measures enable the EU to readjust its cooperation commitments.[48] The country-specific protocols at the end of the Agreement have accompanied the State Parties in the achievement of legal homogeneity in the wider ECAA legal space with a view to establishing a level playing field and equal conditions of competition. A multi-phased approach informed the design of the Agreement to progressively liberalise all of the relevant freedoms of the air, including cabotage. As is often the case with EU proximity policies, further liberalisation was made conditional upon the implementation of the relevant EU *acquis*. Similar mechanisms inform the design and implementation of the TCT.

The ECAA Agreement and the TCT feature far-reaching mechanisms of organisational interaction between the EU neighbourhood law regimes and the EU legal order. Both regimes operate institutional *renvois*. As far as enforcement is concerned, the ECAA extends the powers of EU institutions and particularly of the Commission, the extension ranges from inspection to the monitoring powers for the legislative approximation process.[49] The formula used in the ECAA reads that 'the [EU] institutions shall enjoy the powers specifically granted to them under the provisions of the acts referred to or contained in Annex I.'[50] The TCT operates institutional *renvois* to the Commission for the assessment of the State Parties' implementation of the *acquis* and for the transitional arrangements.[51]

The objective of uniform interpretation and application of the Agreements are pursued through the interpretative *renvois* to CJEU's case law, considered as the authoritative source of interpretation of extended EU law. In that respect also an institutional *renvois* to the CJEU is envisaged. The *renvoi* operates in the context of the legality of the EU institutional acts adopted pursuant to the Agreements[52] and of dispute resolution.[53] As far as the interpretation of the Agreements is concerned, provisions that are identical in substance to those of the EU 'shall be interpreted in conformity with the relevant rulings of the Court of Justice and decisions of the European Commission given before the date of signature' of the Treaties.[54] Similarly to the EEA, this provision is intended to limit the divergent interpretation

[47] Bombay and Gergely (n 23) 222. The authors note also how Regulation 2408/92, listed in Annex I to the agreement is applicable to the Agreement. Now the relevant legislation on market operation has been incorporated into the ECAA Agreement By Decision No 1/19 of the ECAA Joint Committee of 31 July 2019 replacing Annex I to the ECAA Agreement on the rules applicable to civil aviation, [2019] OJ L 211/4.

[48] ECAA Agreement, Arts 21–22.

[49] ibid, Art 13(2) and Annex III.

[50] ibid Art 15(2).

[51] Arts 3 and 40 TCT.

[52] ECAA Agreement, Art 15(3); TCT, Art 18.

[53] ECAA Agreement, Art 20(3); TCT, Art 37(3).

[54] ECAA Agreement, Art 16(1); TCT, Art 19(1).

of extended EU norms in application to the *Polydor* principle. Moreover, post-signature case law shall also inform the interpretation of the Agreement and it shall be communicated to the non-EU contracting parties of the ECAA and the TCT. In particular, the ECAA Joint Committee and the TCT Regional steering committee are in charge of assessing how the dynamic evolution of EU law, stemming from new pieces of legislation and case law, affects the functioning of the Agreement.[55] The attainment of dynamic homogeneity is thus largely left to diplomatic bodies. This was not considered controversial by the Court in *Opinion 1/00*. In the Court's words,

> any divergences in the interpretation of the rules of the ECAA Agreement which may arise as between the [EU] and the States Parties as a result of [the Joint Committee failures to reach decisions] will not, in themselves, have any impact on the [EU] legal order, whose rules, which are identical as to substance but distinct to form, will continue to be interpreted autonomously.[56]

Again, the relationship between EU membership law and EU neighbourhood law is one of extension of the EU's legal space but demarcation among different legal orders. Yet, the demarcation among EU legal orders is tempered through institutional *renvois* that, especially in the single-pillar model, subject third countries legal orders to the reach of the EU institutions powers. The demarcation is also tempered by the provisions of the ECAA Agreement and TCT indicating the effect of extended EU acts, distinguishing between EU regulations,[57] EU directives[58] and decisions.[59] By establishing the obligation to incorporate the acts corresponding to the EU regulations into the parties' legal systems, these Agreements attempt to replicate the effects of EU law in EU neighbourhood law arrangements.[60]

The tenor of the institutional *renvois* renders the ECAA and the TCT unique among the multilateral regimes extending the EU's legal space. Both Agreements recognise the Court of Justice's exclusive jurisdiction over the extended EU law[61] as well as over the decisions of EU institutions under these Agreements.[62] In addition, courts of the Contracting Parties are entitled to submit preliminary questions to the CJEU.[63] The institutional *renvois* to the CJEU are also prominent when one considers the mechanisms of dispute settlement that, as in the case of the EEA, feature a hybrid diplomatic and judicial model: in case of failure of the diplomatic

[55] ECAA Agreement, Art 18(7); TCT, Art 20(2).
[56] *ECAA Opinion* (n 27) [41].
[57] ECAA Agreement, Art 3(a); TCT, Art 3(2)a.
[58] ECAA Agreement, Art 3(b); TCT, Art 3(2)b.
[59] TCT, Art 3(2)c; no corresponding provision in the ECAA Agreement.
[60] See also ECAA Agreement, Art 15(1). The article reads: 'Without prejudice to paragraphs 2 and 3, each Contracting Party shall ensure that the rights which devolve from this Agreement, and in particular from the acts specified in Annex I, may be invoked before national courts.' Similarly see TCT, Art 18(1).
[61] ECAA Agreement, Art 15(3) and TCT, Art 18(2).
[62] ECAA Agreement, Art 15(3).
[63] ECAA Agreement, Art 16(2); TCT, Art 19(2).

body to settle the dispute, the parties may decide to refer the dispute to the Court of Justice. Significantly, the dispute settlement provisions of the ECAA Agreement and the TCT specify that the rulings of the Court of Justice will be final and binding on the parties;[64] a specification that is absent in the EEA Agreement.[65] Moreover, as it is the case in the EEA,[66] both the ECAA Agreement and the TCT present a direct institutional *renvoi* to the CJEU that enables courts of the ECAA and TCT States to ask preliminary rulings to the CJEU on matters of interpretations of extended EU law.[67] The TCT also envisages the possibility of inviting an EU representative to the consultation within the proceedings before the Regional Steering Committee, in case the EU is not party to the dispute.[68] The far-reaching obligations resulting from the high gravitational intensity around the EU legal order are counterbalanced by full market access rights in the domains of aviation and transport. The patterns of inclusions are thus mirrored in the extension of notions of EU law as 'Union carrier' to the Western Balkans.[69]

IV. EU Neighbourhood Law's Continuum in Aviation Law

EU aviation law and policies are fruitful domains in which to assess the ambition and the implementation of *Wider Europe* design of *lato sensu* reconfiguration of the Union's borders through law. Aviation, and transport networks more generally, are a paradigmatic example of how the EU manages interdependence in its proximity. The ensuing EU neighbourhood law functional regimes take various forms. In the aviation sector, a variety of institutional arrangements of EU neighbourhood law emerges in the interplay between multilateral and bilateral regimes. The longer-term goal of the EU's aviation policy in the EU's geographical proximity is that of integrating both the southern and eastern neighbours into a single ECAA.[70] The variety of institutional arrangements produced by the extension of the EU's legal space in aviation law helps us appreciating variations in the EU neighbourhood law continuum on the basis of different echelons of intensity of gravitation around the EU legal order. In these different gradations,

[64] ECAA Agreement, Art 20(3); TCT, Art 37(3).

[65] In the EEA Agreement, Art 111 is the provision corresponding to the articles of the ECAA and TCT mentioned above (n 64). It is difficult to imagine how the CJEU ruling could not be binding, as this would be in breach of the principle of autonomy of EU law.

[66] EEA Agreement, Art 107 and protocol 34.

[67] ECAA Agreement, Art 16(2) and in the TCT, Art 19(2). Also in this case there is an additional specification with respect to the corresponding provision of the EEA Agreement that the CJEU's ruling shall be final and binding.

[68] TCT, Art 37(2).

[69] See ECAA Agreement, Annex II, Art 2(e) and see TCT, Annex II, Arts 2–3.

[70] European Commission 'The EU and its neighbouring regions: A renewed approach to transport cooperation', COM(2011) 415 final, 4.

the ECAA Agreement is the regime that gravitates closest to the EU legal order in the aviation law domain. The other bilateral regimes examined in this section occupy subsequent places in this continuum. As will be discussed further, moreover, these different echelons of intensity of the extension of the EU's legal space correspond to different paradigms of the exercise of sovereignty entailed in the relevant political covenant.

A. The Swiss Air Transport Agreement

The status of Switzerland remains unique and rather exceptional in the context of EU proximity policies. The EU–Swiss Air Transport Agreement confirms this special status. Switzerland is linked to the European Common Aviation Area through a bilateral agreement with the EU signed in 1999 and entered into force in 2002. While a significant part of the complex relationship between the EU and the Confederation is based on equivalence schemes,[71] Switzerland incorporates a significant portion of the EU aviation *acquis* into its domestic legal order. The EU–Swiss bilateral Air Transport Agreement, indeed, envisages overarching substantive *renvois* as well as mechanisms of organisational interaction with the EU legal order.

The objectives of the Agreement set out in the recitals include the desire that 'regulations for intra-European air transport be harmonised'. The Parties also agree that 'it is appropriate to base these rules on the legislation which is in force within the [EU] at the time of the signature of [the] Agreement'. In contrast to the ECAA case, the ultimate objective appears more tenuous than that of achieving an 'homogeneous' legal area. As indicated in the relevant recitals, the objective is to 'arrive at as uniform an interpretation as possible of the provisions of this Agreement and the corresponding provision of [EU] law which are substantially reproduced in [the] Agreement'.[72]

The EU–Swiss Air Transport Agreement is based upon ambitiously granting the first seven freedoms of the air that have been accorded on a progressive basis. An understanding has also been found with respect to the eighth (cabotage) and ninth freedoms. However, its application has been halted: the EU made this conditional upon two other agreements. The first is an agreement which concerned linking the EU–Swiss greenhouse gas emission trading scheme; the second was the EU–Switzerland Institutional Framework Agreement.[73] While the former

[71] Leinarte and Barnard characterise the EU–Swiss mutual recognition agreement (MRA) as the 'broadest MRA ever to have been concluded'. Emilija Leinarte and Catherine Barnard, 'Negotiating Mutual Recognition Agreements: Challenges and Techniques' in Albertina Albors-Llorens, Catherine Barnard and Brigitte Leucht (eds), *Cassis de Dijon: 40 years on* (Hart Publishing, 2021) 224.

[72] EU–Swiss Air Transport Agreement, [2002] OJ L 114/73; hereinafter 'EU–Switzerland ATA'.

[73] See further ch 7 of this work.

has been concluded,[74] negotiations on the latter have stalled.[75] This shows that conditionality is a qualifying aspect of EU proximity policies beyond the ENP. Participation in the extended legal space and the resulting market access is not only made conditional upon legal approximation in that specific sector. With the EU's western neighbours especially, issue-linkage conditionality is becoming increasingly common.

Like the ECAA, the EU–Swiss Air Transport Agreement provides for non-discrimination on the basis of nationality,[76] and no restrictions to the rights of establishment.[77] The substantive *renvois* to EU law can be found in the provisions of the Agreement,[78] as well as in the relevant Annex. The dynamic evolution of EU law is accommodated in the Agreement through the standard mechanism that enables the Joint Committee's assessment to take decisions to incorporate new legislation adopted by the contracting parties (mostly the EU) into the Agreement.[79] The Annex is amended regularly and this process reflects the development of the legislation on the side of the EU. The Agreement replicates some of the mechanisms of organisational interaction present in the ECAA.

The EU–Swiss Aviation Agreement recognises the rulings of the Court of Justice and the decisions of the European Commission as authoritative sources of interpretation of the provisions of the Agreement identical in substance to EU law.[80] Although this applies to rulings and decisions prior to the signature of the Agreement, the EU–Swiss aviation legal framework is kept up to date with the evolution of EU law pursuant to Article 23 of the Agreement. As in the ECAA and the TCT arrangements, the Court of Justice also enjoys exclusive competence to rule on the validity of EU institutions' decisions taken on the basis of their competences under the EU-Swiss Air Transport Agreement.[81]

Several tasks are entrusted upon the EU institutions and particularly to the Commission via institutional *renvois*. The *renvois* are also operated by virtue of amendments to the Agreement. This is confirmed by the amendments to the Annex,[82] sanctioning the extension to Switzerland of the powers enjoyed by Commission pursuant to several pieces of EU legislation. The extension of the powers occurred in the domains of interoperability of the European Air Traffic

[74] EU–Swiss Agreement on the linking of their greenhouse gas emissions trading systems, [2017] OJ L 322/ 3.

[75] See Confédération Swisse and Direction des affaires éuropéennes, 'Transport Aérien' (August 2020), www.eda.admin.ch/dam/dea/fr/documents/fs/09-FS-Luftverkehr_fr.pdf.

[76] EU–Switzerland ATA, Art 3.

[77] ibid Art 4.

[78] For instance *renvois* are made to Arts 4 and 15 of Council Regulation (EEC) No 2407/92 and those in Art 18 to Council Regulation (EEC) No 2408/92. Both Regulations are now repealed by Regulation (EC) No 1008/2008 (n 7).

[79] See EU–Switzerland ATA, ch 6 on new legislation.

[80] EU–Switzerland ATA, Art 1.

[81] ibid Art 20.

[82] See Decision No 2/19 of the Joint European Union/Switzerland Air Transport Committee set up by the EU–Switzerland ATA, [2020] OJ L31/23.

Management network, the performance and sustainability of the European Aviation System,[83] and of aviation safety. Moreover, the amendment also extends to Switzerland many of the EASA (European Union Aviation Safety Agency) powers,[84] given that Switzerland has been a full member of the EASA since 2006.[85]

B. The EU–Ukraine Common Aviation Area

The EU–Ukraine Common Aviation Agreement (CAA)[86] is part of the extension of the EU's legal space. Although more distant from the EU than the EU–Swiss Air Transport Agreement in terms of ideal orbits of gravitation around the EU legal order, it remains one of the most advanced in the neighbourhood. This resonates with the ambitions of the broader framework of association between the EU and Ukraine.[87] Indeed, the Common Aviation Area Agreement concluded with Ukraine envisages and articulates substantive and organisational *renvois* to the EU legal order that locates the Agreement close to the ECAA's design.

On the substantive plane, the CAA Agreement contains provisions on Ukraine's obligation to adopt EU laws and standards. The EU instruments to which the substantive *renvois* are made can be found in the Annexes. They concern the domains of aviation safety,[88] air traffic management,[89] environment,[90] consumer protection,[91] computer reservation systems[92] and social aspects.[93] EU law, however, is not the basis of cooperation on aviation security. In this domain, the basis of the cooperation revolves around international law instruments. The Agreement's substantive *renvois* to EU law are embedded in principles of regulatory cooperation pursuant to Article 5 of the EU–Ukraine CAA Agreement. This provision governs inter alia Ukraine's obligations to incorporate the relevant EU *acquis*

[83] Pursuant to Regulation (EC) No 1070/2009 (n 18).

[84] Pursuant to Regulation (EU) 2018/1139 on common rules in the field of civil aviation and establishing a European Union Aviation Safety Agency, [2018] OJ L 212/1.

[85] Decision No 2/2006 of the EU–Switzerland Air Transport Committee [2006] OJ L 298/25.

[86] EU–Ukraine Common Aviation Area Agreement, [2021] OJ L 387/3. Hereinafter EU–Ukraine CAA Agreement. Interestingly difficulties in the conclusions of the agreement arose due to disagreements between the UK and Spain on the notion of 'territory of Gibraltar'. The tensions seemed to be partially dissolved as the 'references to Gibraltar in the definition of 'territory' have been removed'. See Council of the EU, 'Note from the General Secretariat of the Council to the Permanent Representative of the Council', 9689/21. See also European Commission, Amended Proposal for a Council Decision on the signing, on behalf of the European Union, and provisional application of the Common Aviation Area Agreement between the European Union and its Member States and Ukraine, COM(2021) 158 final.

[87] Guillaume Van der Loo, *The EU–Ukraine Association Agreement and Deep and Comprehensive Free Trade Area: A New Legal Instrument for EU Integration without Membership* (Brill Nijhoff, 2016).

[88] EU–Ukraine CAA Agreement, Art 7.

[89] ibid Art 9.

[90] ibid Art 10.

[91] ibid Art 11.

[92] ibid Art 13.

[93] ibid Art 14.

according to the transitional arrangements envisaged therein.[94] The CAA thus largely replicates the rationale of the ECAA's multi-phased approach whereby the Commission monitors Ukraine's process of adopting EU legislation and transmits its findings to the Joint Committee.

Moreover, the EU–Ukraine CAA Agreement identifies the CJEU's rulings and the Commission's decisions as authoritative sources of interpretation.[95] The requirement of conformity with the CJEU's relevant rulings and decisions is a key aspect of the Agreement.[96] As far as organisation interaction is concerned, far reaching institutional *renvois* envisage the extension of the Commission powers for monitoring the implementation of the standards of the EU acts relating to civil aviation, especially in the transition phase.[97] In addition, Annex I envisages an extension of the Commission's powers in Ukraine especially on aviation safety.[98]

A distinctive feature of the EU–Ukraine CAA pertains to the freedoms of the air. Pursuant to this Agreement, EU carriers are granted full cabotage rights.[99] This is also a feature of the ECAA. However, the CAA Agreement is rather unique as Ukraine *unilaterally* grants to EU carriers the possibility of carrying out stand alone and consecutive cabotage operations in Ukraine.[100]

The EU–Ukraine CAA, although similar to other CAA Agreements, concluded with Moldova and Georgia, remains rather unique in the neighbourhood's bilateral CAA agreements landscape. This is primarily due to the Ukraine's unilateral conferral of cabotage rights to EU carriers and to the overarching substantive and organisational *renvois* to the EU legal order. Indeed, in the Agreements in place with Georgia and Moldova, the reference to the Court of Justice's rulings as authoritative source of interpretation pertains only to interpretation and enforcement provisions.[101] It does not extend to dispute resolution and arbitration as in the case of Ukraine. More importantly, only the EU–Ukraine Agreement envisages a provision on general principles of regulatory cooperation detailing the patterns of gravitation of Ukrainian aviation law around the EU's legal space.[102] Furthermore, in terms of procedural interaction among legal regimes, the Ukrainian CAA Agreement, similarly to the ECAA Agreement, details the effects that different pieces of EU legislation (Directives, Regulations) shall have in the Ukrainian legal order.[103]

[94] ibid Art 33 and Annex III.
[95] ibid Art 28.
[96] ibid Art 30.
[97] ibid Art 33.
[98] Pursuant to Regulation (EC) No 216/2008, now Regulation (EU) 2018/1139 (n 81).
[99] EU–Ukraine CAA Agreement, Annex III, Art 1(a) of section 4.
[100] European Commission, 'Proposal for a Council Decision on the signature, on behalf of the European Union, and provisional application of a Common Aviation Area Agreement between the European Union and its Member States and Ukraine', COM(2014) 18 final, 3.
[101] EU–Georgia CAA Agreement, Art 21, [2012] OJ L 321/1: and Article 21 EU–Moldova ECAA Agreement. [2012] OJ L 292/3.
[102] EU–Ukraine CAA Agreement, Art 5.
[103] ECAA Agreement, Art 3; EU–Ukraine CAA Agreement, Annex I.

C. The EuroMed Air Transport Agreement with Morocco

Morocco was a frontrunner in the bilateral patchworks of bilateral agreements extending the EU's legal space. The EU–Morocco EuroMed Air Transport Agreement was the first bilateral agreement concluded within the framework of the ENP. The Agreement has been portrayed by the Commission as 'an unprecedented example of what can be achieved in transport negotiations between the EU and a third country' as it set 'a benchmark for future agreements in the neighbouring region of the EU'.[104] Although the Euro-Med is less ambitious than the ECAA model, Article 25 is dedicated to the geographic extension of the Agreement. It envisages the possibility of linking the EU–Moroccan pioneering EuroMed Aviation Agreement with similar air transport agreements concluded within the Barcelona process. The Agreement has already served as a model for the subsequent EuroMed aviation arrangements with Israel and Jordan.

The Agreement's objective is not that of a homogeneous aviation area, as is the case with the ECAA. In similarity with the traditional *Open Skies* arrangements concluded at a global level, the EU-Morocco Aviation Agreement promotes gradual liberalisation, a level playing field, increased economic opportunities and better choices and conditions for citizens.[105] The language of the Agreement also appears to be that of an equal partnership based on international law. There are no formal organisational interactions between the EU legal order and the Agreement. There is also no mention of the authoritative interpretation of the CJEU and of the European Commission. Thus, formally, the gravitation of the Moroccan aviation system around the EU legal order is mainly limited to substantive *renvois*.

The gravitation of Morocco's legal framework on aviation to the EU legal order is mediated by the EU–Morocco Association Agreement. An organisational *renvoi* made by the Aviation Agreement to the Association Agreement: in case of impossibility to solve a dispute within the Joint Committee established by the Aviation Agreement, the issue may be referred to the Association Council of the Association Agreement which should act as a Joint Committee.[106] The link with the EU–Morocco Association Agreement is also demonstrated with regard to the suspension and termination of the EuroMed Aviation Agreement. Indeed, the latter shall cease to be in force or may be suspended if the former ceases to be in force or is suspended.[107] The subordination of sectoral cooperation to the broader framework of association also characterises the ECAA Agreement which

[104] European Commission, 'First Steps towards an Extended Single Aviation Market', IP/06/764, ec.europa.eu/commission/presscorner/detail/en/IP_06_764.

[105] See recitals of the EuroMed EU–Morocco Aviation Agreement [2006] OJ L 386/57; hereinafter 'EU–Morocco Aviation Agreement'.

[106] EU–Morocco Aviation Agreement, Art 23. This arrangement has been subsequently replicated in of the EU–Israel EuroMed Aviation Agreement, Art 23 [2013] OJ L 208/3.

[107] EU–Morocco Aviation Agreement, Art 28.

ceases to be in force or is suspended 'with respect to an Associated Party if the corresponding Association Agreement ceases to be in force or is suspended'.[108]

The EuroMed Aviation Agreement differs from agreements with global partners, such as the US: it is premised upon legislative convergence with EU law. The gravitation around the EU legal order especially operates via substantive *renvois* established in the annexes. Yet, the intensity of this gravitation is weaker than in the ECAA or the subsequent bilateral aviation agreements concluded with the EU eastern partners. The lesser intensity of gravitation can be inferred from the comparison of Article 3 of the ECAA Agreement and Article 21 of the Euro-Med Aviation Agreement. The former gives detailed indications on how to incorporate the EU legislation, referred to in the relevant Annex I, in the non-EU parties legal orders. Instead, Article 21 of the Agreement with Morocco establishes each party's responsibility to ensure appropriate enforcement of the Agreement on the respective territories.

There is thus a dissonance between the language of the provisions of the Agreement evoking equal partnership and the paradigm underlying this neighbourhood aviation regime. This emerges from the very last recital of the Agreement mentioning an 'ever closer harmonisation with [EU] legislation' and Annex VI to the Agreement, where the copious substantive *renvois* to the EU legal order can be found. The asymmetry underlying the arrangement is equally evident from the mechanisms of conditionality. On the substantive plane, Annex VI subordinates future cooperation to 'the implementation and application by the Moroccan Party of all the provisions of [Union] legislation … indicated in Annex VI'. On the organisational plane, the evaluation of the above-mentioned implementation and application of Union legislation is under the responsibility of the EU and shall be validated by decisions of the Joint Committee. Moreover, Articles 14–20 of the Agreement puts EU legislation at the basis of this neighbourhood aviation regime.

The Moroccan aviation legal framework's gravitation around the EU legal order also pertains to notions of EU law. Indeed, the principles on ownership and control of the Agreement are oriented towards an extension of the EU's aviation legal space. Article 5 of the Euro-Mediterranean Aviation Agreement allows for majority investment. As was the case firstly with the EU and then the ECAA, the intra-EU nationality barrier to ownership and control was therefore abolished. Such an integration-friendly regime has been extended to Morocco. Differently from the ECAA model, however, issues of bilateral investments of majority participation, or change in the effective control of air carriers of the Contracting Parties, is examined *ad hoc* by the Joint Committee of the EuroMed Aviation Agreement and is not automatic.[109] With regard to the freedoms of the air, the Agreement directly envisages granting third and fourth freedoms rights.

[108] ECAA Agreement, Art 31.

[109] EU– Morocco Aviation Agreement, Arts 5 and 22(10).

The appropriate implementation by Morocco of EU legislation listed in Annex VI of the Agreement, triggers the granting of fifth freedom rights.[110] The Agreement envisages the granting to Morocco consecutive fifth freedom rights in Europe, while for EU carriers the fifth freedom passenger rights will be limited to countries involved in the ENP. This highlights again the regional dimensions of the extension of the EU's legal space.

The EuroMed Agreement is less developed than the ECAA or Ukraine CAA provisions regarding the dynamic evolution of the extended *acquis*. Indeed, the latter are more detailed regarding the procedures for possible amendments of the annexes following the adoption of new legislation by the EU.[111] The Euro-Med Agreement only contemplates that one of the contracting parties (de facto the EU) may propose to the Joint Committee the modification of the Agreement's Annexes detailing the substantive *renvois* to EU law. Moreover, like the Ukrainian CAA, EU legislation at the basis of cooperation does not include EU aviation security laws.[112]

The limited gravitation around the EU legal order governed by the tenuous nature of mechanisms of organisational interaction (circumscribed to the EU institutions assessment of the implementation progress) is somewhat bolstered by networks of cooperation contributing to the socialisation of third countries in the wider European legal space. In Morocco, the Twinning Programme on civil aviation served as the watershed in the process of approximation of Moroccan legislation to EU law. By ensuring training and assistance to Moroccan officials provided from their Spanish counterparts, the Twinning Programme laid the foundations for legislative and regulatory rapprochement.[113] The programme was designed to give effect to the implementation of Annex VI of the Euro-Mediterranean Aviation Agreement. The Twinning report underscores the aim of the project to 'contribute to the harmonisation between the Moroccan and the EU legal system in the aviation domain' conducive to the 'progressive integration of Morocco in the EU Internal Market'.[114]

Regulatory cooperation in the aviation domain is undertaken through an articulated web of bureaucratic networks of supranational, regional and bilateral

[110] ibid, Annex IV. Pursuant to this annex, existing fifth freedoms rights granted by virtue of existing bilateral agreements in force between Morocco and some of the EU Member States 'can continue to be exercised insofar as there is no discrimination on the basis of nationality'.

[111] See particularly, ECAA Agreement, Art 17.

[112] EU–Morocco Aviation Agreement, Art 15 only envisages relevant international law instruments at the basis of cooperation.

[113] Royaume du Maroc, 'Rapport Finale, Projet de Jumelage MA11/ENP-AP/TP24 – Jumelage Institutionnel «Appui Au Renforcement Des Capacités Institutionnelles, Organisationnelles et Techniques Des Institutions de P Aviation Civile Au Maroc » (ENPI/2012/304-891)' (Ministère des Affaires Etrangères Et de la Coopération 2015) V/L n° OPT2/Ares 1940 186 22.

[114] ibid 9. In the Moroccan Presentation to the ICAO, it was highlighted that already the then draft law on the Civil Aviation Code (Loi 40-13) of 2009 had two objectives: creation of a new juridical framework (respondent to international needs in the civil aviation domain); and the convergence to the EU *acquis*: www.icao.int/Meetings/Moroccan-Economic-Forum/Documents/Mr-Manar_pr%C3%A9sentation_D%C3%A9veloppmentTransport.pdf.

nature. The EASA is the hub of this network which introduced the Mediterranean Aviation Safety Cell (MASC) for supervising EuroMed Aviation Projects in the framework of the Barcelona Process, and the harmonisation of aviation safety rules and practices. Besides, the EASA signed a Working Arrangement with the Moroccan *Direction Générale de l'Aviation Civile* (DGAC) in 2011 providing for regulatory cooperation on aviation safety measures.[115] This Working Arrangement provided for the extension of the Safety Assessment of Foreign Aircraft (SAFA) Programme in Morocco.[116]

The administrative networks of cooperation generated by the ENI-funded programmes highlight, here again, the relational aspect of the extension of the EU's legal space. In the same vein, the institutional framework put in place by the Aviation Agreement has also started to foster the networks that were already present during the provisional application of the Agreement. As similarly occurs in other domains of cooperation, economic benefits of the participation in *Wider Europe* are significant and brought about increased competition and number of routes, as well as presenting the potential for triggering economic development.[117] Yet, the process of convergence has been rather slow in the civil aviation domain.[118] More emphasis is the placed on the process of gravitation around the EU legal order than on the results of convergence in the socialisation of the EU's legal space.

Therefore the EU–Morocco Aviation Agreement can be located within the spectrum of the EU neighbourhood law continuum. On the substantive plane, the convergence with EU legislation is less ambitious than the ECAA. This is evident from the different scope of the annexes and the more limited market access envisaged at the end of the transitional arrangement. On the organisational level, the more limited ambition of the EuroMed Aviation Agreement results from the absence of the Court of Justice in dispute settlements, of indications to its case law for interpreting the Agreement and EU relevant legislation, and the absence of explicit mention of the effect of the Agreement. In the composite spectrum of the extension of the EU's legal space, these characteristics locate the Euro-Med Agreement closer to EU-driven compatibility rather than to homogeneity.

[115] Now the legal basis of the Working Arrangement could be found in Regulation (EU) 2018/1139 (80) whose Art 90 provides for the possibility for EASA to establish working arrangements with third countries' competent authorities.

[116] Florin Coman-Kund, *European Union Agencies as Global Actors: A Legal Study of the European Aviation Safety Agency, Frontex, and Europol* (Routledge, 2018) 140. Similar extensions of the SAFA programme were put into place in Australia, Canada, Israel and Singapore.

[117] For the increase in consumer surplus see Valeria Bernardo and Xavier Fageda, 'The Effects of the Morocco–European Union Open Skies Agreement: A Difference-in-Differences Analysis' (2017) 98 *Transportation Research Part E: Logistics and Transportation Review* 24. See also the independent study requested by the Commission Booz & Company: 'Development of the EU's Future External Aviation Policy', Final Report, April 2012.

[118] ARS Progetti, 'Rapport Sur La Mise En Œuvre Du Programme "Réussir Le Statut Avancé II" Du Maroc, Lettre de Marché N. 2017/386192- Request Ref. GestDem 2019/4653' (European Commission–EU Delegation in Rabat 2018) 48.

D. The *Brexit* Disentanglement

The EU–UK Trade and Cooperation Agreement (TCA) includes provisions on air transport. The TCA constitutes a rather unique reversal of the liberalisation waves that international aviation law (and especially EU aviation law) had engendered in the past decades. The Agreement still attempts to preserve the key aspects of the EU–UK aviation market while disconnecting the UK from the ECAA. The general framework of the TCA is based on equal partnership based on international law. It thus marks a departure from the canonical mechanisms EU neighbourhood law.

With respect to the freedoms of the air, the TCA preserves third and fourth freedom traffic rights.[119] The unrestricted rights pursuant to EU law ceased to apply from 1 January 2021. Fifth freedom rights for passengers were removed. While there is the possibility for this freedom to be allowed for cargo, this will be provided for by bilateral arrangements between the UK and the Member States.[120] Cabotage is instead excluded.[121] Non-discrimination is ensured provided that the provisions of Title XI of the Agreement on a level playing field for open and fair competition and sustainable development are respected.[122]

The disentanglement from the EU's legal space and its paradigms also occurred with respect to ownership and control provisions. As a matter of fact, backtracking from the notion of EU carrier as established by Regulation (EC) No 1008/2008, in order for traffic rights to be granted, UK carriers must be owned, directly or through majority ownership, and be effectively controlled by the UK, its nationals, or both. They must have principal place of business in the UK; be licensed according to EU law; and hold an air operating certificate issued by the UK competent authority.[123] For EU air carriers, similar conditions apply with the specificity that ownership and control conditions are extended to EFTA states.

A margin of flexibility for existing UK air carriers has been envisaged in so far as operating authorisations and permissions apply for carriers with their principal place of business in the UK, with a UK operating certificate, but owned and controlled by the EU or EFTA Member States, whether alone or together with the UK and/or its nationals.[124] Also the UK–US Aviation Agreement contains an exception clause on ownership and control for UK carriers.[125] This arrangement may be construed as a manifestation of the 'hysteresis'[126] of the EU membership whereby the effects of the EU legal order remain in UK's legal system. While the

[119] EU–UK TCA, Art 419(2)–(3) [2021] OJ L 149/10.
[120] ibid Art 419(4)(a)–(b).
[121] ibid Art 419(7)–(8).
[122] ibid 427.
[123] ibid Art 422 (1)(a).
[124] EU–UK TCA, Art 422(2).
[125] US-UK Air Transport Agreement, 10 November 2020, annex I.
[126] In physics, hysteresis is 'the phenomenon in which the value of a physical property lags behind changes in the effect causing it, as for instance when magnetic induction lags behind the magnetizing force' (Oxford Dictionary online).

disentanglement has different motives from the gravitational attraction generating the extension of the EU's legal space, some effects are similar.

The clause above especially applies to *British Airways* owned by the *IAG* multinational holding company, and it also allows UK subsidiaries of groups with a majority of EU ownership to operate as UK airlines.[127] The EU–UK TCA envisages that its Specialised Committee on Air Transport assess options for the reciprocal liberalisation of the ownership and control of EU and UK air carriers within 12 months from the entry into force of the EU–UK TCA.[128]

Clearly, the EU–UK TCA challenges the paradigms of the extension of EU aviation legal space in the EU proximity. Not only did a retrenchment occur on air freedom rights and on the clauses of ownership and control, but there was also a turn from EU neighbourhood law's paradigm of gravitation around the EU legal order. Not surprisingly in light of the motives underlying the *Brexit* process, there are no substantive or organisational *renvois* to the EU legal order. Rules on aviation safety are mainly premised on mild mutual recognition schemes.[129] The cooperation in aviation security[130] is largely based on international law conventions. Furthermore, the provision on air traffic management focuses more on global cooperation than on regional interoperability.[131] The UK is no longer a member of the EASA and in contrast to the other countries in the proximity, the only legal instrument presiding over the relationship between the UK authorities and the EASA is the EU–UK TCA: no sectoral agreement has been adopted to date.

The focus on international law conventions, and even more on equivalence of standards, together with the detachment from EU institutions and agencies, characterise the uniqueness of the EU–UK TCA regime in the landscape of the aviation agreements concluded by the EU in its proximity. While the equivalence of standards can be taken for granted in the initial phases of the implementation of the Agreement, this may change over time depending on whether the UK retains most of EU membership law into its legal system.[132]

[127] David Kaminski-Morrow, 'Brexit and Aviation: All's Well That Ends. Well, Almost … | CAPA' (CAPA–Center for Aviation, January 2021), centreforaviation.com/analysis/reports/brexit-and-aviation-alls-well-that-ends-well-almost-548205. Major low-cost air carriers, such as easyJet, had already decided to establish a subsidiary in Vienna holding an EU operating licence. Since at the time of the enaction of the EU–UK TC, non-EU shareholding was at 52.7%, and therefore above the 49.5% limit, easyJet Europe 'commenced to suspend voting rights of non-EU shareholders to comply with the EU air carriers requirements'. Similar measures have been taken by Ryanair and Wizzair. On this see David Kaminski-Morrow, 'EasyJet Restricts Voting Power of Shares Held by Non-EU Interests' (CAPA–Center for Aviation, January 2021), centreforaviation.com/analysis/reports/brexit-and-aviation-alls-well-that-ends-well-almost-548205.

[128] EU–UK TCA, Art 425. Yet in the second meeting of the committee the UK appeared to question the relevant scheme of the TCA, and the Commission 'confirmed its position had not changed', See European Commission 'Specialised Committee on Air Transport – Minutes of the Meeting', London Gatwick and online, 28 June 2022.

[129] EU–UK TCA, Art 434.

[130] ibid Art 435.

[131] ibid Art 436.

[132] EU (Withdrawal) Act 2018 (UK), See also, Union (Withdrawal Agreement) Act 2020 (UK).

V. The *Wider Europe* Energy Community

The legal frameworks of energy governance have been crucial for European integration.[133] Even before the fall of the Berlin Wall, the increasing of natural gas supplies from the East fostered interconnections and material relations countering the divisive logic of the Cold War.[134] The ensuing webs of interdependence arising from technology projects of transport networks and energy supply have been powerfully described as the 'hidden integration' of Europe.[135] The vulnerability of the EU in the energy sector was already apparent at the inception of the *Wider Europe* as a policy design. At that time, the choice of the Prodi Commission was to increase import from Russia.[136] The choice was grounded in the belief that energy supply from the East was more reliable, while Middle Eastern alternatives were considered too unstable.[137]

Energy governance become thus a key domain in the sectoral development of the EU's proximity policies. Energy supply was crucial in achieving its goals of stability, security and prosperity. The signature of the Energy Community Treaty was a landmark step in this process. The geopolitical motives of the extension of the EU's regulatory framework beyond membership animated both the EU's internal and external energy policy.[138] Energy governance brought to the fore competing geopolitical perspectives on the continent. While the EU energy community was premised on the values of liberalism and level playing field, the competing Russian-led Eurasian Economic Union was driven more by economic interests than by openness, liberalisation, and integration.[139]

The Energy Community Treaty[140] was signed in Athens in 2005 between the EU and neighbouring countries of south-eastern Europe.[141] Not dissimilarly from the ECAA, it was initially considered as 'a waiting room for the Balkan countries in the framework of their pre-accession talks with the EU'.[142] The subsequent

[133] See Treaty establishing the European Coal and Steel Community, Paris, 18 April 1951; Treaty creating the European Atomic Energy Community, Rome, 25 March 1957.

[134] Per Högselius, *Red Gas: Russia and the Origins of European Energy Dependence* (Springer, 2012).

[135] Thomas J Misa and Johan Schot, 'Inventing Europe: Technology and the Hidden Integration of Europe' (2005) 21 *History and Technology* 1.

[136] Pami Aalto, *The EU–Russian Energy Dialogue: Europe's Future Energy Security* (Ashgate, 2008).

[137] European Commission, 'Green Paper: Towards a European Strategy for the Security of Energy Supply' COM(2000) 769 final, 44.

[138] European Commission, 'Communication on Security of Energy Supply and International Cooperation – "The EU Energy Policy: Engaging with Partners beyond Our Borders", COM(2011) 539 Final, 5–6.

[139] Rozeta Karova, 'The Energy Community in Its Second Decade: Where Does It Stand and Where Is It Heading ?' in Lucila de Almeida and Marta Cantero Gamito (eds), *The transformation of economic law: essays in honour of Hans-W. Micklitz* (Hart Publishing, 2019) 291.

[140] The Energy Community Treaty, [2006] OJ L 198/18; hereinafter EnCT. See also 2006/500/EC.

[141] At the time Albania, Bulgaria, Bosnia and Herzegovina, Croatia, the former Yugoslav Republic of Macedonia, Montenegro, Romania, Serbia and the United Nations Interim Administration Mission in Kosovo.

[142] Karova (139) 273.

developments of the geographic scope of the EnCT anticipated the processes of *lato sensu* reconfiguration of the EU borders through law undercurrent in the east of the EU. The Energy Community Treaty became 'the reference point' for the EU's neighbours 'willing to be a part of the European energy system'.[143] The accession of Moldova, Ukraine and Georgia to the EnCT[144] not only signalled the increasingly significant eastern orientations of *Wider Europe* and potentially of the EU,[145] it also shows the value of *Wider Europe* as an analytical concept cutting across different EU proximity policies. Indeed, the extension of the EU's legal space via the EnCT encompassed both countries belonging to the pre-accession process (the Western Balkans) and to the Eastern Partnership of the ENP (Georgia, Moldova, and Ukraine).

On the substantive plane, the EnCT is premised upon a strong gravitation around EU law. It establishes clear obligations for non-EU parties to the Agreement to implement sectoral portions of EU law. It differentiates between compulsory *acquis* and legislation where approximation commitments are governed by best endeavours clauses. The provisions governing the substantive *renvois* to the EU legal order are to be found mainly in Title II of the Agreement, named the 'extension of the *acquis communautaire*'. Title II provides for detailed and mandatory commitments to implement EU legislation especially with regard to the *acquis* on energy,[146] environment,[147] competition,[148] and renewables.[149] In these domains, the annexes detail the adoption of new legislation. Looser obligations are enshrined in the Articles 13 and 14 of the EnCT. They pertain to accession to the Kyoto Protocol and EU legislation on pollution prevention and control.[150] In addition, Article 35 EnCT on renewable sources and energy efficiency has been used to incorporate the EU *acquis* into domains rather distant from the original EnCT design.[151] A degree of uniformity is ensured by the 'evolution clause' of Article 25 EnCT providing for a dynamic adaptation to the development of EU law. Moreover, Article 94 EnCT identifies the case law of the CJEU as a mandatory authoritative source of interpretation of the Agreement. This can be thus construed as an interpretative *renvoi*.

On the organisational plane, the EnCT adds further variation to the wide spectrum of arrangements of EU neighbourhood law. It is neither based on a

[143] European Commission, COM(2011) 539 final (n 138) 6.
[144] Karova (n 139).
[145] As it later became evident with the granting of the candidate status.
[146] EnCT, Art 10.
[147] ibid Art 12.
[148] ibid Art 18.
[149] ibid Art 20.
[150] It is mentioned in this respect Council Directive 96/61/EC, now Directive 2010/75/EU of the European on industrial emissions (integrated pollution prevention and control), [2010] OJ L 334/17.
[151] For instance Directive 2012/27/EU of the European Parliament and of the Council of 25 October 2012 on energy efficiency, OJ L 315, 14 November 2012, 1–56; Directive 2010/31/EU of the European Parliament and of the Council of 19 May 2010 on the energy performance of buildings OJ L 153, 18 June 2010, 13–35.

two-pillar model like the EEA, nor on a single-pillar model like the ECAA. In spite of its geographical scope initially similar to that of the ECAA, the EnCT operation is different from a 'single pillar' model where EU institutions also oversee the uniform implementation of extended EU law. In the EnCT, this task is entrusted upon the institutions established by the EnCT. Arguably the EnCT institutional framework is premised on a mimetic imitation of the EU institutional structure.[152] Significantly, the extension of the EU *acquis* is operated by majority voting,[153] although more politically sensitive measures are taken under unanimity.[154] The absence of significant organisational interactions between the EU legal order and the EnCT regime, render the enforcement mechanisms rather shallow. The redress measures envisaged in Title VII EnCT have seemingly been inspired by the procedures of current Article 7 TEU.[155] More articulated dispute settlement procedures were subsequently introduced with the establishment of the advisory Judicial Committee.[156] Although independent from the authorities of the Contracting Parties, its opinions do not bind the Ministerial Council (the main decision-making body of the EnCT).[157] Reliance on political and diplomatic enforcement systems raises a questions on the effectiveness of the implementation of the *acquis*. Already in 2011, the Commission denounced the ineffectiveness of the implementation and enforcement of the extended Union energy *acquis*.[158] Concerns have been also raised by the Parliament advocating for the establishment of 'legal control mechanisms to deal with deficient acquis implementation'.[159] Notwithstanding this, the implementation of the extended EU energy law continues also in the troubled times of Russian aggression of Ukraine and the ensuing challenges that this entailed for the energy sector in Europe.[160]

[152] Steven Blockmans and Bart van Vooren, 'Revitalizing the European Neighbourhood Economic Community: The Case for Legally Binding Sectoral Multilateralism' (2012) 17 *European Foreign Affairs Review* 577.

[153] See EnCT, Art 81 governing measures pursuant to Title II (The Extension of the Acquis Communautaire). This is different from the ECAA model where usually unanimity is generally required (ECAA, Art 18(3)).

[154] Title IV on the Creation of A single Energy Market, see EnCT, Art 85, and crucially on existence of serious and persistent breach, EnCT, Art 92.

[155] Helmut Schmitt von Sydow, 'Die Paneuropäische Energiegemeinschaft Mit Südosteuropa', Die Herausforderung von Grenzen – Le défi des frontières – Challenging Boundaries: Festschrift/ Mélanges en l'honeur de/Essays in honor of Roland Bieber (Nomos, 2013) 13 quoted in Dirk Buschle, 'The Enforcement of European Energy Law Outside the European Union Does the Energy Community Live up to the Expectations?' (2016) 6 *European Energy Journal* 26, 29.

[156] Procedural Act No 2008/01/MC-EnC on the Rules of Procedure for the Dispute Settlement as amended by Procedural Act 2015/04/MC-EnC.

[157] Rules of Procedure for the Dispute Settlement as amended by Procedural Act 2015/04/MC-EnC, Art 32(1).

[158] European Commission, COM(2011) 539 final (n 138) 7.

[159] European Parliament resolution of 23 October 2013 on the European Neighbourhood Policy: towards a strengthening of the partnership. Position of the European Parliament on the 2012 reports (2013/2621(RSP)) 2016, 126.

[160] Energy Community Secretariat, 'Annual Implementation Report', 1 November 2022.

While on the substantive plane, the EnCT gravitation around the EU's legal order is premised on a set of *renvois* similarly to what happens in other sectoral arrangements of EU neighbourhood law, on the organisational plane, the EnCT mirrors some of the political remedies under EU law. The EnCT does not envisage judicial interventions or institutional *renvois* to the EU legal order. This is unlikely to change through the EnCT amendments under discussion. The proposed amendments aim at increasing the EU's engagement in the management of the EnCT by enhancing the role of its decisions and voting,[161] with a particular focus on the EU's role in the monitoring of the implementation and enforcement of the extended *acquis*.[162] The amendments largely leave intact the institutional structures primarily based on diplomatic mechanisms.

The interplay of law and diplomacy in the extension of the EU's legal space brings to the fore the dynamics of inclusion and exclusion characterising *Wider Europe*. Indeed, although the extension of the EU's legal space comes with a degree of solidarity,[163] this does not extend to the far-reaching mechanisms of obligatory solidarity envisaged within the EU.[164] Moreover, exclusion is also evident from the fact that in the EnCT crucial measures as those pertaining to security of supply need a positive vote of the EU in the relevant EnCT decision-making bodies.[165] An increase in the positive vote prerogatives of the EU is under discussion in the reform proposal, this signals the prominent role of the EU in determining patterns of inclusion and exclusion in the extended EU's legal space.

VI. Conclusions

The extension of the EU's legal space in functional regimes resonates with the understanding that in contemporary regulatory regimes, claims to authority respond to functions more than territory.[166] The legal articulations of functional regimes are illustrative of the *lato sensu* reconfiguration of the Union's borders

[161] See EnCT Annex 1, 61st PHLG Meeting Vienna, 1 July 2021, 'Amendments to the Energy Community Treaty', see in particular proposed amendments to Arts 25, 91, 92.

[162] ibid. See proposed amendments in Art 25(3)–(4).

[163] See for instance Council Regulation (EU) 2022/2576 of 19 December 2022 on enhancing solidarity through better coordination of gas purchases, [2022] OJ L 355/1 expressly contemplating some degree of involvement for EnCT contracting parties.

[164] This is clarified in the proposed amendments of the EnCT, See Annex 1, 61st PHLG Meeting Vienna, 1 July 2021, 'Amendments to the Energy Community Treaty', Art 25(1)(e) as compared to those envisaged in Art 13 Regulation (EU) 2017/1938 of the European Parliament and of the Council of 25 October 2017 concerning measures to safeguard the security of gas supply and repealing Regulation (EU) No 994/2010, [2017] OJ L 280/1.

[165] EnCT, Art 83 regulating measures under Title III.

[166] Neil Walker, 'Late Sovereignty in the European Union' in Neil Walker (ed), *Sovereignty in transition* (Hart Publishing, 2003). Walker here refers to functionally bounded polities to highlight the functional limits on claims to authority of the EU (over the Member States).

through arrangements of EU neighbourhood law. The one-pillar structure of the ECAA Agreement and the TCT combines the substantive extension of the EU *acquis* in civil aviation and transport with advanced mechanisms of organisational interaction amounting to institutional *renvois*. The one-pillar model is predicated upon a more significant extraterritorial extension of the powers of the EU institutions (including those of the Court of Justice). The resulting arrangement epitomises the patterns of inclusion and exclusion in *Wider Europe*. Similarly to the two-pillar configuration, exclusion is primarily governed by the principle of autonomy of EU law. In *Opinion 1/00*, the ECJ clarified that autonomy requires not only third country exclusion from the decision-making process of (extended) EU law, but also that the (extended) powers of the EU institutions remain unaltered. These requirements stem from the different nature of ECAA arrangement and the EU legal order. The constraining obligations entailed in being subject to the substantive and institutional reach of the EU legal order are mirrored by equally far-reaching rights entailed in the inclusion of the ECAA (and TCT) countries in the relevant domains of the EU internal market at the same conditions as EU Member States. These complex dynamics of inclusion and exclusion are reflected in the reconfiguration of sovereignty that the ECAA and the TCT entail. The significant restriction of sovereignty stemming from the one-pillar structure does not only pertain to the extraterritorial reach of the powers of EU institutions but also to the reconfigurations of sovereignty entailed in distinctive notions of EU law as that of 'Union carrier'. The significant reconfiguration of sovereignty entailed in the ECAA and the TCT for the Western Balkans can also be explained from the link of these instruments of EU neighbourhood law with the pre-accession process. The review of the EU neighbourhood law continuum in the aviation domain shows how to a decreasing scope and intensity of gravitation around the EU's legal order corresponds a progressively more limited set of benefits (and freedoms of the air) associated to the participation in the extended EU's legal space.

The EnCT exemplifies yet another institutional arrangement of EU neighbourhood law. The extensive substantive scope of the extended EU *acquis* is not combined with mechanisms of organisational interaction with the EU legal order. The lack of these mechanisms has resulted in difficulties in the implementation and enforcement of the extended EU's *acquis*. In spite of the similarity in the geographical scope of the ECAA Agreement and the EnCT, the difference in the institutional arrangements can be explained considering the political sensitivity of the energy sector as compared to that of civil aviation. Indeed, the far-reaching reconfiguration of sovereignty entailed in the one-pillar model would have been difficult to accept for the non-EU members in the aviation domain. The organisation of the EnCT is instead premised upon a partial mimetic imitation on the EU institutional structure. Although some majority voting arrangement may suggest a degree of supranationalism, unanimity is required for the most crucial decisions. This has also led to some vetoes coalitions against measures attempting to redress the failure of implementation of the *acquis*.[167] The extension of the geographical scope of the EnCT as to include the countries of the ENP Eastern partnership (well before their status of candidates to membership had been on the table) in addition to the Western Balkans, validates the value of *Wider Europe* as an analytical concept capturing the interplay of law and geopolitics in different types of EU's proximity policies.

[167] See EnCT, Conclusions of the 55th Permanent High Level Group, Chisinau, 12 December 2019, para 17: 'Request by the Secretariat under Art 92 against Bosnia and Herzegovina in Cases ECS-g/1 1SEcs-2/13s, Ecs-6/16s was not endorsed. Serbia voted against' and para 18. 'Request by the secretariat under Art 92 against Serbia in cases ECS-3/ogs and ECS-g/13s was not endorsed. Bosnia and Herzegovina voted against'. See also EnCT, 17th Ministerial Council Conclusion, Chisinau, 13 December 2019.

PART III

Wider Europe Through Bilateral Partnerships

6

Ukraine at the Crossroad between a *Wider* and *Narrower Europe*

I. Introduction

The study of the reconfiguration of the Union's frontiers through the interplay of law and geopolitics cannot be undertaken without reflecting on the place of Ukraine in *Wider Europe*. In its complex and often tragic history,[1] Ukraine may be construed as a conceptual and geographic borderland between the East and the West.[2] In that light, this chapter discusses the development of the EU's relations with Ukraine as a borderland between Brussels' *Wider Europe* and the Kremlin's *Russkiy mir* (section II). The reflection continues by examining the convoluted process of the signature of the EU–Ukraine new generation Association Agreement, with Ukraine initially embarking on a tightrope walking between Brussels and the Kremlin (section III). The core of the chapter is devoted to examining the EU–Ukraine Association Agreement as a paradigm of EU neighbourhood law (section IV). A particular focus is placed on the techniques of extension of the EU's legal space in the DCFTA part of the Agreement (section IV.A). The chapter subsequently reviews the developments in the EU–Ukraine relations following the Russian aggression in Ukraine and the ensuing EU enlargement momentum (section V). Finally, it discusses the political covenant underlying the Ukraine's place in *Wider Europe*, contrasting it with the Kremlin's *Russkiy mir*.

II. Ukraine as a Borderland: Between *Wider Europe* and the *Russkiy Mir*

The study of Ukraine's place and role in *Wider Europe* brings to the fore issues at the intersection between geography, history and law. The very meaning of the word

[1] Timothy Snyder, *Bloodlands: Europe between Hitler and Stalin* (Bodley Head, 2010); Timothy Snyder, *The Reconstruction of Nations: Poland, Ukraine, Lithuania, Belarus, 1569–1999* (Yale University Press, 2004); Andrea Graziosi, *Guerra e rivoluzione in Europa. 1905–1956* (Il Mulino, 2002).

[2] Andrea Graziosi, 'Viewing the Twentieth Century through the Prism of Ukraine: Reflections on the Heuristic Potential of Ukrainian History' (2015) 34 *Harvard Ukrainian Studies* 107.

Ukraine is 'march' or 'border area'.[3] Its unique twentieth-century history further illustrates Ukraine's nature as a borderland. As Graziosi put it, Ukraine was a territory where 'people, languages, cultures, different modes of production, and different historical "epochs" [coexisted] within the same time'. This helps explaining 'the richness and fascinating nature'[4] of Ukraine and its geographical and conceptual position as an (often problematic) encounter between the East and the West.[5]

The development of the EU–Ukraine association has been far from linear and has been entangled with the even more troubled EU's relations with Russia. At the inception of the *Wider Europe* design, the EU's partnership with Russia was thought to be more ambitious than the one in place with Ukraine. Arguably, however, Russia's scepticism towards the ENP and the essence of *Wider Europe* more in general[6] could be considered as a harbinger of the conceptual limits of the design of the EU's proximity policies. It signalled the inability to overcome the EU-centrism of its approaches and a rather distracted attitude with regards to the geopolitical implications of the extension of the EU's legal space. Indeed, on the part of the EU there was a certain uneasiness in describing the enlargement, and relatedly *Wider Europe*, as a border making exercise with power balance consequences. The definition of frontiers has traditionally remained a taboo in the EU thinking,[7] and more generally in Europe after WWII. The knotty issue of borders *in* Europe was partly addressed during the negotiation of the Helsinki Final Act in 1975.[8] The Act sanctioned the inviolability of (the post WWII) frontiers dear to the Soviet Union,[9] while remaining open to peaceful change of frontiers. This latter element was particularly of interest to the Bonn Government in light of a possible elimination of 'the border between the FRG [Federal Republic of Germany] and the GDR [Germany Democratic Republic] through a peaceful decision of the German people'.[10] The compromise solution found in the Helsinki Final Act on the borders *in* Europe was still different from addressing the even more contentious issue *of* the European external frontiers, not least because this would entail a reappraisal of the universalistic ambitions entailed in the very notion of *Europe*.

[3] Michel Foucher, 'The Geopolitics of European Frontier' in Eberhard Bort and Malcolm Anderson (eds), *The frontiers of Europe* (Pinter, 1998) 236.

[4] Graziosi (n 2) 109.

[5] ibid 109–10.

[6] See Hannes Adomeit, 'Russia, ENP Competitor' in Erwan Lannon (ed), *The European Neighbourhood Policy challenges. Les défis de la politique européenne de voisinage* (Peter Lang, 2012).

[7] Luuk van Middelaar, 'L'Union européenne face aux voisins russe et turc: la frontière' in *Le réveil géopolitique de l'Europe* (Collège de France, 2022).

[8] See Organisation for Security and Cooperation in Europe, Final act of the 1st CSCE Summit of Heads of State or Government, 1 August 1975.

[9] Oliver Bange and Gottfried Niedhart, *Helsinki 1975 and the Transformation of Europe* (Berghahn Books, 2008).

[10] NARA, RG 59, Subject Numeric Files, 1970–1973, box 2306, memcon RogersScheel/Bahr/ Brunner, 1 May 1973 quoted in Stephan Kieninger, 'Transformation or Status Quo: The Conflict of Stratagems in Washington over the Meaning and Purpose of the CSCE and MBFR, 1969–1973' in Bange and Niedhart (n 9) 67.

Prodi's speech was adamant in including Russia among the target countries of the *Wider Europe* design. *Wider Europe* would consist of 'a ring of friends surrounding the Union … from Morocco to Russia'.[11] The Partnership and Cooperation Agreement with Russia, entered into force at the end of 1997, had already sketched the rather blurred contours of the association referred to in the preamble as a 'a gradual rapprochement between Russia and a wider area of cooperation in Europe and neighbouring regions'. This was echoed in Article 1 PCA, which established the aim of 'providing an appropriate framework for the gradual integration between Russia and a wider area of cooperation in Europe'. It is worth stressing that the integration language was somewhat specific to the partnership with Russia and absent from other coeval PCAs as that with Ukraine.

The EU efforts of rapprochement with Russia have been especially oriented towards energy cooperation. Russia was considered by the EU to be a relatively reliable partner in energy relations when compared to the more unstable Middle East. EU–Russia partnership in this domain was intended to bring about 'approximation of legislation and standards between Russia and the European Union' particularly on customs, standards and certification, competition policy and the environment.[12] In line with the canons of the EU's proximity policies, this approximation would be largely asymmetric and based on EU standards. As a matter of fact, in a relevant country strategy paper, it was clarified that 'Legislative, regulatory and institutional convergence' would develop 'on the basis of European models and standards'[13] with a view of enabling Russian regulatory framework to be 'more in line with the legal framework of the single European market'.[14] Yet, EU–Russia integration would be progressively operationalised through working methods that moved away from the EU-centric attitude typical of the ENP. For instance, the common spaces[15] would be described in the relevant concept papers as based on 'common and compatible rules'[16] more than on EU rules. Therefore, although the PCA was predicated upon a language of gravitation around the EU legal order,[17] some timid attempts were made to establish a more equal partnership by downplaying the de facto superordination of EU law.

The motives underlying Russia's uneasiness and contestation of *Wider Europe* as a policy design can be construed as part of a broader crisis related to the

[11] Romano Prodi, European Commission 'A Wider Europe – A Proximity Policy as the Key to Stability', Speech/02/61.

[12] European Council, 'Common Strategy of the European Union on Russia', Cologne, 3–4 June 1999', 23 November 1999) 10; 17.

[13] European Union, 'Country Strategy Paper 2002–2006, National Indicative Programme 2002–2003 Russian Federation', 27 December 2001, 2.

[14] ibid 3.

[15] See ch 1.IV (of this work).

[16] EU– Russia Summit, 'Joint Statement' Rome 6 November 2003, 13990/03 (Presse 313), Annex 1, CEES Concept paper, 6, www.consilium.europa.eu/uedocs/cms_data/docs/pressdata/en/declarations/77846.pdfv.

[17] See for instance EU–Russia PCA [1997] OJ L 327/3, Art 55 establishing that 'Russia shall endeavour to ensure that its legislation will be gradually made compatible with that of the [Union]'.

redefinition of Russia's role in Europe. It has been noted how 'Russia's identity crises after the cold war … become deeply intertwined with a litany of spatial projects attempting to define its relationship with the historical neighbours'.[18] The tones of the contestation of the *Wider Europe* gradually developed in purported civilisational fractures. In that regard, it is key to reflect on the turning of the Russian concept of the 'near abroad' into the *Russkiy mir* (the Russian world). Graziosi highlights that while the concept of 'near abroad' could imply degrees of subordination to Russia, it recognises the distinct identity of the other post-soviet states. Instead, the *Russkiy mir*, especially as reformulated by Putin starting from 2007, emerges as a 'political and cultural instrument' to reshape the ex-soviet states along new lines resonating with Putin's understanding of Russia as 'a great patrimonial power'.[19] As pointed out by Graziosi, painful historical, intellectual and political processes had led major European capitals to abandon the attitudes of their imperial past favouring cooperation, integration and respect of 'small states'.[20] Conversely, Putin has re-interpreted the double tzarist and soviet 'imperial heritage' of Russia subscribing to the early nineteenth-century conceptual and operational paradigms of European great powers, paradigms that were premised on power politics and spheres of influences.[21] Moreover, the Kremlin's rhetoric surrounding the *Russkiy mir* has been progressively inflated with a harsh contempt of the 'West', of its alleged degeneration and corruption following the demise of 'traditional values'. In that light, the *Russkiy mir* is presented as a 'civilisational' enterprise and its vocation is that of safeguarding and upholding what are conceived to be Russian traditional values antithetic to those pursued by the West.[22]

The conceptualisation of the *Russkiy mir* has been thus accompanied with a 'civilisational turn' shaping Putin's return to the presidency in 2012.[23] In the view of the Russian leadership, Ukraine would belong to this *Russkiy mir*. Suslov has argued that concept of 'Holy Russia' employed by Patriarch Kirill, starting from his enthronement in 2009 and his extended visit to Ukraine, could be seen as a 'territorial projection of Russia's civilisational identity, its basic cultural and moral values' which largely coincides with the concept of 'Russian world', and which would certainly include the Russian Federation,

[18] David G Lewis, *Russia's New Authoritarianism: Putin and the Politics of Order* (Edinburgh University Press, 2020) 166.

[19] Andrea Graziosi, *L'Ucraina e Putin tra storia e ideologia* (Laterza, 2022) 159.

[20] ibid 158.

[21] ibid.

[22] Illustrative in this respect, Putin's speech in Valdai in 2013: 'many of the Euro-Atlantic countries have effectively gone down the path of rejecting their roots, including the Christian values that constitute the basis of Western civilisation. [They] reject moral principles and any traditional identities: national, cultural, religious and even sexual. Policies are being implemented that equate large families with same-sex partnerships, and belief in God with belief in Satan'. Quoted in Lewis (n 18) 182.

[23] Fabian Linde, 'The Civilizational Turn in Russian Political Discourse: From Pan-Europeanism to Civilizational Distinctiveness' (2016) 75 *The Russian Review* 604.

Ukraine and Belarus.[24] In the Kremlin's understanding, the *Russkiy mir* was thus not compatible with the 'European choice' of Ukraine.

In some Russian circles, the development of the concept of the *Russkiy mir* would be intended as competing with the *Wider Europe* design. The ensuing reading would be one of geopolitical rivalries among regional centres. Illustrative in this respect is a Report of the Institute of National Strategy on Conservatism in 2014[25] mentioning how 'Geoeconomic confrontation more and more clearly is shifting from the inter-state level to the level of struggle between macro-regions' and this would increase the significance for Russia 'to pursue its integration project in the Eurasian space'.[26] In the same crucial year for the Ukraine' s 'European choice', Putin further articulated this conception. He affirmed that 'in order to develop … a dialogue, we need to begin with the idea that all regional centres, which have formed integration projects around them, should have equal rights to development'.[27]

Ukraine attempted to maintain an equilibrium between the two regional integration projects. New EU Member States that were sensitive to developments at the EU eastern borders contributed to the process of making Ukraine a frontrunner of the European Neighbourhood Policy. In that regard, Poland attempted to 'Europeanise' its foreign policy objectives by enhancing the eastern regional dimension of the ENP.[28] The increasing attention placed on the eastern dimension of the ENP could be traced back to EU constitutional provisions indicating that EU membership is generally open to European states. In fact, in pursuance of Article 49 TEU, any 'European State' committed to respecting and upholding EU values enshrined in Article 2 TEU may apply for membership. These legal and geographic elements contribute nourishing the membership aspirations of Eastern European States, and particularly of Ukraine.

In EU circles, different cooperation prospects between the southern and the eastern dimensions of the ENP were already captured by the former Polish foreign minister Radowslaw Sikorski. He maintained: 'We in Poland make a distinction between the southern dimension and the eastern dimension [of the ENP] and it consists in this: to the South, we have neighbours of Europe, to the East we have European neighbours'.[29] Yet, the membership aspirations of Eastern European

[24] Mikhail Suslov, '"Russian World" Concept: Post-Soviet Geopolitical Ideology and the Logic of "Spheres of Influence"' (2018) 23 *Geopolitics* 330, 345.

[25] The year in which the new generation EU–Ukraine Association Agreement (hereinafter EU–Ukraine AA) was signed.

[26] Institute of National Strategy (2014), 'Konservatizm kak faktor myagkoi sily Rossii', 2 *Tetradi po konservatizmu* 93, 110–11 quoted in Lewis (n 18) 169.

[27] Vladimir Putin, 'Zasedanie Mezhdunarodnogo diskussionnogo kluba "Valdai"', 24 October 2014, quoted in Lewis (n 18) 170.

[28] Karolina Pomorska, 'The Impact of Enlargement: Europeanisation of Polish Foreign Policy? Tracking Adaptation and Change in the Ministry of Foreign Affairs' (2007) 2 *The Hague Journal of Diplomacy* 25.

[29] Quoted in Ahto Lobjakas, 'New Life For Eastern Neighborhood; EU: Poland, Sweden Breathe New Life Into Eastern Neighborhood' (*RadioFreeEurope/RadioLiberty*, 26 May 2008), www.rferl.org/a/1144495.html.

countries were initially glossed over. The Joint Declaration of the Prague Eastern Partnership summit vaguely recognised that the eastern dimension of the ENP would 'be developed without prejudice to individual countries' aspirations for their future relationship with the European Union'.[30]

As is often the case for the ENP, more than in the regional dimension, it is in the bilateral relations that the special partnership with Ukraine stood out. The legislative approximation clause in the EU–Ukraine Partnership and Cooperation Agreement that pre-dated the ENP was more detailed than the corresponding provisions in place with the Southern neighbours. While the EuroMed Agreements indicated, for instance, that 'Cooperation shall be aimed at helping Morocco to bring its legislation closer to that of the Community',[31] the PCA singled out Ukraine's obligation 'to endeavour to ensure that its legislation [would] be gradually made compatible with that of the Community': the 'approximation of Ukraine's *existing and future* legislation' would be at the basis of the 'strengthening of the economic links'[32] between the partners. From the outset, Ukraine chose to converge on a spectrum of *acquis* larger than had been envisaged by the Agreement. It also adopted a method of convergence which was similar to that of the pre-enlargement process, 'position[ing] itself as a would be-candidate preparing for the accession'.[33]

Notwithstanding the frontrunner status of Ukraine within the ENP, the choice to be associated with the EU's legal space has not always been linear or taken for granted. In fact, it has often been fraught. The initially convoluted posture of Ukraine towards the European Neighbourhood Policy can be read against the background of the intricacies of its relationship with Russia; its peculiar geographical position within Europe; and its fascinating albeit troubled history.

III. The Origin of a Special Partnership: Tightrope Walking between Brussels and the Kremlin

The Ukrainian 'European choice' has progressively emerged in the context of rather intricated relations of the EU with the post-soviet space. The different conceptions and political visions on the common neighbourhood between the EU and Russia had more evident economic and legal implications in the context of the EU–Russia energy cooperation efforts. Ukraine had thus to orient itself among different geopolitical projects and visions with different legal implications.

[30] Council of the EU, 'Joint Declaration of the Prague Eastern Partnership Summit', 8435/09 (Presse 78) 5.

[31] EU–Morocco EuroMed Agreement [2000] OJ L 70/2, art 52.

[32] EU–Ukraine PCA [1998] OJ L 49/3, art 51 (emphasis added).

[33] Laure Delcour, 'Does the European Neighbourhood Policy Make a Difference? Policy Patterns and Reception in Ukraine and Russia' (2007) 7 *European Political Economy Review* 118, 146.

The EU–Russia energy dialogue initiated in 2000 proved dismal. One commentator highlighted how the failure of cooperation efforts was based on the lack of a 'proper conceptual vision' triggered by a mutual misunderstanding of the parties' assumptions and objectives and incapacity to find a common ground of discussion.[34] In addition to Russia's unresponsiveness and different outlook on energy policy, the EU's strategy was also undermined by the big Member States' reluctance to let the Commission manage their internal energy choices. In fact, they often preferred to strengthen their ties with Russia bilaterally. Besides, the Russia's strategy was more centred on investment than on legislative convergence.[35]

The EU's third energy package and its liberalisation ambitions featured among the principal bones of contention between the EU and Russia. The Kremlin received with hostility the requirements envisaged by EU law for foreign companies wishing to operate in the EU markets. The demand of 'unbundling' production and distribution assets was characterised by Putin as 'confiscation of Russian property'[36] and its retrospective application considered unacceptable.[37] Russia submitted a complaint to the WTO on the compatibility of the EU's third energy package with multilateral trade rules. In August 2018, the WTO panel found that the unbundling requirements were not in contrast with GATS rules, albeit they recognised limited incompatibilities between WTO rules and EU energy policy.[38]

Putin's ascent to power marked the reinforcement of a statist vision which was particularly evident in energy matters. As noticed by Talseth:

> [T]his 'statism' was diametrically opposed to Brussels' European narrative, which called for the liberalisation of the energy sector. In this respect, both the Statist and the European narratives sought authority. The Statist and Post-Imperial narratives on the one hand, and the European narrative on the other, were by nature expansionistic (centripetal), thus creating a zero-sum environment between them.[39]

Energy cooperation was thus a terrain where different geopolitical implications of *Wider Europe* and the *Russkiy mir* would be confronted.

Against the backdrop of this zero-sum climate, Ukraine initially undertook an attitude of political tightrope walking between the East and West. Ukraine's energy sector has always played a significant part in the country's economy, being

[34] Lars-Christian U Talseth, *The Politics of Power EU–Russia Energy Relations in the 21st Century* (Springer, 2017) 254.

[35] ibid 125.

[36] 'Putin and Barroso in Public Scrap on EU Energy Law' (*EUobserver*), euobserver.com/foreign/31869.

[37] President of Russia, 'Transcript, Joint News Conference Following Russia–EU Summit, June 2012', en.kremlin.ru/events/president/transcripts/15541.

[38] WTO, 'European Union and Its Member States – Certain Measures Relating to the Energy Sector' (2018) Panel Reports WT/DS476/R, www.wto-ilibrary.org/dispute-settlement/european-union-and-its-member-states-certain-measures-relating-to-the-energy-sector_ca3abb32-en.

[39] Talseth (n 34) 258.

a prominent source of the Ukrainian GDP,[40] with significant economic and political interests involved.[41] Ukrainian elites played a rather contradictory role in their relationship with the EU and Russia on energy matters. While apparently backing economic integration with the EU and also advocating for EU membership, Ukraine maintained its energy dependency on Russia thus failing to reform its energy sector. This rendered the country particularly exposed to the Russian issue linkage of political and economic interests.[42] Indeed the Kremlin made energy prices for the Ukrainian market conditional upon Russia's control of assets and infrastructure.[43] In particular, in the period 2005–2013 that policy of tightrope walking became more evident. Although manifesting the intention to meet the EU's demands, Ukrainian leaders attempted to obtain low gas prices from Russia. Moreover, they temporised on the Kremlin's requests to concede control over strategic assets and to reintegrate into a Russian-led economic and geopolitical space.[44]

Within this intricated context, in 2009 the EU and Ukraine wished to convey greater momentum to their partnership. The EU–Ukraine Cooperation Council adopted the Association Agenda.[45] The Agenda's objective 'to prepare and facilitate the implementation of the [new generation] Association Agreement'.[46] Energy was regarded as a crucial sector of cooperation. Ukraine was asked to accelerate the unbundling and restructuring of its energy giant *Naftogaz* in line with the EU's third Energy Package.[47] Moreover, a focus was also placed on Ukraine's commitments to the Energy Community Treaty.

The process of signature of the new Association Agreement was fraught with difficulties, especially arising as a result of Russian pressure aimed at regaining Ukraine in its orbit of influence. The Kremlin launched an initiative to counteract the EU's schemes in the Eastern dimension of the ENP.[48] In this context, a European Parliament Resolution condemned Russian interference as 'unacceptable' and admonished the Kremlin 'to refrain from putting pressure on Ukraine to join the Russia-Kazakhstan-Belarus customs union'.[49] The Kremlin's moves reflected the

[40] See OECD, 'Supporting energy sector reform in Ukraine 2019–2021', www.oecd.org/eurasia/competitiveness-programme/eastern-partners/supporting-energy-sector-reform-ukraine.htm.

[41] Anton Antonenko Takac Roman Nitsovych, Olena Pavlenko, Kristian, 'Reforming Ukraine's Energy Sector: Critical Unfinished Business' (2018) *Carnegie Europe*.

[42] Kataryna Wolczuk, 'Managing the Flows of Gas and Rules: Ukraine between the EU and Russia' (2016) 57 *Eurasian Geography and Economics* 113, 14.

[43] Roman Olearchyk, 'Moscow Lures Ukraine with Cheap Gas' *Financial Times* (7 April 2011), ww.ft.com/content/9d5f8f0c-6106-11e0-8899-00144feab49a.

[44] Wolczuk (n 42) 124.

[45] EU–Ukraine Cooperation Council, 'Recommendation on the implementation of the EU–Ukraine Association Agenda to prepare and facilitate the implementation of the Association Agreement', UE-UA 1057/0923, 23 November 2009.

[46] ibid 2.

[47] ibid 7.

[48] See Agreement for a Free Trade Zone, signed on 18 October 2011 in St Petersburg by Armenia, Belarus, Kazakhstan, the Kyrgyz Republic, the Republic of Moldova, Ukraine and Tajikistan. See also Pasquale de Micco, 'When Choosing Means Losing: The Eastern Partners, the EU and the Eurasian Economic Union', European Parliament, Directorate-General for External Policies, March 2015.

[49] European Parliament, 'Resolution adopted on 9 June 2011 in Strasbourg on the EU–Russia summit', P7_TA(2011)0268, para 22.

progressive ripening of Putin's understanding of international relations predicated upon potentially hostile centres of influence and civilisational alliances functioning according to distinctive 'ideas and principles that correspond to their cultural, historical, geographical features'.[50]

The Kremlin's role as a competitor of the ENP had been highlighted with foresight by Adomeit. Already at the times of the launch of *Wider Europe*, the Kremlin had made it clear that it would reserve to itself a prominent standing in the Commonwealth of Independent States (CIS) in the context of the dissolution of the USSR was described by Putin as the 'greatest geopolitical catastrophe of the twentieth century'.[51] The Kremlin was particularly keen in asserting its room for manoeuvre in what it was referred to as Russia's 'Near Abroad' of the post-soviet space in a reading of international politics as 'an arena of competition and conflict'.[52] The Russian mid-term strategy (2000–2010) on the relationship with the EU highlighted how Moscow would 'counteract any attempt at hampering economic integration in the CIS. In particular, it [would oppose] "special relations" of the EU with individual countries of the CIS to the detriment of Russia's interests'.[53] Touching perhaps the most profound chords of the Kremlin's world vision, Adomeit captured the meaning of the ENP for Russia:

> [Moscow] has chosen not to become a participant in the ENP, emphatically rejecting, from its perspective, the *degrading notion* that Russia was *not* an integral part of Europe but its *neighbour*. It also objected to being treated like an object of EU policies, and to having the same status as countries like Moldova or Morocco, rather than as an *equal*.[54]

Against this background, in the period of the Kremlin-backed Viktor Yanukovych's presidency, beginning in February 2010, EU–Ukraine relations began deteriorating after the parenthesis of the more pro-European presidency of Viktor Yushchenko. On its part, the Union clarified that its engagement with Ukraine could not be taken for granted. Its engagement would depend on Ukraine's progress in addressing the issue of selective justice (principally related to the trial of the former prime minister Tymoshenko), and on the implementation of the reforms envisioned in the Association Agenda.[55]

Notwithstanding signs of reconciliation, Yanukovych eventually announced on 21 November 2013 that Ukraine would not sign the Agreement. This abrupt

[50] Vladimir Putin, 'Zasedanie mezhdunarodnogo diskussionnogo kluba "Valdai"', 19 October 2017, quoted in Lewis (n 18) 169.

[51] See Gerard Toal, 'Geopolitical Catastrophe' in *Near Abroad: Putin, the West and the Contest over Ukraine and the Caucasus* (Oxford University Press, 2017).

[52] Adomeit (n 6) 393.

[53] Strategy for the Development of Relations between the Russian Federation and the European Union in Medium-Term Perspective (2000–2010), in Diplomaticheskii vestnik, Moscow, November 1999 quoted and translated in Adomeit (n 6) 394.

[54] Adomeit (n 6) 407 (emphasis added). Crucially, Adomeit continued by saying: 'Yet Russia's attitude to the EU and the ENP(I) shows that, on the one hand, it does not want to be included in the project of European integration but, on the other hand, it does not want to be excluded'.

[55] Council of the EU, 'Press Release, Foreign Affairs Meeting', 7438/1/12 REV 1, Brussels 10 December 2012.

change, shortly before the Vilnius Summit, where the signature of the Association Agreement was envisaged, reinvigorated threads of political tightrope walking of a part of the Ukrainian elite. The EU did not manage to counteract what European Parliament had denounced as 'unacceptable pressures' rejecting 'the zero-sum game as a paradigm for EU and Russian relations with the Eastern Partnership countries'.[56] The Ukrainian Government's press release adduced reasons of 'Ukraine's national security' to justify its unwillingness to sign the Agreement. It expressed its intention to 'restore the lost production and output and areas of trade and economic relations with Russia and other CIS member states'. Crucially, the *communiqué* stressed the objective of achieving '*equal relations* between Ukraine and the EU member states that is the fundamental principle of *international law*'. It also envisioned the establishment of tripartite commission between Ukraine, Russia and the EU to solve common problems.[57] This choice triggered profound popular unrest and political turmoil, including the Euromaidan protests, named in Ukraine as the 'Revolution of Dignity', and an abrupt change in government.

With the installation of a new pro-EU government in February 2014, the EU decided to sign 'the political chapters' of the AA during the European Council on 21 March 2014. The gesture was heralded by the President of the European Council as 'symbolis[ing] the importance that both sides attached to this relationship'.[58] The Association Agreement was eventually signed in June 2014 while Russia continued to apply trade restrictions.[59] Disapproval of the EU–Ukraine Deep and Comprehensive Trade Area included in the AA was also demonstrated by the Kremlin during the trilateral meetings (UE, Ukraine, Russia) that took place after the signature of the Agreement.[60] Russia–Ukraine relations further worsened with the Russia's unilateral suspension of trade preferences.[61] Trade frictions were exacerbated by the dreadful events culminating in the Russia's annexation of Crimea.[62]

[56] European Parliament, 'Resolution of 12 September 2013 on the pressure exerted by Russia on Eastern Partnership countries' (in the context of the upcoming Eastern Partnership Summit in Vilnius), P7_TA(2013)0383.

[57] Government of Ukraine, 'Resolution on Suspension of Preparation Process to Conclude Association Agreement with EU' (21 November 2013), old.kmu.gov.ua/kmu/control/en/publish/printable_article?art_id=246867400 (emphasis added).

[58] European Council, 'Statement by President of the European Council Herman Van Rompuy at the occasion of the signing ceremony of the political provisions of EU–Ukraine AA', EUCO 68/14 (emphasis added).

[59] Guillaume Van der Loo, *The EU–Ukraine Association Agreement and Deep and Comprehensive Free Trade Area : A New Legal Instrument for EU Integration without Membership* (Brill Nijhoff, 2016) 137.

[60] European Commission, 'Joint Ministerial Statement on the Implementation of the EU–Ukraine AA/DCFTA', STATEMENT/14/276, Brussels 12 September 2014; European Commission, 'Joint conclusions, EU–Russian Federation-Ukraine ministerial meeting on the effects of implementation of the EU–Ukraine AA/DCFTA', STATEMENT/14/223, Brussels, 11 July 2014.

[61] European Commission, 'Trilateral Talks on EU–Ukraine DCFTA: distinguishing between myths & reality', December 2015, myth 1, web.archive.org/web/20151223235739/http://trade.ec.europa.eu/doclib/docs/2015/december/tradoc_154127.pdf..

[62] Hugh Carnegy, Kathrin Hille and Roman Olearchyk, 'Vladimir Putin Signs Treaty to Annex Crimea' *Financial Times* (18 March 2014), www.ft.com/content/d93e4c7c-ae6d-11e3-8e41-00144feab7de.

The Euromaidan has been convincingly portrayed as 'Putin's first, veritable and great defeat'.[63] In the meantime, in Russia the 'civilisationist' discourse was supplanting the 'statist' one. A key difference among the two discourses pertains to the geopolitical posture of Russia especially towards the West. Based on the realist school of international relations theory, 'statist' views firmly advocated for the recognition of Russia's distinctive role in the post-soviet space. Yet they are 'not inherently anti-Western' and promoted "'equidistant' relations with both Western and non-Western powers'.[64] The 'civilisationist' discourse, instead, regards 'the multipolar world as divided into large regions, centered on great powers, considered to be the bearers of certain civilisational values and histories'.[65] Arguably, the civilisational reading of the relationship between Russia and the West exacerbated the zero-sum logic already somewhat inherent in the statist view. Crucially for Putin, the Ukrainian 'European choice' was a major danger for the geopolitical dimension of the *Russkiy mir*. As Graziosi posits, more than the alleged expansion of NATO, the danger for Putin was thus the EU and its culture, 'against which Putin's Moscow had undertaken a long-term fight by supporting and financing "sovranist" movements'.[66]

IV. The EU–Ukraine AA: A Legal Paradigm for Borderlands in *Wider Europe*

The troubled events surrounding the signature of the Agreement did not overshadow the potential of the EU–Ukraine new generation Association Agreement. The Agreement was heralded by the Commission as a 'pioneering document', and 'unprecedented in its breadth and depth'.[67] Several elements qualify it as such. It was the first Association Agreement concluded pursuant to a Council Decision featuring both a TFEU (Article 217) and CFSP legal basis (Articles 31(1)–37 TEU).[68] Moreover, it brought about a shift from soft law

[63] Graziosi (n 19) 48 (my traslation).

[64] Lewis (n 18) 167.

[65] ibid.

[66] Graziosi (n 19) 116.

[67] Johannes Hahn, European Commission, 'Opening Address to the Ukraine Financial Forum of the Vienna Initiative', SPEECH/14/1760.

[68] See the first Decision for the signature of the 'political parts' of the agreement: Council Decision 2014/295/EU on the signature of the EU–Ukraine AA, as regards the Preamble, Art 1, and Titles I, II and VII thereof, [2014] OJ L 161/1; the remaining parts of the Agreement including the DCFTA were signed subsequently with other two Council Decisions: Council Decision 2014/668/EU on the signature of the EU–Ukraine AA as regards Title III (with the exception of the provisions relating to the treatment of third-country nationals legally employed as workers in the territory of the other Party) and Titles IV, V, VI and VII thereof, as well as the related Annexes and Protocols [2014] OJ L 278/1; Council Decision 2014/669/EU on the signature of the EU–Ukraine AA as regards the provisions relating to the treatment of third-country nationals legally employed as workers in the territory of the other party [2014] OJ L 278/6.

to hard law in the practices of the ENP. This holds particularly true for ENP conditionality whereby EU market access is made conditional upon legislative approximation to EU law. In the EU–Ukraine AA, this conditionality is no longer enshrined in the ENP's soft law documents, such as action plans or association agendas, but in a legally binding bilateral agreement. To be sure, this pattern of legally binding conditionality in the framework of the ENP has been present at the multilateral level with the European Common Aviation Area.[69] The ECAA, however, is limited to sectoral approximation in aviation law for Western-Balkans countries within the pre-accession strategy. The novelty of the EU–Ukraine AA lies in the breadth of approximation commitments in a bilateral instrument concerning a county that at that time was not candidate for EU accession.

The ambition of the EU–Ukraine AA is captured by Article 1 EU–Ukraine AA. The Article sets out the objectives of the partnership, which include 'increasing Ukraine's association with EU policies and participation in programmes and agencies', and establishing conditions that would lead to 'the Ukraine's gradual integration in the EU Internal Market'. In this process, the 'progressive approximation' of Ukraine's legislation to that of the Union is intended as a tool for 'support[ing] Ukrainian efforts to complete the transition into a functioning market economy'.[70] The tenets of the association are also perceivable in the recitals of the Agreement. They identify Ukraine as 'a European country shar[ing] a common history and common values with the Member States of the European Union' and emphasise Ukrainian commitments in 'convergence with the EU in political, economic and legal areas'.[71]

Read together with Article 1, these passages of the Association Agreement originally located Ukraine in a rather vague path; a path oscillating between prospects of membership and a permanent borderland status. The former status would be possible pursuant to Article 49 of the TEU and the eventual fulfilment of the Copenhagen criteria. Yet, in the Agreement there is only an acknowledgment of 'the European aspirations of Ukraine', or 'the importance that Ukraine attaches to its European identity', welcoming 'its European choice'.[72] On the EU's side, this possible permanent status of Ukraine as a borderland would be congruent with the *Wider Europe* geopolitical aspirations and the EU exercise in borders reconfiguration through law resulting in the creation of buffer zones at its borders.[73] While the candidate status to EU membership granted to Ukraine[74] might lead to a clearer path for Ukraine in *Wider Europe*, the Western Balkan case may suggest a lengthy and indefinite *interregnum* between friendship

[69] See ch 4 of this work.
[70] EU–Ukraine AA [2014] OJ L 161/3, Art 1.
[71] ibid, recitals 3 and 8.
[72] ibid, recitals 5–6.
[73] Andreas Marchetti, 'Of Borders and Boundaries The Neighbourhood as the EU's Buffer Zone' in Tobias Schumacher, Andreas Marchetti and Thomas Demmelhuber (eds), *The Routledge handbook on the European neighbourhood policy* (Routledge, 2018).
[74] European Council, Conclusions, EUCO 24/22, Brussels, 23–24 June 2022.

and membership. Understandably, the current Ukrainian leadership adversely sees the characterisation of Ukraine as a borderland. Emphatically, President Zelensky has called for an elimination of the 'grey geopolitical zones' in a process whereby 'the borders of the European Union will be the borders of the continent of Europe'.[75]

The EU–Ukraine Association Agreement makes often the use of the notion of 'integration'.[76] This stands in contrast with the language of the EEA, which evokes instead a 'homogeneous' economic area and uniform interpretation of the Agreement.[77] While the language of 'integration' remains somewhat blurred, clearer legal effects are attached to homogeneity. Nevertheless, the Agreement possesses a robust governance framework. Several horizontal provisions of the AA, not specific to the DCFTA, are charged with governing the general aspects of bilateral relations. As far as the institutional provisions of the EU–Ukraine AA are concerned, Article 479 AA establishes that 'Existing agreements relating to specific areas of cooperation falling within the scope of this Agreement shall be considered part of the overall bilateral relations as governed by this Agreement and as *forming part of a common institutional framework*'.[78] The same applies to future agreements.[79] The dynamic evolution of the bilateral relations is also provided for in Article 463 AA where the powers of the Association Council are detailed.[80] They include the power to adopt decisions binding upon the parties and to amend or update the annexes to the Agreement 'taking into account the evolution of EU law'.[81] In addition, the horizontal provisions pertain to organisational interaction between the Ukrainian legal system and the EU legal order. An example of this is provided for in Article 475 AA, which governs the monitoring of the Agreement and operates an institutional *renvoi* to the EU legal order. Indeed, EU institutions may be entrusted to carry out 'on-the spot missions'. This is particularly the case for the assessment of the approximation commitments undertaken by Ukraine.[82]

A. *Wider Europe*'s Novel Techniques: The Deep and Comprehensive Free Trade Area

Borrowing from Santi Romano's theoretical corpus, the relevance of the EU legal order for the Ukrainian legal system is multifarious. Within the same EU

[75] Volodymyr Zelenskyy, 'Speech at the meeting of the College of the European Commission', 24 October 2023, www.president.gov.ua/en/news/yaksho-mozhemo-pozbutisya-sirih-geopolitichnih-zon-mi-povinn-86549.

[76] EU–Ukraine AA, Art 1; see also the Preamble and Art 337 on Energy Cooperation.

[77] See for instance EEA Agreement [1994] OJ L1/3, Art 1.

[78] EU–Ukraine AA, Art 479(4) (emphasis added).

[79] ibid Art Article 479(5).

[80] ibid Art 463(1).

[81] ibid Art 63(3).

[82] ibid Art 475(2)–(3).

neighbourhood regime ensuing from the Association Agreement, different types of substantive *renvois* and organisational interactions between the EU neighbourhood regime and the EU are envisaged. Especially the Deep and Comprehensive Free Trade Area (DCFTA) is governed by a distinctive regime within the law of association. Such a regime is based on far-reaching substantive *renvois* and organisational interactions with the EU legal order.

The overall rationale of the Agreement is informed by the motive of liberalisation characterising the agreements concluded in *Wider Europe*. Market access conditionality predicated upon the approximation to EU law characterises asymmetrical relations between the EU and its partners which are dependent on the EU market. In turn, this asymmetry is partly counterbalanced with more significant market opening on the part of the EU with respect to that initially required from its neighbours. Especially for trade in goods, the EU opens its market more comprehensively and at a faster pace than it generally requires from its partners.[83]

An example of mechanisms of legislative approximation on the basis of market access conditionality may be found in the sector of Technical Barriers to Trade (TBT) part of the DCFTA. In that regard, Article 56 AA highlights how Ukraine 'undertakes to follow the principles and the practices laid down in relevant EU Decision and Regulations'. The legislation is listed of in Annex III of the Agreement. The substantive *renvois* operated by these Articles do not refer directly to pieces of EU legislation. In the Annex, only the titles of the 'horizontal (framework)' and 'vertical (sectoral) legislation' are specified. These are adopted through the 'New legislative framework' and they concern the conditions allowing for the marketing of industrial products into the EU.[84] As put forward by van der Loo, the reasons for this rather open-ended *renvoi* can be found in the circumstance that the pieces of legislation were in the process of being drafted during negotiations for the Agreement between the EU and Ukraine.[85] Market access conditionality is already indicated in Article 56(3) AA where reference is made to the timeline detailed in Annex III.

The Association Agreement provides for the negotiations of agreements on Conformity Assessment and Acceptance of Industrial Products (ACAA) which may occur 'following a check by the EU party on the state of alignment of relevant Ukrainian technical legislation, standards and infrastructure'.[86] Significantly,

[83] Van der Loo (n 59) 223–27.

[84] Comprising Regulation (EC) No 765/2008 setting out the requirements for accreditation and market surveillance relating to the marketing of products [2008] OJ L 218/30; and Decision No 768/2008/EC a common framework for the marketing of products [2008] OJ L 218/82.

[85] Van der Loo (n 59) 250, and in particular his fn 1018. The similar agreements concluded shortly after with Georgia [2014] OJ L 261/4 and Moldova [2014] OJ L 260/4 contain more detailed Annexes with the list of relevant legislation. See Annex XVI EU–Moldova AA and Annex III-A of the EU–Georgia AA, updated respectively by Decision No 1/16 of the EU–Moldova Joint Trade Committee [2017] OJ L 39/45 and Decision No 1/18 of the EU–Georgia trade committee [2018] OJ L140/107.

[86] EU–Ukraine AA, Art 57.

Mutual Recognition Agreements (MRA) are based on legislative approximation. This is not the case for mutual recognition schemes envisioned in the agreements with other EU trade partners.[87] For instance, the EU–Canada Comprehensive Economic and Trade Agreement (CETA) adopts a different approach as it does not envisage the future conclusion of an MRA, but incorporates elements of mutual recognition in the Agreement itself.[88] The CETA framework does not require legislative approximation to EU law. Instead, the EU–Ukraine AA establishes that the conclusion of the ACAA is made conditional upon Ukrainian alignment to EU laws, standards, and infrastructure.[89]

The mechanisms of conditionality established by the Association regime further complicate the patterns of 'relevance' of the EU's legal order for the Ukrainian system. In Santi Romano's understanding, not only does the association regime presuppose the EU legal order for its '*existence*' and '*content*', as in the case of the ACAA, it also requires '*action*' by Ukraine for the depth and breadth of cooperation to progress.[90] Besides, this action is monitored by EU institutions through mechanisms of organisational interaction among the EU and the Ukrainian legal orders.

An even more articulated mechanism of legislative approximation pertains to the services chapter of the DCFTA. A significant path of liberalisation was envisaged despite reservations on audio-visual services, national maritime cabotage, and some domestic and international transport services.[91] Besides, the liberalisation of cross-border supply of services (GATS mode 1) had a 'reversed asymmetry' pattern: in accordance with its previous WTO commitments, Ukraine liberalises more services than the EU.[92] Furthermore, the EU has maintained more reservations than Ukraine for the sensitive GATS mode 4 services, such as the presence of natural persons for the purpose of providing a service.[93]

This is yet another manifestation of the dynamics of inclusion and exclusion characterising the *Wider Europe* design. On the one hand, the EU encourages a gravitation around its legal order for legislative approximation and convergence. On the other hand, liberalisation of modes of supply of services entailing the presence of natural persons in the EU is more restricted due to the potential detrimental effects that it could have on the employment markets for foreign workers in EU Member States. Notwithstanding this, EU liberalisation remains significant: reservations were restricted to a relatively limited negative list of instances

[87] For instance, see EU–Korea FTA [2011] OJ L127/6, Arts 4.6 and 7.21(4).

[88] See Protocol on Mutual acceptance of conformity assessment results of the EU–Canada Comprehensive Economic and Trade Agreement EU–Canada CETA [2017] OJ L 11/23 (hereinafter CETA).

[89] EU–Ukraine AA, Art 57(3).

[90] This is not specific to Ukraine, but pertains more generally to agreements based on market access conditionality; see also chs 5 and 7 of this work.

[91] EU–Ukraine AA, Arts 92 and 95.

[92] For the respective services reciprocally liberalised see EU–Ukraine AA, Annex XVI-B for the EU and Annex XVI-E for Ukraine; Van der Loo (n 59) 260–62.

[93] See EU–Ukraine AA, Annexes XVI-C and XVI-F.

whereby liberalisation can be eschewed.[94] This rather novel practice, which was also adopted in the CETA arrangement,[95] departs from the more usual and restrictive posture of detailing the limited sectors to be liberalised in a 'positive' list.

The peculiarity of services liberalisation in proximity policies also lies in the conditionality mechanisms of market access. The chapter on trade in services and on right of establishment is a case in point, especially in the sectors of postal services, electronic communications, financial services and transport.[96] In these domains, 'internal market treatment' is granted upon legislative approximation to EU law.[97] This aspect is rather unique for non-EEA members and it is substantiated by a robust set of substantive *renvois* and organisational interactions between the Ukrainian legal order and EU law vehiculated through the association regime.

The substantive *renvois* to EU law detailed in Annex XVII are made in the body of the Agreement through provisions that have a dynamic character. Indeed, they refer to the approximation and incorporation of the EU's 'existing laws and future legislations' into the EU legal order.[98] The Annex, echoing the EAA's model, also specifies the differences between the nature of directives and regulations into the Ukrainian legal order, and provides timelines for their implementation.[99] At the organisational level, the Agreement envisages an extension of the powers of the Commission to monitor the transposition of the *acquis* in Ukraine. In the case of positive assessment, the Commission proposes that the Joint Trade Committee, established by the Agreement, issues a decision on 'internal market treatment'.[100] Hence, the association regime itself envisions not only substantive *renvois* and organisational interaction *per se*. It again requires 'action' on the part of Ukraine to enhance the partnership and include Ukraine, to a certain degree, on equal footing as an EU Member State.

The organisational interactions between the EU legal order and Ukraine's legal system are particularly significant in the DCFTA title of the Agreement and especially in dispute settlement provisions.[101] Indeed, they have been used as a model for governing arrangements on the extension and retrenchment of the EU's legal space.[102] Like the subsequent EU–UK Trade and Cooperation Agreement (TCA),[103] the EU–Ukraine DCFTA dispute settlement mechanism[104] envisages

[94] See ibid Annexes XVI-A and D.

[95] See CETA (n 88), Annex II.

[96] EU–Ukraine AA, postal services: sub-section 4 (Arts 109–14); electronic communications: sub-s 5 (Arts 115–24); financial services: sub-s 6 (Arts 125–33); transport sector: sub-s 7 (Arts 134–37).

[97] EU–Ukraine AA, Annex XVII, Art 4.

[98] See EU–Ukraine AA, Arts 114(1), 124(1), 133(1).

[99] EU–Ukraine AA, Annex XVII, art 2.

[100] ibid Annex XVII, art 4(2-3).

[101] EU–Ukraine, Title IV DCFTA.

[102] See further chapter 7 of this work.

[103] See EU–UK TCA [2021] OJ L 140/10, art 738 EU–UK TCA.

[104] The general dispute settlement mechanism for the Agreement is governed by EU–Ukraine AA, art 477.

a consultation among the parties.[105] Such a consultation precedes the establishment of the arbitration procedure.[106] Interestingly, both the EU–Ukraine AA and the EU–UK TCA, as well as the EU–Switzerland draft Institutional Framework Agreement, contemplate the possibility of failure by the parties to nominate the arbitrators.[107] This circumstance actually occurred when Ukraine refused to appoint the arbitrators in pursuance of Article 96 of the Partnership and Cooperation Agreement which was then in force with the EU.[108]

The paradigmatic character of the EU–Ukraine institutional arrangements in the *Wider Europe* design emerges in the special procedure which applies to disputes relating to regulatory approximation. In these cases, 'where a dispute raises a question of interpretation of a provision of EU law', 'the arbitration panel shall not decide on the question but request the Court of Justice of the European Union to give a ruling on the question'. The CJEU's ruling is binding upon the arbitration panel.[109] The foregoing amounts to an institutional *renvoi* extending the powers and tasks of the CJEU to the regime of EU–Ukraine bilateral relations. Remarkably, it has also been a blueprint for the EU–UK Withdrawal Agreement and the EU–Switzerland Draft Institutional Agreement.[110] It strikes a balance between the requirements of the principle of autonomy of EU law and the political necessity that 'the court of one party cannot resolve disputes between the two'.[111] In fact, the arrangement is deferent to the CJEU's exclusive jurisdiction to interpret EU (neighbourhood) law. Yet, the CJEU's ruling is binding on the jointly established arbitration panel which remains the ultimate authority on the dispute.

It is worth stressing that the EU–Ukraine AA is far from being a monolith with a single institutional and governance framework. Several domains of cooperation present some specificities with respect to the general institutional arrangement. For instance, the Agreement presents a strong mimetism to the EU competition law framework. In this domain the text of the Agreement itself replicates provisions of EU law.[112] Substantive *renvois* thus do not operate through the annexes. This, although apparently based on an error,[113] detaches the sector from the mechanisms of dynamic adaptation of the Agreement via annex amendments.[114]

[105] EU–Ukraine AA, art 305.
[106] EU–Ukraine, art 306 and EU–UK TCA, art 739.
[107] EU–Ukraine AA, art 307; EU–UK TCA, art 740 ; EU Switzerland draft Institutional Framework Agreement Protocol 3, art II.2 'Accord Facilitant Les Relations Bilatérales Entre l'Union Européenne et La Confédération Suisse Dans Les Parties Du Marché Intérieur Auxquelles La Suisse Participe (Institutional Agreement- Draft Text) (23 November 2018) www.eda.admin.ch/dam/dea/fr/documents/abkommen/Acccord-inst-Projet-de-texte_fr.pdf accessed 8 February 2019.
[108] Van der Loo (n 59) 294; See references in his fn 1246.
[109] EU–Ukraine AA, Art 322.
[110] See further chs 7 and 9 of this work.
[111] This was the expression used in the Chequers plan on the EU–UK Future Relations drafted by Theresa May's Government; see ch 7 of this work.
[112] See for instance, EU–Ukraine AA, Art 256.
[113] Van der Loo (n 59) 278.
[114] EU–Ukraine AA, Art 463.

A different type of arrangement is in place in the energy sector whereby the relationship between the DCFTA and EnCT provisions is at play. In fact, the DCFTA includes a chapter on trade-related energy encompassing transport in electricity and gas and third-party access to fixed infrastructure. The chapter operates substantive *renvois* to EU law not only by referring to the annexes of the AA but also via the *acquis* referred to in the EnCT.[115] In Santi Romano's understanding, the 'relevance' of the EU legal order for the EU–Ukraine association regime is also mediated through an additional EU-led multilateral sectoral regime. This demonstrates a complex interaction among parallel regimes of the extension of the EU's legal space. Although they feature different geographical extensions and vary in substantive scope, they have the EU legal order as a common gravitational fulcrum. In the event of a conflict between the provisions of the energy-related DCFTA and the provisions of the EnCT, or the provisions of the EU legislation made applicable under the EnCT, the EnCT provisions shall prevail to the extent of such conflict.[116] Disputes concerning energy provisions in the DCFTA's energy chapter may be subject to a faster procedure to remedy interruptions to transport or energy, which may result in suspension of cooperation.[117] Moreover, the breadth of the EU *acquis* referred to in the DCFTA is greater than that of the EnCT (to which Ukraine is also party). Besides, Title V of the EU–Ukraine AA includes a separate chapter on energy cooperation, including nuclear issues, which is not comprised in the DCFTA section of the Association Agreement. This separate chapter is premised upon political and security-focused dialogue complementing the more strictly legal and market-oriented domains DCFTA. The dialogue is intended to respond to emergency situations or contingent energy security threats. Certainly, EU law and legislative cooperation also play a major role in this chapter,[118] but here EU law-based commitments are embedded in a broader international framework comprising the Energy Charter Treaty and other international instruments and UN initiatives.[119]

V. Russian Aggression on Ukraine and the EU Membership Application

On 24 February 2022, Russia started an armed aggression on Ukraine with the preposterous aim of 'de-nazifying' Ukraine. Arguably, the timing of the aggression may have been influenced by the Kremlin's perception of weakness of the West. Europe was experiencing somewhat problematic governments transitions and

[115] ibid Arts 314, 305(5), 307(8), 308(4) and 310(3).
[116] ibid Art 278.
[117] ibid Art 273.
[118] ibid Annex XXVII to Chapter I Energy Cooperation, including nuclear issues.
[119] EU–Ukraine AA, Arts 337–38.

elections in its Member States. Moreover, the perception of a weak and divided West was grounded on the timid response to the annexation of Crimea and on the hasty and chaotic withdrawal of the US and allies' troops from Afghanistan at the end of August 2021. It is hardly a coincidence that escalation of Russian military pressure around Ukraine began in the autumn following the US withdrawal from Kabul.[120]

Beyond these specific circumstances, deeper roots of the aggression can be found in Putin's ambitions concerning the *Russkiy mir*, a space that would include Ukraine. The 2022 aggression can thus be read as a continuation of the Kremlin's attempt to frustrate with military force the 'European choice' of Ukraine. It brought to a larger scale the military aggression initiated with the annexation of Crimea following Ukraine's decision to proceed with the strengthening of EU association in 2014. In that regard, Graziosi has perceptively highlighted how the preposterous aim of 'de-nazifying' Ukraine can be construed, in fact, as an attempt of its 'de-Europeanisation'.[121]

In Putin's own reinterpretation of history, nations and statehood, Russia and Ukraine are inhabited by one single people. He spelled out this belief on multiple occasions. In the wake of the annexation of Crimea, by referring to Kyiv as the 'mother of Russian cities', Putin contended that Russia and Ukraine are not 'not simply close neighbours' but the expression of 'one people'.[122] This stance was reiterated in Putin's 'essay' on the 'Historical Unity of Russians and Ukrainians', in which he attempted to offer an explanation of this claim.[123] He mentioned that the 'Ukraine and Russia have developed a single economic system over decades and centuries. The profound cooperation [Russia and Ukraine] had 30 years ago is an example for the European Union to look up.'[124] The claim was further developed with a portrayal of an alleged US and EU attempt to 'curtail and limit [Ukraine's] cooperation with Russia' well before 2014, a crucial year considered by Putin as a watershed.[125] In his words, 'Ukraine was dragged into a dangerous geopolitical game aimed at turning Ukraine into a barrier between Europe and Russia. Inevitably, there came a

[120] Carl Bildt, 'Did the Afghan Failure Lead to the Ukraine War?' *Project Syndicate* (16 August 2022), www.project-syndicate.org/commentary/afghanistan-us-failure-set-stage-for-russia-invasion-ukraine-by-carl-bildt-2022-08.

[121] Graziosi (n 19) 17, 101, 116. In April 2022, an article in *Ria Novosti* (a Russian state-owned news agency made the appalling link between 'de-nazification' and 'de- Europeanisation': Timofej Sergejcev, 'What Should Russia Do with Ukraine? – RIA Novosti' *Medium* (11 April 2022), medium.com/@kravchenko_mm/what-should-russia-do-with-ukraine-translation-of-a-propaganda-article-by-a-russian-journalist-a3e92e3cb64.

[122] Prague Post, 'Full Text of Putin's Speech on Crimea, 18 March 2014' (19 March 2014), www.praguepost.com/eu-news/37854-full-text-of-putin-s-speech-on-crimea.

[123] For a contextualization, see Harvard Ukrainian Research Institute, 'Contextualizing Putin's "On the Historical Unity of Russians and Ukrainians"', huri.harvard.edu/news/putin-historical-unity.

[124] Vladimir Putin, 'On the Historical Unity of Russians and Ukrainians' *Office of the President of Russia*, 12 July 2021, 16.

[125] ibid 13.

time when the concept of "Ukraine is not Russia" was no longer an option. There was a need for the "anti-Russia" concept that we will never accept'.[126]

The foregoing passages are illustrative of how the 'European choice' of Ukraine was considered by Putin as a 'forced change of identity'[127] perpetrated by the 'new "Maidan authorities"'.[128] As highlighted by Timothy Snyder, the 'de-nazification' of Ukraine 'operates within the special Russian definition of "Nazi": a Nazi is a Ukrainian who refuses to admit being a Russian'.[129] Snyder also highlights how in Putin's vision of a broken world where Ukraine and Russia are separated, restoration would occur 'through violence. Russia becomes itself only by annihilating Ukraine'.[130] In that light, some commentators have brought to the fore the potential genocidal nature that the Kremlin's visions and policies in Ukraine might entail.[131]

In less than a week from the Russian aggression, Ukraine reaffirmed its European choice with an EU membership application. The application was presented in very exceptional circumstances during frantic and harsh days. Yet, there is a deep meaning in the Ukrainian application. It can be argued that the Ukrainian leadership wanted to convey an existential message to the EU and to the world: the fight for survival of Ukraine was inherently linked to the EU membership prospects. Such a reading is not surprising in light of the appalling links made between de-nazification and de-Europeanisation of Ukraine.

The exceptional circumstances of the Ukrainian application were met with an equally swift timeframe for handling the procedure pursuant to Article 49 TEU. The relevant Commission opinion was delivered as early as 17 June 2022. The Opinion stressed the development of the Ukraine's 'aspiration to belong to the European Union' portraying it as 'an underlying motive for [its] democratic changes … and a driver of key reforms founded on European values'.[132] The Commission review of the relations between the EU and Ukraine chronicled the fundamental moments of the 'Ukrainian path towards the European Union', including the *Orange revolution* portrayed as being 'about the orientation towards the West and integration with the EU', and the process of signature of the new generation Association Agreement, with the *Revolution of Dignity* marking the support for the European choice and the deepening of the EU–Ukraine political and economic ties. Moreover, the context of the review

[126] ibid.

[127] ibid 14.

[128] ibid 13.

[129] Timothy Snyder, 'Russia's Genocide Handbook' (*Thinking about* …, 8 April 2022), snyder.substack.com/p/russias-genocide-handbook.

[130] Timothy Snyder, 'The War in Ukraine Is a Colonial War' *The New Yorker* (28 April 2022), www.newyorker.com/news/essay/the-war-in-ukraine-is-a-colonial-war.

[131] In that sense the above-noted work of Timothy Snyder, see also Graziosi (n 19) 124.

[132] European Commission, 'Opinion on Ukraine's application for membership of the European Union', COM(2022) 407 final.

of Ukraine's membership application was one where the dynamics of exclusion proper to *Wider Europe* were tempered. This holds especially true for the welcoming of Ukraine refugees by the EU and its Member States.[133]

The Commission recommended to the Council that 'Ukraine should be given the perspective to become a member of the European Union' with the granting of the candidate status.[134] The Commission singled out seven points to be part of the conditions attached to the granting of the candidate country status to Ukraine. These pertained to the enactment of reforms related to the Rule of Law concerning the selection of judges (two points were identified in this area), the fight against corruption, anti-money laundering legislation, anti-oligarch legislation, media law, and protection of minority legislations.[135] In June 2022, the European Council swiftly granted the candidate status to Ukraine.[136] The EU canonical ambiguous parlance emerged in the immediately subsequent passage where it was affirmed that the 'progress of each country towards the European Union will depend on its own merit in meeting the Copenhagen criteria, taking into consideration the EU's capacity to absorb new members'.[137]

Notwithstanding the general positive outlook surrounding the attainment of that status, the Commission recommendation on the reforms to be taken by Ukraine summarises critical issues already largely highlighted in previous reports on the implementation of the Association Agreement.[138] The 2021 implementation report mentioned 'notable reform progress … in a wide range of areas relation to the Association Agreement'. Yet, a significant attention was placed on issues relating to the rule of law and fight against corruption, with a particular emphasis on the critical reform of Ukraine's judiciary.[139] In the subsequent analytical report on Ukraine application for membership of February 2023, the Commission offered a detailed account of the status of adoption and implementation of the EU *acquis* subdivided in the well-established format of accession chapters. From the analytical report, it can be discerned that even in the chapters of the internal market cluster, the core of EU law and the law of the extension of the EU's legal space, significant progress remains to be made on the part of Ukraine. In the crucial area of free movement of goods largely covered by the DCFTA of

[133] See Council Implementing Decision (EU) 2022/382 establishing the existence of a mass influx of displaced persons from Ukraine within the meaning of Art 5 of Directive 2001/55/EC, and having the effect of introducing temporary protection, [2022] OJ L 71/1.

[134] European Commission, 'Opinion on Ukraine's application for membership' (n 132) 20.

[135] ibid 20–21.

[136] European Council, Conclusions, EUCO 24/22, Brussels, 23–24 June 2022, 4. The European Council also granted the candidate country status the Republic of Moldova, and affirmed its willingness to do the same with Georgia 'once the priorities specified in the Commission's opinion on Georgia's membership application have been addressed'.

[137] ibid.

[138] European Commission, 'Ukraine 2023 Report' SWD(2023) 699 final.

[139] European Commission and EU High Representative, 'Association Implementation Report on Ukraine' 2020 SWD(2020) 329 final. See also European Commission and EU High Representative, Association Implementation Report on Ukraine, SWD(2022) 202 final.

the AA, the report acknowledges that Ukraine 'is moderately prepared' and it exhorts Ukraine to 'complete its alignment with the EU acquis for the legislative framework, i.e. standardisation, accreditation, conformity assessment, metrology and market surveillance'.[140] Less advanced is the Ukrainian progress with respect to the *acquis* in the free movement of persons where the Commission recognised only an 'early stage of preparation'.[141] In the areas of right of establishment and freedom to provide services; and free movement of capital, the Commission recognised 'some level of preparation' in the Ukrainian alignment with the relevant *acquis*.[142]

The Commission Report on Ukraine of 8 November 2023 highlighted the acceleration of the Ukrainian 'reform efforts' following its granting of the candidate country status, while substantially reiterating the findings of the previous February 2023 analytical report on the implementation of the EU *acquis*.[143] In that date, in a new enlargement momentum, the Commission recommended the Council to open accession negotiations with Ukraine, stressing the importance of continuing the efforts on the seven points singled out in June 2022.[144] The European Council of December 2023 endorsed the Council conclusions[145] on enlargement and opened accession negotiations with Ukraine inviting the Commission to adopt the relative negotiation framework.[146] The European Council of December 2023 also reaffirmed the EU unwavering support for Ukraine.[147]

In their *Common Market Law Review* editorial on 'integration through war', Petrov and Hillion have magisterially captured the tensions and opportunities arising from the dreadful circumstances of Ukraine's EU membership application. Noticing the mixed implementation results of the Association Agreement and the overall Ukrainian commitments of the implementation of the EU *acquis*, the authors convincingly argue that

> the EU Member States and institutions have granted the candidate status to Ukraine essentially as an act of moral support, to boost the country's resistance to the

[140] European Commission, 'Analytical Report Following the Commission Opinion on Ukraine's Application for Membership of the European Union' (2023) SWD(2023) 30 final, 16–17.

[141] ibid 18.

[142] ibid 20–21.

[143] European Commission, 'Ukraine 2023 Report' (n 137).

[144] European Commission, '2023 Communication on EU Enlargement Policy', COM(2023) 690 final, 22 ff. For the seven points see text to n 134 above.

[145] Council of the EU, Conclusions, 16707/23, Brussels 12 December 2023.

[146] The European Council of December 2023 also granted the status of candidate country to Georgia and mentioned that it would open accession negotiations with Bosnia and Herzegovina, once the necessary degree of compliance with the membership criteria is achieved. European Council, Conclusions, CO EUR 16, Brussels 14–15 December 2023.

[147] Although Hungary blocked a significant aid package for Ukraine in December 2023 and the European Council decision on opening membership negotiations was taken by consensus without the Hungarian vote. Matina Stevis-Gridneff and Steven Erlanger, 'Hungary Blocks Ukraine Aid After E.U. Opens Door to Membership' *The New York Times* (14 December 2023), www.nytimes.com/2023/12/14/world/europe/eu-ukraine-hungary-aid.html; 'Hungary Blocks €50 Billion in EU Aid for Ukraine' *Le Monde.fr* (14 December 2023), www.lemonde.fr/en/international/article/2023/12/14/eu-agrees-to-open-ukraine-and-moldova-accession-talks_6344057_4.html.

> aggression and, perhaps more than ever in the history of EU enlargement, as a (geo) political decision rather than a scrupulous legal application of the conditions related to Article 49 TEU.[148]

It can be thus maintained that the tragic circumstances of the war have fostered the turning of the eastern dimension of the ENP into a recognised path for possible EU membership. The *Wider Europe* design is thus confirmed as a geopolitical engagement that, albeit largely inadvertently, elicits a border reconfiguration through law.

VI. Political Covenants Confronting Aggression

The Ukrainian case is illustrative of the value of *Wider Europe* as an analytical framework capable of capturing the patterns of extension of the EU's legal space across different EU's proximity policies. In fact, although veritable membership prospects may appear distant from the horizon, it can be argued that the war in Ukraine has accelerated the trend of turning the eastern dimension of the ENP into a pre-accession policy. For its historic and geographic characteristics, the Ukrainian case is also conducive to refining the reflection on the political covenants of EU neighbourhood law and their complex relationship with EU membership law.

The tragic events of the Russian aggression have corroborated the nature of Ukraine as a geographic and conceptual borderland where two opposed conceptions of conducting international relations are competing: *Wider Europe* and the *Russkiy mir*. The juxtaposition of *Wider Europe* and the Kremlin's take on the *Russkiy mir* in this reflection does certainly not imply that the extension of the EU's legal space can be compared to a military aggression on a moral ground. Besides, the considerations on the geopolitical tenor of EU neighbourhood law shall by no means be read as to sustain the Kremlin's propaganda on a preventive war to respond to the potential threats posed by NATO and the West. The very shaky grounds on which this propaganda rests have been highlighted by Graziosi, who chronicled the main events bringing to the fore the fallacies of the Kremlin's discourse on the 'preventive war'.[149] Suffice here to mention the Budapest memorandum of 1994 sanctioning the commitment of the Russian Federation, the United Kingdom, and the United States of America 'to respect the independence and sovereignty and the existing borders of Ukraine' and 'to refrain from the threat or use of force against the territorial integrity or political independence of Ukraine'.[150] Russia has thus breached this agreement by annexing Crimea in 2014

[148] Roman Petrov and Christophe Hillion, 'Guest Editorial: "Accession through War" – Ukraine's Road to the EU' (2022) 59 *Common Market Law Review* 1289, 1291.

[149] Graziosi (n 19) 113–16.

[150] Memorandum on security assurances in connection with Ukraine's accession to the Treaty on the Non-Proliferation of Nuclear Weapons, Budapest, 5 December 1994, UN Treaties registration number 52241.

and launching a large-scale aggression in 2022. More bitterly, the memorandum's implementation led to the transfer of Ukrainian nuclear weapons from Ukraine to Russia, with US funds.[151] In that regard, Graziosi posits that, more than NATO, the greatest threat to Putin was perhaps Ukraine itself: Ukraine was following an independent path oriented towards the West, preferring the European Union to the *Russky mir*.[152] In that light, there is a certain consensus, also from scholars who are critical on the foreign policy of the West, that Ukraine's membership of the EU would be unacceptable for the Kremlin.[153]

The brutal challenge posed by the Russian aggression to *Wider Europe* invites us again to reflect on the interaction between sovereignty, politics and law. Examining the political covenants underlying *Wider Europe* and the *Russkiy mir* sheds light on the differences in their geopolitical nature. In his address to the nation before the aggression on Ukraine, Putin contended that Ukraine 'is not just a neighbouring country for us. It is an inalienable part of our history, culture and spiritual space.'[154] He went on to contend that Ukraine 'never had a stable tradition of statehood'.[155] These considerations should be read against the background of the above-mentioned Putin's own 'historical essay' of July 2021 where he insisted on his belief that 'true sovereignty of Ukraine is possible only in partnership with Russia';[156] and that Ukraine's European choice would entail a 'forced change of identity'.[157]

Russia's claims to authority in Ukraine are hence based on an interpretation of history imbued with ideological flavour[158] and implemented through a war of aggression in blatant violation of international law.[159] In the Kremlin's understanding of the *Russky mir*, the asymmetry in the relations between Russia and Ukraine goes far beyond authoritarianism. As Khodarkovsky notes, 'it is about imperial

[151] Nadia Schadlow, 'The Denuclearization of Ukraine: Consolidating Ukrainian Security' (1996) 20 *Harvard Ukrainian Studies* 271. Note that even a scholar increasingly critical of the Western attitude towards Russia then advocated against a denuclearisation of Ukraine, see John J Mearsheimer, 'The Case for a Ukrainian Nuclear Deterrent' [1993] *Foreign Affairs*, www.foreignaffairs.com/articles/ukraine/1993-06-01/case-ukrainian-nuclear-deterrent.

[152] Graziosi (n 19) 116.

[153] Isaac Chotiner, 'Why John Mearsheimer Blames the U.S. for the Crisis in Ukraine' *New Yorker* (1 March 2022), www.newyorker.com/news/q-and-a/why-john-mearsheimer-blames-the-us-for-the-crisis-in-ukraine.

[154] Address by the President of the Russian Federation (21 February 2022), en.kremlin.ru/events/president/transcripts/67828.

[155] ibid.

[156] Putin (n 124) 18.

[157] ibid 14.

[158] See inter alia Graziosi (n 19); Snyder, 'The War in Ukraine Is a Colonial War' (n 130).

[159] Ingrid Brunk and Monica Hakimi, 'Russia, Ukraine, and the Future World Order' (2022) 116 *American Journal of International Law* 687. To be sure, the Western claim of defending a rule-based international order is far from immune from double-standards critiques: see Kai Ambos, 'Ukraine and the double standards of the West' (2022) 20 *Journal of International Criminal Justice* 875. See also Patryk I Labuda, 'Beyond rhetoric: Interrogating the Eurocentric critique of international criminal law's selectivity in the wake of the 2022 Ukraine invasion' (2023) 36 *Leiden Journal of International Law* 1095.

nostalgia, restoration and expansionism'.[160] The 'spiritual unity' referred to by Putin entails the rejection of self-determination for Ukrainians,[161] and a repression of Ukrainian identity.[162] The expansionist project underlying the Kremlin's *Russkiy mir* in Ukraine is thus grounded on military force disguised as deceptively charged narratives of civilisational and spiritual unity.

The *Wider Europe* design can certainly be read in terms of spheres of influence: the extension of the EU's legal space has geopolitical implications. Although the issue of borders remained vague in all the *Wider Europe* documents, the geographic tenor of the projects and the pursuance of the political objectives of stability and security were evident from the start. Moreover, as it has been argued and problematised in Chapter 2 of this book, the interaction of EU neighbourhood law regimes with the EU legal order and the ensuing relations of asymmetry and dependence, together with the indefinite nature of EU borders, present characteristics that are reminiscent of the empires of the past. Yet the means through which the EU vehiculates its power and channels its magnetism is law, not armed aggression. It is worth stressing that although *Wider Europe* entails a *lato sensu* reconfiguration of the EU's borders through law, it does not challenge the territorial integrity of the states participating in the extended EU's legal space. Similarly to EU enlargement, the *lato sensu* reconfiguration of the EU borders entailed in *Wider Europe* is premised on the free choice of states wishing to partake in the extended EU's legal space.

The troubled signature process of the EU–Ukraine AA qualifies the status of Ukraine as a borderland not only on the geographical plane, but also in the intersection of two competing *ethos* on how to conduct international relations. The Kremlin's stance is based on a statist and civilisational conceptions of the world order, power-politics and military territorial extension. In that view, trade is instrumental to geopolitical influence. Conversely, the Brussels' vision is largely agnostic to territory as it is premised on a functional and legal extension of the EU's legal space. Trade is still intended to be instrumental to geopolitical influence. The calibre of the Union's power, however, chiefly lies in its laws.

Ukraine's belonging in the 'European family', as the adherence of Ukraine to *Wider Europe* has been defined,[163] is extraneous to the use of force. The tension between openness and closeness in the EU has been resolved with a combination of wide areas of inclusion entailed in open functional confines combined with patterns of exclusion in the migration domain. The generally open nature of the

[160] Michael Khodarkovsky, 'Russia's War in Ukraine: How the 19th Century Imperialism and 20th Century Fascism Found Home in the 21st Century Russia' (2022) 35 *The Journal of East Asian Affairs* 95, 106. The ensuing understanding and implementation of the *Russky mir* in the post-soviet space is entrenched in imperialist, colonial and fascist conceptions, on this see Timothy Snyder, *The Road to Unfreedom: Russia, Europe, America* (Tim Duggan Books, 2018).

[161] Brunk and Hakimi (n 159).

[162] See n 131.

[163] Natalia Drozdiak and Daryna Kranolutska 'Ukraine Belongs in the "European Family," EU Chief Says on Kyiv Trip' *Bloomberg.com* (8 April 2022), www.bloomberg.com/news/articles/2022-04-08/ukraine-belongs-in-european-family-eu-chief-says-on-kyiv-trip.

EU stems from its development as an antidote to the antagonism and the abuses of European nation-states especially in the first half of the twentieth century.[164] Although with rather mixed results,[165] the EU thus attempted to extend the internal paradigm of peaceful relations in the *Wider Europe*. As happens internally within EU membership law, in *Wider Europe*, diplomacy is somewhat replaced by law,[166] with the extension of EU law becoming a major component of the conduct of international relations.

Certainly, the extension of the EU's legal space operates through patterns of exclusion and not only of inclusion. Non-EU members participating in the *Wider Europe* are excluded from the decision-making process of the law they ultimately adopt. And citizens of non-EU countries can hardly benefit from the rights of EU citizenship law. Yet, the belonging to the European family allows third countries to participate in international networks of administrative cooperation sustained by EU funds.[167] These networks play a role in the modernisation of the legal and administrative system of third countries participating in the extended EU legal space. They also allow the governing of transnational issues at a wider level beyond the state. Significantly, moreover, although there are some indirect pressures to align to EU law, ensuing from the power and the size of the EU market,[168] these pressures mainly operate through conditionality and stand in stark opposition to violent coercion. The prospects of EU membership can be seen as a driver for change and as a fulfilment of the aspirations of the EU's partners in *Wider Europe*.

The events in Ukraine have revealed not only the political covenant underlying *Wider Europe* but shed light also on the political covenant of EU membership law itself, and its limits. When it comes to military deterrence, the political covenants promoted by the EU are underdeveloped at best. Indeed, although the EU has devised complex financing mechanisms to support Ukraine's defence efforts,[169]

[164] Joseph HH Weiler, 'The Transformation of Europe' (1991) 100 *The Yale Law Journal* 24o3.

[165] Charlemagne, 'Europe's Ring of Fire' *The Economist* (20 September 2014), www.economist.com/europe/2014/09/20/europes-ring-of-fire.

[166] Especially for the internal sphere, see Jozef Bátora, 'Does the European Union Transform the Institution of Diplomacy?' (2005) 12 *Journal of European Public Policy* 44.

[167] For an overview of the packages of EU financial assistance to Ukraine both before and after the war, see neighbourhood-enlargement.ec.europa.eu/european-neighbourhood-policy/countries-region/ukraine_en. In the Commission Opinion on Ukraine's membership application (n 132) 3–4, the Commission noted that 'The EU has provided significant financial assistance to Ukraine, which over the years 2014 to 2021 amounted to EUR 1.7 billion in grants under the European Neighbourhood Instrument, EUR 5.6 billion under five macro-financial assistance programmes in the form of loans, EUR 194 million in humanitarian aid and EUR 355 million from foreign policy instruments'.

[168] Chad Damro, 'Market Power Europe' (2012) 19 *Journal of European Public Policy* 682; Anu Bradford, *The Brussels Effect: How the European Union Rules the World* (Oxford University Press, 2020).

[169] Support has been given under the European Peace Facility Council Decision (CFSP) 2021/519, [2021] OJ L102/14. See in particular Council Decision (CFSP) 338/2022 on an assistance measure under the European Peace Facility for the supply to the Ukrainian Armed Forces of military equipment, [2022] OJ L 60/1 and Council Decision (CFSP) 2022/339 on an assistance measure under the European Peace Facility to support the Ukrainian Armed Forces, [2022] OJ L 60/6. See further the Commission proposal for a 'Regulation on establishing the Act in Support of Ammunition Production' COM(2023) 237 final, 2023/0140 (COD).

and set up an unprecedented sanction regime targeting Russian entities,[170] its absence as a veritable security actor has been blatant. This certainly constitute a noble feature of the EU project especially as the Union was born from the ashes of military devastation in the continent; but it now also stands out as a limit of the EU to defend and uphold its values and interests, not the least through deterrence. Interestingly, the EU–Russia PCA continues to be formally in force. The EU relied on Article 99 of the Agreement to adopt the complex set of sanctions targeting entities and institutions in Russia.[171] In the relevant EU documents, EU–Russia relations are described as 'strained since the illegal annexation of Crimea' in 2014 with the remaining areas of cooperation suspended after the armed aggression of Ukraine in 2022.[172]

At the time of writing, it seems that the destiny of Ukraine and its belonging to the 'European Family' or to a distorted and dreadful implementation of the *Russky mir* is being decided on the battlefield, with the appalling toll of human losses it entails. The destiny of Ukraine will shape the future of a *Wider* or *Narrower Europe*. The war is further fragmenting and deteriorating increasingly precarious geopolitical equilibria and is bringing to the fore the profound inadequacy of the Union's capacity of deterrence as a geopolitical actor.

VII. Conclusions

The chapter has construed Ukraine as a key geographic, conceptual and legal borderland for understanding the geopolitical tenor of the extension of the EU's legal space. Ukraine has been a frontrunner in the ENP and its path in *Wider Europe* has been convoluted due to the Kremlin's competing claims to authority in its 'Near Abroad'. The tortuous process of signature of the new-generation EU-Ukraine AA reflected the strong influence of the Kremlin in the orientations of the Yanukovych's regime. The sealing of the 'European choice' of the Ukrainian people, with the Revolution of Dignity and the events in Maidan, delineated a clear path towards the EU sanctioned by the eventual conclusion of the Association Agreement. The techniques of extension of the EU's legal space of the Agreement govern Ukraine's gravitation around the EU legal order. The DCFTA chapters represent a far-reaching paradigm of EU neighbourhood law, with EU market access envisaged in some specific domains, such as trade in services and right of

[170] Frank Hoffmeister, 'Strategic Autonomy in the European Union's External Relations' (2023) 60 *Common Market Law Review* 667; Luigi Lonardo, 'Weapons, Humanitarian Assistance, Sanctions: A Legal Analysis of the EU's Immediate Response to the Russian Invasion of Ukraine of 2022' (2022) 47 *European Law Review* 410.

[171] See Case C-72/15 *Rosneft*, EU:C:2017:236. See also Christophe Hillion, 'The EU External Action as Mandate to Uphold the Rule of Law Outside and inside the Union' (2023) 29 *Columbia Journal of European Law* 228, 237.

[172] European Parliament, Russia Factsheet, June 2023, www.europarl.europa.eu/erpl-app-public/factsheets/pdf/en/FTU_5.6.3.pdf.

establishment. The innovative nature of the Agreement emerges from the dispute settlement mechanism governing some of the DCFTA's chapters and from the enshrining of ENP conditionality of EU *acquis* incorporation into a legally binding framework originally detached from EU accession. As the next chapters of this work will show, the distinctive dispute settlement mechanism of some of the DCFTA's chapters amounting to an institutional *renvoi* to the CJEU has been used in other arrangements of EU neighbourhood law. This highlights the value of *Wider Europe* as an analytical concept capturing the interplay of law and diplomacy in a variety of EU's proximity policy.

The EU's responses to the Russian aggression in Ukraine have further diluted the confines among the different proximity policies in the *Wider Europe* framework, with the EU granting the candidate country status to the Eastern Partners of the EU. Tragically, the Ukrainian future in *Wider Europe* will be largely decided on the battlefield. While the war is certainly not the terrain for the expression of the political covenant of *Wider Europe*, it is the principal venue for the expression of the Kremlin's stance on the *Russkiy mir*. By precluding Ukraine from claiming and developing an identity distinct from the one of Russia, the Kremlin's grasp on the *Russkiy mir* is frustrating with violence the Ukrainian aspirations and its 'European choice'.

In the EU, the enlargement momentum brought about by the war is orienting *Wider Europe* towards the East. This is in line with the interplay of law and geography resulting from the constitutional mandate of Article 49 TEU. Yet the Union's capacity to make a difference in a deteriorating wartime scenario and meet the increased membership expectations of its Eastern friends appears limited.

7

Narrower Europe? The EU's Relations with the UK and Switzerland Through *Brexit*

I. Introduction

This chapter addresses the significance of *Brexit* for *Wider Europe. Brexit* has questioned the belief in an ever-expanding Union membership and has challenged the inevitability of the EU's proximity relations based on patterns of gravitation around the EU legal order. Yet this chapter brings to the fore how EU neighbourhood law has played a role not only in the process of withdrawal, but also in the EU–UK future relations pertaining to Northern Ireland. The UK withdrawal and the EU's desire to avoid *à la carte* involvements in the EU internal market have led the EU to rationalise its bilateral partnerships by clarifying the balance between benefits and obligations for third country participation in *Wider Europe*. This has been particularly the case of Switzerland (section II). In that light, the chapter discusses the evolution of EU–Switzerland convoluted relations (section II.A). A particular emphasis is placed on the techniques of extension of the EU's legal space in the framework of the EU–Swiss Free Movement of Persons Agreement (section II.B) and on the attempts to rationalise the fragmented EU–Swiss bilateral partnership (section II.C).

The core sections of the chapter are devoted to unravelling the purport of the *Brexit* process in the *Wider Europe* context (section III). By discussing the similarities between the neighbourhood clause enshrined in Article 8 TEU and the withdrawal clause of Article 50 TEU, the chapter illustrates how the UK's withdrawal has been embedded in techniques of retrenchment of the EU's legal space not dissimilar from those of the extension of the EU's legal space (section III.A). In the context of *Brexit*, the use of techniques of EU neighbourhood law is further examined with respect to the Withdrawal Agreement (section III.B) and to the Protocol on Ireland and Northern Ireland (section III.C). The chapter argues that both these arrangements are a faithful manifestation of the everything but institutions' formula characterising the *Wider Europe design*. The chapter then accounts for the progressive detachment of the EU–UK relations from the patterns of gravitation around the EU legal order proper to EU neighbourhood law. Indeed, while the Chequer's plan negotiated under Theresa May's Government would not significantly challenge the paradigm of extension of the EU's legal space (section III.D), the Trade and Cooperation Agreement negotiated by Boris Johnson's Government marks a rupture with the canonical forms of EU neighbourhood law and its techniques (section III.E). The more recent developments in EU–UK relations including the *Windsor Framework* are then discussed (section III.F). Finally the chapter offers some insights on the political covenant of EU membership and neighbourhood law inferred from *Brexit* (section IV).

II. The Swiss Conundrum and the EU's Quest for a Governance Framework

A. The Context of a Convoluted Relationship

The relationship between the EU and Switzerland features among the most far-reaching bilateral partnerships in *Wider Europe*. Its development has been rather convoluted. The initial fervour of the Swiss elites towards the EU project was in fact tempered by the negative result of a 1992 referendum concerning the Swiss participation in the EEA as a transitional stage towards EU membership.[1] Switzerland's 'dormant application' to join the EU was formally withdrawn only in 2016.[2] This indicates a not casual temporal intertwining of the development of the EU–Swiss relationship with the *Brexit* process. The non-participation of Switzerland in the EEA resulted in the Confederation's rather singular entanglement in the wider European legal space through a complex patchwork of bilateral agreements that started to operate alongside the 1972 Free Trade Agreement, which is still in force.[3]

The first package of Bilateral Agreements was signed in 1999. It encompassed the domains of free movement of persons (FMPA),[4] air transport,[5] land transport,[6] trade in agricultural products,[7] mutual recognition and conformity assessment,[8] government procurement,[9] and scientific and technological cooperation.[10] Although

[1] Rapport du Conseil fédéral du 18 mai 1992 sur la question d'une adhésion de la Suisse à la Communauté européenne, Feuille Fédérale, 1992 III 1125. See also Benedikt Pirker, 'Switzerland and the EEA' in Finn Arnesen *et al Agreement on the European Economic Area* (CH Beck, 2018) 84.

[2] Hortense Goulard 'Switzerland Withdraws Application to Join the EU' (*Politico*, 15 June 2016), www.politico.eu/article/switzerland-withdraws-application-to-join-the-eu.

[3] EU–Switzerland FTA [1972] OJ L 300/189.

[4] Now amended, EU–Switzerland Agreement on the Free Movement of Persons [2009] OJ L 353/ 71; hereinafter 'EU–Switzerland FMPA'.

[5] EU–Switzerland Air Transport Agreement, [2002] OJ L 114/73; see further ch 5 of this work.

[6] EU–Switzerland Agreement on the Carriage of Goods and Passengers by Rail and Road, [2002] OJ L 114/91.

[7] EU Switzerland Agreement on trade in agricultural products [2002] OJ L 114/132.

[8] EU–Switzerland Agreement on mutual recognition in relation to conformity assessment [2002] OJ L 114/369.

[9] Agreement between the European Community and the Swiss Confederation on certain aspects of government procurement [2002] OJ L 114/430.

[10] EU–Switzerland Agreement on Scientific and Technological Cooperation [2002] OJ L 114/468. See more recently the Agreement for scientific and technological cooperation between the European Union and European Atomic Energy Community and the Swiss Confederation associating the Swiss Confederation to Horizon 2020, [2014] OJ L 370/3.

mostly covering economic domains, the relevant EU acts for the conclusion of the agreements were adopted pursuant to the overarching association legal basis, now enshrined in Article 217 TFEU.[11] The special nature of the EU's bilateral relations with Switzerland arises in light of the operation of both formal substantive *renvois* to EU law present in the different agreements and of processes of mimetic imitation of EU law. These processes are referred to as 'autonomous adaptation' whereby Switzerland 'approaches or aligns Swiss law with the relevant EU law despite the absence of any legal obligation to do so'.[12] Legislative mimetism to EU law is also mediated by Swiss participation in the EFTA. Indeed, Swiss courts are often inspired by the case law of the EFTA Court when interpreting extended EU law, while not obliged to do so. This has led Pirker to speak of a 'triple parallelism' between EFTA norms, norms in the bilateral agreements, and the EEA norms.[13] For its complex and fragmented articulation, the EU–Swiss bilateral law has been eloquently characterised as 'complex, almost beyond comprehension'.[14]

The above-described fragmented pattern of extension of the EU's legal space has hardly encountered the favour of the EU institutions. In 2014, the Council brought to the fore the need for an overarching institutional framework agreement (InstA) presiding over the patchwork of sectoral relations. The Council stressed that 'a precondition for further developing the sectoral approach remain[ed] the establishment of a common institutional framework for existing and future agreements through which Switzerland participates in the EU's Single Market'.[15] The momentum for the InstA negotiations grew progressively as the EU–Swiss negotiation became intertwined with the Brexit talks and the ensuing EU's emphasis on the indivisibility of the four freedoms.[16] The requests made on the EU side have been compellingly summarised by Tobler in four points:

> 1) a system of continued updating of the bilateral market access law in view of changes in the relevant EU law; 2) an interpretation of this law in line with the case law of the

[11] See for instance Decision 2002/309/EC, Euratom as regards the Agreement on Scientific and Technological Cooperation, of 4 April 2002 on the conclusion of seven Agreements with the Swiss Confederation, [2002] OJ L 114/1. The substantive legal basis was Art 310 TEC and the procedural Art 300 TEC, now respectively Arts 217 and 218 TFEU. See further Christa Tobler, 'The EU–Swiss Sectoral Approach Under Pressure: Not Least Because of Brexit' in Stefan Lorenzmeier, Roman Petrov and Christoph Vedder (eds), *EU External Relations Law: Shared Competences and Shared Values in Agreements Between the EU and Its Eastern Neighbourhood* (Springer, 2021) 108.

[12] Christa Tobler, 'A Look at the EEA from Switzerland' in EFTA Court, *The EEA and the EFTA court: decentred integration* (Hart Publishing, 2014) 41–42.

[13] Pirker (n 1) 8.

[14] Andrea Ott, 'Free Movement Rights in an Enlarged European Union' in Bruno de Witte, Andrea Ott and Ellen Vos, *Between flexibility and disintegration: the trajectory of differentiation in EU law* (Edward Elgar, 2017) 170; Guillaume Van der Loo, *The EU–Ukraine Association Agreement and Deep and Comprehensive Free Trade Area: A New Legal Instrument for EU Integration without Membership* (Brill Nijhoff, 2016) 357; Adam Łazowski, 'The End of Chocolate Box-Style Integration? EU–Swiss Relations after the Referendum' (2014) CEPS Paper.

[15] See for instance Council of the EU, 'Conclusions on a homogeneous extended single market and EU relations with Non-EU Western European countries', General Affairs Council meeting, Brussels, 16 December 2014.

[16] For a discussion on the indivisibility of the four freedoms see Editorial Comments, 'Is the Indivisibility of the Four Freedoms a Principle of EU Law?' (2019) 56 *Common Market Law Review* 1189. See contra Stephen Weatherill, 'The Several Internal Markets' (2017) 36 *Yearbook of European Law* 125.

European Court of Justice on the same EU law matters; 3) an effective mechanism to supervise the application of this law; 4) a supranational agreement for resolution of disputes between parties.[17]

B. *Wider Europe* Techniques in the Free Movement of Persons Framework

The Air Transport Agreement[18] and the Free Movement of Persons Agreement (FMPA) were the most significant agreements concluded in the first round of Bilaterals. The first bilateral packages extended the EU law rights and obligations associated with the free movement of workers and self-employed persons to Switzerland. It also aimed to facilitate the provisions of services, especially of a brief duration. The FMPA was later complemented with additional agreements on the free movement of people relating to the Swiss Confederation's association with the implementation, application and development of the Schengen *acquis*,[19] and the Dublin system.[20]

As with the other agreements included in the Bilaterals I, the FMPA is considered a 'static' agreement. The EU legislation at the basis of the substantive *renvois* should be applied taking into account of the CJEU's case law prior to the date of the signature of the Agreement.[21] The general EU–Swiss free movement scheme, however, risks being oversimplified under the 'static' label. First, the FMPA has been updated with several pieces of legislation related to free movement, including the already mentioned Regulation 833/2004 on the coordination of social security systems.[22] Second, the satellite Bilaterals (especially the Schengen Agreement) feature highly in the echelons of intensity of the extension of the EU's legal space for their far-reaching substantive and organisational interactions with the EU legal order. The EU–Swiss Schengen agreement is premised upon the willingness to associate the Swiss Confederation 'on equal footing with Iceland and Norway in the implementation, application, and development of the Schengen acquis'. This has led 'to set up a committee in accordance with the institutional model established for the association of Iceland and Norway'.[23] The overarching substantive *renvois* to the EU legal order referred to in Article 2(1)–(2) of the Schengen Agreement are complemented

[17] Tobler (n 12) 543.

[18] See ch 5 of this work.

[19] EU–Switzerland Agreement on application and development of the Schengen *acquis* [2008] OJ L 53/52; hereinafter 'EU–Switzerland Schengen Agreement'.

[20] Agreement between the European Community and the Swiss Confederation concerning the criteria and mechanisms for establishing the State responsible for examining a request for asylum lodged in a Member State or in Switzerland [2008] OJ L 53/5.

[21] EU–Switzerland FMPA, Art 16(2).

[22] For a list of the updated *acquis* incorporated see the 'Recueil de textes juridiques sur les accords sectoriels avec l'UE, Accord du 21 juin 1999 entre la Confédération suisse d'une part, et la Communauté européenne et ses Etats membres, d'autre part, sur la libre circulation des personnes' at www.fedlex.admin.ch/fr/sector-specific-agreements/EU-acts-register/7.

[23] EU–Swiss Schengen Agreement, recitals 6 and 9.

by mechanisms ensuring the dynamic adaptation of the extended Schengen regime to Switzerland.[24] Some room for manoeuvre is left to Switzerland with a view to fulfilling its constitutional requirements to hold referenda to validate the adoption of the amended *acquis*. The Agreement sets up precise deadlines for this process. In case Switzerland does not accept the adoption of the new EU *acquis*, the Agreement may be terminated unless the Mixed Committee established thereof considers otherwise.[25] This applies also if Swiss refusal is due to the result of a referendum.

The substantive gravitation of the EU–Swiss Schengen framework is complemented by shallow interpretative *renvois* intended to ensure the 'most uniform possible application and interpretation' of the *acquis* referred to by the Agreement. With that aim, 'the Mixed Committee shall keep under constant review developments in the case-law of the Court of Justice'.[26] Contrarily to most of the EU–Swiss Bilaterals, conformity of interpretation is not formally limited to the pre-signature case law: account is taken also of the dynamic evolution of the *acquis*.[27] Yet, no specific mechanism of organisational interaction with the EU legal order is envisaged for the implementation and the enforcement of the Agreement. In case of failure to settle the dispute within the Mixed Committee, no appeal is envisaged, and the Agreement will be terminated.[28] The focus of the InstA would also be placed on ensuring greater organisational interaction between the EU legal order and the regimes extending EU law to Switzerland.

Together with the Air Transport Agreement, the free movement of persons framework remains thus rather exceptional in its complex patchwork of EU–Swiss mostly static bilateral agreements.[29] Its special nature also arises from the fact that it has been granted direct effect by Swiss tribunals,[30] while some provisions of the EU–Swiss Free Trade Agreement have not.[31]

C. Streamlining the Techniques of the Extension of the EU Legal Space Throughout the Bilateral Partnership

The EU's focus on the negotiation of a framework institutional arrangement has arisen from the desire to rationalise Swiss participation in the extended EU's legal space by clarifying the balance to be struck between benefit and obligations. The negotiations of the new institutional framework was intended to enhance

[24] ibid Arts 2(3), 6 and 7(2).
[25] ibid Art 4.
[26] ibid Art 8.
[27] See ibid Arts 4(4) and 9.
[28] ibid Art 10.
[29] The Bilaterals also encompass a second package concluded in 2004. For an overview see Pirker (n 1).
[30] See in this respect BGE 129 II 249 s 251.
[31] For instance in cases concerning Art13 FTA on quantitative restrictions on import. BGE 105 II 49, and a case concerning competition BGE 104 IV 175. For a discussion see Christa Tobler, Jeroen Hardenbol and Balázs Mellár, 'Internal Market beyond the EU: EEA and Switzerland' (European Parliament, 2010); Alan F Tatham, 'Diffusing EU Law beyond the Borders of the Union: The Judicialization of the European Trading Area' (2014) 81 *Colombia Internacional* 27. See further ch 9 of this work.

Switzerland's binding commitment to incorporate EU law in its legal system and increase the mechanisms of organisational interaction between the relevant bilateral agreements and the EU legal order. The EU's requests were mainly met with Switzerland's refusal to be entangled with the EU through specific monitoring and enforcement mechanisms along the lines of the EEA model.

The draft InstA aims to achieve greater legal certainty and equal treatment in the sectors of the internal market in which Switzerland participates. The InstA specifies the objective of ensuring 'legal certainty and homogeneity' in the application of the bilateral agreements thus in indirect deference to the EU legal order. It also envisages mechanisms to guarantee the dynamic evolution of the sectoral regimes by rapidly incorporating new EU legal acts into the agreements.[32] The semantics of the institutional arrangement oscillates between homogeneity,[33] harmonious application,[34] and uniform interpretation.[35] Article 4(2) InstA provides for the uniform interpretation of the extended EU rules in Switzerland. This provision requires uniform interpretation of the agreements in conformity with CJEU case law, both prior and after the date of their signature.[36]

To sustain these dynamic efforts of homogeneity and uniform interpretation, the draft Agreement establishes far-reaching mechanisms of organisational interactions between the EU–Swiss Agreements and the EU legal order. In disputes where the interpretation of (extended) EU law is at stake, the arbitral tribunal entrusted to resolve the dispute shall ask the CJEU to deliver a pronouncement on the issue which shall be binding on the arbitration panel.[37] The above-mentioned institutional *renvoi* to the CJEU is borrowed from the arrangement of the EU–Ukraine Association Agreement. It was also adopted in the EU–UK Withdrawal Agreement.[38] After the arbitration decision, if one of the parties believes considers that the other is not acting in conformity with the findings of the arbitration panel, remedial and compensatory measures are envisioned. These may also involve the suspension of the Agreement.

In addition to this, the InstA establishes procedural interactions to the benefit of Switzerland during the phases of preparation for EU legislative and delegated acts in the areas covered by the Agreement. These cover consultation of Swiss experts[39] and far-reaching involvement of Switzerland in procedures before the CJEU.[40] In this way, the EU attempts to counterbalance the pervasive substantive

[32] EU–Switzerland draft Institutional Framework Agreement, 'Accord Facilitant Les Relations Bilatérales Entre l'Union Européenne et La Confédération Suisse Dans Les Parties Du Marché Intérieur Auxquelles La Suisse Participe' (Institutional Agreement- Draft Text) (23 November 2018), www.eda.admin.ch/dam/dea/fr/documents/abkommen/Acccord-inst-Projet-de-texte_fr.pdf; hereinafter 'EU–Switzerland InstA', Art 5.

[33] EU– Switzerland InstA, Arts 5 and 8a.

[34] ibid Art 7.

[35] ibid Art 4.

[36] ibid Art 4(2).

[37] ibid Art 10(3).

[38] See further section III.B of this chapter.

[39] EU–Switzerland InstA, Art 12(1), (4)–(5).

[40] ibid Art 10(4).

renvois and organisational interactions with the EU legal order with Switzerland's enhanced participation in *Wider Europe*.

Several issues related to the InstA, considered contentious by Switzerland, have led to the stalling of negotiations. They mainly revolve around the EU Citizenship Directive,[41] the protection of labour and the state aid regimes.[42] The EU Citizenship Directive[43] has been a bone of contention between the EU and Switzerland for several years. In fact, Switzerland rejected the update of the FMPA with this piece of legislation. The Directive at issue relates both to economically active and inactive persons, and also includes equal treatment provisions for social assistance. Besides, it codifies the Court of Justice's rich case law on Union citizenship. This case law largely 'release(s) the rights of citizenship from economic considerations attached to freedom of movement in the realm of the internal market', embedding them in a more social dimension.[44] Switzerland does not intend to subscribe to this understanding of free movement. The European Commission's view is different. In the negotiations, the Commission maintained that the Directive should be part of the *acquis* included in the dynamic adaptation envisaged by the draft Agreement.[45]

The overall partnership on the free movement of persons in Switzerland has been problematic. Tensions were exacerbated especially after the 2014 referendum following the 'Against Mass Immigration' initiative promoted by a Swiss nationalist party that used a discourse which was largely similar to the one that would shortly after fuel the *Brexit* process.[46] The referendum resulted in an amendment to the Swiss Constitution providing for the autonomous control of immigration of foreign nationals.[47] After a difficult political process, a compromise was found to implement the constitutional provisions without breaching the EU–Swiss FMPA.[48] Subsequent attempts to contest the FMPA and its related provisions on the basis of the new constitutional provisions through referenda have not produced any effect. This is either through failure to reach the minimum number of signatures for the referendum or due to a negative vote.[49]

[41] Directive 2004/38/EC on the right of citizens of the Union and their family members to move and reside freely within the territory of the Member States amending [2004] OJ L 158/77.

[42] Christa Tobler, 'Switzerland-EU: Whereto with the Draft Institutional Agreement?' (*EFTA-Studies*, 19 February 2020), www.efta-studies.org/post/whereto-with-the-draft-institutional-agreement.

[43] Directive 2004/38(41).

[44] Loïc Azoulai, '"Euro-Bonds" The Ruiz Zambrano Judgment or the Real Invention of EU Citizenship' (2011) 3 *Perspectives on federalism* 35.

[45] Tobler (n 42).

[46] Tobler (n 11) 118.

[47] Federal Constitution of Switzerland, Art 121a.

[48] Samuel Osborne and Matt Broomfield, 'Switzerland Waters down Immigration Referendum to Protect EU Relationship' *The Independent* (15 December 2016), www.independent.co.uk/news/world/europe/switzerland-immigration-referendum-result-reduce-water-down-protect-eu-relationship-migrant-a7476801.html.

[49] See Confédération suisse, Initiative populaire « Pour une immigration modérée » : Le 27 septembre 2020 les citoyennes et les citoyens ont refusé l'initiative populaire « Pour une immigration modérée (initiative de limitation) », www.admin.ch/gov/fr/accueil/documentation/votations/20200927/initiative-populaire-pour-une-immigration-moderee.html.

The InstA negotiation has been intertwined with salient political issues that are not limited to the free movement of persons. As a matter of fact, issue linkages in the InstA negotiations related to inter alia the regime of state aid strongly advocated by the EU;[50] the equivalence decision for the Swiss stock exchange pursuant to the MiFID II Directive[51] and MiFIR Regulation.[52] The reviewed adequacy determination pursuant to the GDPR has also been sensitive on a political plane.[53] While the adequacy determination pursuant to the Data Protection Directive is still in force,[54] the Commission's Implementing Decision on the equivalence of the legal and supervisory framework applicable to stock exchanges in Switzerland[55] is not. Moreover, in the context of the bilateral Agreement on Conformity Assessment with respect to the EU legislation on medical devices pursuant to Regulation (EU) No 2017/745,[56] parts of the EU–Switzerland Mutual Recognition Agreement should have been updated. The EU, pending progress on the conclusion of the InstA, has however proven unwilling to endorse the update.[57] For the same reasons the new equivalence decision pursuant to the GDPR has been delayed.[58] Besides, the unwillingness to conclude a draft institutional arrangement has had repercussion also on the research sector, with Switzerland being sidelined in the EU's research and education projects.[59]

III. *Brexit* and the Challenges to *Wider Europe*

A. The Legal Context of Withdrawal

Brexit certainly poses a major challenge to the *Wider Europe* design. From the outset of the withdrawal negotiations, the UK advocated for a 'bespoke' arrangement: the

[50] On State Aid see also EU–Switzerland InstA, Art 8b(3).

[51] Directive 2014/65/EU on markets in financial instruments [2014] OJ L 173/ 349.

[52] See specifically Regulation (EU) No 600/2014 of on markets in financial instruments [2014] OJ L 173/84, Arts 23 and 28(4).

[53] See Regulation (EU) 2016/679 on the protection of natural persons with regard to the processing of personal data and on the free movement of such data [2016] OJ L 119/1 (hereinafter 'GDPR'), Arts 45 and 97(2). Note that Switzerland already possesses an adequacy determination pursuant to Commission Decision (EC) 2000/520 of 26 July 2000 pursuant to Directive 95/46/EC of the European Parliament and of the Council on the adequacy of the protection provided by the safe harbour privacy principles and related frequently asked questions issued by the US Department of Commerce (notified under document number C(2000) 2441), [2000] OJ L 215/7.

[54] Now replaced by an adequacy decision pursuant to the GDPR.

[55] Commission Implementing Decision (EU) 2018/2047 of 20 December 2018 on the equivalence of the legal and supervisory framework applicable to stock exchanges in Switzerland in accordance with Directive 2014/65/EU of the European Parliament and of the Council [2018] OJ L 327/77.

[56] Regulation (EU) 2017/745 on medical devices [2017] OJ L 117/1.

[57] See Tobler (n 11) 117–18. See also Swiss Confederation, Federal Office of Public Health, Medical Devices Legislation, pending MRA update, www.bag.admin.ch/bag/en/home/medizin-und-forschung/heilmittel/revision-med-prod-verord-mepv.html.

[58] Tobler (n 42). The adequacy has been confirmed in European Commission, "Report on the first review of the functioning of adequacy decisions", COM(2024) 7 final.

[59] Universität Bern, 'Universities pay a high price for Switzerland's sidelining in the European Union's research and education projects', 25 January 2022, mediarelations.unibe.ch/media_releases/2022/

existing models of EU proximity relations based on the *Wider Europe* design were not considered suitable by the UK negotiators for the EU–UK future relations. The UK's quest to 'tak[e] back control' was predicated upon the desire to eschew the EU's regulatory and legislative magnetism of the EU legal order.

Notwithstanding this, the *Brexit* process has often been characterised by techniques of EU neighbourhood law similar to those operating for the extension of the EU's legal space. Reflecting on the correspondence between Article 8 and Article 50 TEU helps us to expound the similarity of techniques of the extension and retrenchment of the EU's legal space. As aptly noted by Hillion, Article 50 TEU serves to 'manage the reduction of the [EU's *acquis*] *geographical* scope of application'.[60] Article 8 of the TEU mandates shaping the EU's geographical neighbourhood according to EU values and norms.[61] Although operating in the opposite direction, Article 50 TEU shares the ultimate rationale of the extension of the EU's legal space. It is concerned with a geographical reconfiguration of the EU's legal space whereby the EU *acquis* is not extended but reduced in its geographical scope of application.[62] The correspondence between Articles 8 and 50 TEU stems also from their horizontal nature,[63] covering potentially all the policies of the Union. Yet, notable differences may be found in their procedural dimensions. The neighbourhood clause is explicit with regard to the values of the Union as being the basis of neighbourhood partnerships, while silent on the procedure. Instead, the withdrawal clause is largely silent on the principles and substantive aspects, while more detailed on the procedural dimension of withdrawal.

The similarities between the *Brexit* process and the law of the EU's proximity policies emerged also on the methodological plane. The sequencing of negotiations was based on a phased conditionality approach.[64] The European Council had clarified that in the process of withdrawal, the settlement of 'the disentanglement of the United Kingdom from the Union' and from the rights and obligations deriving from its membership status was paramount. Only after 'sufficient progress' had been attained on disentanglement issues would the European Council 'allow

media_releases_2022/universities_pay_a_high_price_for_switzerland_s_sidelining_in_the_european_union_s_research_and_education_projects/index_eng.html.

[60] Christophe Hillion, 'Withdrawal under Article 50 TEU: An Integration-Friendly Process' (2018) 55 *Common Market Law Review* 29, 35; emphasis in the original.

[61] Christophe Hillion, 'Anatomy of EU Norm Export towards the Neighbourhood: The Impact of Article 8 TEU' in Peter Van Elsuwege and Roman Petrov (eds), *Legislative approximation and application of EU law in the Eastern neighbourhood of the European Union: towards a common regulatory space?* (Routledge, 2014).

[62] On the geographical scope of application of extended EU law see the CJEU's findings in *Opinion 1/00* on the European Common Aviation Area EU:C:2002:231, para 3. See further ch 5 of this work.

[63] The Council directives qualify Art 50 TEU as 'conferring on the Union an exceptional horizontal competence to cover in this agreement all matters necessary to arrange the withdrawal'. Council of the EU, 'Directives for the negotiation of an agreement with the United Kingdom of Great Britain and Northern Ireland setting out the arrangements for its withdrawal from the European Union', Brussels, 22 May 2017, XT 21016/17 ADD 1 REV 2, para 5.

[64] Hillion (n 60) 45 ff.

negotiations to proceed to the next phase'.[65] The novelty in the conditionality paradigm brought about by *Brexit* could be found in the enhanced role of the European Council. In fact, this chief EU political institution was also entrusted with monitoring tasks. This aspect, although resulting from the specificities of Article 50 of the TEU, is rather atypical when considered against the background of the procedural canons for the negotiation and conclusion of international agreements enshrined in Article 218 TFEU.

The significance of the procedural dimension of withdrawal was stressed by the EU through the requirement of unity in the EU negotiating process. The European Council emphasised that the EU would 'act as one' so that the Union 'would approach the negotiations with unified positions, and [would] engage with the United Kingdom exclusively through the channels set out in [the European Council] guidelines and in the negotiating directives'.[66] The emphasis of unity results also from the fact that the Withdrawal Agreement and the EU–UK Trade and Cooperation Agreement have not been concluded as mixed agreements, as is very often the case for agreements in place the context of the EU's proximity policies.[67]

B. The EU–UK Withdrawal Agreement and the *Wider Europe* Techniques

The place of the *Brexit* process in the *Wider Europe* templates is governed by the principle of autonomy of EU law. This holds true both for decision-making and the judicial dimension. The principle of autonomy has located the *Brexit* process within the frameworks of EU proximity policies. In that regard, the European Council's Guidelines made it clear the EU's willingness to preserve EU 'autonomy as regards its decision making as well as the role of the Court of Justice of the European Union'.[68] The European Council stressed the demarcation between the internal and the external highlighting how the relationship between the Union and a non-Member State 'cannot offer the same benefits as Union membership'. It further highlighted that any arrangement with the UK would be based 'on a balance of rights and obligations, and ensure a level playing field.'[69] In that light, the EU–UK Withdrawal Agreement (WA) of 17 October 2019 entered into force on 1 February 2020 can be scrutinised with the same analytical tools adopted for the study of the extension of the EU's legal space. As a matter of fact, the WA is

[65] European Council, European Council (Art 50) guidelines for Brexit negotiations, Brussels, 29 April 2017, EUCO XT 20004/17, Part II, para 4.

[66] ibid para 2.

[67] With the notable exceptions of the Energy Community Treaty, [2006] OJ L 198/18, and the Transport Community Treaty, [2017], OJ L 278/3.

[68] European Council (n 65).

[69] ibid. para 1.

largely predicated on techniques of geographical reconfiguration of the EU's legal space in a phase of transition from EU membership to non-membership.

With respect to the substantive *renvois* to EU law, Article 6 EU–UK WA clarifies the scope and the nature of the references to Union law. These are numerous and can be found in all of the chapters of the Agreement. Moreover, Article 127 EU–UK WA can be construed as an interpretative *renvois* as it mandates that the provisions of EU law referred to in the Agreement shall be interpreted and applied according to the principles of Union law.[70] Remarkably, the Agreement also provides that 'the provisions of Union law made applicable [by the Agreement] shall produce in respect of and in the United Kingdom the same legal effects as those which they produce within the Union and its Member States'.[71] In a manner comparable to what happens in other institutional arrangements of EU neighbourhood law, substantive *renvois* are reinforced by mechanisms ensuring the dynamic adaptation of the neighbourhood regime to the evolving EU *acquis*.[72]

The mismatch between the geographical scope of application of EU law and the decision-making structures is an additional feature drawing the WA near to the experiences of extension of the EU's legal space. Indeed, the pervasive extension of the EU's legal space to the UK as a non-member of the EU is not matched by an extension of the EU's institutional structure: the UK representatives were excluded from the EU law decision-making. To be sure, the Agreement is managed, as it is usually the case in EU association agreements, by a Joint Committee. However, the UK representatives have no say in matters of EU law. Article 128(3) WA reads: 'during the transitional period, provisions of the Treaties which grant institutional rights to Member States … shall be understood as *not* including the United Kingdom'.[73] The organisational interaction between the withdrawal regime and the EU legal order is overarching: the EU institutions are granted supervision and enforcement rights in the UK in the transition period. Significantly, Article 7 clarifies that for the purposes of the Agreement, the references to Member States and relevant competent authorities shall be understood as including the UK *except* with regards to 'participation in the decision-making and the attendance in meetings of the institutions'. These arrangements led Dougan to single out the 'UK's institutional non-existence'.[74]

One could hardly think of a better application of Prodi's *Wider Europe* formula 'everything but institutions' than the operation of the EU–UK Withdrawal Agreement. Indeed, the 'everything' part of the formula applies also to direct effect and primacy. While in the transition period the UK was left outside of the EU institutional machinery, the UK was treated de facto as a member when it comes to the

[70] EU–UK Withdrawal Agreement (hereinafter 'EU–UK WA') [2019] OJ C 384I/1, Art 4(3).
[71] EU–UK WA, Art 4(1).
[72] ibid Arts 6(1) and 36(1).
[73] Emphasis added.
[74] Michael Dougan, 'So Long, Farewell, Auf Wiedersehen, Goodbye: The UK's Withdrawal Package' (2020) 57 *Common Market Law Review* 631, 659.

application of EU law, and the bindingness and enforceability of judgments and orders.[75] The role of the European Commission within the Agreement is significant for monitoring the UK's fulfilment of its obligations especially under Part IV of the Agreement on the transition period.[76] The same applies to state aid and competition procedures.[77] The WA also envisages participation of the European Commission in pending cases in UK where the interpretation of the Agreement is at stake.[78] Moreover, Article 131 WA sanctions the authority of EU institutions and bodies, including the CJEU, in the UK during the transition period. The organisational interactions between legal regimes continue after the transition period especially with regard to new state aid and European Anti-Fraud office procedures.[79] Similarly, the jurisdiction of the Court of Justice will be maintained after the transition period in the second part of the Withdrawal Agreement concerning Citizens' Rights.[80]

On the plane of organisational interactions, the dispute settlement mechanism occupies a prominent role. It is the product of a compromise between the CJEU's exclusive jurisdiction and interpretation on matters of Union law pursuant to Article 344 of the TFEU on the one hand, and the UK's desire to end the 'direct' jurisdiction of the Court of Justice on the other.[81] Disputes arising from the implementation or application of the Agreement should primarily be dealt with by the Joint Committee through diplomatic consultations.[82] Only if no solution is found, the dispute may be brought before an arbitration panel. The Agreement sets out detailed provisions on the establishment of the arbitration panel,[83] on its functioning, the timeframe of the procedure before it,[84] and on compliance with its rulings. The WA clarifies that rulings of the arbitration panel shall be binding on the Union and the United Kingdom under international law.[85]

The drafting of the dispute-settlement mechanism in the EU–UK WA borrows from the EU–Ukraine DCFTA: when disputes concern matters of Union law, the 'arbitration panel shall not decide on any such question' but it 'shall request the Court of Justice of the European Union to give a ruling on the question … which shall be binding on the arbitration panel'.[86] This also extends to cases where the CJEU finds that the UK has failed to fulfil its obligation under the Treaties or the Withdrawal Agreement with respect to orders and judgments of the CJEU.[87] It has

[75] EU–UK WA, Arts 86–90.
[76] ibid Art 87.
[77] ibid Arts 92–93.
[78] ibid Art 162.
[79] ibid Art 93.
[80] ibid Art 158(1).
[81] UK Parliament, European Union Committee, Dispute resolution and enforcement after Brexit, 15th Report of Session 2017–19 (3 May 2018) HL Paper 130, para 30.
[82] EU–UK WA, Art 169.
[83] ibid Art 171.
[84] ibid Art 173.
[85] ibid Art 175, see also Arts 177 and 178 respectively on the review of measures taken to comply with the arbitration panel ruling and on temporary remedies in case of non-compliance.
[86] ibid Art 174(1).
[87] ibid Art 174 (2) and Arts 89(2) and 86–87.

been noted that the role of the CJEU is stronger than the one envisaged by the draft agreement for the Union's accession to the European Convention of Human Rights: the latter did not envisage the bindingness of the CJEU's ruling on the Strasbourg Court.[88]

C. The Protocol on Ireland and Northern Ireland (PINI): Techniques for Extending the EU's Legal Space

The techniques of extension of the EU's legal space informing the *Brexit* process are particularly apparent in the Protocol on Ireland and Northern Ireland (PINI). The Protocol came last in a series of attempts to avoid a 'hard border' between Northern Ireland and the Republic of Ireland. Both parties wished to safeguard the Belfast Good Friday Agreement that succeeded in managing the violent tensions characterising the Northern Ireland conflict in the second half of the twentieth century. As the European Council Guidelines put it, the balance to be struck would require 'flexible and imaginative solutions' aiming to avoid 'a hard border, while respecting the integrity of the Union legal order'.[89]

The original draft protocol envisaged Northern Ireland to be included in the EU's customs territory.[90] A 'common regulatory area comprising the Union and the United Kingdom'[91] was therefore envisioned. Boris Johnson's cabinet, however, soon demonstrated its aversion to the arrangement. From the UK's perspective, the risk would have been that of a contractual relationship entailing gravitation around the EU legal order. In a letter addressed to the President of the European Council, Johnson posited that the 'backstop' arrangement envisaged for Northern Ireland would lock 'the UK, potentially indefinitely, into an international treaty which will bind [the UK] into a customs union and which applies large areas of single market legislation in Northern Ireland'. Instead 'the point of [UK] exit' was to enact laws and regulations which 'will potentially diverge from those of the EU'.[92]

In pursuance to the revised Protocol, Northern Ireland is de jure part of the United Kingdom's customs territory,[93] while de facto embedded in the law and practices of the EU customs zone, especially for goods liable to move to the

[88] Joris Larik, 'Decision-Making and Dispute Settlement' in Federico Fabbrini, *The withdrawal agreement* (Oxford University Press, 2020) 206. See also Council of Europe, Fifth Negotiation Meeting between the CDDH and the Ad Hoc Negotiation Group and the European Commission on the Accession of the European Union to the European Convention on Human Rights, Final report to the CDDH, Strasbourg, 10 June 2013, Appendix V: Draft explanatory report to the Agreement on the Accession of the European Union to the Convention for the Protection of Human Rights and Fundamental Freedoms, pt 68.

[89] European Council (n 65) Part III, para 11.

[90] EU–UK Protocol on Ireland and Northern Ireland, [2020] OJ L 29/7 (hereinafter 'EU–UK PINI'), Art 4(1).

[91] ibid Art 3.

[92] Prime Minister Boris Johnson letter to Donald Tusk: 19 August 2019, available at www.gov.uk/government/publications/pm-letter-to-donald-tusk-19-august-2019.

[93] EU–UK PINI, Art 4.

Republic of Ireland.[94] *Renvois* cover matters such as customs, free movement of goods, where Articles 30 and 110 of the TFEU will remain applicable[95] as well as the relevant EU legislation.[96] Extensive *renvois* are envisaged in customs and trade law, manufacture and marketing of goods as well as VAT.[97] The placement of goods on the market of Northern Ireland is governed by Articles 34 and 36 of the TFEU for goods imported from the Union.[98] Moreover, the PINI allows for a more dynamic adaptation to the evolution of EU law with respect to the EU–UK WA. In that regard, Article 13(3) establishes that 'where the Protocol makes reference to a Union act, that reference shall be read as referring to that Union act *amended or replaced*'.[99]

The extension of the EU *acquis* to the territory of Northern Ireland is not dissimilar from the instances of extension of the EU's legal space in the proximity. Notwithstanding the formal elimination of the backstop and the fact that Great Britain is outside of the EU customs union, the absence of a hard border between Ireland and Northern Ireland entails a significant degree of regulatory alignment to EU law. The UK Government's explanatory memorandum to the Protocol recognises that Article 5 thereof 'establishes a single regulatory zone on the Island of Ireland' and that 'This involves Northern Ireland aligning with … specific EU regulations … on agri-food products and manufactured goods'.[100] A number of more detailed substantive *renvois* to EU law can be found in Annex 2 to the PINI.

The Protocol establishes that in the EU domains singled out above, the acts of EU institutions 'shall produce in respect of and in the United Kingdom the same legal effects as those which they produce within the Union and its Member States',[101] including primacy and direct effect.[102] Furthermore, in contrast to the Withdrawal Agreement and the previous 'backstop', the Protocol was not designed as a temporary arrangement.[103] As a matter of fact, the EU–UK Trade and Cooperation Agreement presiding over the future relationship between the EU and the UK does not change the regime in place between the EU and Northern Ireland. Although with minor operational developments, the Protocol continues to be in force.

[94] Paola Mariani and Giorgio Sacerdoti, 'Trade in Goods and Level Playing Field' in Federico Fabbrini (ed), *The Law & Politics of Brexit: Volume III* (Oxford University Press, 2021) 95–96.
[95] EU–UK PINI, Art 5(5).
[96] ibid Art 5(3)–(4).
[97] ibid Arts 5, 7, 8 and 10.
[98] ibid Art 7(1).
[99] Emphasis added. See further discussion in section III.F of this chapter.
[100] UK Government, Explainer for the new Ireland/Northern Ireland Protocol and the Political Declaration on the Future Relationship, 18 October 2019, para 15, assets.publishing.service.gov.uk/government/uploads/system/uploads/attachment_data/file/840653/EXPLAINER_FOR_THE_NEW_IRELAND_NORTHERN_IRELAND_PROTOCOL_AND_THE_POLITICAL_DECLARATION_ON_THE_FUTURE_RELATIONSHIP.pdf.
[101] EU–UK PINI, Art 12 (5).
[102] Dougan (n 74) 685.
[103] ibid 687; Oliver Garner, 'New Irish Protocol Could Lead to Indefinite Jurisdiction of EU Court in the UK' *Scottish Legal News* (31 October 2019), www.scottishlegal.com/article/oliver-garner-new-irish-protocol-could-lead-to-indefinite-jurisdiction-of-eu-court-in-the-uk.

A notable organisational element of the PINI relates to the implementation, supervision and enforcement of Union law. Article 12 PINI provides that 'the authorities of the United Kingdom shall be responsible for implementing and applying the provisions of Union law made applicable [by] the protocol to and in the United Kingdom with respect to Northern Ireland'. As noted by Dougan, the fact that Union's borders will be policed by a third country is a remarkable concession in light of the complaints regarding the UK's abilities to tackle border frauds.[104] The tasks attributed to the UK institutions in the implementation of the PINI do not release the UK from its gravitation around the EU legal order. In fact, the extensive powers entrusted upon the UK authorities are corresponded by an equally overarching role envisaged for Union's institutions in the monitoring of the UK authorities' activities related to the implementation and applications of the provisions of Union law.[105] The organisational interaction between the international law regime envisaged by the Agreement is also evident with respect to the role that EU institutions enjoy in the domain of state aid,[106] technical regulations and certificates,[107] customs and movement of goods.[108]

The PINI envisages organisational interactions between the regime created by the Protocol and the EU legal order. This occurs via far reaching institutional *renvois*. Especially for the interpretation and application of extended EU law operated by the Protocol, the 'institutions, bodies, offices, and agencies of the Union in relation to the United Kingdom … shall have the powers conferred upon them by Union law' and that 'the Court of Justice … shall have the jurisdiction provided for in the Treaties in this respect'.[109] Also the system of CJEU's preliminary reference procedure pursuant to Article 267 of the TFEU applies to the UK with respect to the Protocol.[110] In light of the absence of a termination date for the PINI, the CJEU's jurisdiction over the UK pursuant to the Protocol is likely to remain permanent.[111] Such a pervasive institutional *renvoi* to the EU legal order is rather atypical even in the most developed forms of the extension of the EU's legal space. A distinctive trait of the PINI pertains to the mechanisms for democratic control of the arrangement. In fact, the PINI envisages a rather unique instrument for assessing the democratic viability of the Agreement over time: Article 18 PINI provides for the monitoring of the democratic consent of the application of the provisions of the Protocol providing for the extension of the EU's legal space.[112]

The PINI can be certainly regarded as an instrument of EU neighbourhood law. It presents several substantive *renvois* to EU law and far-reaching organisational interactions between the PINI regime and the EU legal order, including

[104] Dougan (n 74) 684. Case C-213/19 *Commission v UK*, EU:C:2022:167.
[105] See particularly EU–UK PINI, Art 12(2).
[106] ibid Art 10.
[107] ibid Art 7.
[108] ibid Art 5.
[109] ibid Art 12(4).
[110] ibid.
[111] Garner (n 103).
[112] In particular EU–UK PINI, Arts 5 and 7–10.

institutional *renvois* potentially extending to the whole of the UK.[113] The extent to which the UK will be in the position to significantly diverge from EU law in accordance with the *Brexit* rhetoric is doubted. Should the UK wish to fulfil its desire of regulatory divergence from the EU, this may well result in problems in the viability of the PINI and more generally of the UK single market.[114]

It comes thus with no surprise that the PINI has occupied the centre stage of the negotiating battles in the post-*Brexit* scenario. The UK Brexit Minister, David Frost, denounced the difficulty of operating the PINI while maintaining the regulatory autonomy that had inspired the *Brexit* process. In his words, the 'EU needs a new playbook for dealing with neighbours, one that involves pragmatic solutions between friends, not the imposition of one side's rules on the other and legal purism'.[115] A contentious moment in the fraught EU–UK relations occurred with the launch of the Northern Ireland Protocol Bill, through which the UK intended to unilaterally limit the implementation of the Northern Ireland Protocol in the United Kingdom. The Bill inter alia envisaged to limit the role of the CJEU in disputes over the Protocol.[116] This resulted in infringement procedures brought by the European Commission pursuant to Article 12(4) PINI.[117]

D. Further Exit? From the Chequers Plan to the EU–UK Trade and Cooperation Agreement

Unlike the previous arrangements envisaged in the wake of *Brexit*, the EU–UK Trade and Cooperation Agreement stands apart from the models of *Wider Europe*. Such a departure has developed gradually in the negotiation process on the future arrangements between the EU and UK. Indeed, Under Theresa May's cabinet, the Chequers Plan[118] included the option for regulatory alignment in certain sectors: these would mainly be achieved through 'common rulebooks' that would practically be based on substantive *renvois* to EU law.

The Plan envisioned that the 'the UK would maintain common rules with the EU in several domains, including the Union customs code and rules related to safety and security. The UK would apply and interpret those rules *consistently* with

[113] ibid Arts 12(4) and (6)–(7).
[114] Colin Harvey, 'The Irish Protocol' in Federico Fabbrini (ed), *The withdrawal agreement* (Oxford University Press, 2020) 166.
[115] 'David Frost: The EU Must Revisit the Northern Ireland Protocol' *Financial Times* (6 June 2021), www.ft.com/content/eb35a108-6186-42a4-b401-5e1df0e2c64a.
[116] See UK Parliament, proposed Northern Ireland Protocol Bill, publications.parliament.uk/pa/bills/lbill/58-03/052/5803052_en_2.html#pb1-l1g1.
[117] See European Commission Press Release, 'Commission launches infringement proceedings against the UK for breaking international law and provides further details on possible solutions to facilitate the movement of goods between Great Britain and Northern Ireland', Brussels 15 June 2022. See further discussion in section III.F of this chapter.
[118] UK Government, *The Future Relationship between the United Kingdom and the European Union* (Chequers Plan), presented to Parliament by the Prime Minister, July 2018.

the EU'.[119] The Plan clarified that the substantive *renvois* to EU law would have a dynamic nature.[120] It was thus acknowledged that this would 'limit the UK's ability to make changes to regulation in those areas covered by the rulebook'.[121] According to the original plan, the UK would remain in the EU-led administrative networks of cooperation and specifically in the EU bodies such as Europol, Eurojust and the EASA whilst also making appropriate financial contributions for its participation in this framework.

Interpretative *renvois* would also be at play insofar as the Plan envisaged that 'where the UK had agreed to retain[122] a common rulebook with the EU, the UK would commit by treaty that its courts would pay due regard to the CJEU case law'. While direct preliminary references were not envisaged,[123] there was a possibility that a preliminary reference to the CJEU could be triggered via the Joint Committee by mutual consent. Alternatively, the reference could be triggered by the arbitration panel for the interpretations of EU rules to which the UK 'had agreed to adhere as a matter of international law'. In these cases, the Joint Committee or the arbitration panel 'would have to resolve the dispute in a way that is consistent with [the CJEU's] interpretation. This would respect the principle that the court of one party cannot resolve disputes between the two.'[124] Theresa May's cabinet's plan thus left room for 'some form of indirect jurisdiction'.[125] Such an arrangement would have been similar to the EU–Ukraine DCFTA, the proposed InstA with Switzerland, as well as the EU–UK WA. May's stance is illustrative of how, in spite of the lofty declarations on taking back control, is difficult to eschew the magnetism of the EU legal order. The UK's wish to base the future relationship on 'international law', predicated upon sovereign equality between the two parties, became more evident with Johnson's cabinet.

E. The EU–UK TCA: Ever Distant from *Wider Europe*?

The green light to the Chequers Plan would have been problematic for the EU as it envisaged free movement of goods while terminating free movement of people. In June 2016, the EU had made it clear that 'Access to the Single Market requires acceptance of all four freedoms'.[126] The 2017 European Council guidelines stressed that 'the four freedoms of the Single Market are indivisible and that there can be

[119] ibid 18 (emphasis added).
[120] ibid.
[121] ibid 49.
[122] Note that the word 'retain' with respect to EU law is the same of the 'retained EU law' under the UK's European Union (Withdrawal) Act which is telling of the fact that the Plan's drafter by 'common rulebook' would possibly intend 'EU *acquis*'.
[123] UK Government (n 118) 92.
[124] ibid 93.
[125] UK Parliament, European Union Committee, Dispute resolution and enforcement after Brexit, 15th Report of Session 2017–19 (3 May 2018) HL Paper 130, para 30.
[126] Informal Meeting of the Heads of State or Government of 27 Member States and of the Presidents of the European Council and the European Commission, 29 June 2016, para.4.

no "cherry picking"'.[127] Yet, the largely rhetoric nature of this stance was revealed by the PINI itself. As a matter of fact, the PINI envisages the extension of the EU's legal space for rules on the movement of goods, not of persons.

Major hopes were placed on the future relations both by the EU and the UK. The Political Declaration on the future relations envisioned an 'ambitious, broad, deep and flexible partnership across trade and economic cooperation, law enforcement and criminal justice, foreign policy, security and defence and wider areas of cooperation'.[128] Along these lines, the European Parliament Resolution called for the signature of a comprehensive agreement 'pursuant to Article 8 TEU and Article 217 TFEU'. The robust governance framework with an overarching dispute resolution mechanism would be intended to avoid 'a proliferation of bilateral agreements and the shortcomings which characterise the EU's relationship with Switzerland'.[129]

For its reference to the values of the Union, the use of Article 8 would hardly be accepted by the UK. Moreover, the UK's negotiating stance under Boris Johnson's Government was that of reaching a 'comprehensive free trade agreement, similar to Canada's',[130] without alignment to EU law. The UK's negotiating stance was that of basing the future relations on international law, avoiding the gravitation around the EU's legal order. The EU–UK Trade and Cooperation Agreement has been eventually adopted pursuant to the association's legal basis in Article 217 of the TFEU, which is primarily used in EU neighbourhood agreements.[131] Differently from the UK's stance, it was not adopted under Article 207 TFEU, the common commercial policy legal basis for the conclusion of the EU– Canada CETA.[132] The TCA's scope is significantly wider than a typical EU trade agreement concluded with global partners. It contemplates an even wider framework of association with possible future supplementing agreements.[133]

The compromise between the two different standpoints of the EU and the UK is evident from the first provision reading that the Agreement 'establishes the basis for a broad relationship between the Parties, within an area of prosperity and good neighbourliness characterised by close and peaceful relations based on cooperation, respectful of the Parties' autonomy and sovereignty'.[134] On the one hand, this provision reflects the UK's willingness to depart from the paradigms of the extension of the EU's legal space. Such a willingness can be inferred from the

[127] European Council (n 65) Part I, para 1.

[128] EU–UK Political declaration setting out the framework for the future relationship between the European Union and the United Kingdom [2019] OJ C 384 I/178.

[129] European Parliament, 'Guidelines on the framework of future EU–UK relations', European Parliament resolution of 14 March 2018 on the framework of the future EU–UK relationship 2018/2573(RSP, point 5).

[130] UK Government, Prime Minister Boris Johnson's speech in Greenwich, 3 February 2020.

[131] Council Decision (EU) 2020/2252 on the signing, on behalf of the Union, and on provisional application of the EU–UK Trade and Cooperation Agreement [2020] OJ L 444 /2.

[132] Council Decision (EU) 2017/37 of 28 October 2016 on the signing on behalf of the European Union of the EU–Canada Comprehensive Economic and Trade Agreement (CETA) [2017] OJ L 111. For the Trade Agreement itself see EU–Canada CETA [2017] OJ L 11/23.

[133] EU–UK Trade and Cooperation Agreement, [2021] OJ L 149/10 (hereinafter 'EU–UK TCA'), Art 2: Supplementing agreements.

[134] ibid Art 1.

emphasis on the autonomy and sovereignty of both Parties. It is also apparent from Title II of the first part of the Agreement, which states that its provisions shall be interpreted 'in accordance with customary rules of interpretation of public international law, including those codified in the Vienna Convention on the Law of the Treaties'.[135] Interpretative *renvois* to EU law would not be thus contemplated in the EU–UK TCA. Yet, the first provision of the TCA, referring to the 'area of prosperity and good neighbourliness', replicates the wording of Article 8 of the TEU. Differently from Article 8 TEU, it does not mention that cooperation in this area is 'founded on the values of the Union'. It underscores instead that the relationship will be grounded on the respect of the 'Parties' autonomy and sovereignty'. In a more neutral fashion, the TCA recognises the basis as cooperation 'shared values and principles'.[136] From the EU side, pursuant to the constitutional mandate of Article 8 of the TEU, the EU would need to halt such neighbourhood cooperation, should it depart from the values of the EU.[137]

The Agreement is more detailed than standard association agreements with regard to the governance framework. It envisages a political Partnership Council which gathers representatives of the EU and UK at ministerial level and is co-chaired by a member of the European Commission and a representative of the UK Government.[138] The Partnership Council is the ultimate body presiding over the Agreement.[139] The day-to-day management of the Agreement is then operated by the Specialised Committees[140] that supervise the role of the Working Groups.[141] There are in total 24 bodies set up by the Agreement for the bilateral cooperation between the EU and the UK stemming from the Agreement.

The model of partnership based on 'international law' is made clear from the outset of the Agreement.[142] This is intended to mark the choice of premising the new legal relations on an equal partnership, as opposed to the canons of EU neighbourhood law predicated on third country gravitation around the EU legal order. Yet, some of the salient features of EU neighbourhood law emerge from closer scrutiny of the EU–UK TCA. The interdependence of EU–UK relations and the former membership of the latter in the EU renders the UK's participation in the EU's extended legal space unsurprising. Indeed, substantive *renvois*, although indirect, to EU law are to be found in the Part III, Title II of the Agreement where cooperation is established between the UK and Member States' competent law enforcement authorities and on the automated transfer of DNA profiles, dactyloscopy data and domestic vehicle registration data.[143] This part of cooperation originated with

[135] ibid Art 4: Public International Law.
[136] EU–UK TCA, Art 763(2).
[137] Hillion (n 61).
[138] ibid Annex I.
[139] EU–UK TCA, Art 7: Partnership Council.
[140] ibid Art 8: Committees.
[141] ibid Art 9: Working Groups.
[142] ibid Art 4: Public International Law.
[143] EU–UK TCA, Title II: Exchanges of DNA, Fingerprints, and Vehicle Registration Data, Article LAW.PRUM.5.

the EU Member States *inter se* agreement of the 2005 Prüm Convention.[144] As an *inter se* treaty complementing the EU legal order, the Convention was initially concluded under international law. It was subsequently adopted and transposed into the EU Treaty Framework through a Council Decision.[145] The resulting Area of Freedom, Security and Justice (AFSJ) cooperation developed from the Prüm Convention is largely replicated in the TC Agreement.[146] Title II thus evokes some characteristics largely resembling EU neighbourhood law. This derives primarily from the asymmetry between the EU-27 and the UK, as well as their strong interdependence.

In particular, Article 541TCA contemplates that in case

> the Union considers it necessary to amend this Title because Union law relating to the subject matter governed by this Title is amended substantially, … it may notify the United Kingdom accordingly with a view to agreeing on a formal amendment of this Agreement in relation to this Title.'

In case an agreement is not found within nine months of the notification, the Union (and not the UK) may suspend partially or entirely the cooperation under Title II.[147] Such a possibility derogates from the general rules on the suspension of the Agreement detailed in Title XII. Moreover, the Agreement specifies that declarations made by Member States pursuant to the Council Decisions[148] incorporating the Prüm Convention shall also extend to the UK.[149]

Additional substantive *renvois* to EU law are also present with respect to the EU Europol Agency for cooperating to prevent and combat serious crime and terrorism, although the UK is no longer a member of the EU Agency. Here, the notions and mechanisms underpinning cooperation are modelled along the lines of the Europol Regulation.[150] As anticipated, the Regulation is explicitly referred to in the Agreement.[151] With some foresight, the UK, while still a member of the EU, was entitled not to take part in the AFSJ area pursuant to Protocol 21 of the

[144] Convention between the Kingdom of Belgium, the Federal Republic of Germany, the Kingdom of Spain, the French Republic, the Grand Duchy of Luxembourg, the Kingdom of the Netherlands and the Republic of Austria on the stepping up of cross-border cooperation, particularly in combating terrorism, cross-border crime and illegal migration, Prüm, 27 May 2005.

[145] Council Decision 2008/616/JHA on the stepping up of cross-border cooperation, particularly in combating terrorism and cross-border crime [2008] OJ L 210/12.

[146] Oliver Garner, 'Part Three of the EU–UK TCA – From a "Disrupted" Area of Freedom, Security and Justice to "New Old" Intergovernmentalism in Justice and Home Affairs?' [2021] DCU Brexit Institute 5. He notices how 'Title II mandates a simulacrum of access to AFSJ cooperation rather than a construction of a new species of cooperation'.

[147] EU–UK TCA, Art 541(2).

[148] Council Decision 2008/615/JHA on the stepping up of cross-border cooperation, particularly in combating terrorism and cross-border crime; and Council Decision 2008/616/JHA on the implementation of Decision 2008/615/JHA on the stepping up of cross-border cooperation, particularly in combating terrorism and cross-border crime [2008] OJ L 210/1 and 12.

[149] EU–UK TCA, Art 539.

[150] Regulation (EU) 2016/794 of the European Parliament and of the Council of 11 May 2016 on the European Union Agency for Law Enforcement Cooperation (Europol) [2016] OJ L 135/53.

[151] EU–UK TCA, Art 565.

TFEU and decided instead to adhere to the renewed Europol framework. This opt-in occurred after the *Brexit* notification.[152] Similar patterns are replicated for cooperation with the Eurojust Agency.[153] It is worth stressing how these *renvois* in the domain of AFSJ actually pertain to core state functions. Moreover, although not directly operating substantive *renvois*, a certain mimetism also applies to state aid rules that replicate and evoke notions and mechanisms of EU law.[154]

In accordance with the UK's desire to base the relationship on international law and not upon the canons of the extension of the EU's legal space, the Agreement does not envisage particular organisational interactions between the TCA regime and the EU legal order. Nevertheless, in addition to the CJEU's role pursuant to the WA and the PINI, the Commission and the CJEU's tasks are extended to the UK via the TCA with respect to matters relating to the UK's participation in Union programmes, activities, or projects. Here, 'Judgments and orders of the Court of Justice … delivered in application of an arbitration clause contained in a contract or agreement in relation to Union programmes, activities … shall be enforceable in the United Kingdom'.[155] In this domain, the CJEU's powers shall also include the review of the legality of the Commission's decisions to impose a pecuniary obligation on legal or natural persons other than States in relations to claims stemming from Union programmes.[156]

The general dispute settlement provisions envisage mainly diplomatic channels and political consultations before triggering the arbitration mechanism.[157] This applies also to the many special clauses and derogations in different parts of the Agreement. For instance, Part III envisages that the parties may agree to solve the dispute via consultations in the framework of the Specialised Committees or the Partnership Council. The latter may resolve the dispute by a decision[158] which will be considered as a mutually agreed solution.[159] Significantly, the TCA's dispute

[152] UK Government, Home Office, 'Explanatory Memorandum on the UK Government's Intention to Opt-in to Regulation (EU) 2016/794 of the European Parliament and of the Council on 11 May 2016 on the European Union Agency for Law Enforcement Cooperation (Europol), available at european-memoranda.cabinetoffice.gov.uk/files/2016/11/EM_Europol_Opt_in.pdf.

[153] EU–UK TCA, Art 581 ff. See also Regulation (EU) 2018/1727 on the European Union Agency for Criminal Justice Cooperation (Eurojust) [2018] OJ EU L 295/138. Also in this case the UK Government, while member of the EU, decided to opt in According to Protocol 21 TFEU.

[154] EU–UK TCA, Art 3.1(b), Catherine Barnard noted 'the similarity … between the state aid regime that is currently applied in the text' in her intervention at House of Commons, 'Committee on the Future Relationship with the European Union, Oral evidence: Progress of the negotiations on the UK's future relationship with the EU, HC 203', 6 January 2021. See also Regulation (EU) 2016/1037 on protection against subsidised imports from countries not members of the European Union, [2016] OJ L 176/55, Art 3 definition of subsidy.

[155] EU–UK TCA, Art 728.

[156] ibid.

[157] Konstantinidis Mark and Poula Vasiliki, 'From Brexit to Eternity: The Institutional Landscape under the EU–UK Trade and Cooperation Agreement' (*European Law Blog*, 14 January 2021), europeanlawblog.eu/2021/01/14/from-brexit-to-eternity-the-institutional-landscape-under-the-eu-uk-trade-and-cooperation-agreement.

[158] EU–UK TCA, Art 698(5).

[159] ibid Art 699.

settlement mechanisms endeavour to detach the TCA regime from domestic legal orders.[160] This stems directly from the 'international law' basis of the Agreement excluding that a pronouncement of a court of one party could be binding on a court of another party.[161] Such a detachment resonates with the Court's reasoning in the *CETA Opinion*.[162] In the *Opinion*, the CJEU manifested a greater acceptance towards international law dispute settlement mechanisms with respect to its previous pronouncements that emphasised the autonomy of the EU's judicial bodies.[163] As argued by the Commission and the Council, this was possible in light of the circumstance that the CETA does not aim to 'extend a part of the EU law *acquis* to Canada'.[164] Indeed the Court found that the CETA 'does not confer on the envisaged tribunals any jurisdiction to interpret or apply EU law other than that regulating to the provision of the agreement'.[165] The parties' domestic law may only be taken into account as 'a matter of fact'.[166] In the Court's view, this does not amount to an interpretation of domestic law.[167]

The EU–UK relations are thus grounded on allegedly more classical patterns of international law rather than EU neighbourhood law. The TCA free movement of goods regime is a case in point. It operates as 'zero tariff' arrangement.[168] Yet, the arrangement is closer to the WTO model than to the mechanisms governing EU internal market law. As noted by Barnard and Leinarte especially with regard to technical barriers to trade, the TCA is primarily grounded on non-discrimination rather than on market access operating through equivalence or mutual recognition.[169] The international nature of the TCA and its departure from the canons of EU neighbourhood law is also reflected in the dispute settlement. The articulated enforcement mechanisms of the TCA will be discussed further in the chapter 9 of this book. Suffice here to mention that the increased emphasis on the level playing field regimes is illustrative of the desire to safeguard the autonomy and sovereignty of the parties while ensuring that EU–UK relations be informed by equal conditions of competition. The TCA thus distances itself from institutional arrangements pursuing homogeneity typical of EU neighbourhood law agreements extending the EU internal market.[170]

[160] Nicolas Levrat, 'Governance: Managing Bilateral Relations', *Brexit Institute Working Paper Series, No 10/2021* (2021) 12, http://dx.doi.org/10.2139/ssrn.3811236. He notes: 'There is thus an internationally based two-tiered legal system, with no connecting mechanism between on the one hand the international law regime between the parties, and on the other the domestic legal regimes of each parties'.

[161] See in this sense EU–UK TCA, Art 4(3) 'Public International Law'.

[162] Opinion 1/17 *CETA* EU:C:2019:341.

[163] Cécile Rapoport, 'Balancing on a Tightrope: Opinion 1/17 and the ECJ's Narrow and Tortuous Path for Compatibility of the EU's Investment Court System (ICS)' (2020) 57 *Common Market Law Review* 1725, 1744.

[164] *Opinion 1/17* (n 162) para 78.

[165] ibid 136.

[166] EU–Canada CETA (n 132), Art 8.31.2.

[167] *Opinion 1/17* (n 162) para 131. For a problematisation of this see Rapoport (n 163) 1745 ff.

[168] TCA Arts 21–22, Arts 37–53 and Annex 3.

[169] Catherine Barnard and Emilija Leinarte, 'Movement of Goods Under the TCA' *Legal Studies Research Papers*, University of Cambridge, Paper 31/2021.

[170] For a broader discussion and comparison between the TCA and other trade agreements concluded by the EU at a regional and global level see Marise Cremona and Alessandro Petti, 'Extending the

F. The Windsor Framework and Developments in EU–UK Relations

Evoking the language of the EU enlargement process, top EU officials have denounced a certain *Brexit fatigue* well before the conclusion of the negotiations.[171] Arguably, a significant part of such a fatigue was due to the negotiations on the legal framework governing the exchanges between Ireland and Northen Ireland. These negotiations proved to be lengthy and with a rapidly changing orientation and focus. Arguably, the border between Ireland and Northern Ireland has become a legal and conceptual borderland liable to further define the future of the EU–UK relations while shedding light on EU membership law itself. Northern Ireland in particular has found itself at the crossroad between the Brussels' regulatory space and London's ambitions of regulatory autonomy. Due to its mechanisms of gravitation around the EU legal order, the Protocol has been at the centre stage of the UK's criticism of the EU–UK post-*Brexit* relations. On the UK's side, criticism has developed with varying intensity ranging from an overt dissatisfaction,[172] to attempts to rewrite it,[173] to specious endeavours, likely to be in breach of international law,[174] to unilaterally suspend it.[175]

The latest attempt to review and smoothen the operation of the PINI has occurred in the context of the *Windsor Framework* announced on 27 February 2023. Beyond its grandiloquent label, the new framework for the operation of the PINI has its legal basis in a Decision of the Joint Committee of the EU–UK Withdrawal Agreement (Decision 1/23).[176] Pursuant to Article 164(4)d of the EU–UK WA, the Joint Committee is empowered to adopt decisions amending the Agreement especially in so far as the amendments are necessary to correct errors, address

Internal Market Through Free Trade Agreements' in Robert Schütze, Takis Tridimas (eds), *Oxford Principles of European Union Law*, vol 2 (Oxford University Press, forthcoming).

[171] For Jan Claude Junker, then President of the Commission see Alastair Macdonald and Gabriela Baczynska, 'Good Riddance? EU's "Brexit Fatigue" Limits UK Extension Options' *Reuters* (28 February 2019), https://www.reuters.com/article/us-britain-eu-delay/good-riddance-eus-brexit-fatigue-limits-uk-extension-options-idUSKCN1QH242. For Michel Barnier, chief *Brexit* negotiator, Michel Barnier and Robin Mackay, *My Secret Brexit Diary: A Glorious Illusion* (Polity Press, 2021).

[172] George Parker, 'Defiant Johnson "Will Not Hesitate" to Suspend Northern Ireland Protocol' *Financial Times* (12 June 2021), www.ft.com/content/78115941-afa1-4d98-82d1-719a53d451f9. Peter Foster, 'How to Solve Brexit's Northern Ireland Protocol Stalemate' *Financial Times* (15 July 2021), www.ft.com/content/22f617a1-f481-4d81-9687-a482803b6a44.

[173] Lisa O'Carrol, Jessica Elgot and Jennifer Rankin, 'UK Says It Wants to Substantially Rewrite Northern Ireland Protocol' *The Guardian* (21 July 2021), www.theguardian.com/politics/2021/jul/21/uk-substantially-rewrite-northern-ireland-brexit-protocol.

[174] Billy Melo Araujo, 'An Analysis of the UK Government's Defence of the Northern Ireland Protocol Bill under International Law' (2022) 73 *Northern Ireland Legal Quarterly* 89.

[175] This is the case of The Northern Ireland Protocol Bill, Originated in the House of Commons, Session 2022–23, a proposed act of the Parliament of the United Kingdom, now withdrawn. See n 117 and text thereto, Art 12(4) PINI. For an additional critical comment see Mark Elliott, 'The Northern Ireland Protocol Bill' *Public Law for Everyone* (13 June 2022), publiclawforeveryone.com/2022/06/13/the-northern-ireland-protocol-bill.

[176] See Decision No 1/2023 of the Joint Committee of the WA laying down arrangements relating to the Windsor Framework [2023] OJ L 102/61, Art 1.

omissions or respond to unforeseen situations, 'provided that such decisions may not amend the essential elements of this Agreement'. The Decision at issue indicates that the amended PINI should be referred to as the 'Windsor Framework'.[177]

The *Windsor Framework* has thus introduced some operational amendments to the PINI. It has given substance to the original Article 6(2) of the WA that enshrined a best endeavour clause to facilitate the trade between Northern Ireland. In particular, the Decision articulates specific arrangements for the movement of goods within the UK's internal market, when the goods are destined for final consumption in Northern Ireland, provided that necessary safeguards are in place to protect the EU internal market.[178] In that regard, the major novelty introduced are to be found in section 2 of Decision 1/23. The section simplifies the criteria for considering that a good brought into Northern Ireland from outside the Union is not at risk of subsequently being moved into the EU.[179]

The new criteria widen the spectrum of goods not raising the risk of being subsequently moved into the EU compared to those previously established.[180] The extension of the new green lane of goods not at risk of movement into the EU facilitates trade of these goods between Great Britain and Northern Ireland.[181] Yet, as noted by Murray and Robb,

> Northern Ireland is left with a somewhat moth-eaten set of EU rules applicable to trade in goods from Great Britain (provided the goods' ultimate destination is Northern Ireland) and a rather more extensive list of EU rules applicable to the production or processing of goods in Northern Ireland.[182]

The changes from the perspective of EU law brought about by the framework are rather limited.[183] In light of the foregoing, Northern Ireland's gravitation around the EU's legal order remains strong notwithstanding the facilitations introduced by the extended green lane arrangement.

A significant component of the *Windsor Framework* is its attempt to further remedy the democratic deficit and sovereignty threats attributed to the PINI[184] by overhauling and better operationalising existing rules. It does so though an interaction between unilateral and bilateral arrangements underlying the operation of

[177] ibid recital 4.
[178] ibid.
[179] ibid, see in particular Arts 6 and 7.
[180] See previous criteria in EU–UK WA Joint Committee Decision No 4/2020 on the determination of goods not at risk [2023] OJ L 443/6.
[181] For a broader discussion Steve Peers, 'EU Law Analysis: The Windsor Framework: Limiting the Scope of EU Law in Northern Ireland in Practice, Though Not in Theory (Part 1)' *EU Law Analysis* (4 March 2023), eulawanalysis.blogspot.com/2023/03/the-windsor-framework-limiting-scope-of.html.
[182] Colin RG Murray and Niall Robb, 'From the Protocol to the Windsor Framework' (2023) 74 *Northern Ireland Legal Quarterly* 1, 10. Basing their argument on the insights offered by Jude Webber and Andy Bounds, 'New EU Arsenic Rules Catch Northern Ireland between Brussels and London' *Financial Times* (9 March 2023), www.ft.com/content/30d7aae0-49ed-4398-bea3-e2483a882207.
[183] Editorial Comments, 'Unfinished Brexit Business: The Windsor Framework on the Northern Ireland Protocol' (2023) 60 *Common Market Law Review* 1224.
[184] Anurag Deb, 'Parliamentary Sovereignty and the Protocol Pincer' (2023) 43 *Legal Studies* 47.

the *Framework*.[185] An articulated mechanism has been designed to enhance the UK's parliamentary input in the management of the *Windsor Framework* and in the dynamic extension of EU law into the Agreement. The newly introduced paragraph (3)(a) of Article 13 of the *Windsor Framework*,[186] in conjunction with the UK's unilateral declaration to be found Annex I of Decision 1/2023, gives rise to what it has been called the 'Stormont Brake'.[187]

The original PINI already envisioned the possibility for the UK to somehow review the development of EU law to be incorporated into the Protocol. It is worth remembering that Article 13(3) PINI explicates the dynamic substantive *renvoi* to EU law by establishing that 'where this Protocol makes reference to a Union act, that reference shall be read as referring to that Union act as amended or replaced'. The original PINI then moved to paragraph (4) of Article 13 establishing a procedure to discuss within the Joint Committee whether to incorporate into the Protocol a *new* act adopted by the Union 'that falls within the scope of this Protocol, but which neither amends nor replaces a Union act listed in the Annexes'. The UK representatives could therefore oppose to the introduction of new Union acts into the Protocol, which would in turn trigger the possibility for the EU to take 'appropriate remedial measures'.[188]

The *Windsor Framework* bridges paragraphs (3) and (4) of Article 13 PINI with the introduction of a new subparagraph (3)(a). Derogating to paragraph (3), the new subparagraph allows the UK to trigger a brake in the application into the agreement of 'a Union act … that has been amended or replaced by a specific Union act'. The procedure triggered by Article 13(3)(a) operates in conjunction with the UK's unilateral declaration present in Annex I of the *Windsor Framework*. The brake has been introduced with a view to reinforcing the democratic control in the development of the EU–UK relations relating to Northern Ireland with regard to the evolution of EU law. Such an element, read together with the simplification of the green lane for the movement of goods not liable to be moved further in the EU internal market, could in practice reduce the marked gravitation around the EU legal order originally envisioned by the PINI.

It is worth stressing that the smoothening of the operation of the extended EU legal regimes applicable to Northern Ireland does not obliterate the patterns of gravitation around the EU legal order. With regard to the Stormont Brake, the scope and conditions of its activation are quite restrictive. The brake mainly covers only parts of Annex II.[189] It also applies to the third subparagraph of Article 5(1), EU–UK PINI concerning reliefs from customs duty for personal property of

[185] Some early signs of this approach could be found in Directive (EU) 2022/642 concerning derogations regarding certain medicinal products for human use made available in the United Kingdom in respect of Northern Ireland and in Cyprus, Ireland and Malta [2022] OJ L 118/ 4.

[186] Decision 1/23 (n 176) Art 2.

[187] The Brake has been then named after the Parliament Buildings of Northern Ireland in Belfast.

[188] EU–UK PINI, Art 13(4).

[189] Excluding inter alia EU anti-fraud law, EU trade defence instruments and EU regulations on bilateral safeguard.

residents of the UK. The brake thus excludes several domains.[190] With regard to the conditions to be met, Article 13(3)(a) mandates the combined fulfilment of two requirements: a) the amended or replaced EU act shall significantly differ from the content or scope of that Union act before it was amended or replaced; and b) the application in Northern Ireland of the Union act as amended or replaced 'would have a significant impact specific to everyday life of communities in Northern Ireland in a way that is liable to persist'. Although this language leaves room for interpretation, it is clear that the UK will have to support the activation of the brake with adequate evidence and argumentation. Moreover, on the UK's side it is necessary that the executive of Northern Ireland and the Northern Ireland Assembly are fully functioning.[191] The fulfilment of this conditions cannot be taken for granted.[192] Moreover, the break can be only invoked as a matter of last resort,[193] and the EU could take remedial measures if it finds that the non-application of the act at issue is liable to undermine the proper functioning of the Protocol.[194]

The *Windsor Framework* has introduced novelties in the way in which the extension of the EU's legal space in Northern Ireland operates with respect to the PINI. It modifies, and potentially reduces, the gravitation around the EU legal order of the regimes of free movement of goods in Northern Ireland, especially for goods not liable to be transferred in the EU. It also introduces a break in the automatisms related to the dynamic incorporation into the PINI of extended EU law. Yet, the basics patterns of gravitation around the EU's legal order in the EU–Northern Ireland regime remain in place. Similar to other institutional arrangements of *Wider Europe*, moreover, binding legal relations are enriched by soft law instruments. The novelty of the *Windsor Framework* lies perhaps in the modalities in which the interaction of hard law and soft law operates, namely through an articulated interaction of unilateral declarations and bilateral agreements.[195] Significantly, unilateral instruments do not only come from the EU but also the UK.

The amendments of the *Windsor Framework* have been welcomed as a success by the UK Government.[196] Indeed, they are likely to bring about a relative normalisation of the EU–UK novel contractual framework. Such a normalisation is illustrative of the interplay between law and diplomacy, and of the importance

[190] Such as those in EU–UK PINI, Annex I (EU equality and non-discrimination law), Annex III (EU tax and excise law), Annex IV (EU electricity law) and Annex V (EU State aid law).

[191] See the UK's unilateral declaration regarding the involvement of the institutions of the 1988 Agreement attached to Decision 1/2023 (n 176).

[192] Jess Sargeant, 'Northern Ireland: Functioning of Government without Ministers' *Institute for Government*, 14 November 2022, www.instituteforgovernment.org.uk/article/explainer/northern-ireland-functioning-government-without-ministers.

[193] Decision 1/2023 (n 176) Annex I, 1(c)i.

[194] EU–UK PINI, Art 13(4).

[195] Steve Peers, 'EU Law Analysis: Just Say No? The New "Stormont Brake" in the Windsor Framework (Part 2 of the Analysis of the Framework)' *EU Law Analysis*, 5 March 2023, eulawanalysis.blogspot.com/2023/03/just-say-no-new-stormont-brake-in.html.

[196] UK Government, *The Windsor Framework: A New Way Forward* (February 2023) CP 806, para 12.

of the political covenant underlying legal relations between the EU and its neighbours. Arguably, the concessions made by the EU to the UK in the negotiation of the *Windsor Framework* arose out of the change in the political approach to the Protocol brought about by Rishi Sunak's Government and its less confrontational stance on post-*Brexit* issues.[197]

The positive negotiation outcomes of the *Windsor Framework* may shed new light on the implementation of the post-*Brexit* EU–UK partnership. In 2023, the Commission implementation report of the EU–UK TCA highlighted the deadlocks and strains in the EU–UK relations attributing them primarily to the UK's 'persistent refusal to uphold its legal obligations under the Withdrawal Agreement'. Nevertheless, the Report heralded the Windsor Political Declaration[198] as a positive 'intention to fully exploit in the future the potential of the Trade and Cooperation Agreement'.[199] This positive outlook is enriched by the fact that the TCA institutional framework was completed and became fully operational in 2022. Notwithstanding the tabling by the UK of the Retained EU Law (Revocation and Reform) Bill, EU law magnetism in the UK is likely to remain. Indeed, the UK repeatedly postponed a series of deadlines for UK SPS checks for products from the EU. With respect to conformity assessment markings for products placed on the market of Great Britain, the EU certificates and CE marking will remain valid until the end of 2027.[200] Moreover, after the adoption of the UK data protection framework,[201] the EU has granted an adequacy determination pursuant to the GDPR.[202] In this case, the EU continuous magnetism and mimetic imitation of EU law emerges from the fact that many of the legal notions of the EU GDPR have been retained in the UK GDPR.[203] The Commission implementation report still highlights room for improvement inter alia in trading arrangement for electricity flows,[204] better communication with regard to fisheries measures,[205] and the association of the UK to certain Union programmes.[206]

[197] Murray and Robb (n 182) 3.

[198] European Commission and UK Government, 'Windsor Political Declaration, 27 February 2023,. europa.eu/system/files/2023-02/political%20declaration.pdf.

[199] European Commission, 'Report on the implementation of the EU–UK TCA', COM(2023) 118 final, 18.

[200] ibid 5.

[201] UK Data Protection and Digital Information Bill, 143 58/3 2022–23.

[202] Commission Implementing Decision on the adequate protection of personal data by the United Kingdom (EU) 2021/1772, [2021] OJ L 360/1.

[203] The very Commission adequacy decision (n 202) highlights inter alia the identical definitions of 'personal data', of 'data subject' and of 'processing' (see recital 20); the identical provisions regarding the principle of integrity and confidentiality and the provision on security of processing (recital 48), the identical substance of the regimes of international transfer of personal data (recital 75) and the identical rules on compensation and liability (recital 108).

[204] European Commission (n 199) 7.

[205] ibid 8.

[206] ibid 10.

IV. *Narrower Europe*, EU Neighbourhood Law and Sovereignty

The non-replicability of the EU membership law covenant in EU arrangements of EU neighbourhood law was a central theme of the EU's negotiating stance on *Brexit*. The EU's chief negotiator posited that

> by creating, or joining the EU, Member States accepted to put together certain parts of their sovereignty to create a body of law which applies to them and their citizens. It is this community of law, based on reciprocal trust, which the UK is about to leave.[207]

As Barnier had spelled out in a previous speech, 'being a Member of the European Union comes with rights and benefits. Third countries can never have the same rights and benefits, since they are not subject to the same obligations'.[208]

Arguably, the frictions between the UK and the EU on EU membership law and EU neighbourhood law largely originate from different understandings of the interplay between the political and the legal/judicial in the exercise of sovereignty. Indeed, a significant part of the UK's scepticism towards EU membership law pertained the extensive judicial interpretation of citizenship rights.[209] In contrast to the stance of the EU chief negotiator on *Brexit*,[210] Boris Johnson contested the extensive interpretation of the free movement of people. Probably overlooking the role of the CJEU in the development of EU primary law, he posited: 'It's a total myth-nonsense. It is stupid to say that freedom of movement is a fundamental right. It's something that has been acquired by a series of decisions by the Courts.'[211] 'Taking back control' was thus a claim for the UK's reconquest of its lost political autonomy, and of its traditional parliamentary sovereignty.

In the UK legal system, parliamentary sovereignty is understood as the 'dominant characteristic of [the UK's] political institutions'.[212] As Dicey put it, the Parliament: 'has, under the English constitution, the right to make or unmake any law whatever; and, further, that no person of body is recognised by the law of England as having a right to override or set aside the legislation of Parliament'.[213] Moreover, the singularity of the UK's (unwritten) constitution also lies in its characterisation as a 'political constitution' whereby the 'principle of parliament

[207] European Commission, Michel Barnier, 'Speech at the 28th Congress of the International Federation for European Law (FIDE), SPEECH/18/3962, Estoril 26 May 2018.

[208] European Commission, Michel Barnier 'Introductory Comments', Press Briefing Brussels, 6 December 2016, ec.europa.eu/info/news/introductory-comments-michel-barnier-2016-dec-06_en.

[209] Susanne K Schmidt, 'No Match Made in Heaven. Parliamentary Sovereignty, EU over-Constitutionalization and Brexit' (2020) 27 *Journal of European Public Policy* 779.

[210] European Commission, Michel Barnier, 'Protecting Citizens' Rights in the Negotiations with the UK', speech delivered at the European University Institute, Florence, 5 May 2017.

[211] Ashley Cowburn, 'Free movement of people as a founding principle of Eu is a 'total myth' says foreign Secretary Boris Johnson' *The Independent* (15 November 2016), www.independent.co.uk/news/uk/politics/brexit-boris-johnson-freedom-of-movement-myth-immigration-eu-uk-a7419026.html.

[212] Albert V Dicey, *Introduction to the Study of the Law of the Constitution* (Macmillan, 1989) 37.

[213] ibid 38.

sovereignty ... lie in *realpolitik* as distinct from law'.[214] As Elliot puts it, the 'political' nature of the UK constitution derives from the 'deeply pragmatic mindset that prioritises "what works" from conceptual tidiness'. It is also derived from the fact that 'the legal authority of constitutional actors [is] controlled in important part not by law or courts, but by the entrenchment of fundamental values in institutional practices that are "enforced" by political rather than judicial means'.[215] The EU's identity and functioning, instead, are predicated upon an understanding where law stands over politics. This premise, as Floris de Witte puts it, 'Not only does [the centrality of law] suggest that law can replace politics *for the purpose of managing interdependence between States* – in political agreement on the European level is no longer necessary to push forward integration; but also that the use of law in and of itself can somehow stabilise that process integration.'[216] These differences in the interplay between law and politics are also evident in the different underpinning and functioning of the EU and UK's internal markets. It has been noted that differently from the UK internal market, which is mostly based on a higher law originating in ancient provisions of UK's constitutionalism and the informal arrangements of UK intergovernmental relations, the EU internal market is 'law-given'.[217]

EU membership has thus challenged, or at least redesigned, some of the principal tenets of UK constitutionalism. By introducing the primacy of EU law, the UK 1972 European Communities Act had brought about a change in the principle of equality of primary legislation.[218] It had established different patterns of hierarchy in the UK legal system.[219] With its complex hierarchies of sources of law and institutional legal structures, EU membership thus questioned the strict conception of UK Parliamentary sovereignty. As a member of the EU, the UK was part of a regime characterised by a dense constellation of institutional, legal and diplomatic relations stemming from 'the basic fact of mutual membership'.[220]

[214] Mark Elliot, 'The United Kingdom Constitution' in Roger Masterman and Robert Schütze (eds), *The Cambridge Companion to Comparative Constitutional Law* (Cambridge University Press, 2019) 72.

[215] ibid 74–75.

[216] Floris de Witte, 'Interdependence and Contestation in European Integration' (2018) Vol 3 European Papers 2499, 484 (emphasis in the original). Later quoting Loïc Azoulai: 'law not only as a functional tool but as a cultural or symbolic form, as a carrier of a new spirit of cooperation and solidarity, and as the medium capable of containing political, economic, and social forces, as well as the cement capable of holding these divergent forces together' Loïc Azoulai, 'Integration through Law and Us' (2016) 14 *International Journal of Constitutional Law* 449, 450.

[217] Catherine Barnard, 'Protection of the UK Internal Market: Article 6 of the Ireland/Northern Ireland Protocol' in Federico Fabbrini (ed), *The Law & Politics of Brexit: The Protocol on Ireland / Northern Ireland* (Oxford University Press, 2022) 163, 168. Barnard reflects on the fact that the EU internal market has been a (tacit) source of inspiration of the UK Internal Market Act of 2020; see 172.

[218] Elliot (n 214) 80. See also Dicey (n 211) 145: 'neither the Act of Union with Scotland nor the Dentists Act 1878 has more claim than the other to be considered a supreme law'.

[219] *See R (HS2 Action Alliance Ltd) v Secretary of State for Transport* [2014] UKSC 3, [2014] 1 WLR 32 and further, Mark Elliot, 'Reflections on the HS2 Case: A Hierarchy of Domestic Constitutional Norms and the Qualified Primacy of EU Law' *UK Constitutional Law Association* (23 January 2014), ukconstitutionallaw.org/2014/01/23/mark-elliott-reflections-on-the-hs2-case-a-hierarchy-of-domestic-constitutional-norms-and-the-qualified-primacy-of-eu-law.

[220] Loïc Azoulai and Edwina Jaeger, 'Book Review: The Passage to Europe, by Luuk van Middelaar (New Haven: Yale University Press, 2013)' (2014) 51 *Common Market Law Review* 311, 312.

The entanglement in such legal system, not entirely cognate to the UK legal tradition, was compensated by the leverage in the decision-making of one most prosperous market in the world, which is often characterized as a global standard setter.[221]

Paradoxically, the UK's quest for regulatory autonomy leads to a reduction in its political capacity to influence the laws of what is currently its largest trade partner.[222] The benefit of membership, compared to mere participation in the extension of the EU's legal space typical of the EU's proximity policies, lies in full participation in the EU's decision-making process and the political leverage it entails. Arguably a similar quest for autonomy has characterised Switzerland's convoluted relation with the EU, in the attempt to safeguard the distinctive constitutional characteristics of Swiss Federal Law.[223] The choice between EU membership and participation in the EU's extended legal space is thus a difficult one for advanced economies like the UK and Switzerland. The EU's increased emphasis on the importance of a robust governance framework presiding over the bilateral relations adds to this difficulty. The ensuing overarching institutional setup ultimately intends to establish a balance between benefits and obligations for external participation in the EU internal market or for international cooperation with the EU.

By embracing international law-based cooperation in an attempt to disentangle itself from the gravitation around the EU's legal order, the UK chose to challenge the paradigms of gravitation around the EU legal order which underly *Wider Europe* and its institutional arrangements. Despite becoming a potential laboratory for proximity relations,[224] it is questionable whether *Brexit* will significantly change the paradigms and techniques of the extension of the EU's legal space. In light of PINI and subsequent *Windsor Framework*, divergence between EU and UK law especially in free movement of goods would undermine the unity and uniformity of the UK's legal order. This could also result in gloomy prospects for the stability of Ireland and the maintenance of the peace process of the Good Friday Agreement.[225] Moreover, the essence of the 'non-regression clauses' in the domains of competition, environmental and social standards would hardly allow for any significant regulatory divergence. Furthermore, the main motive rendering divergence unlikely in the EU–UK relations is the asymmetry characterising EU relations in the proximity. Such an asymmetry stems from the size of the EU

[221] Anu Bradford, *The Brussels Effect: How the European Union Rules the World* (Oxford University Press, 2020).

[222] Matthew Ward, 'Statistics on UK–EU Trade' [2020] Research Briefing, commonslibrary.parliament.uk/research-briefings/cbp-7851.

[223] On this see Marc Maresceau and Christa Tobler, *Switzerland and the EU, a challenging relationship* (Brill Nijhoff, 2023) and in particular the editors' introduction 33; the chapter by Christine Kaddous, 'Switzerland and the EU: the failure of the Institutional Agreement from a legal perspective', 318.

[224] Joseph HH Weiler, Daniel Sarmiento and Jonathan Faull, 'An Offer the EU and UK Cannot Refuse' *Verfassungsblog* (22 August 2019), verfassungsblog.de/an-offer-the-eu-and-uk-cannot-refuse; Kalypso Nicolaidis, 'Schroedinger's Backstop' *Verfassungsblog* (4 September 2019), verfassungsblog.de/schroedingers-backstop.

[225] Laura Noonan and Peter Foster, 'Resurgence of Violence Threatens to Drag N Ireland Back to Past' *Financial Times*, 9 April 2021, www.ft.com/content/d57085a8-e8b1-47e9-b030-1ece759aeef1.

market,[226] and relatedly, from the capacity of regulatory influence of the EU legal order over foreign jurisdictions.[227] Although the UK apparently expected that future relations would be based on mutual recognition arrangements, this prospect has not materialised. Thus, it seems difficult to imagine a replication of the EU–Canada relations in the proximity without alignment to EU law.[228]

Both the *Brexit* process and the *Wider Europe* paradigms of the extension of the EU's legal space are driven by a quest for autonomy. In the UK, this quest takes the forms of the desire of a 'full legal autonomy'[229] consisting in regulatory independence and the avoidance of the CJEU's influence. In the EU, it takes the form of the imperatives of the principle of autonomy of EU law requiring decision-making independence. It is also premised upon a balance between rights and obligations in proximity cooperation which is often cast in terms of the indivisibility of the four freedoms. These similar but opposing quests have already found accommodations in the existing arrangements in EU–UK relations. On the EU's part, the PINI is a clear example of the fact that, beyond the preconceived formula of the indivisibility of the four freedoms, a sectorial application of EU law focused on free movement of goods but not entailing movement of services and persons is possible.[230] On the UK's side, it is an intimation that the management of interdependence in the EU's proximity within and outside the UK can hardly disregard the paradigms of gravitation around the EU's legal order.

The foregoing illustrates the hiatus between the EU and the UK's visions of sovereignty and power. Given the economic asymmetry between the EU and UK, it is difficult to imagine that this asymmetry will not reverberate in the EU–UK legal relations. By disentangling itself from EU membership law, the UK has deprived itself of the prime venue for the exercise of sovereignty and political autonomy in the wider European legal space: participation in EU law-making. As shown by the paradigms of *Wider Europe* and more generally the global reach of EU law, the EU's capacity to regulate results in geopolitical power. In light of the asymmetry described above, with its *exit*, the UK has lost a privileged venue from which to exercise its sovereignty. In *Wider Europe*, political autonomy seems hardly detachable from the capacity to exercise legal sovereignty through relational law-making within EU structures. Arguably, for advanced economies in the EU's proximity, sovereignty and regulatory autonomy are best exercised through law within EU membership.

[226] Chad Damro, 'Market Power Europe' (2012) 19 *Journal of European Public Policy* 682.

[227] Bradford (n 221).

[228] For the mutual recognition arrangements envisaged by the EU–Canada CETA (n 132), see its 'Protocol on the mutual acceptance of the results of conformity assessment' and 'Protocol on the mutual recognition of the compliance and enforcement programme regarding good manufacturing practices for pharmaceutical products and see envisages a mutual recognition arrangement'.

[229] Kenneth Armstrong, 'Long Read | It's the Autonomy, Stupid – Can the EU and UK Agree the Rules of a Future Relationship?' *LSE BREXIT* (10 February 2020), blogs.lse.ac.uk/brexit/2020/02/10/long-read-its-the-autonomy-stupid-can-the-eu-and-uk-agree-the-rules-of-a-future-relationship.

[230] Stephen Weatherill, 'The Protocol on Ireland/Northern Ireland: Protecting the EU's Internal Market at the Expense of the UK's' (2020) 45 *European Law Review* 222.

V. Conclusions

This chapter has advanced the three lines of inquiry of the book with insights from the *Brexit* process and from the convoluted framework of EU-Switzerland relations. *Brexit* has influenced the EU's attempt to rationalise the bilateral partnership in the EU's proximity by clarifying the balance struck between benefits and obligations entailed in the participation in *Wider Europe*. When the UK's place in the extended EU's legal space was still an option after its withdrawal from the Union, the emphasis on the indivisibility of the four freedoms can be construed as an attempt by the EU to spell out the demarcation between EU membership and EU neighbourhood law. The EU's willingness to uphold the stance that the EU's relations with a non-Member State could not entail the same benefits as Union membership was at the core of the EU's engagement in the negotiation of an Institutional Framework Agreement with Switzerland. The objective was precisely that of overhauling the EU–Switzerland fragmented partnership with binding and dynamic techniques of gravitation around the EU legal order.

With regard to the techniques of extension of EU neighbourhood law, the chapter has enriched the value of *Wider Europe* as an analytical concept in a twofold manner. First, the *Brexit* process has shown the similarity between the techniques of extension and retrenchment of the EU's legal space. Both are concerned with the extension or reduction of the scope of application of the EU *acquis* in regimes different from EU membership law. The chapter has argued that one cannot think of a better example of the *Wider Europe* 'everything but institutions' formula than the EU–UK Withdrawal Agreement. Relatedly, the chapter has further highlighted how techniques of EU neighbourhood law might be used across different institutional arrangements. This is the case of the specific dispute settlement mechanism borrowed from the EU–Ukraine DCFTA chapters: it was included in the EU–UK Withdrawal Agreement and in the EU–Switzerland draft Institutional Agreement. The value of *Wider Europe* as an analytical concept capturing the interplay between law and diplomacy across the new and old EU's proximity policies has thus been corroborated.

By discussing the techniques of extension of the EU's legal space in the complex EU partnerships with the UK and Switzerland, this chapter has also shed light on the relevant political covenants. The convoluted nature of the EU's bilateral partnerships with the UK and Switzerland can be read in light of the prominent role played by autonomy: autonomy as a principle of EU law and as an objective of the UK and Switzerland to safeguard their sovereignty and distinctive constitutional traditions. Beyond dubious populist stances that have significantly affected both the *Brexit* process and the evolution of the EU's relations with Switzerland, the posture of the two countries in *Wider Europe* resulted in an attempt to calibrate distance with the EU. These intimations of sovereignty on their part have met with an increased rigidity of the EU's own interpretation of autonomy of EU membership law. In the case of Switzerland, the EU has insisted on rationalising the patterns of gravitation around the EU legal order to balance with clear obligations the benefits entailed in Switzerland's sectoral and fragmented participation in the extended internal market. The obligations also include those relating to the EU Citizenship Directive. Swiss refusal to conclude the Institutional Agreement is likely to result in a reduced EU market access. In the case of the UK, the possibilities of an *à la carte* participation in the internal market have been ruled out through an increased emphasis on the indivisibility of the four freedoms. In the novel EU–UK relations governed by the Trade and Cooperation Agreement, the EU has stressed that close trade interdependence with the EU come with the requirement not to undercut levels of protection in labour and environmental standards and with competition rules ensuring a level playing field. Yet, the strong UK's interdependence from the EU shows the difficulty of eschewing the techniques of EU neighbourhood law, which in fact still govern the EU–UK arrangement pertaining to Ireland and Northern Ireland. The reality of interdependence in the EU's proximity demonstrates that in spite of the motives characterising the quest for a *Narrower Europe*, it is hard to eschew the paradigms of EU neighbourhood law and the ensuing gravitation around the EU legal order. Moreover, this chapter has argued that for advanced economies in *Wider Europe* the quest for regulatory autonomy is best attained through membership, with the access to the decision-making of EU law and the relational exercise of sovereignty it entails.

8

Wider and Yet *Distant* Europe in Morocco: Cross-dependence at the Bridge between the EU and Africa

I. Introduction

The original intent of *Wider Europe* as a policy design was that of promoting a ring of friends surrounding the EU form Morocco to Russia. The extreme edges of this ring of friends are increasingly under strain. While the war in Ukraine has arguably accelerated and emphasised the inclusive dimension of *Wider Europe* in the East, the EU's relations with the southern neighbours have lost momentum, with a progressive political disengagement after the Arab Springs. The EU's engagement with the south is now largely oriented towards migration control. Notwithstanding the rejection of its application to EU membership, the Moroccan case is interesting as it reflects the paradigms of cross-dependence in *Wider Europe*. It is also telling of the evolution of the *Wider Europe* design in the south. Moroccan dependence on the EU is principally due to trade. Morocco is the 21st trade partner of the EU, while the EU is the principal trading partner of Morocco.[1] Moroccan dependence on the EU market is counterbalanced by the EU's dependence on Morocco on the management of migration flows. In 2018 the number of what is classified by Frontex as irregular border crossing of migrants to Europe via Morocco reached a record high, with a further increase in recent times.[2] Morocco continues to shrewdly weaponise migration[3] for more benefits in the extended EU's legal space and to have its territorial claims on the territories of Western Sahara recognised. Moreover, the EU is dependent on Morocco for combatting terrorism.

These patterns of dependence and cross-dependence are intertwined with the dynamics of inclusion and exclusion proper to the *Wider Europe*. Following the contextualisation of the origins of the EU–Morocco relations (section II),

[1] European Commission, EU trade relations with Morocco. Facts, figures and latest developments (2022 data), policy.trade.ec.europa.eu/eu-trade-relationships-country-and-region/countries-and-regions/morocco_en.

[2] Frontex, 'Risk Analysis for 2019', (European Border and Coast Guard Agency, 2019) 6. See more recently European Council, Council of the EU, Migration flows on the Western Routes, www.consilium.europa.eu/en/policies/eu-migration-policy/western-routes.

[3] 'King Muhammad of Morocco Weaponises Migration' *The Economist* (22 May 2021), www.economist.com/middle-east-and-africa/2021/05/22/king-muhammad-of-morocco-weaponises-migration.

section III addresses the inclusion of Morocco in the extended EU's legal space through trade. In *Wider Europe*, trade is considered as a vector of stabilisation that would trigger convergence to EU norms and increase its influence in the neighbourhood. Interdependence is engendered and fostered by trade. This paradigm continues today. The gravitation of Morocco around the EU legal order is mainly provided for in soft law instruments. This is the case of the EU–Morocco Advanced Status (section III.A.i), and of the Moroccan National Programme of Regulatory Convergence (section III.A.ii). The chapter shows how these instruments, largely managed through EU funds, result in a process of socialisation of Morocco in *Wider Europe* (section III.A.iii).

Sections IV looks at the EU's dependence on Morocco in the migration domain. The extension of the EU's legal space in EU–Morocco migration cooperation amounts to an externalisation of EU border controls. Dynamics of inclusion and exclusion are simultaneously at play. Both dynamics contribute to the 'transporting of actual borders beyond the borderline'.[4] In the words of Balibar, this dual phenomenon is an aspect of what he calls a

> *would-be 'power politics'* of Europe, following the model of the capacity to 'project power' beyond the mere territory of the new superstate, but, in fact, illustrating its incapacity to regulate differences and conflicts *within* its own limits, using the capacities of its domestic institutions and societies.[5]

The resulting techniques of EU neighbourhood law can be again traced back to the processes of socialisation of Morocco in the wider European legal space. These are reflected in Moroccan mimetic imitation of EU law and the laws of the EU Member States (section IV.A.i); in the tortuous dynamics of inclusion and exclusions of the negotiations of visa facilitation and readmission agreement (section IV.A.ii); and in EU-led international cooperative arrangements of migration containment (section IV.A.iii). The chapter further discusses the failure of the existing categories of EU law and international law to capture responsibility in cooperative migration containment frameworks. It highlights how the cooperative practices of migration containment are characterised by accountability gaps in the allocation of responsibility for wrongdoings (section IV.B).

Finally, the chapter discusses Moroccan geopolitical positioning in *Wider Europe* (section V) through the convoluted judicial and political saga concerning the application of the EU–Morocco trade and fisheries agreements to the contested territories of Western Sahara (section V.A). The foregoing reflection paves that way for examining the patterns of reversed conditionality weaponised by Morocco (section V.B).

[4] Etienne Balibar, 'Europe as Borderland' (2009) 27 *Environment and Planning D: Society and Space* 190, 203.

[5] ibid 203–04 (emphasis in the original).

II. *Wider Europe* and Morocco

In EU–Morocco relations, motives relating to material interdependence and geography have been often juxtaposed with ideational dimensions of the partnership. On the material plane, as posited by an adviser to King Mohammed VI: 'Geographically, historically and culturally, Morocco is closer to Western Europe than most of Eastern Europe. The Strait of Gibraltar is just a geographical accident'.[6] On the ideational plane, the monarchy[7] and a large part of the Moroccan elite have often demonstrated a 'profession of the European faith'.[8] In this respect, the monarchy's identity discourses have managed to foster the Kingdom's pro-European orientation while not impinging upon the distinctive Moroccan socio-cultural identity.[9]

The Royal Palace's ambitions to forge a privileged partnership with the EU were clearly manifested in 1984. On the occasion the European Council of Fontainebleau, King Hassan II formally submitted a request for the Accession of the Kingdom of Morocco to the European Economic Community. Geographical, geopolitical and economic factors as well as the democratic credentials of the Kingdom were put at the forefront for the membership application formalised in 1987.[10] The application was rejected on the grounds that Morocco is not a European country.[11] The EU's refusal was soon met with the Moroccan monarchy's acrimony. King Hassan II himself declared that:

> On the cultural level the West and the Moslem world have contributed equally to world cultures. We are just as cultivated as the West … [But Europeans] think of themselves as the whites, the colonisers, while we are the former colonies. We are not full citizens … And so they look for allies more to the East, because people there are white, … because it's one big family.[12]

[6] Bahar Rumelili, 'Constructing Identity and Relating to Difference: Understanding the EU's Mode of Differentiation' (2004) 30 *Review of International Studies* 30, 42–43.

[7] The Morocco Government website states that Mohammed VI is 'Docteur en Droit avec la mention « très honorable », suite à la soutenance, le 29 octobre 1993, à l'Université de Nice Sophia-Antipolis en France, d'une thèse sur le thème: « La coopération entre la Communauté Economique Européenne et l'Union du Maghreb Arabe »' 'Biographie de Sa Majesté Mohammed VI' (13 April 2013), www.maroc.ma/fr/content/biographie-de-sa-majest%C3%A9-mohammed-vi.

[8] Irene Fernández-Molina, *Moroccan Foreign Policy Under Mohammed VI, 1999–2014* (Routledge, 2016) 99.

[9] Raffaella Del Sarto, *Contested State Identities and Regional Security in the Euro-Mediterranean Area* (Palgrave Macmillan, 2006) 209.

[10] Maurice Flory, 'Note Sur La Demande d'adhésion Du Maroc à La Communauté Économique Européenne', *Annuaire de l'Afrique du Nord* (Editions du CNRS, 1986).

[11] Council Decision of 1 October 1976, quoted in Europa-archiv, 1987, 207, and in Briefing No 23 'Legal questions of enlargement', European Parliament 19 May 1998, www.europarl.europa.eu/enlargement/briefings/23a2_en.htm.

[12] Interview with Hassan II, *Financial Times* (28 October 1994), quoted in Jan Zielonka, *Explaining Euro-Paralysis: Why Europe Is Unable to Act in International Politics* (Springer, 1998) 77. Note how King Hassan described with foresight what would become the common language in the EU to refer to Ukraine and to the 'European Family', see further ch 6, section VI of this work.

EU relations with the southern neighbours received renewed hopes from the Barcelona Process. The process was intended to rebalance the equilibrium between the East and the West following the focus on post-1989 eastward enlargement.[13] Held in November 1995, the Barcelona Conference gathered the then 15 EU Member States and 12 Mediterranean non-Member countries.[14] The ensuing Barcelona Declaration[15] was based on three pillars of cooperation: the political and security partnership, the economic and financial cooperation, and the partnership in social, cultural and human affairs.

The Euro-Mediterranean Partnership (EMP) inaugurated with the Barcelona Declaration thus set high goals with the regional dimension described as an innovative aspect of the EU's renewed engagement with the South.[16] As pointed out by Del Sarto, the Kingdom of Morocco proved capable of 'playing the "Euro-Mediterranean game"' rather shrewdly in this context, and it '"used" the EMP to support its developmental strategy and to foster a stronger attachment to the EU'.[17] In fact, it was in the bilateral relations, within the EMP, where privileged partnerships providing for the extension of the EU's legal space would emerge. The Euro-Mediterranean Agreements (EMAs) reflected the spirit of the Barcelona Process and covered the three pillars of the relevant declaration. Signed in 1996, the EU–Morocco Association Agreement with the EU entered into force in 2000 and still presides over EU–Moroccan relations.[18]

The principal element of the *Wider Europe* design as articulated by the Barcelona process was that of creating an EU-led trade regime: the actual economic, development and convergence performance of the partners was largely secondary to this project. It has been contended that EU-led regional trade initiatives, such as the subsequent Agadir Agreement,[19] resulted in furthering patterns dependence from the EU. As highlighted by Kourtelis, this was mainly due to a rigid concatenation of Southern Mediterranean production in low-added value inputs to the Euro-Mediterranean value chains. Such a dependence arguably prevented trade reorientation among the southern countries of the Mediterranean.[20] It can thus be argued that the Agadir Agreement contributes 'to the reproduction of the hub-spoke effect',[21] exacerbating the asymmetric

[13] Erwoan Lannon et al, 'Barcelona Plus: Towards a Euro-Mediterranean Community of Democratic States' (2005) *IEMed- EuroMeSCo*, 15.

[14] Algeria, Cyprus, Egypt, Israel, Jordan, Lebanon, Malta, Morocco, Syria, Tunisia, Turkey and the Palestinian Authority.

[15] Barcelona declaration adopted at the Euro-Mediterranean Conference, 27–28 November 1995, eeas.europa.eu/archives/docs/euromed/docs/bd_en.pdf.

[16] European Commission, *Europe and the Mediterranean – Towards a closer partnership – An overview of the Barcelona Process in 2002* (Publications Office, 2003) 5.

[17] Del Sarto (n 9) 203.

[18] EU–Morocco EuroMed Agreement [2000] OJ L 70/2.

[19] The Agreement on the Establishment of the Free Trade Area between the Arab Mediterranean States, signed on 25 February 2004 between Morocco, Tunisia, Egypt and Jordan.

[20] Christos Kourtelis, 'The Agadir Agreement: The Capability Traps of Isomorphic Mimicry' (2021) *World Trade Review* 1, 10.

[21] ibid 12.

relations between the centre and the periphery. The relation of dependence and Morocco's gravitation around the EU legal order has also been sustained by substantial EU financial assistance. Morocco has been the first beneficiary of the MEDA (*Mesures d'accompagnement*) funds the principal financial instrument of the Euro Mediterranean Partnership.[22]

The mixed results of the multilateral ecosystem of the Barcelona process were superseded by more promising privileged bilateral relationships. The boost to the bilateral partnership primarily occurred with the launch of the ENP, which was based on differentiated bilateralism. As a matter of fact the ENP was not based on the region-building drive upon which the Barcelona Process was premised[23] or the subsequent regional initiatives as the Union for the Mediterranean.[24] The bilateral turn was considered necessary as the regional design evoked unresolved tensions, like the convoluted relations between Morocco and Algeria over the contested territories of Western Sahara, and the Arab-Palestinian conflict.[25]

Interestingly, in Morocco the ruling elite somewhat anticipated the spirit of *Wider Europe*. Shortly before the EU–Morocco Euro-Mediterranean (EuroMed) Association Agreement entered into force in 2000, King Mohammed VI outlined the elements that should define relations between Morocco and the EU:

> A partnership that would be at the same time:
>
> - more and better than the revised and corrected association we undertook,
> - and perhaps still for some time, a little less than accession dictated to us by reason, geography and the everyday realities of economic social and cultural life in our country.[26]

The King's Parisian address anticipated key elements of the *Wider Europe* speech by Romano Prodi. Two years later the Commission President maintained that '[accession] was not the only game in town'. Increased market access and prospects of political stability were perceived to still be appealing for the new EU

[22] Council Regulation (EC) No 1488/96 on financial and technical measures to accompany (MEDA) the reform of economic and social structures in the framework of the Euro-Mediterranean partnership [1996] OJ L 189/1 (no longer in force). European Commission, 'Country Strategy Paper Morocco 2007–2013', European Neighbourhood and Partnership Instrument (ENPI) (2007) 17; Michal Natorski, 'CIDOB – The Meda Programme in Morocco 12 Years on: Results, Experiences and Trends.' (CIDOB edition, 2008) 38.

[23] Raffaella A Del Sarto and Tobias Schumacher, 'From EMP to ENP: What's at Stake with the European Neighbourhood Policy towards the Southern Mediterranean?' (2005) 10 *European Foreign Affairs Review* 17, 21.

[24] Taib Fassi Fhiri, 'The Union for the Mediterranean: An Active Commitment for Ambitious Accomplishments' (IEMed/CIDOB Mediterranean Yearbook, 2009) 27, 28.

[25] Abderrahman Youssoufi, 'Allocution du Premier Ministre Du Royaume Du Maroc, Prononcée à l'occasion Du Colloque Maroc-Europe: Un Destin Commun, Brussels' (21 August 1999), quoted in Del Sarto (n 9) 201.

[26] Moroccan Government website, 'Allocution de S.M Le Roi Mohammed VI Lors Du Dîner Offert En l'honneur Du Souverain Par Le Président Jacques Chirac' (22 March 2000), www.maroc.ma/fr/discours-royaux/allocution-de-sm-le-roi-mohammed-vi-lors-du-d%C3%AEner-offert-en-lhonneur-du-souverain.

neighbourhood.[27] The new proximity policy would '*not* start with the promise of membership and it would *not exclude eventual* membership'.[28]

From the speeches of both Prodi and King Mohammed, key elements of the *Wider Europe* design emerge, entailing patterns of exclusion from membership and of inclusion in the extended EU's legal space. The extension of the EU's legal space ultimately results in an exercise in reconfiguration of borders through law. As noted by Del Sarto and Schumacher, the ENP discourse characterised by reference to a *Wider Europe* or to the *ring of friends* aims 'at blurring the EU's external borders'[29] while preventing instability.[30] The European Neighbourhood Instrument (ENPI) Country Strategy Paper for Morocco for the years 2007–2013 offers insights on the tenor of the bilateral relations. The ENP's underlying preoccupation regarding the EU's security interests in the south is evident from the outset of the policy. The ENPI, later replaced by the European Neighbourhood Instrument (ENI),[31] defined the framework for governing financial assistance and cooperation projects between the EU and its neighbourhood. Notwithstanding the asymmetric traits of the ENP deriving from Morocco's trade dependence, the Kingdom managed to orient the cooperation to its advantage. This has been especially the case in the migration domain and with regard to the EU's posture towards the territories of Western Sahara.

III. Trade and its Ecosystem: Moroccan Dependence on the EU

EU–Morocco bilateral relations are largely governed by the Euro-Mediterranean Association Agreement and its structures. As several other Euro-Mediterranean agreements and, more broadly, agreements concluded in the EU neighbourhood, the EU–Morocco Association Agreement contains a clause on the legislative approximation. In particular, Article 52 of the EU–Morocco AA reads that 'cooperation shall be aimed at helping Morocco to bring its legislation closer to that of the [EU] in the areas covered by this Agreement'.[32] This best-endeavours clause

[27] Romano Prodi, European Commission 'A Wider Europe – A Proximity Policy as the Key to Stability', Speech/02/619, 3–5.

[28] ibid 5 (emphasis in the original).

[29] Del Sarto and Schumacher (n 23) 25–26.

[30] ibid 26–28.

[31] Regulation (EU) No 232/2014 establishing a European Neighbourhood Instrument (ENI), [2014] OJ L 77/27 (no longer in force). Replaced by the NDICI see n 73.

[32] The wording of the approximation clauses varies in language. Art 49 of the EU–Lebanon Association Agreements reads (and similarly Art 55 of the EU–Israel Association Agreement): 'The Parties shall use their best endeavours to approximate their respective laws in order to facilitate the implementation of this Agreement' The latter would suggest a bi-directional approximation. The practice, however, is that of a uni-directional approximation of the third countries law to those of the EU (see also Art 52 of the EU–Tunisia Association Agreement and Arts 10 and 16 of the EU–Turkey Association Agreement).

promotes Morocco's gravitation around the EU legal order. However, in contrast to other multilateral and bilateral international agreements of EU neighbourhood law,[33] extension of the EU's legal space does not occur via legally binding substantive *renvois* or mechanisms of organisational interaction with the EU legal order. It operates, instead, via more flexible mechanisms of socialisation in the wider European legal space. This socialisation revolves primarily around the economic and legal relations ensuing from trade with the EU, which are predicated around the EU standards and norms. The commitment of alignment to EU law is fostered through technical assistance programmes and EU funds to the benefit of Morocco.

A. Techniques of EU Neighbourhood Law

i. The Privileged Partnership Through the Advanced Status

The EU–Morocco privileged partnership has taken the form of the Advanced Status. In October 2008, a joint document paving the way for the Advanced Status was adopted at the 7th session of the EU–Morocco Association Council.[34] Fernandez-Molina convincingly explains how in the Advanced Status, 'its *ideational* power or *symbolic dimension* carried far more weight than its *practical* content'.[35] Nevertheless, the document has played a part in shaping Moroccan institutional set-up, legal developments and system of governance.

The document starts with a focus on the legislative approximation to the EU *acquis* advocating for the systematisation of the convergence process.[36] The adoption of an EU–Morocco DCFTA would be considered a key step for promoting regulatory alignment to EU law. Interestingly, the language of the document is predicated upon the establishment of common spaces, not dissimilarly from what had been attempted with Russia. The Advanced Status paves the way for the participation of Morocco in EU agencies and programmes accompanied with significant financial support. The document recognises that Morocco had been the first recipient of the EU financial assistance in the Southern neighbourhood. A potentially breakthrough dimension of the partnership, mentioned in the document, is that of 'accompany[ing] Morocco in the logic of EU regional and cohesion policy'.[37]

The EU–Morocco Action Plan 2013–2017 for the implementation of the Advanced Status has been the 'living instrument' of the Advanced Status. The Action Plan is still applicable in an extended version and has been adopted as

[33] See for instance the EEA in ch 1, the ECAA and EnCT in ch 4, and the bilateral relations with Switzerland and Ukraine examined in ch 6.

[34] EU–Morocco Association Council, 'Document conjoint UE-Maroc sur le renforcement des relations bilatérales/ Statut Avancé', 13 October 2008.

[35] Fernández-Molina (n 8) 132.

[36] EU–Morocco Association Council, 'Document conjoint UE-Maroc sur le renforcement des relations bilatérales/Statut Avancé' (2008) 4.

[37] ibid 14.

a Recommendation of the Association Council.[38] The legal link between soft law instruments adopted by the Association Council and the EU legal order are Council Decisions pursuant to Article 218(9) TFEU. The Article at issue, in fact, allows the establishment of the EU's position in bodies set up by the Agreements. The Action Plan starts by emphasising a space of shared values to be fostered by continuous political dialogue. This space is sustained by numerous, although scattered, references to EU law and pieces of EU legislation. In addition, mechanisms for ensuring coordination at multilateral meetings are envisaged, as well as participation of Moroccan officials to some Council meetings, such as the PSC (Political and Security Committee) and the MaMa (Maghreb Mashreq) Group.

The Action Plan makes manifold references to EU law. Reference is made to the EU Charter of Fundamental Rights, EU legislation and Conventions of the Council of Europe deemed relevant for the development of a space of shared values. Cooperation is envisioned in domains including police matters, counter-terrorism, organised crime and border management. The more technical Part B of the Action Plan is dedicated to the promotion of a common economic space featuring an ambitious modernisation plan for Morocco in terms of fiscal policy, public finances, regional and local development, employment and structural reforms. With respect to the convergence to the EU *acquis*, a wide-ranging section titled 'trade, market and regulatory reform' envisages the establishment of a DCFTA and regulatory convergence in the sectors of consumer protection, Sanitary and Phytosanitary Standards (SPS), fisheries and agriculture, right of establishment, company law, financial services and competition law. The Action Plan therefore covers practically all the domains of the EU *acquis* including coordination in political, security and educational issues with a strong focus on the promotion of reform elements conducive to the modernisation of Morocco.

Morocco's gravitation around the EU legal order is highlighted in the various references to EU legislation operated by the Action Plan. The references are not legally binding and cannot thus be construed as formal *renvois* to the EU legal order. The document is drafted in a rather vague fashion. It envisages the gradual adoption (*reprise*) of the EU *acquis* in certain sectors, the incorporation of sectoral portions of the *acquis* in Morocco (*transposition*), as well as the adoption of the general principles of the *acquis* and good practices. The Annexes to the Action Plan detail only in limited sectors the specific pieces of EU legislation at the basis of convergence.[39]

The main tenet of the partnership is thus that of the *Wider Europe* Communication. Commercial relations would be the basis for triggering cooperation in related sectors while promoting the extension of the EU's legal space. Following the launch of Global Europe Commission Strategy of 2006, the EU tried

[38] EU–Morocco Association Council, Recommandation n° 1/2013 du Conseil d'association UE-Maroc du 16 décembre 2013 portant sur la mise en œuvre du plan "action UE–Maroc dans le cadre de la PEV mettant en œuvre le statut avancé (2013–2017), [2013] OJ 352/78.

[39] Mainly financial services, postal services, Intellectual and industrial property.

to expand trade liberalisation to the services sectors.[40] The target countries to be prioritised for these new FTAs were chosen on the basis of two economic criteria: their 'market potential (economic size and growth) and the level of protection against EU export interests (tariffs and non-tariff barriers)'.[41] ENP countries were clearly not a priority as they accounted for less than eight per cent of total EU trade.[42] Yet, trade, especially when coupled with regulatory convergence, is utilised by the EU as a vehicle for the political objective of increased prosperity, security and stability in the neighbourhood.[43]

The negotiations of the DCFTAs were expected to provide new impetus for trade liberalisation, as envisaged by the EU–Morocco Action Plan. The adoption of DCFTA with the EU's southern partners were authorised in a Council Foreign Affairs Meeting in Geneva in 2011.[44] Negotiations were interrupted by the Moroccan authorities' decision to conduct an impact assessment on the benefits of the arrangement. The costs of adopting EU regulations were believed to be very high in a number of sectors and accompanying and adaptation measures were needed to manage a possible transitional period.[45] After the Moroccan impact assessment, which has not been made public, negotiations on the DCFTA were halted. This shows that although generally perceived as a vector of stabilisation, trade and particularly ensuing convergence to EU law may also have significant costs and a destabilising effect on domestic societies.[46]

The EU attempted to ensure the maintenance of the privileged partnership following the EU's controversial judicial pronouncements on the application of liberalisation protocols of agricultural products and fisheries agreements to the contested territories of Western Sahara. The EU–Morocco Association Council meeting of 28 June 2019 was a public affirmation of the re-establishment of the privileged partnership[47] and the special role that the EU and Morocco attach to their alliance as a model for the region.[48] In the new momentum of the EU–Moroccan

[40] European Commission, 'Global Europe: Competing in the World, A Contribution to the EU's Growth and Jobs Strategy' COM(2006) 567 Final.

[41] ibid 9.

[42] Guillaume van der Loo, 'Mapping out the Scope and Contents of the DCFTAs with Tunisia and Morocco' (2016) *IEMed- EuroMeSCo*.

[43] ibid 41.

[44] Council of the EU, 3136th Council Meeting, Foreign Affairs Trade, Geneva, 14 December 2011, 8.

[45] Guillaume van der Loo, 'Enhancing the Prospects of the EU's Deep and Comprehensive Free Trade Areas in the Mediterranean: Lessons from the Eastern Partnership' (2015) CEPS Commentary. See also 'Négociations Sur l'ALECA: Le Maroc Toujours En «stand-By»', www.leseco.ma/economie/53670-negociations-sur-l-aleca-le-maroc-toujours-en-stand-by.html.

[46] This happens also internally in the EU: see Fritz W Scharpf, 'The Asymmetry of European Integration, or Why the EU Cannot Be a "Social Market Economy"' (2010) 8 *Socio-Economic Review* 211. For the experience of enlargement see Paul Copeland, 'EU Enlargement, the Clash of Capitalisms and the European Social Model' (2012) 10 *Comparative European Politics* 476.

[47] EU–Morocco Association Council, 'Joint Declaration by the European Union and Morocco for the Fourteenth Meeting of the Association Council' (27 June 2019), www.consilium.europa.eu/en/press/press-releases/2019/06/27/joint-declaration-by-the-european-union-and-the-kingdom-of-morocco-for-the-fourteenth-meeting-of-the-association-council.

[48] James Moran, 'Winds of Change for EU–Morocco Relations', *CEPS* (23 October 2019).

partnership in 2019, the Association Council relaunched the DCFTA negotiations grounding them

> on the basis of the expected benefits for both parties, the gradual move towards regulatory convergence, close bilateral cooperation regarding customs, good fiscal governance, the protection of personal data and a strengthening of the connectivity of physical and digital infrastructures.[49]

In line with the *Wider Europe* design, the 2019 Association Council meeting has highlighted how trade talks would foster the Moroccan legal system's convergence with the EU legal order. The EU hence attempted to gain leverage from Morocco's dependence on economic relations with the EU. Morocco, in turn, proved itself quite able to astutely interpret its role in the Wider European legal space by reorienting EU offers in favour of Moroccan interests.[50]

Notwithstanding the lofty declarations following the 2019 Association Council, the bilateral relations are de facto under a stalemate. Tensions in diplomatic relations following the controversial line of cases over the application of EU–Morocco Agreements over the territories of Western Sahara play a part in the uncertain path of relations. The old Advanced Status bilateral contractual framework has been only extended but not truly upgraded or reconsidered.[51] The lack of vitality in the bilateral partnership has not been altered by the rather timid attempt of the EU to establish 'a new agenda for the Mediterranean'.[52] Sectoral initiatives continue to be launched, such as the signature of the first 'Green Partnership' of this kind by the EU in October 2022 to accompany the ecological transition with significant EU funds.[53]

ii. The National Programme of Regulatory Convergence

The distinctive way in which Morocco interprets its role in the wider European legal space is illustrated by the set-up of the National Programme of Legislative Convergence with the EU (PNCR). As it is often the case in the context of EU–Morocco relations, the ideational component of the PNCR is prominent while the concrete results are not always tangible. In spite of being drafted in 2015, the Plan has remained a political document as it has no formal legislative or executive

[49] EU–Morocco Association Council (n 47).

[50] For a broader discussion on the strategies of Moroccan interlocution with the EU, see Sylvia I Bergh, 'Public Sector Governance Reforms and "advanced Regionalization" in Morocco: What Role for the European Union?' *EUI RSCAS 2016/ 56 Working Paper 5*.

[51] Council Decision (EU) 2019/2156 on the extension of the EU–Morocco Advanced Status [2019] OJ L 327/75 and Recommendation No 1/2019 of the EU Morocco Association Council of 4 December 2019 Approving the Extension of the EU–Morocco Action Plan Implementing the Advanced Status (2013–2017) by Two Years [2019] OJ L 327/108.

[52] European Commission and EU High Representative for CFSP, 'Renewed Partnership with the Southern Neighbourhood: a new Agenda for the Mediterranean', JOIN(2021) 2 final.

[53] EEAS, Partenariat Vert UE-Maroc, +www.eeas.europa.eu/sites/default/files/documents/2023/ Partenariat%20Vert_FR.pdf.

status.[54] The PNCR has been designed by the Moroccan administration[55] and is illustrative of the broad range of techniques of extension of the EU legal space and how the socialisation processes of mimetic imitation operate in third countries' legal systems. The PNCR is thus an instrument through which Morocco calibrates its *proximité optimale* with the EU in the EU's extended legal space.

The elaboration and setup of the PNCR has been promoted by the EU with programmes mainly funded through the ENI. The first was the one labelled *Réussir le Statut Avancé* (RSA I) that aimed to sustain Moroccan sectoral policies with funds mainly deployed through direct budget support to the Moroccan Government.[56] A subsequent funding and technical support package was launched in 2013 by the Commission, after the elaboration of the EU–Morocco 2013–2017 Action Plan and the commitments by Morocco to engage in the development of the PNCR with a view to determining the priorities, the scope and the rhythm of such a convergence.[57] These commitments were welcomed by the EU. Through the Programme *Réussir le Statut Avancé II* (RSA II), the Union highlighted the need to support the efforts to speed up and render more dynamic the process of convergence from a strategic perspective with a focus on its governance.[58]

The Moroccan PNCR is endowed with an institutional set-up presiding over its design and implementation. Building upon the experience of the RSA I programme, the PNCR involves various actors of Moroccan administration and in particular the Government General Secretariat (Secretariat General du Gouvernement; SGG), the Ministry for Foreign Affairs and Cooperation (MFA) and the Ministry of Finance (MoF). The MoF had already established a specific institutional body (*cellule de convergence*) of six officials in charge of operationalising the convergence process within the framework of the programme RSA I. This support body, in cooperation with the other relevant ministries, has developed a methodological document for the elaboration of the PNCR. The *cellule de convergence* has evolved over time. It now entails being the secretariat and 'steering committee' of the process. Besides, a central part of the role includes managing and coordinating, in partnership with the relevant sectoral ministries, the actions designed to identify the priorities of the convergence path. The *cellule* is also in charge of executing and monitoring the implementation of the process.[59]

The identification of priorities for alignment with EU law in sectoral domains is followed by a study considering the gap between Moroccan and EU legislation.

[54] Although it is highly institutionalised in the Moroccan state structures.

[55] In February 2021 some documents of the PNCR were made available online: convergence-maroc-ue.gov.ma/fr/Pages/index.aspx.

[56] European Commission, 'Fiche d'action Reussir Le Statut Avancé' (Brussels, 2011), ec.europa.eu/neighbourhood-enlargement/sites/near/files/aap_maroc_2011_ad3.pdf.

[57] Council of the EU, 'Relations avec le Maroc: projet de plan d'action Maroc pour la mise en œuvre du statut avancé (2013–2017) adopted by the EU–Morocco Association Council on 17 December 2013.

[58] European Commission, 'Convention de Financement Entre l'Union Européenne et Le Royaume Du Maroc', Programme "Réussir Le Statut Avancé II", "RSA II", DG NEAR, Brussels, GestDem No 2018/4333.

[59] ibid.

The convergence priorities insist on a three-year time period. Following the requests of the Commission, attention is placed on impact assessments intended to highlight the possible negative impacts of convergence on local economic structures, and especially on informal economic structures upon which part of the fabric of Moroccan society is based.[60] In addition to this, institutionalisation of the convergence process has been achieved through the set-up of a high-level Steering Committee (Comité de Pilotage; CoPIL) composed by the MoF, the MFA, the SGG and the EU Delegation in Rabat as an observer.

The EU funding distributed has been made conditional, inter alia, upon the Moroccan Government's adoption of three indicative action plans in three different sectoral domains, and on it setting clear deadlines to submit legislative texts for approval. The fulfilment of performance indicators set out the pace for the disbursement of the variable tranches of funding.[61] The monitoring of the envisaged initiatives takes place especially through dialogue between the parties. Moreover, the Moroccan MoF submits an annual report to the EU on the convergence process. External monitoring missions, managed by the EU delegation in Rabat, are envisaged with a view to assessing the advancement status of the programme and to provide elements to enhance the political dialogue on convergence.[62] In the PNCR, regulatory convergence and legislative approximation are seen as 'essential element[s] of anchoring to the European Union, … not only in terms of trade or investment, but also in terms of the more general *integration* between Morocco and Europe'.[63] In the *Wider Europe* conception, trade would foster the extension of the EU's legal space which in turn would enhance political stability through a (thin) integration of Morocco in some sectors of the internal market.[64]

Notwithstanding declaratory commitments, the practical results of the privileged partnership are rather dismal. In awareness of the foregoing, the Commission stressed the need for *ex ante* evaluation of the socioeconomic effect of the convergence priorities and measures. Among other lesson learned from the RSA I programme, the lack of a dedicated institutional structure was highlighted. It found that greater institutionalisation would embed isolated initiatives in an overarching strategy but also better assess *ex ante* and verify *ex post* the impact of convergence measures.[65]

The reports made by the EU Court of Auditors equally highlighted the unsatisfactory results of the budget support delivered to Morocco to implement the special partnership with the EU. In particular, the Court of Auditors pointed

[60] ibid.
[61] ibid 8–12.
[62] ibid 14.
[63] European Commission, 'Fiche d'action Pour Le Programme "Réussir Le Statut Avancé II, Maroc" "RSA II", Annexe II de La Décision d'exécution de La Commission [Implementig Decision] Approuvant Le Programme d'action Annuel 2013 (partie 2) En Faveur Du Maroc à Financer Sur Le Budget Général de l'Union Européenne' Request GestDem 2018/3765, 4.
[64] ibid 25.
[65] ibid 10.

out that budget supports targets were 'not ambitious enough to support reforms'. Besides, benchmarks on the creation of institutions, drafting legislation and national plans did not sufficiently focus on outcomes. Shortcomings in the reform process were also highlighted with respect to the Commission's monitoring efforts as well as those of the EEAS delegation in Rabat. These considerations led the Court of Auditors to recommend a better use of conditionality by improving the design of targets and performance indicators, as well as by enhancing disbursement verification procedures.[66]

iii. The Socialisation of Morocco in the Wider European Legal Space

The participation of Morocco in *Wider Europe* can be distinguished from the extension of the EU's legal space occurring via multilateral and bilateral international agreements led by the EU. Unlike the EEA arrangement and the agreements modelled upon it,[67] in Morocco the extension of the EU's legal space mainly takes the form of socialisation in *Wider Europe*. The EU's attention is not so much placed on the establishment of a homogeneous legal area[68] or on legal certainty.[69] This partly explains the shortcomings resulting from actual EU–Moroccan relations.[70] On the one hand, the dismal results of convergence may suggest the inefficiency, if not the irrelevance, of ENP policy design. It has been argued that Action Plans are little more than a political 'wish list'[71] and they are often criticised insofar as they raise expectations without being able to bring about change.[72] The political and soft law documents established with Morocco are no exception. Yet, although the ambition of the *Wider Europe* design is that of fulfilling the transformative mandate in the neighbourhood, as now enshrined in Article 8 TEU, the ultimate motive of EU neighbourhood law is EU borders security and stability. The concrete results of the implementation of the *acquis* are secondary although important. What matters most appears to be the process of engagement with the EU and the gravitation around the EU legal order. This enables the EU to have third countries' participating in EU policy objectives.

The process of socialisation is the product of multiple interactions between the EU and Morocco's officials facilitated through the implementation of the

[66] European Court of Auditors, 'Special Report: EU Support to Morocco-Limited Results so Far, Brussels, 2019' (2019), www.eca.europa.eu/Lists/ECADocuments/SR19_09/SR_Morocco_EN.pdf.

[67] See ch 4 of this work.

[68] See in particular the EEA Agreement and the ECAA Agreement discussed respectively in chs 4 and 5 and more generally in Ch 9 of this work.

[69] As in the case of the EU–Switzerland Draft Institutional Arrangement; see ch 7 of this work.

[70] Iván Martín, 'The EU Has Strengthened Its Relations with Morocco, but Not to the Extent Required to Bring about Real Change in the Country' (EUROPP–London School of Economics, 2014).

[71] Nariné Ghazaryan, *The European Neighbourhood Policy and the Democratic Values of the EU: A Legal Analysis* (Hart Publishing, 2014) 69.

[72] For a discussion see David M Trubek, Patrick Cottrell and Mark Nance, '"Soft Law", "Hard Law" and EU Integration' in Gráinne De Búrca and Joanne Scott, *Law and New Governance in the EU and the US* (Hart Publishing, 2006) 66.

EU–Morocco Association Agreement. The iterative interactions mainly revolve around Morocco's implementation of EU-funded programmes and Moroccan participation in Twinning and TAIEX (Technical Assistance and Information Exchanges).[73] In these programmes, EU Member State officials train Moroccan officials in EU practices and promote convergence to EU law. In Schimmelfenning's understanding, these programmes foster *social influence*, imitation and social *learning*.[74] In fact, in terms of social influence, image and status have been paramount for Morocco in its quest for the Advanced Status signalling its privileged partnership with the EU. In terms of imitation, it is apparent how in the relevant instruments of the ENP, EU law is used as a template for Moroccan legislation. Finally, the Moroccan case is a good example of social learning and normative internalisation,[75] as evident from the PNCR.

These processes of socialisation thus amount to techniques of extension of the EU's legal space. Morocco's limited progress with respect to convergence and adoption of EU law may also be explained by the processes of *bargaining*[76] that operate along the patterns of dependence and cross-dependence between the EU and Morocco. The migration domain is illustrative of how Morocco attempts to receive further financial, geopolitical and trade-related rewards for participating in the attainment of EU migration policy objectives.

IV. Migration: EU's Dependence on Morocco

The *Wider Europe* Communication made it clear that interdependence between the EU and its new neighbours was already a reality. This part of the chapter attempts to show how the patterns of dependence are far from being unidirectional. Indeed, EU–Moroccan relations show patterns of dependence and cross-dependence. On the one hand, Morocco is dependent on market access and trade is seen as a vector for promoting legislative convergence with the EU and thus as enhancing the extension of the EU's legal space. On the other hand, the EU is heavily dependent on Morocco for the management of migration. Both these patterns of dependence result in the extension of the EU's legal space and in different techniques of EU neighbourhood law.

[73] For an overview of how these instruments have been gradually extended to the ENP and Western Balkans via ENP and IPA (Pre-accession) instruments see Elsa Tulmets, 'Policy adaptation from the enlargement to the neighbourhood policy: a way to improve the EU's external capabilities?'(2007) 2 *Politique européenne* 55. Now the previous instruments have been largely replaced by the EU Regulation (EU) 2021/947 the Neighbourhood, Development and International Cooperation Instrument – Global Europe (NDICI), [2021] OJ L 209/1.

[74] Frank Schimmelfennig, 'Transnational Socialization Community-Building in an Integrated Europe' in Wolfram Kaiser and Peter Starie, *Transnational European Union: Towards a Common Political Space* (Taylor & Francis, 2005).

[75] Harold H Koh, 'Internalization through Socialization' (2005) 54 *Duke Law Journal* 975.

[76] Schimmelfennig (n 74) 62.

A. Techniques of Extension of the EU's Legal Space

In the migration domain, the techniques of extension of the EU's legal space aim at the externalisation of EU border management. This resonates with the dynamics of exclusion in the *Wider Europe* design: the primary objective of the extension of the EU's legal space is that of excluding 'undesired' migrants from the EU. This objective predates the launch of the European Neighbourhood Policy. In the years 2002–2004, the National Indicative Programme for Morocco envisaged a substantive EU financial contribution under the heading 'migration management'.[77] The EU focus was on the establishment of an institution in Morocco which was in charge of applying the laws on migrations and borders, training of police and the necessary equipment for coastal and land frontiers.[78]

The process of externalisation of EU border controls to Morocco already started in the wake of Spain's entry into the Schengen system.[79] The extended EU's legal space in the migration domain would result in Morocco's engagement in the Schengen framework. Moroccan elites were well aware of this. In the words of the former Ministry of the Interior Driss Basri, 'Moroccan primary objective is that of becoming a key stakeholder in the European migration policy following the establishment of the Schengen regime … The defence of the European space cannot be effective without Moroccan contribution'.[80] Border control externalisation practices through cooperative arrangements with Morocco were not only motivated by EU security needs, but also sought to reduce administrative burdens on Schengen states and allow for pre-screening procedures of 'undesired migrants', which involved the Moroccan administration as well as private agencies.[81]

i. *Mimetic Imitation of EU Member States Law*

Several techniques are in place for the extension of the EU's legal space into the migration domain. The legislative results of Morocco's socialisation in the wider European legal space in the early 2000s was the adoption of Bill No 02-03 of

[77] The EU assigned €187 million: European Commission, 'Partenariat EuroMed, Programme Indicatif National, Maroc, 2005–2006', eeas.europa.eu/archives/docs/morocco/csp/nip_05_06_fr.pdf; see particularly 'Orientation du Document de Strategie Pays 2002–2006 et du PIN 2002–2004' 3 ff.

[78] 'European Commission, 'Partenariat EuroMed EU–Maroc, Document de Strategie, 2002–2006 et Programme Indicatif National (PIN), 2002–2004', (6 December 2001) 25, www.eeas.europa.eu/archives/docs/morocco/csp/02_06_fr.pdf.

[79] Sergio Carrera et al, *EU–Morocco Cooperation on Readmission, Borders and Protection: A Model to Follow?* (2016) *CEPS* 4.

[80] D Basri, *L'Opinion*, 24 February 1999 quoted in Abdelkrim Belguendouz, 'Expansion et sous-traitance des logiques d'enfermement de l'Union européenne: l'exemple du Maroc' (2005) 57 *Cultures & conflits* 155, 184 (my translation).

[81] Federica Infantino, 'La frontière au guichet. Politiques et pratiques des visas Schengen à l'Ambassade et au Consulat d'Italie au Maroc' (2010) 7 *Champ pénal/Penal field*, journals.openedition.org/champpenal/7864.

11 November 2003.[82] The securitarian character of this piece of legislation was intensified to respond to the terrorist attacks in Casablanca on 16 May 2003.[83] As a result of its repressive nature, the Bill has been considered 'emergency legislation' and regarded as a 'Moroccan–European co-sovereignty law inasmuch as it falls primarily within the will of the EU to protect itself from illegal migration bound from one of its major passage points towards Europe'.[84] Indeed, the sanction regime envisaged by the Bill not only covers 'irregular immigration', but also 'irregular emigration',[85] mostly directed towards Europe. The Bill was explicitly devised with a view to 'allowing Morocco to fulfil its commitments towards its partners, particularly with respect to [the] fight against transnational irregular migration, both in its national and international dimension'.[86]

The controversial Bill replicates some of the principles and provisions present in the legal regimes of EU Member States exemplifying the imitation processes proper to third country socialisation in the wider European legal space. As far as the criminalisation of irregular migration is concerned, a mimetic attitude has been noticed between the Moroccan and French regimes.[87] Indeed, the definition of the Moroccan waiting zone as well as the conditions for its maintenance and prolongation were inspired by French law.[88] This is especially the case in instances of illegal return on Moroccan territory[89] and administrative procedures concerning waiting zones.[90] The influence of European partners also led to the establishment of hosting centres, which followed the model of

[82] Loi n° 02-03 relative à l'entrée et du séjour des étrangers au Royaume du Maroc, à l'émigration et l'immigration irrégulières, 2013, Bulletin Officiel n° 5162 du jeudi 20 novembre 2003; hereinafter Loi n° 02-03.

[83] Douglas Jehl, 'Morocco Suicide Bombs Kill at Least 14 In Casablanca' *The New York Times* (17 May 2003), nytimes.com/2003/05/17/world/aftereffects-morocco-suicide-bombs-kill-at-least-14-in-casablanca.html.

[84] Mehdi Lahlou, 'Morocco's Experience of Migration as a Sending, Transit and Receiving Country' (2015) Istituto Italiano Affari Internazionali, Working Papers 7.

[85] Loi n° 02-03, Art 50: 'Est punie d'une amende de 3000 à 10.000 dirhams et d'un emprisonnement de un mois à six mois, ou de l'une de ces deux peines seulement, sans préjudice des dispositions du code pénal applicables en la matière, toute personne qui quitte le territoire marocain d'une façon clandestine, en utilisant, au moment de traverser l'un des postes frontières terrestres, maritimes ou aériens, un moyen frauduleux pour se soustraire à la présentation des pièces officielles nécessaires ou à l'accomplissement des formalités prescrites par la loi et les règlements en vigueur, ou en utilisant des pièces falsifiées ou par usurpation de nom, ainsi que toute personne qui s'introduit dans le territoire marocain ou le quitte par des issues ou des lieux autres que les postes frontières créés à cet effet'.

[86] Note de présentation du projet de loi n°02-03 relative à l'entrée au séjour des étrangers au Maroc, à l'émigration et limmigration irrégulière, quoted in Belguendouz (n 80) (my translation).

[87] Ludivine Richefeu, 'Le droit pénal face à la migration transfrontière' (Université Panthéon-Sorbonne – Paris I, 2 2018) 227 ff.

[88] ibid 228–29.

[89] Loi n° 02-03, Art 42 of the French Code de l'entrée et du séjour des étrangers et du droit d'asile, Art L624-1 (in force until 1 May 2021). Richefeu points out also instances of criminalisation of illegal stay in Morocco taken from French legislation, now abrogated.

[90] See Loi n° 02-03, Art 38 and the French Code de l'entrée et du séjour des étrangers et du droit d'asile, Art L221-1 (in force until 1 May 2021).

Spanish Migrant Temporary Stay centres.[91] The waiting areas are zones principally located at ports and airports where migrants are hosted awaiting their possible expulsion.[92]

Moroccan legislative mimetic imitation of EU Member State laws, however, does not encompass the safeguards and remedies that would be accorded to migrants in the legal systems of the Member States. The securitarian character of this piece of legislation thus appears to fall short of guaranteeing full respect for Morocco's international commitments. For instance, unlike French law, the Moroccan Act does not envisage adequate legal remedies against abuses or injustices on the part of the Moroccan administration.[93] Moreover, human rights safeguards are contemplated to protect aliens who cannot be subjects to expulsion measures under the 1951 Geneva Convention relating to the status of refugees, such as pregnant women and minors.[94] Although Morocco is a party to the Geneva Convention, its domestic regime envisages several exceptions and derogations to the Convention's provisions.[95] Furthermore, it has been noted that the Bill appears to overlook Moroccan international commitments relating to the 1990 International Convention on the Protection of the Rights of All Migrant Workers and Members of Their Families guaranteeing protection to irregular workers.[96] As a matter of fact, notwithstanding the Moroccan ratification of said Convention, it is difficult for the Kingdom to meet its own and EU's securitarian objectives, and its own commitments with regard to International Conventions.[97]

ii. Inclusion and Exclusion: Visa Facilitation and Readmission Agreement

A key component of the externalisation of EU's border is the dual process of negotiation of mobility partnerships and readmissions agreements. This twofold carrot-and-stick paradigm has been at the basis of the EU Global Approach to

[91] 'Report Submitted by Ms. Gabriela Rodríquez Pizarro, Special Rapporteur on the Human Rights of Migrants, Addendum: Visit to Morocco' (United Nations Economic and Social Council, 2004) E/CN.4/2004/76/Add.3 17, digitallibrary.un.org/record/518530?ln=en.

[92] Loi n° 02-03, Art 38.

[93] Khadija Elmadmad, 'Migration irrégulière et migrations illégale: l'example des migrants subsharien aux Maroc' EUI Working Paper RSCAS 2008, 7.

[94] Loi n° 02-03, Arts 26 and 29; see also of the 1951 Geneva Convention relating to the status of refugees, Art 33.

[95] Safeguards can be superseded pursuant Loi n° 02-03, Art 27 'when expulsion constitutes an imperative necessity of the State or for public order': Lahlou (n 84) 7. Nadia Khrouz, Adila Ouardi and Hicham Rachidi, 'Le Cadre Juridique Relatif à La Condition Des Étrangers Au Regard de l'interprétation Du Juge Judiciaire et de l'application Du Pouvoir Exécutif' (GADEM – Groupe antiraciste d'accompagnement et de défense des étrangers et migrants 2008) 5, www.lacimade.org/wp-content/uploads/2009/02/ETUDE-GADEM-janv2009.pdf.

[96] Khadija Elmadmad, 'La nouvelle loi marocaine du 11 novembre 2003 relative à l'entrée et au séjour des étrangers au maroc, et à l'émigration et l'immigration irrégulières' EUI RSCAS CARIM 2004/01, 6.

[97] Khadija Elmadmad, 'Le Maroc et la Convention sur la protection des droits de tous les travailleurs migrants et des membres de leur famille', EUI RSCAS CARIM, 2009/11, 5 (my translation).

Migration, described as 'a comprehensive approach which combines measures aimed at facilitating legal migration opportunities with those reducing illegal migrations'.[98] Mobility Partnerships were devised as soft law instruments within which hard law instruments, such as visa facilitation (inclusion) and readmission agreements (exclusion) would be negotiated. In the EU's understanding, the promotion of the EU's securitarian interests would be achieved through a conditionality-based approach whereby 'renewed Mobility Partnerships [would offer] visa facilitation based on a simultaneously negotiated readmission agreement'.[99]

Moroccan officials perceived a difference in attitude between the conditionality schemes used in the East and in the South. Their perception was that in contrast with the approach in the East, the EU wanted readmission agreements to be negotiated first.[100] Moreover, the benefits of the facilitation were regarded as minor in so far as they affect people with skills and qualifications who already enjoy relatively high mobility opportunities.[101] Although readmission agreements have been constantly at the top of the EU priorities,[102] the Moroccan side did not consider Mobility Partnerships as sufficient to overcome its reservations.[103] In the multiple rounds of negotiations,[104] a key bone of contention has been a clause contemplating readmission of third country nationals.[105] Furthermore, Moroccan diplomats often questioned the added value that such an agreement could bring for Morocco in light of those that had already concluded with some of the EU Member States.[106] While important for the EU Member States, the inclusion of a third country national clause in the agreement has proved controversial for Morocco. With respect to the citizens of the parties to the readmission agreement, readmission may be seen as a way to facilitate the right of return in one's own country ensuing

[98] Council of the EU, Conclusions on the Global Approach to Migration, 2807th Justice and Home Affairs Council Meeting, Luxembourg', 12 June 2007.

[99] European Commission, 'The Global Approach to Migration and Mobility', Brussels, 28 November 2011, COM(2011) 743 Final, 11.

[100] Nora El Qadim, 'The Symbolic Meaning of International Mobility: EU–Morocco Negotiations on Visa Facilitation' (2018) 6 *Migration Studies* 279, 293.

[101] Tasnim Abderrahim, 'A Tale of Two Agreements: EU Migration Cooperation with Morocco and Tunisia' (2019) 41 *IEMed-EuroMeSCo*, 22. This elitist approach seems confirmed by the Commissions initiatives on the 'Talent Partnerships', see European Commission, 'Communication on an New Pact on Migration and Asylum' COM(2020) 609 final.

[102] See for instance European Council, Presidency Conclusions, Seville European Council, 22 June 20023, DOC/02/13. See Also EU–Morocco EuroMed Agreement, Art 69(3c).

[103] The issue incentives has also been addressed in European Court of Auditors, 'EU readmission cooperation with third countries: relevant actions yielded limited results', 2021, paras 47–72.

[104] Sergio Carrera, Jean-Pierre Cassarino and Mehdi Lahlou, 'EU–Morocco Cooperation on Readmission, Borders and Protection' (2016) 87 *CEPS Paper in Liberty and Security in Europe* 21; Sarah Wolff, 'The Politics of Negotiating EU Readmission Agreements: Insights from Morocco and Turkey' (2014) 16 *European Journal of Migration and Law* 69.

[105] This is a protracted bone of contention between the EU and Morocco. See recently 'Morocco Rebuffs EU Request to Re-Admit Third-Country Migrants', *Reuters* (15 December 2020), www.reuters.com/article/morocco-eu-migration-int-idUSKBN28P252.

[106] Nora El Qadim, *Le gouvernement asymétrique des migrations: Maroc-Union européenne* (Dalloz, 2015).

from Article 13 of the Universal Declaration of Human Rights.[107] This right entails with a duty upon states to receive nationals who 'are not allowed to remain on the territory of other States'.[108] When it comes to non-Moroccan migrants transiting through the Kingdom to reach the EU, it is questionable whether international law establishes any legal obligation. The principle of good neighbourliness enshrined in Article 74 of the UN Charter has been considered by one commentator as entailing an obligation to readmit third country nationals.[109] As convincingly noticed by Coleman, however, 'the proposed application [of the principle of neighbourliness] in the field of migration is decidedly political' and defining what constitutes good neighbourly conduct in relation to cross-border migration is prone to political or subjective interpretation, and therefore unsuitable as a basis for establishing related international obligations'.[110] In Morocco, the unfavourable political climate to such an extensive interpretation of the principle of good neighbourliness is manifested by the unwillingness to act as a '*gendarme de l'Europe*'.

Another major reason for the failure to sign the readmission agreement with the EU was the presence of bilateral agreements in place with Member States. The bilateral Spain–Morocco readmission agreement includes a third-county nationals clause.[111] The agreement at issue was an element of the reconciliation process following the signature of a Treaty of Good Neighbourliness and Friendly Cooperation on 4 July 1991.[112] The Agreement with Spain, together with the one signed with Italy in 1998 is one of the few instances of international law Agreements concluded by Morocco on readmission featuring an explicit third country nationals clause. Part of the exceptionality of the readmission framework lies in the fact that most of the cooperation on readmission happens through informal channels and rather opaque instances of *procès-verbaux*, administrative arrangements and exchanges of letters.[113] Indeed, EU Member States have learned how readmission cooperation is part of a broader diplomatic landscape where issue linkage

[107] Annabelle Roig and Thomas Huddleston, 'EC Readmission Agreements: A Re-Evaluation of the Political Impasse.' (2007) 9 *European Journal of Migration and Law* 364. Art 13 of the UN Universal Declaration of Human Rights establishes that 'everyone has the right to leave any country, including his own, and to return to his country'.

[108] Robert Jennings and Arthur Watts (eds), *Oppenheim's International Law* (Longman, 1992) 857.

[109] Kay Hailbronner, 'Readmission Agreements and the Obligation on States under Public International Law to Readmit Their Own and Foreign Nationals' (1997) 57 *Zeitschrift für ausländisches öffentliches Recht und Völkerrecht* 1, 25.

[110] Nils Coleman, *European Readmission Policy: Third Country Interests and Refugee Rights* (Brill, 2009) 45.

[111] Spain–Morocco Readmission Agreement, 'Acuerdo entre el Reino de España y el Reino de Marruecos relativo a la circulación de personas, el tránsito y la readmisión de extranjeros entrados ilegalmente, firmado en Madrid el 13 de febrero de 1992' [BOE-A-1992–8976].

[112] Jean-Pierre Cassarino, 'Informalising Readmission Agreements in the EU Neighbourhood' (2007) 42 *The International Spectator* 179, 184.

[113] El Qadim (n 106) 73. Lorenzo Gabrielli, 'Cooperation on Readmission in the Western Mediterranean Migration Route' in Jean-Pierre Cassarino, Lorenzo Gabrielli and Delphine Perrin, *Cooperation on readmission in the Euro-Mediterranean Area and Beyond: lessons learned and unlearned* (2023) *IEMed-EuroMeSCo*.

is crucial, and it is hardly captured in a single bilateral instrument.[114] Moreover, with migration flows significantly increased after 2014, readmission is at any rate difficult to manage by Morocco.[115]

Notwithstanding Moroccan unwillingness to sign a legally binding instruments at the EU level, Morocco was the first country in the EU southern neighbourhood to conclude Mobility Partnership with the EU and nine of its Member States in June 2013.[116] As it is customary with Mobility Partnerships, the EU–Morocco joint declaration clarifies that it does not produce binding effects under international law.[117] The objectives of the MP are thus pursued with other means. The proliferation of soft law instruments and the informalisation of legal arrangements in the migration domain[118] are predicated upon the argument of efficiency and on the desire of enhancing the margin of discretion in the ways objective are fulfilled especially in politically sensitive domains.[119] This is highlighted in Commission documents mentioning that 'the paramount priority is to achieve fast and operational returns and not necessarily formal readmission agreements'.[120] This is not specific to Morocco and it applies also to the EU relationship with other countries on migration matters.[121]

iii. Cooperation Networks: EU Financial Assistance in Migration Management

EU funds and programmes hence foster networks of cooperation between EU and Morocco officials with training, exchanges of expertise and monitoring. The panoply of EU financial instruments used by the Union to socialise neighbouring countries in the externalisation of migration control has evolved over time.[122]

[114] Jean-Pierre Cassarino, 'Informalising EU Readmission Policy' in Adriana Ripoll Servent and Florian Trauner, *The Routledge Handbook of Justice and Home Affairs Research* (Routledge, 2018) 86.

[115] El Qadim (n 106) 88.

[116] Namely the Kingdom of Belgium, the French Republic, the Federal Republic of Germany, the Italian Republic, the Kingdom of the Netherlands, the Portuguese Republic, the Kingdom of Spain, the Kingdom of Sweden and the UK.

[117] General Secretariat of the Council, 'Joint Declaration Establishing a Mobility Partnership between the Kingdom of Morocco and the European Union and Its Member States', Brussels, 3 June 2013, 6139/13, para 41.

[118] Cassarin. (n 114).

[119] Paula García Andrade, 'The Distribution of Powers Between EU Institutions for Conducting External Affairs through Non-Binding Instruments' (2016) 1 *European Papers* 115, 116.

[120] European Commission, 'On Circular Migration and Mobility Partnerships between the European Union and Third Countries' COM(2007) 248 Final.

[121] See Asli Okyay and Jonathan Zaragoza-Cristiani, 'The Leverage of the Gatekeeper: Power and Interdependence in the Migration Nexus between the EU and Turkey' (2016) 51 *The International Spectator* 51.

[122] These included Council Regulation (EC) No 1488/96 on financial and technical measures to accompany (MEDA) the reform of economic and social structures in the framework of the Euro-Mediterranean partnership [1996] OJ L 189/1; Regulation (EC) No 1638/2006 laying down general provisions establishing a European Neighbourhood and Partnership Instrument, OJ [2006] L310/1; Regulation (EU) No 232/2014 of the European Parliament and of the Council of 11 March 2014 establishing a European Neighbourhood Instrument, OJ [2014], L 77/27, These Regulations are no longer in force and they have been largely replaced by the NDICI Regulation (n 73).

In the context of the Valletta Summit in 2015, the Emergency Trust Fund (TF) for Africa was launched on the legal bases of the EU Financial Regulation[123] and the Financial Regulation applicable to the European Development Fund.[124] The Fund comprises financial allocations from the EU budget and a variety of donors, including EU Member States and non-EU countries, with the European Commission playing a major role in its governance.[125] While it has been praised for its flexibility and the swift allocation of funds, concerns have been raised over the duplication of or overlapping with other EU forms of support.[126] The Trust Fund was extended for another year until the end of 2021,[127] and the implementation of its programmes in Morocco is expected to last until 2025.[128] From the second half of 2021, the EU financial support to Morocco, including in the migration domain, is vehiculated primarily through the Neighbourhood, Development and International Cooperation Instrument (NDICI) – 'Global Europe', replacing the ENI and rationalising a host of EU external financial instruments.[129]

EU-led networks of cooperation also arise through the upgrade of already existing networks initiated by EU Member States. A case in point in the migration domain was the integrated system of external vigilance (SIVE).[130] Initiated by Spain to monitor the Spanish–Moroccan border, the project was subsequently funded by the EU[131] and developed further with the participation of Moroccan forces.[132] Moreover, the Seahorse programme, which was mainly financed by the EU and implemented by Spain, envisaged setting up an expert network, and the development of transnational coordination for the fight against illegal immigration.[133] This project has been subsequently upgraded through

[123] See in particular Regulation (EU, Euratom) 2018/1046 on the financial rules applicable to the general budget of the Union, OJ [2018] L 193/ 1, Art 234, and, previously Regulation No 966/2012, OJ [2012] L 298/ 1, Art 187.

[124] Council Regulation (EU) 2015/323 on the financial regulation applicable to the 11th European Development Fund, OJ [2015] l 58/17. See Art 42 (no longer in force).

[125] See European Commission, 'Decision of 20 October 2015 on the establishment of a European Union Emergency Trust Fund for stability and addressing root causes of irregular migration and displaced persons in Africa on the establishment of a European Union Emergency Trust Fund for stability and addressing root causes of irregular migration and displaced persons in Africa, C(2015) 7293 final and the Constitutive Agreement of the EU Trust Fund for Africa', trust-fund-for-africa.europa.eu/system/files/2019-07/original_constitutive_agreement_en_with_signatures.pdf.

[126] European Court of Auditors, Special Report, 'European Union Emergency Trust Fund for Africa: flexible but lacking focus', Report pursuant to Article 278(4) TFEU, 2018.

[127] Council Regulation (EU) 2015/323 of 2 March 2015 on the financial regulation applicable to the 11th European Development Fund, [2015] OJ L 58/17, Art 42.

[128] European Commission, Factsheet, EU Migration support in Morocco, February 2023.

[129] NDICI Regulation (n 73).

[130] Dirección General de la Guardia Guardia Civil, 'Sistema Integrado de Vigilancia Exterior (SIVE)', www.guardiacivil.es/es/prensa/especiales/sive/index.html.

[131] European Commission, 'EU Project, Seahorse Network, 2006–2008', ec.europa.eu/anti-trafficking/eu-projects/seahorse-network_en.

[132] Dirección General de la Guardia Guardia Civil, 'El Director General de la Guardia Civil presenta en Málaga los medios que participarán en la operación INDALO' (2015), www.guardiacivil.es/ga/prensa/historico_prensa/5363.html. El Qadim (n 106) 353–54.

[133] European Commission (n 131).

the Eurosur framework[134] led by Frontex.[135] A working arrangement between Frontex and the Moroccan Ministry of Interior for operational cooperation was signed in December 2015.[136]

The Western-European Mediterranean continues to occupy a crucial place in EU migration management. After the five-fold increase of departures from Morocco from 2017 to 2018,[137] EU–Morocco cooperation has brought about a progressive reduction in migration flows.[138] In 2020–2021,[139] and particularly in 2023, arrivals have surged again.[140] In that light, the cooperation networks ensuing from Frontex's partnership with Morocco have been extended to risk analysis, technology and innovation, and coastguard cooperation.[141] The EU thus supports the modernisation of the Moroccan legal framework through EU funds contributing to the socialisation of Morocco in cooperative arrangements extending the EU's legal space.[142]

A key dimension of the EU-Morocco cooperation networks in migration control occurred in the context of the National Strategy for Immigration and Asylum (SNIA) launched by Morocco in 2013. The strategy envisages a regularisation programme for migrants, the management of migration flows ensuring respect for human rights, and the reinforcement of the Moroccan institutional framework. These objectives were accompanied by significant developments in the Moroccan legislative framework.[143] A migration strategy to improve coordination among different sectors of Moroccan administration had been at the

[134] Regulation (EU) No 1052/2013 establishing the European Border Surveillance System (Eurosur) [2013] OJ L 295/11.

[135] Julien Jeandesboz, 'European Border Policing: EUROSUR, Knowledge, Calculation' (2017) 18 *Global Crime* 256, 274.

[136] Frontex, Management Board Decision 53/2015 of 10 December 2015 Adopting the Working Arrangement between Frontex and the Ministry of the Interior of the Kingdom of Morocco (Directorate for General Affairs), frontex.europa.eu/assets/Management_Board/decisions/WA/MB_Decision_53_2015_adopting_the_WA_between_Frontex_and_the_Ministry_of_the_Interior_of_the_Kingdom_of_Morocco.pdf.

[137] Frontex, 'Risk Analysis for 2019' (European Border and Coast Guard Agency 2019) 6. However, a significant decrease was witnessed in 2019 (57% for the sea route): Frontex, 'Risk Analysis for 2020' (European Border and Coast Guard Agency 2020) 26.

[138] European Council, Council of the EU, Migration flows on the Western Routes, www.consilium.europa.eu/en/policies/eu-migration-policy/western-routes.

[139] Frontex, 'Situation at EU External Borders, News Release 16 December 2020', frontex.europa.eu/media-centre/news-release/situation-at-eu-external-borders-western-african-route-at-record-highs-yzD0DS.

[140] Frontex, Record arrivals on Western African route in October 2023, www.frontex.europa.eu/media-centre/news/news-release/record-arrivals-on-western-african-route-in-october-uNCHfO.

[141] Frontex, 'International Border and Coast Guard Community Gathers in Warsaw' (31 October 2019), www.frontex.europa.eu/media-centre/news/news-release/international-border-and-coast-guard-community-gathers-in-warsaw-oIfoTR.

[142] European Commission, 'Document d'action Pour Le Programme d'appui Aux Politiques Migratoires Du Royaume Du Maroc, Annexe 1 à La Décision d'exécution de La Commission Relative Au Programme d'action Annuel 2016 – Partie 3 En Faveur Du Maroc' (Bruxelles, 2016) CRIS: ENI/2016/39-372, neighbourhood-enlargement.ec.europa.eu/system/files/2017-04/c_2016_8836_morocco_aap_2016_part_3_annex_1.pdf.

[143] Dahir N° 1-16-127 du 25 aout 2016 portant promulgation de la Loi n° 27-14 relative à la lutte contre la traite des êtres humains 2016 (Bulletin Officiel du Maroc n° 6526 du 12 Decembre 2016).

centre of the cooperation programmes financed by the EU in Morocco for several years.[144] Arguably, the launch of the SNIA can be thus construed as responding to EU processes of socialisation, resulting in Moroccan internalisation of EU's policy objectives and nurturing Morocco's desire to enhance its international image with respect to upholding of human rights.

The EU funds the implementation of the SNIA primarily through the ENI and the North Africa window of the EU TF. In the framework of the ENI, at the end of 2016, the EU earmarked a significant proportion of its budget support to the overhaul of the Moroccan legislative framework following the adoption of the Moroccan migration strategy.[145] The EU's financial contribution thus fostered networks of cooperation between Morocco and NGOs, Member States and UN agencies.[146] The objectives of the EU's support included the reinforcement of the legislative and institutional foundations of Moroccan migration policies, the development of knowledge on migration issues and, significantly, the reinforcement of the national system of voluntary return to countries of origin.[147]

Several cooperation networks have been developed under the aegis of the EU TF.[148] In 2019, the EU set up a comprehensive programme to support integrated border management and migration in Morocco under the request of Spain. Its primary objective was to combat irregular migration.[149] This initiative was intended to support the programmes of budget support in the domain of integrated border management already envisaged in the RSA II.[150] The programme also envisioned assistance and training of Moroccan official for the purchase and use of relevant land and sea equipment. Training was intended to exchange best practices with the EU on the matter of irregular migration management and to foster cooperation schemes with Frontex.[151]

While recognising the reduction in migration flows reflecting the positive results in EU–Moroccan cooperation, EU funding documents highlight the rather slow implementation of the Moroccan migration policy, especially with regard to the adoption and application of the legislative framework to address the

[144] Daniel Wunderlich, 'Differentiation and Policy Convergence against Long Odds: Lessons from Implementing EU Migration Policy in Morocco' (2010) 15 *Mediterranean Politics* 249, 265; European Commission, 'Staff Working Document Accompanying the Communication from the Commission: Strengthening the European Neighbourhood Policy, ENP Progress Report – Morocco' (2006) COM(2006) 726 Final.

[145] European Commission (n 142).

[146] Expertise France, GIZ (Gesellschaft für Technishe Zusammenarbeit), AECID (Agencia Española la Cooperación Internacional y el Desarrollo), UNICEF, IOM.

[147] European Commission, 'Décision d'éxecution Du 15 Decembre 2016 Relative Au Programme d'action Annuel 2016 – Partie 3 En Faveur Du Maroc à Financer Sur Le Budget Général de l'Union, C(2016) 8836 Final' 2–3.

[148] European Union, 'EU Support on Migration in Morocco' February 2023, trust-fund-for-africa.europa.eu/system/files/2023-03/EU_support_migration_morocco_Kostas.pdf.

[149] European Commission, 'Contrat T05-EUTF-NOA-MA-05 (T05.888), Description de l'action « Soutien à La Gestion Intégrée Des Frontières et de La Migration Au Maroc », Réf Ares(2019)2624518; N° Réf GestDem 2020/7898' (2019) 9.

[150] ibid 11.

[151] ibid.

precarious status of migrants in Morocco in line with the Kingdom's international commitments.[152]

B. Accountability Gap in the Externalisation of EU Border Controls

The externalisation of the EU's border controls has often problematic implications in terms of human rights protection. A study commissioned by the European Parliament, highlighted how a readmission agreement between the EU and Morocco would transfer the management of migration flows to Morocco with the risk of exposing migrants sent back to Morocco to treatments not compliant with human rights. This was pointed out after the repression exercised by Moroccan police of migrants attempting to reach Europe through the border fences separating Morocco to the Spanish enclaves of Ceuta and Melilla.[153] The European Commission itself highlighted instances of breaches of the rights of migrants with sub-Saharan origin that have been illegally detained after a repression campaign launched by Moroccan forces.[154]

Concerns have been raised in the Council of Europe fora by the Special Representative on Migration and Refugees, Tomáš Boček. Several practices have been condemned in the framework of extended networks of migration management. These practices entail that 'whenever boats of migrants moving towards the Spanish waters are detected the [Spanish] *Guardia Civil* notifies the Royal Moroccan Navy which often intercepts migrants before they cross the border and returns them to Morocco'. Challenges were pointed out to the principle of non-refoulement as 'a keystone of international human rights law and essential to the obligations to which member states have committed themselves under Article 2 … and Article 3 … of the European Convention on Human Rights (ECHR)'.[155]

Migration containment practices in the border area between Spain and Morocco have also raised questions of jurisdiction, notably in *ND and NT v Spain* before the ECtHR.[156] In the appeal case, a strand of Spain's submission built on the

[152] See for instance European Commission, EU emergency trust fund for Africa, Référence: T05-EUTF-NOA-MA-07, 'Appui aux actions des autorités marocaines sur la gestion des flux migratoires' 9, storage.googleapis.com/akvo-rsr-production-media-files/db/project/8634/document/T05-EUTF-NOA-MA-07_2020.pdf.

[153] Claire Rodier, 'Analyse de La Dimension Externe Des Politiques d́asile et d́immigration de ĺUE – Synthèse et Recommandations Pour Le Parlement Européen', European Parliament, 8 June 2006, www.europarl.europa.eu/meetdocs/2004_2009/documents/dt/619/619330/619330fr.pdf.

[154] See European Commission, 'Décision d'exécution Du 19 Decembre 2019 Relative Au Financement Du Programme d'action Pluriannuel En Faveur Du Maroc Pour Les Années 2019 et 2020 Partie I, C(2019) 9148 Final', Annex IV, 7.

[155] Tomáš Boček, Report of the Fact-Finding Mission by Ambassador Tomáš Boček, Special Representative of the UN Secretary General on Migration and Refugees, to Spain, SG/Inf(2018)25, rm.coe.int/09000016808d2c31#_ftnref6.

[156] ECtHR, *ND and NT v Spain* nos 8675/15 and 8697/15, judgment of 3 October 2017; and ECtHR, *ND and NT v Spain*, judgment of 13 February 2020 (appeal).

notion of 'operational border' which was introduced by the Spanish *Guardia Civil's* border control operation protocol of 26 February 2014.[157] The tenor of this notion may be construed as attempting to limiting Spanish jurisdiction especially in its African enclaves of Ceuta and Melilla, and with respect to the fences at the border of Morocco.[158] The Guardia Civil protocol envisages that:

> [W]here attempts by migrants to cross this line illegally are contained and repelled by the law-enforcement agencies responsible for controlling the border, no actual illegal entry is deemed to have taken place. Entry is deemed to have been affected only where a migrant has penetrated beyond the above-mentioned internal fence, thereby entering the national territory and coming within the scope of the rules governing aliens.[159]

In the appeal, the ECtHR highlighted that the Chamber had not assessed 'whether the fences scaled by the applicants were located on Spanish or Moroccan territory', and it reviewed whether the actions it undertook were in pursuance of Article 13 of the Schengen Borders Code.[160] The Strasbourg Court held that 'the special nature of the context as regards migration cannot justify an area outside the law where individuals are covered by no legal system' and 'the Convention cannot be selectively restricted to only parts of the territory of a State by means of an artificial reduction in scope of its territorial jurisdiction'.[161] Therefore the Spanish Government's objection on its lack of jurisdiction was dismissed. Yet, the ECtHR was unpersuaded by the findings of collective expulsion by the previous Chamber's judgment. It posited that that states may

> refuse entry to their territory to aliens, including potential asylum-seekers, who have failed, without cogent reasons …, to comply with [the Schengen Borders Code] arrangements by seeking to cross the border at a different location, especially, as happened in this case, by taking advantage of their large numbers and using force.[162]

In that regard, Carrera highlights how, although in principle it is prohibiting the artificial restriction of States' territorial jurisdiction, the Strasbourg Court seems to limit the operations of border control envisaged by EU law to those occurring at 'border crossing points'.[163] Instead, EU law also explicitly envisages 'border

[157] ECtHR, *ND and NT v Spain* (appeal) [37].

[158] The Ministry of Interior Spain website refers to 'a *special legal regime* in Ceuta and Melilla so that foreigners who are detected on the border line of the territorial demarcation of Ceuta or Melilla, attempting an unauthorized crossing of the border in a violent, flagrant or clandestine manner, are rejected in order to prevent their illegal entry into Spain', my translation (emphasis added), MoI of Spain, 'El Ministerio del Interior culmina un protocolo de actuación integral en los perímetros fronterizos de Ceuta y Melilla' *Ministerio del Interior* (22 October 2014), www.interior.gob.es/noticias/detalle.

[159] Quoted ECtHR, *ND and NT v Spain* (appeal) (n 156) [37].

[160] ibid [90]–[91].

[161] ibid [110].

[162] ibid [210], see [231].

[163] Sergio Carrera, 'The Strasbourg Court Judgement ND and NT v Spain. A Carte Blanche to Push Backs at EU External Borders?' EUI RSCAS Working Paper, 2020/21, 7.

surveillance activities'.[164] The combined reading of Articles 2(12) and 4 of the Border Schengen Code suggests that both the activities of border control and border surveillance shall be subject to relevant EU and international human rights instruments.

The reasoning behind the practices of migration containment emerging in the case now informs the New Immigration and Asylum Pact proposed by the European Commission. The pact envisages a pre-entry screening 'applicable to all third-country nationals who cross the external border without authorisation'.[165] Such a screening would be operated at the EU's external borders and during the screening, and the persons concerned 'shall not be authorised to enter the territory of a Member State'.[166] The 'no legal system area' evoked by the ECtHR might thus be legitimised by an EU law proposal which, although through a legal fiction, aims to keep migrants outside of the EU legal system.[167]

The development of these international cooperative arrangements and networks to tackle migration matters raises questions on the ultimate responsibility for joint operations devised to manage migration flows and possible breaches of human rights.[168] It has been proposed that the international law concept of refoulement be adapted to the concept of *containment* to respond to the burgeoning practices of migration management. This would also hold accountable sponsoring destination states and international organisations (such as the EU) when providing assistance to transit states.[169]

These accountability and responsibility gaps call for novel efforts to capture the reality of relationships and cooperative arrangements in migration control. The notions of EU neighbourhood law and extension of the EU's legal space attempting to capture the legal relations in place in the EU's proximity are a step in this direction. International responsibility for activities of third countries carried out in pursuance of programmes of containment could in part be attributable to the EU on the basis of the legal link that the EU financial instruments and regulations generate between EU law and the programmes of return that could result in breaches of human rights. This understanding would require a paradigm shift in the understanding of the exercise of sovereignty in cooperative networks and arrangements. The challenges inherent to such a change of paradigm relate to the fact that EU neighbourhood law is not emerging from membership to an

[164] Regulation (EU) 2016/399 of the European Parliament and of the Council of 9 March 2016 on a Union Code on the rules governing the movement of persons across borders (Schengen Borders Code) [2016] OJ L 77/1.

[165] Commission Communication, 'A New Pact on Migration and Asylum', COM(2020) 609 Final, 4.

[166] European Commission, 'Proposal for a Regulation Introducing a Screening of Third Country Nationals at the External Borders and Amending Regulations (EC) No 767/2008, (EU) 2017/2226, (EU) 2018/1240 and (EU) 2019/817', COM(2020) 612 Final, 2020/0278(COD), Art 4.

[167] Editorial Comments, 'Europe Is Trembling. Looking for a Safe Place in EU Law' (2020) 56 *Common Market Law Review* 1675, 1687.

[168] See extensively Melanie Fink, *Frontex and Human Rights: Responsibility in 'multi-Actor Situations' under the ECHR and EU Public Liability Law* (Oxford University Press, 2018).

[169] Annick Pijnenburg, 'Containment Instead of Refoulement: Shifting State Responsibility in the Age of Cooperative Migration Control?' (2020) 20 *Human Rights Law Review* 306.

international organisation (the EU) that could mobilise ARIO clauses, but instead from a set of practices and norms that gravitate around the EU legal order but that are not properly EU law. The broader range of activities gravitating around the EU law with respect to EU law proper is exemplified by the EU–Turkey statement adopted in the context of the Syrian refugee crisis. Questionably, the EU General Court of the EU found that the statement, published by means of a press release, was adopted by the Heads of State and Government of the members of the EU in their international law capacity and not by the European Council acting as an EU institution.[170] Through a legal fiction, the Agreement was thus deemed to be outside the EU legal order. The externalisation of EU border controls in *Wider Europe* thus brings to the fore a reconfiguration of jurisdiction and sovereignty not entirely captured by the existing categories of international law.

V. Moroccan Geopolitical Positioning

A. The Judicial and Political Saga of Western Sahara in EU–Moroccan Relations

The controversial application of EU–Morocco Agreements to the territories of Western Sahara is key for understanding the geopolitical challenges in the evolution of the EU–Morocco relations. A long-lasting judicial-political saga is bringing to the fore delicate and complex issues at the interface between EU law and international law. A former Spanish colony, Western Sahara is a non-self-governing-territory under Article 73 UN Charter since 1963.[171] In its Advisory Opinion of 1975, while acknowledging some old ties of allegiance between the Sultan of Morocco and some of the tribes of Western Sahara, the International Court of Justice did not find 'ties of such a nature as might affect the application of … the principle of self-determination', similar considerations were drawn for Mauritania.[172]

A complex scenario emerged with armed confrontations and annexations, which followed the Madrid Agreements sanctioning the partition of the Spanish Sahara between Morocco and Mauritania in 1975.[173] Currently, Morocco controls about 80 per cent of the territory, while the Sahrawi Arab Democratic Republic (SADR) led by the Polisario Front the rest. Mauritania had retreated from the Sahara conflict and withdrew its sovereignty claim in 1979 and recognised the SADR in 1984.[174]

[170] Case T-192/16, *NF v European Council* EU:T:2017:128 [69].

[171] UNGA, Report on the Committee on information from non-self-governing territories, Official Records Records: eighteenth session, supplement No 14, UN doc A/5514, 1963. For the withdrawal of Spain as a colonial power see UN GA, Resolution 2072 Spanish Sahara (XX), 16 December 1965.

[172] ICJ, *Western Sahara (Advisory Opinion)* [1975] ICJ Rep 68 [162].

[173] Declaration of Principles on Western Sahara by Spain Morocco and Mauritania, 19 November 1975, peacemaker.un.org/sites/peacemaker.un.org/files/MA-MR-ES_751114_DeclarationPrinciplesOnWesternSahara_0.pdf.

[174] Zekeria Ould Ahmed Salem 'Mauritania: A Saharan Frontier-State' (2005) *10 The Journal of North African Studies* 491.

The UN has recognised the Polisario Front as 'the representative of the people of Western Sahara' that 'should participate fully in any search for a just, lasting and definitive political solution of the question of Western Sahara'.[175] A long and unconclusive UN-led process for a referendum on self-determination ensued with the deployment of the United Nations Mission for the Referendum in Western Sahara (MINURSO)[176] still in place today. A major reason of the stalemate is the identification of the people entitled to participate in the referendum. Moreover, from late 2020 also the ceasefire has been put in jeopardy.[177] In the resulting entanglement, Morocco is engaging in a diplomatic strategy aiming at having its sovereignty claims recognised in several fora, including the African Union.[178] In turn, Polisario is pursuing a path of legal mobilisation of EU law and international law in EU judicial venues to challenge Moroccan claims to sovereignty.

In Case T-512/12, Polisario challenged before the General Court the Decision on Reciprocal Liberalisation of agricultural and fisheries products in the framework of the EU–Morocco Association Agreement.[179] The General Court found that, in exercising its discretion as to whether to conclude the contested Agreement, the Council should have ascertained that 'there was no evidence of an exploitation of the natural resources of the territory of Western Sahara under Moroccan control likely to be to the detriment of its inhabitants and to infringe their fundamental rights'.[180] The Council challenged the ensuing annulment of the contested decision before the ECJ.

In Case C-104/16P, the ECJ detached itself from the reasoning and findings of the General Court. Largely following the Opinion of AG Wathelet, the ECJ relied on international law sources. On the basis of the principle of self-determination, it established that Western Sahara has 'a separate and distinct status' under international law in relation to the Kingdom of Morocco.[181] On the basis of the pacta *pacta tertiis* principle, it established that without the consent of the people of Western Sahara as a third party to the EU–Morocco Agreement and therefore the said Agreement could not apply to Western Sahara without its people's consent.[182] The ECJ posited that the General Court 'incorrectly held that the Liberalisation Agreement had to be interpreted as applicable to the territory of Western Sahara'.[183] Similar findings informed the preliminary reference procedure

[175] UNGA Res 34/37 (21 November 1979) UN Doc A/RES/34/37, point 7.

[176] UNGA Res 690 (29 April 1991) UN Doc S/RES/690.

[177] UN SG Report on the situation of Western Sahara 1 October 2021, S/2021/843.

[178] Morocco is a founding member of the African Union. It withdrew in 1984, following the SADR admission to the Union, and rejoined in 2017.

[179] Council Decision (EU) 2012/497 on the conclusion of an Agreement between the European Union and Morocco concerning reciprocal liberalisation measures on agricultural products, processed agricultural products, fish and fishery products, [2012] OJ L 241/2.

[180] Case T-512/12 *Front Polisario v Council*, EU:T:2015:953 [241].

[181] Case C-104/16P, *Council v Front Polisario*, EU:C:2016:973 [90]–[92].

[182] ibid [106].

[183] ibid [126]–[127]. For a critique of the Court's argument see Enzo Cannizzaro, 'In Defence of *Front Polisario*: The ECJ as a Global *Jus Cogens* Maker' (2018) 55 *Common Market Law Review* 569, 578; François Dubuisson and Ghislain Poissonnier, 'La Cour de Justice de l'Union européenne et la question du Sahara occidental: cachez cette pratique (illégale) que je ne saurais voir' (2016) 2 *Revue belge de droit international* 601, 630.

in the *Western Sahara UK* judgment.[184] Here, it was questioned the validity of the EU–Morocco Fisheries Partnership Agreement[185] and the EU–Morocco arrangements setting out fishing opportunity.[186] The judgment is particularly interesting in light of the different conclusions of the Advocate General Wathelet. He found that the contested acts 'breach the European Union's obligation to respect the right to self-determination of the people of that territory and its obligation not to recognise an illegal situation resulting from a breach of that right'.[187]

Considering that neither the General Court[188] nor the ECJ[189] ruled out the possibility of extending the contested liberalisation and fisheries Agreements to the non-self-governing territory of Western Sahara, the EU political institutions eventually decided to pursue this controversial route. The Council adopted two decisions extending the EU–Morocco agreements to Western Sahara.[190] The move of the EU political institutions been arguably predicated on the *Wider Europe* paradigm whereby trade liberalisation is a regarded as a vector for stability and convergence to EU law. In the Commission words, the aim was 'to foster the economic development of Western Sahara by treating it export to the EU the same as export of products of Moroccan origin'.[191]

The original EU–Morocco Agreement later extended to Western Sahara displays characteristics typical of the extension of the EU's legal space. Although the Agreement envisages cooperation on the basis of the relevant WTO rules,[192] a closer look reveals how cooperation is in fact predicated upon the extension of the EU's legal space. The liberalisation arrangements are to be considered in the framework of the EU–Morocco EuroMed Agreement, which envisages in its Article 40(1) that the 'Parties shall take appropriate steps to promote the use by Morocco of [EU] technical rules and European standards for industrial and agri-food products and certification procedures'. The SPS sector is one of the domains in which the Moroccan Government envisaged convergence to EU norms in the framework of the PNCR in the implementation of the EU–Morocco Advanced Status.[193]

[184] Case C-266/16, *Western Sahara Campaign UK*, EU:C:2018:118.

[185] Through Council Regulation (EC) No 764/2006 on the conclusion of the Fisheries Partnership Agreement between the European Community and the Kingdom of Morocco, [2006] OJ, L 141/1.

[186] Through Council Decision (EU) 2013/785/EU on the conclusion of the EU–Morocco Protocol setting out the fishing opportunities and financial contribution provided for in the Fisheries Partnership Agreement, [2013] OJ L349/1.

[187] Case C-266/16 *Western Sahara Campaign UK*, Opinion of AG Wathelet, EU:C:2018:1 [293].

[188] *Front Polisario v Council* (n 180) [215].

[189] *Council v Front Polisario* (n 181) [106].

[190] See Council Decision (EU) 2019/217 on the conclusion of the Agreement amending Protocols 1 and 4 of the EU–Morocco EuroMed Agreement, [2019] OJ L 34/1; and Council Decision (EU) 2019/441 on the conclusion of the Sustainable Fisheries Partnership Agreement between the European Union and the Kingdom of Morocco, [2019] OJ L 77/4.

[191] European Commission, 'Proposal for a Council Decision Relating to the Signature, on Behalf of the European Union, of the Agreement in the Form of an Exchange of Letters between the European Union and the Kingdom of Morocco on the Amendment of Protocols 1 and 4 EU–Morocco EuroMed Agreement' COM(2018) 479 Final.

[192] EU–Morocco liberalisation Agreement amending the EU–Morocco EuroMed Agreement [2012] OJ L 241/4, Art 8.

[193] European Commission (n 63) 9; European Commission (n 58) 16.

The Council Decisions leading to the extension of the Agreements to Western Sahara were preceded by a consultation by the Commission. Here, the Commission uses the term Western Sahara to refer to the part of the territory administered de facto by Morocco.[194] Significantly, the consultation was used as a proxy for the expression of consent of the people of Western Sahara. Moreover, the target of the Commission consultation was the 'population concerned' rather than the people of Western Sahara.[195] The motive adduced for this approach is that 'Although the people of Western Sahra have the right to self-determination, … it is not on the EU to conduct a census on them', and that also UN documents relating to non-self-governing territories refer to socio-economic benefits of the inhabitants.[196]

In order to fulfil the Council's mandate, thus the Commission 'detached the political aspects from the economic ones and declared the former irrelevant'.[197] The detachment of politics from legal and economic instruments appears to be grounded on a thin understanding of procedural requirements.[198] The impact of the extension of the EU–Morocco legal and economic instruments to Western Sahara on the political developments of this self-governing territory is disregarded under the veil of political agnosticism and neutrality on the final status of the territory. The Council decisions leading to the extension of the Agreements to Western Sahara have been successfully challenged before the General Court, which annulled the decisions on the grounds that *consultation* was not enough to ascertain the *consent* of the people of Western Sahara.[199] A new episode of this convoluted saga is in the making in the pending appeals of the GC judgments before the ECJ.[200]

It is worth stressing that no EU Member State has formally recognised Moroccan claims over Western Sahara. Yet, the Council Decisions analysed above do not pose an obstacle to Moroccan use of Western Sahara natural resources in the trade with the EU. The composite political orientations within the EU are indeed hard to discern. Spain newspapers have leaked a letter by the Spanish Head of Government addressed to King Mohammed VI expressing appreciation for

[194] European Commission, 'Report on Benefits for the People of Western Sahara and Public Consultation on Extending Tariff Preferences to Products from Western Sahara', SWD(2018) 346 Final/2, 6.

[195] The Commission attempted to somewhat elaborate on the problems and reasons underlying this approach. European Commission, Document accompagnant le document: 'Proposition de décision du Conseil relative à la signature, au nom de l'Union, de l'accord de partenariat dans le domaine de la pêche durable entre l'Union européenne et le Royaume du Maroc', SWD(2018) 433 final, 11.

[196] European Commission (n 191) 5; European Commission (n 194) 7.

[197] Pål Wrange, 'Western Sahara, the European Commission and the Politics of International Legal Argument' in Antoine Duval and Eva Kassoti, *The legality of economic activities in occupied territories: international, EU law and business and human rights perspectives* (Routledge, 2020) 190.

[198] Alessandro Petti, 'The Polisario saga: the principle of good administration and the interface between EU law and international law' in Diane Fromage (ed), *Jacques Ziller a European scholar* (EUI Cadmus, 2022).

[199] Case T-279/19 *Polisario v Council*, EU:T:2021:639; Joined Cases T-344/19 and T-356/19, *Polisario v Council*, EU:T:2021:640.

[200] Case C-799/21 P *Council v Polisario*, pending; Case C-778/21P, *Commission v Polisario*, pending.

the Moroccan plan for autonomy of Western Sahara.[201] In official fora, however, Madrid continues to support a mutually acceptable political solution within the UN framework.[202] In turn, France has intervened in support of the Council in the recent pronouncements before the General Court, although its relations with Morocco are increasingly under strain, not the least for Rabat mounting expectations on Paris's recognition of its sovereignty claims.[203] Moreover, in the Council proceedings leading to the adoption of the Decision extending the Agreement, some Member States[204] have submitted a peculiar declaration in which they highlighted that they had taken a report drafted by the Council legal service on the issue 'as evidence that the Council Legal Service considers that entering into the presented agreement is fully consistent with the judgment of the [ECJ] and does not prejudice the status of Western Sahara'.[205] Only Sweden manifestly expressed its dissent. It stressed that it 'is not satisfied that the outcome of the consultation process can be said to constitute the free and informed consent of the people of Western Sahara', especially in light of the objections of Polisario to that consultation.[206]

Pending the ECJ's pronouncements, in a report issued in early 2023, the Commission highlighted the benefit of the agricultural and fishing sectors of Western Sahara from the extension of the tariff preferences.[207] The report recognised the 'mixed' results of Moroccan reforms to promote and protect human rights and fundamental freedom in a section of the report devoted to EU–Morocco cooperation on fundamental rights. However, the report brings to the fore the ambiguous and logically tortuous position of the EU on Western Sahara. The Commission highlights that 'Western Sahara is considered by Morocco as an integral part of its territory' and 'as a consequence', the 'human rights situation in Western Sahara has traditionally been monitored by the EU pursuant to the institutional framework of the [EU–Morocco EuroMed Agreement]'. In the words of the Commission,

[201] Miguel González, 'La carta de Pedro Sánchez a Mohamed VI: "Debemos construir una nueva relación que evite futuras crisis"' (*El País*, 23 March 2022), elpais.com/espana/2022-03-23/la-carta-de-pedro-sanchez-a-mohamed-vi-debemos-construir-una-nueva-relacion-que-evite-futuras-crisis.html. Raphael Minder, *The New York Times*, 'Spain, Seeking Better Ties With Morocco, Shifts Stance on Western Sahara' (19 March 2022), www.nytimes.com/2022/03/19/world/europe/spain-morocco-western-sahara.html.

[202] 'Statement by His Excellency Pedro Sánchez Pérez-Castejón President of the Government 20 September 2023', gadebate.un.org/sites/default/files/gastatements/%5Bvariable%3Acurrent_session%5D/es_en.pdf.

[203] Aboubakr Jamaï, 'Les dessous d'une fâcherie franco-marocaine' (*Le Monde diplomatique*, 1 October 2023), www.monde-diplomatique.fr/2023/10/JAMAI/66190. Frédéric Bobin, *Le Monde*, 'Entre la France et le Maroc, des réseaux sur le déclin' (Paris, 5 October 2023) 22; Frédéric Bobin, 'Paris et Rabat, deux capitales en froid' *Le Monde* (4 October 2023) 16; Julia Pascual, 'Paris et Rabat, aux frontières de la discorde' *Le Monde* (6 October 2023).

[204] Denmark, Finland, Germany and Ireland.

[205] Council of the EU, Summary Record, Permanent Representative Committee, Brussels 11 and 13 July 2018, 11441/18 CRS CRP 26.

[206] ibid.

[207] European Commission '2022 Report on the impact and benefits for the people of Western Sahara on extending tariff preferences to products originating in Western Sahara' SWD(2022) 448 final, 25.

this is 'without prejudice to EU's own position on Western Sahara'.[208] Such an ambiguous EU's stance stems from the coexistence of a formal *non-recognition* of Moroccan claims on Western Shara, in conformity to the pronouncements of the CJEU,[209] with a de facto *recognition* of these claims ensuing from the management of the EU–Western Shara relations within the framework of the EU–Morocco Association Agreement.

There has been thus a progressive (and largely informal) rapprochement to the Moroccan claims on Western Sahara by the EU, especially since December 2011, when the European Parliament originally rejected giving its consent the conclusion of the EU–Morocco Fisheries Agreement for concerns over the Western Sahara issue.[210] An even more radical change of approach occurred on the part of the US: during the Trump administration, the United States has recognised Moroccan claims over Western Sahara.[211] This move has not been overturned by the subsequent administration and marks an abrupt change from the previous stance, whereby products originating from Western Sahara would not be considering as falling under the US–Morocco Free Trade Area.[212] The US recognition was part of a broader negotiation package chaperoned by American diplomacy, which included the stabilisation of Moroccan–Israeli relations.[213] This move might have played a role in the fact that the US has overtaken France as the first source of foreign direct investment in Morocco.[214]

In her Opinion concerning the pending cases,[215] AG Ćapeta found that the General Court had misinterpreted the ECJ's judgment in *Council v Polisario*, with

[208] ibid 22.

[209] The pronouncements are relegated to a footnote of the report (n 17).

[210] European Parliament, Legislative resolution of 14 December 2011 on the draft Council decision on the conclusion of a Protocol between the European Union and the Kingdom of Morocco setting out the fishing opportunities and financial compensation provided for in the Fisheries Partnership Agreement between the European Community and the Kingdom of Morocco (11226/2011 – C7-0201/2011–2011/0139(NLE)), [2013] OJ C 168E/155; See also European Parliament, 'Extension of EU–Morocco Fisheries Agreement Rejected – Call for a Better Deal | News |' (14 December 2011), www.europarl.europa.eu/news/en/press-room/20111213IPR34070/extension-of-eu-morocco-fisheries-agreement-rejected-call-for-a-better-deal. See also the more articulated position in the Council in 2011 Council of the EU, Press Release 3070th Council Meeting Agriculture and Fisheries, 6655/11 PRESSE 30 PR CO, 12.

[211] US Embassy in Morocco, 'Proclamation on Recognizing The Sovereignty Of The Kingdom Of Morocco Over The Western Sahara' (10 December 2020), ma.usembassy.gov/proclamation-on-recognizing-the-sovereignty-of-the-kingdom-of-morocco-over-the-western-sahara.

[212] US Congress, 'United States, Executive Office of the President, The United States Trade Representative, Letter to the Honorable J.R. Pitts, U.S. House of Representatives Concerning the Free Trade Agreement (FTA) between the United States and Morocco, Washington, 20 July 2004', Congressional Record, V. 150, PT. 13, 22 July 2004 to 14 September 2004 (Government Printing Office, 2009) 17273.

[213] 'Israel, Morocco Agree to Normalise Relations in US-Brokered Deal' *Al Jazeera* (10 December 2020), www.aljazeera.com/news/2020/12/10/israel-morocco-agree-to-normalise-relations-in-us-brokered-deal.

[214] Brendan Murray, 'As West Battles China, a Trade Ally Tries to Keep Both Doors Open' *Bloomberg* (22 June 2023), www.bloomberg.com/news/articles/2023-06-22/as-west-battles-china-a-trade-ally-tries-to-keep-both-doors-open.

[215] See (n 200).

regard to the expression of consent.[216] She argued that the Kingdom of Morocco is capable of consenting on behalf of Western Sahara to the extension of the agreement at issue.[217] The AG's reasoning was informed by her recognition of the role of Morocco as the administering power in Western Sahara;[218] on some qualifications on the status of *Polisario* in Western Sahara;[219] and the inability of the Saharawi people to give consent to be bound by an international agreement before exercising the right to self-determination.[220] Nevertheless, the Advocate General suggested that the ECJ should return the case to the General Court in order to assess the EU's obligations stemming from the right of self-determination of the Saharawi people. These obligations revolve around ensuring that the extended arrangements entered into by Morocco are exclusively to the benefit of the inhabitants of the territory of Western Sahara.[221] This is particularly relevant in light of the different position of Morocco and the EU on the matter, with the former claiming sovereign rights on Western Sahara and the latter considering Morocco as an administering power of that territory.[222] This new controversial episode of the saga is liable to add a new layer of complexity to the issues at stake.

B. Calibrating the *Proximité Optimale* and Reversed Conditionality

The EU's position on the controversial issue of Western Sahara plays a key role in Morocco's calibration of its *proximité optimale* with the Union. Morocco suspended its diplomatic relations with the EU after the judgment of the General Court in 2016.[223] The Moroccan political elite has often linked the application of the EU–Morocco Agreements to Western Sahara to its cooperation with the EU in the domain of migration control highlighting the costs attached to this cooperation.[224] Indeed, in May 2021 Morocco weaponised migration to respond to what it considered hostile acts on the part of Spain with respect to Moroccan claims on Western Sahara.[225]

Moroccan cooperation with the EU in the domain of migration control should be read with a dual perspective. On the one hand, the internalisation of migration

[216] Case C-104/16P (n 181) [106].
[217] Joined Cases C-779/21 P and C-799/21 P, Opinion of AG Ćapeta, EU:C:2024:260 [159].
[218] ibid [156].
[219] ibid [81]–[86].
[220] ibid [133]–[134].
[221] ibid [181]–[185].
[222] ibid [168]; [186].
[223] El Yaakoubi, 'Morocco Suspends Contacts with EU over Court Ruling on Farm Trade' *Reuters* (26 February 2016), www.reuters.com/article/us-eu-morocco-westernsahara-idUSKCN0VY26X.
[224] Gabrielli (n 113). Jesus Cañas and Francisco Peregil, 'Incursions at Spain's North African Exclaves Triple after Moroccan Threats' *El Pais* (27 February 2017), english.elpais.com/elpais/2017/02/27/inenglish/1488185422_295555.html.
[225] 'King Muhammad of Morocco Weaponises Migration' (n 3).

priorities in the Moroccan political agenda reflects the externalisation of the EU's border controls entailed in the socialisation processes of *Wider Europe*. In that regard both internalisation processes and socialisation incentives such as image and status are at play. The Moroccan migration strategy overhauled with EU financial assistance served to counteract the 'international shaming'[226] originating, from a series of reports and analyses denouncing the appalling conditions of sub-Saharan migrants 'trapped at the gates of Europe'.[227] On the other hand, the EU–Morocco cooperation on migration control should be read against the background of the Union's dependence on Morocco to manage and reduce migration flows. In this understanding, EU neighbouring countries are increasingly seen as 'gatekeepers' of the EU.[228] The leverage enjoyed by the EU gatekeepers[229] often leads to 'reversed conditionality'[230] between the EU and its partners premised upon the latter 'geographical rent'.[231] In that light, the narrative of externalisation of EU border controls alone is not sufficient to capture the shifting equilibria in the Moroccan attitude towards migration.[232]

Moreover, the redesign of Moroccan international image through the development of a policy framework on migration was not only intended to enhance its standing in the eyes of its European partners,[233] but was equally intended to reconfigure Morocco's relationship with its Southern neighbours.[234] The King progressively redefined the positioning of Morocco in light of a new 'politique africaine'.[235] As Cherti and Collyer highlight, this marked 'a genuine break from the period in which Moroccan migration policy could be dictated from Europe'.[236]

The economic rationale for what has been powerfully defined as a 'geopolitical rebordering' responded to projects to enhance Moroccan firms' presence and

[226] Kelsey P Norman, 'Between Europe and Africa: Morocco as a Country of Immigration' (2016) 7 *The Journal of the Middle East and Africa* 421, 430.

[227] Médecins Sans Frontières (MSF) International, 'Violence, Vulnerability and Migration: Trapped at the Gates of Europe | MSF', www.msf.org/violence-vulnerability-and-migration-trapped-gates-europe. Rodier (n 153).

[228] Fanny Tittel-Mosser, 'Mobility Partnerships: A Tool for the Externalisation of EU Migration Policy? A Comparative Study of Morocco and Cape Verde' in Sergio Carrera, Juan Santos Vara and Martina Hermina Antonia Strik, *Constitutionalising the External Dimensions of EU Migration Policies in Times of Crisis* (Edward Elgar Publishing, 2019) 243.

[229] Okyay and Zaragoza-Cristiani (n 121).

[230] Fanny Tittel-Mosser, 'Reversed Conditionality in EU External Migration Policy: The Case of Morocco' (2018) 14 *Journal of Contemporary European Research* 349.

[231] Katharina Natter, 'The Formation of Morocco's Policy Towards Irregular Migration (2000–2007): Political Rationale and Policy Processes' (2014) 52 *International Migration* 15.

[232] Leslie Gross-Wyrtzen and Lorena Gazzotti, 'Telling Histories of the Present: Postcolonial Perspectives on Morocco's "Radically New" Migration Policy' (2021) 26 *The Journal of North African Studies* 827.

[233] Katharina Natter, 'Crafting a "Liberal Monarchy": Regime Consolidation and Immigration Policy Reform in Morocco' (2021) *The Journal of North African Studies* 850.

[234] Myriam Cherti and Michael Collyer, 'Immigration and Pensée d'Etat: Moroccan Migration Policy Changes as Transformation of "Geopolitical Culture"' (2015) 20 *The Journal of North African Studies* 590, 602.

[235] El Qadim (n 123).

[236] Cherti and Collyer (n 226) 602.

investments in Africa.[237] At the political level, 'geopolitical rebordering' resulted in the Kingdom's return to the African Union (AU) after 32 years in 2017. King Mohammed VI heralded the return to the AU stressing the Kingdom's decision to be back in the '[African] family … at a time when the Kingdom is among the most developed African nations' and after having strangthened its ties with African partners through several cooperation agreements.[238] This well-planned return was part of an articulated diplomatic and economic strategy principally aimed at gaining African countries' support for Moroccan claims over Western Sahara.[239] It was also intended to marginalise the Saharawi Arab Democratic Republic from the AU.[240] Migration cooperation with its African partners is a key aspect of this strategy.[241]

In the new Moroccan migration policy, the oscillation between the humanitarian aspiration and a rather weak legal framework[242] appears to respond to a precise rationale. As contended by some commentators, 'The SNIA conforms to Morocco's formal alignment to the international human rights regime, but the lack of legal harmonisation grants the state the flexibility to manoeuvre the policy according to its European and African foreign political interests'.[243] Therefore, the safeguard and progresses in the protection of migrants' rights remain 'vulnerable to sudden setbacks'.[244] These conflicting interests thus influence the content and the process of law-making. A visible third country national clause in the EU-level readmission agreement, for instance, could potentially compromise Moroccan relations with the countries of origin of migrants attempting to reach Europe. Instead, more informal arrangements of administrative cooperation between EU agencies and Moroccan forces usually prove more effective for both parties. The EU mainly aims to stem the flow of irregular entry in its territory. In turn, the Kingdom is interested in the EU's financial and technical assistance but maintains independence in positioning itself in the African continent according to its geopolitical interests.

[237] Natter (n 235) 856. Moubarack Lo, 'Relations Maroc-Afrique subsaharienne: quel bilan pour les 15 dernières années ?' *OCP Policy Center* 2016. Moroccan Ministry of Finance 'Relations Maroc-Afrique L'ambition d'une Nouvelle Frontière Actualisation' (July 2015).

[238] Moroccan Government, 'Full Speech of HM the King at 28th African Union Summit' (31 January 2017), www.maroc.ma/en/royal-activities/full-speech-hm-king-28th-african-union-summit.

[239] Liesl Louw-Vaudran, 'The Meaning of Morocco's Return to the African Union' Institute for Security Studies (17 January 2018).

[240] 'Sahara occidental: le Maroc veut déposer une motion visant à exclure la RASD de l'Union africaine' JeuneAfrique.com (8 February 2018), www.jeuneafrique.com/mag/527061/politique/sahara-occidental-le-maroc-veut-deposer-une-motion-visant-a-exclure-la-rasdde-lunion-africaine. 'Comment le Maroc organise le lobbying anti-RASD à l'UA' JeuneAfrique.com (4 February 2023), www.jeuneafrique.com/1414695/politique/comment-le-maroc-organise-le-lobbying-anti-rasd-a-lua.

[241] Moroccan Ministry of Foreign Affairs, 'Politique Nationale d'Immigration et d'Asile – Rapport 2018–2020' (2018).

[242] Leslie Gross-Wyrtzen and Lorena Gazzotti, 'Telling Histories of the Present: Postcolonial Perspectives on Morocco's "Radically New" Migration Policy' (2021) 26 *The Journal of North African Studies* 827, 833.

[243] Mercedes G Jiménez-Alvarez, Keina Espiñeira and Lorena Gazzotti, 'Migration Policy and International Human Rights Frameworks in Morocco: Tensions and Contradictions' (2021) 26 *The Journal of North African Studies* 893, 906.

[244] ibid.

VI. Conclusions

The study of the Moroccan case has illustrated the hiatus between *Wider Europe* and a wider EU. The Moroccan application to EU membership was refused due to geographical motives (now enshrined in Article 49 TEU) delineating the gulf between *Wider Europe* and an enlarged EU. While Morocco was and is a target of *Wider Europe*, the distance between the regimes of EU neighbourhood law governing the EU–Morocco relations and the EU legal order is significant. This is illustrated by the techniques of extension of the EU's legal space. In the EU's relations with Morocco, and more broadly within the ENP, the techniques of extension of the EU's legal space are not operating through articulated substantive *renvois* or mechanisms of organisational interaction with the EU legal order. EU neighbourhood law resides in Morocco's socialisation in the wider European legal space primarily stemming from trade intended as a vector of stabilisation. It is thus the process of gravitation of Morocco around the EU legal order more than the results of tangible convergence that inform the EU–Morocco partnership. As indirectly pointed out by Prodi in his 2002 speech, the objective of the ENP was not necessarily that of establishing a homogeneous legal space, as the one in place with the EEA. It was, instead, that of promoting the formation of a 'ring of friends' surrounding the Union. In its relationship with Morocco, the EU is hence primarily oriented towards cooperation in matters of migration, counterterrorism, and intelligence cooperation.[245] In that light, Morocco has proved capable of leveraging on these sectors and aimed to achieve a *proximité optimale* with the EU while not disregarding its broader interests in the African continent.

This chapter has shown how migration is a sector where patterns of dependence are reversed. While Morocco certainly leverages upon this dependence and often weaponises migration to achieve its geopolitical aims, the extension of the EU's legal space operates also in this domain. The extension of the EU's legal space mainly takes form of the externalisation of EU border controls that are embedded in the mechanisms for Morocco's socialisation into *Wider Europe*.

The political covenant presiding over the EU–Morocco relationship is largely premised upon soft law arrangements and cooperative administrative networks. These networks are illustrative of the relational reconfiguration of sovereignty exercise in *Wider Europe*. Morocco has not formally entered into a covenant with the EU entailing the reconfiguration of its sovereign rights. It is largely for Morocco to determine the extent and the pace of its convergence process with the EU. Yet, the EU–Morocco cooperative arrangements of migration return reconfigure the way sovereignty is exercised. Indeed, the cooperative arrangements in the migration domain reveal intricate patterns of the principal–agent relationship between Morocco, the EU and its Member States (especially Spain) in the extended regime of externalisation of the EU's border controls. The EU exercises a significant role

[245] Bergh (n 50).

in orienting the objectives of Moroccan migration policy, financial resources, technical assistance and coordination of migration operations under the aegis of Frontex. Notwithstanding this, the EU eschews responsibility for human rights violations in the cooperative practices of migration containment. This is partly due to the fact that it is often Morocco's responsibility to carry out operations of 'migration management'. Besides, when EU Member States partake in these operations, regional human rights courts, such as the ECHR are reticent to allocate responsibility to Spain or the EU. This relational reconfiguration of sovereignty creates accountability gaps as there are no adequate judicial venues for sanctioning human rights violations which occur in multi-actor arrangements of migration containment outside the EU borders. This qualifies the EU–Morocco political covenant as rather elusive on both sides of the partnership.

Crucially, the study of the Moroccan case brings to the fore how the edges of *Wider Europe* are liable to shift their international orientation. While at the inception of *Wider Europe* the EU was an uncontested model of international and regional cooperation, in the current fragmented geopolitical landscape, the EU is only one of the possible models. Against this background, Morocco has proven capable to leverage on its 'geographical rent' as a bridge between the EU and Africa promoting its economic interests and advancing its geopolitical objectives in Western Sahara.

PART IV

A Distinctive and Yet Contested Type of Regional Law

9

EU Neighbourhood Law: Gravitation and Contestation in the Extended EU's Legal Space

I. Introduction

This chapter attempts to delineate the defining features of EU neighbourhood law, reflecting on the findings of the previous chapters. By unravelling the interplay between law and diplomacy in calibrating proximity to (and distance from) the EU legal order, the chapter attempts to assess the varying patterns of gravitation around the EU. While examining the *repertoires* of techniques of EU neighbourhood law, the chapter further problematises the existing categories of integration 'beyond membership' in light of the multifaceted nature of EU neighbourhood law regimes. It offers a description of the extension of the EU's legal space through the elements of *scope* of extended EU *acquis* and the *intensity* of gravitation around the EU legal order (section II). It brings to the fore how proximity to and distance from the EU legal order varies in function of the objectives of the regimes of EU neighbourhood law nourishing the relevant political covenants. A particular focus is placed on the legal and political dynamics sustaining the principle and objective of homogeneity in the EU neighbourhood law arrangements that are closest to the EU legal order. This paves the way for discussing the passage from EEA homogeneity to the EU–UK TCA level playing field (section III). The reflection on the nature of the different institutional arrangements of EU neighbourhood law is enriched with a study on how distance from the EU legal order can be calibrated through (the lack of) direct effect of agreements extending the EU's legal space (section IV). The chapter also reviews the motives of contestation of political covenants of EU neighbourhood law (section V). Contestation of EU neighbourhood law includes instances whereby third countries invoke more classical forms of international law in the attempt to downplay the role of the European Union and the magnetism of its law (section V.A).

II. Proximity to the EU Through Repertoires of EU Neighbourhood Law

The arrangements of EU neighbourhood law provide for different echelons of gravitation around the EU's legal order. Proximity to the EU is calibrated through different techniques of extension of the EU's legal space. Delineating a definitive typology or repertoire of techniques of EU neighbourhood law defies simplifications. The categories crafted by the EU legal scholarship on 'external differentiated integration'[1] and 'integration without membership'[2] offer some guidance on the relevance of EU law in *Wider Europe*. The scholarship on integration 'beyond membership' highlights the difference between 'soft law' and 'hard law', distinguishing whether the third country commitment to 'incorporate' EU law into their legal systems is binding or not. Additional guidance pertains to the distinction between 'static' and 'dynamic' adaptation to EU law and on the presence of 'homogeneity clauses' for the interpretation of EU law.[3] The language of the relevant provisions extending the EU *acquis* has also been identified as a variable capable of indicating the *strength* of the obligation.[4]

Yet, beyond the fact that these categories do not make justice to the demarcation between EU law and EU neighbourhood law,[5] the explicatory potential of these categories is limited by a panoply of qualifications. As a matter of fact, the distinction between hard law and soft law gets blurred when one considers the interplay between the two. Soft law instruments as Action Plans and Partnership Priorities are often issued from Decisions of the Association Councils of the relevant association agreements. In that respect, different relationships between soft and hard law instruments in EU bilateral partnerships are telling of the echelons of gravitational intensity around the EU's legal order. The EU's partnerships with both Morocco and Ukraine have been characterised by special soft law instruments, respectively the Advanced Status and the Association Agenda.[6] The former is a declaratory instrument signalling commitments towards reinforced cooperation that would

[1] Luigi Pedreschi and Joanne Scott, 'External Differentiated Integration: Legal Feasibility and Constitutional Acceptability', EUI Working Paper RSCAS 2020/54.

[2] Marc Maresceau, 'Les Accords d'intégration Dans Les Rélations de Proximité de l'Union Europeénne' in Claude Blumann, *Les frontières de l'Union européenne* (Bruylant, 2013); Guillaume Van der Loo, *The EU–Ukraine Association Agreement and Deep and Comprehensive Free Trade Area: A New Legal Instrument for EU Integration without Membership* (Brill Nijhoff, 2016).

[3] The label 'homogeneity clause' is particularly used by Andrea Ott in her perceptive Andrea Ott, 'The EU–Turkey Association and Other EU Parallel Legal Orders in the European Legal Space' (2015) 42 *Legal Issues of Economic Integration* 5.

[4] Pedreschi and Scott (n 1).

[5] As discussed in ch 3, section IV of this work.

[6] EU–Ukraine Cooperation Council, 'Recommendation on the implementation of the EU–Ukraine Association Agenda to prepare and facilitate the implementation of the Association Agreement', UE-UA 1057/0923, 23 November 2009. See also Recommendation (EU) 2015/2419 on the implementation of the EU–Ukraine Association Agenda [2015] OJ L333/150.

nevertheless continue along already established tracks.[7] Instead, the latter served as the harbinger of a new generation of association agreements embedding ENP conditionality in legally binding commitments of gravitation around the EU legal order. The Agenda identified priorities of cooperation 'on a sector-by-sector basis which [would] require action in anticipation of the entry into force of the Agreement'.[8] The relationship between soft law and hard law instruments is strengthened by the fact that the funding of EU actions in support of processes of convergence carried out through soft law is often subject to conditionality schemes envisaged, inter alia, in binding EU unilateral regulations.[9] New forms of interplay between soft law and hard law are emerging, also in the framework of the new EU–UK relations.[10] In the Western Balkans, the development of *Wider Europe* in the accession talks is being overhauled in a way that mixes regional[11] and bilateral[12] soft law instruments with possible amendments of the relevant association agreements.[13]

The very distinction between 'static' and 'dynamic' is in itself reductive as exemplified by the composite nature of the EU partnership with Switzerland. The limits of the static/dynamic dichotomy can be also inferred from the fact that in the different parts and chapters of the EU–Ukraine Association Agreement, the intensity and dynamism of gravitation varies. Moreover, 'homogeneity' clauses may carry different meanings in different life stages of the agreements. The EEA Agreement is a case in point. Whereas the homogeneity clauses would suggest an interpretation of extended EU rules 'in conformity with the relevant rules of the Court of Justice' given prior to the signature of the agreement,[14] recently some EFTA Court judgments have been oriented towards a uniformity of results, more than on uniformity of interpretation. In light of the constitutional asymmetries between the EEA and EU law, the uniformity of results may entail interpreting extended EU law provisions in the EEA Agreement differently from the corresponding provisions of EU law.[15]

[7] As a matter of fact the instruments for the conduct of the ENP remained unchanged after the adoption of the Advanced Status which also entailed the adoption of a more ambitious EU–Morocco Action Plan. See Recommandation n ° 1/2013 du Conseil d'association UE-Maroc du 16 décembre 2013 portant sur la mise en œuvre du plan d'action UE-Maroc dans le cadre de la PEV mettant en œuvre le statut avancé (2013–2017), [2013] OJ 352/78.

[8] EU–Ukraine Cooperation Council, UE-UA 1057/0923 (n 6) 2.

[9] See for instance Regulation (EU) 2021/947 establishing the Neighbourhood, Development and International Cooperation Instrument – Global Europe (NDICI), [2021] OJ L 209/1, Art 27.

[10] Steve Peers, 'EU Law Analysis: Just Say No? The New "Stormont Brake" in the Windsor Framework (Part 2 of the Analysis of the Framework)' (EU Law Analysis, 5 March 2023), eulawanalysis.blogspot.com/2023/03/just-say-no-new-stormont-brake-in.html.

[11] On 10 November 2020 the six Western Balkans countries adopted the Common Regional Market Action Plan at the Berlin Process Summit in Sofia. The plan was intended to facilitate the establishment of the four freedoms in the region.

[12] See for instance the Proposed Reform Agendas, referred to in European Commission, 'New Growth Plan for the Western Balkans', COM(2023) 691 final, 8.

[13] ibid 5.

[14] See in particular, EEA Agreement [1994] OJ L1/3 (hereinafter EEA Agreement), Arts 6 and 105–106; see also Agreement between the EFTA states on the establishment of a Surveillance Authority and a Court of Justice [1994] OJ L 344/3, Art 3.

[15] See discussion in ch 4 of this work, particularly in section IV.

More than compiling a definite typology of techniques of EU neighbourhood law, this study has assessed the role played by these techniques in shaping the interactions between the EU legal order and the arrangements extending the EU's legal space. An account of the different patterns of gravitation around the EU legal order can be clustered around the elements of *scope* and *intensity* of gravitation.[16] The scope of gravitation reflects the range of the substantive *acquis* that is extended in arrangements of EU neighbourhood law. The intensity of gravitation pertains to the level of organisational interaction between the EU legal order and EU neighbourhood law regime. It includes considerations on the enforcement and the effects of extended EU law.

On the substantive plane, the very notion of *renvoi* is indicative of the interactions among legal orders. Different types of substantive *renvois* at play. In the text of agreements of EU neighbourhood law, it is rare to find a direct *renvoi* to articles of the EU Founding Treaties,[17] it is also rare to find direct *renvois* to secondary provisions of EU law in the main text of the agreements.[18] Usually the text of EU neighbourhood law agreements provides for the mimetic imitation of EU primary law provisions.[19] More commonly, the gravitational mechanics operate through the EU legislation at the basis of the annexes of the EU neighbourhood agreements, which are often updated by the decisions of the relevant Joint Committees.

The indeterminate legal drafting and a certain incoherence in the language of the legal provisions presiding over the extension of the EU's legal space does not help in defining a typology of substantive mechanisms of the extension of the EU's legal space. Although the wording of the convergence clauses may give some hints on the patterns of gravitation in different regimes, the language of the provisions mandating the extension of the EU *acquis* is not indicative per se of the intensity of the obligation. The EU–Ukraine Association Agreement is a case in point. While the objectives of the partnership stated in the preamble refer to 'legislative approximation' or 'regulatory approximation', the modalities of extension of the EU's legal space are named in a panoply of different ways in the text of the Agreement. As highlighted by Van der Loo, various terms are used in the Agreement to indicate Ukraine's commitment to converge to EU laws and

[16] The variables of scope and intensity are used by Dirk Leuffen, Berthold Rittberger and Frank Schimmelfennig, *Differentiated Integration: Explaining Variation in the European Union* (Palgrave MacMillan, 2012). Differently from the present study, however, the above-mentioned authors equate (largely) intensity with centralisation of the decision-making.

[17] See, however, the rules applicable to free movement of capital and payments in the EU–Ukraine Association Agreement [2014] OJ L 161/3 listed in Appendix II of Annex XVII indicating the relevant TFEU provisions.

[18] See, however, EU–Ukraine AA, Art 256 detailing the relevant EU secondary law instruments in the Competition chapter, and notably in the Antitrust and mergers section.

[19] For the EU–Ukraine AA see Art 254 mirroring Arts 101 and 102 TFEU. The EEA Agreement offers multiple examples. See inter alia EEA, Arts 11, 12 and 13 that largely replicate the wordings of Arts 34, 35, 36 TFEU. See also the correspondence between EEA, Arts 28, 31, 36 and 45, 49 and 56 TFEU respectively.

regulations. They vary from 'approximate to',[20] 'align to' and[21] 'made compatible with'[22] to 'incorporate the *acquis* in the domestic legal order'.[23] In the proximity policies, these terms are indeed increasingly used interchangeably.[24] The relevant clause of the EU–Morocco Association Agreement reads that 'cooperation shall *be aimed* at helping Morocco to bring its legislation closer to that of the [EU] in the areas covered by this Agreement'.[25] The clause of the EU–Morocco EuroMed Agreement might be construed as an open-ended *renvoi* providing for less defined processes of legislative mimetic imitation of EU law. It could be argued that a greater degree of accuracy is to be found in the clauses of the DCFTA chapters of the EU–Ukraine AA, establishing that 'Ukraine shall *ensure* that its *existing* laws and *future* legislation will be gradually made compatible with the EU *acquis*'.[26] In addition to the different obligations of 'aiming' and 'ensuring', the latter clause is clearer than the EuroMed convergence clause with regard to the dynamic adaptation to the EU *acquis*. Yet, the 'compatibility' language of the EU–Ukraine clause is misleading: the patterns of gravitation around the EU legal order entailed in the DCFTA sections where this clause is included resemble the EEA-like homogeneity more than an open-ended compatibility. In fact, the DCFTA sections covered by the above-mentioned clause of the EU–Ukraine Association Agreement are also governed by Annex XVII, whose Article 6 mandates the interpretation of the provisions of extended EU law 'in conformity with the relevant rulings of the Court of Justice of the European Union', echoing the homogeneity paradigms of the EEA Agreement.[27]

The scope and the language of gravitation alone are thus not per se sufficient to appreciate of the patterns of gravitation around the EU legal order, without assessing the mechanisms of organisational interaction. Mechanisms of organisational interaction are hence key for identifying the patterns of gravitation around the EU legal order. The EnCT is an example of how the absence of mechanism of organisational interaction with the EU legal order goes to the detriment of the intensity of gravitation in spite of the significant scope of *renvois* to the EU *acquis*. As the province of enforcement methods of extended EU law, the techniques of organisational interaction give a better account of the legal relations engendered

[20] See for instance, EU–Ukraine AA. Art 64 on Sanitary and Phytosanitary Standards (SPS); Art 256 AA on competition; Art 290 (2) on Trade and Sustainable development.

[21] See ibid Arts 56(5); 57 (1)–(3) on Technical Barriers to Trade (TBT).

[22] ibid Annex VII, Arts 114(1), 124(1) and 133(1) on trade in services and establishment.

[23] See ibid Annex VII(a).

[24] Van der Loo (n 2) 321. Van der Loo also notes that Commission documents add to the confusion with the terminology of alignment with the EU acquis', 'adoption of elements of the EU acquis', to 'approximation of EU rules and practices' and 'convergence to regulatory areas', see for instance European Commission, 'ENP-A path towards further economic integration. Non-Paper expanding on the proposals contained in the Communication "Strengthening the ENP"' COM(2006) 726 final.

[25] EuroMed Agreement with Morocco, [2000] OJ L70/2, Art 52 (emphasis added). As highlighted in ch 2 (in its n 39), the wording of the approximation clauses in EuroMed Agreements varies.

[26] See EU–Ukraine AA, Arts 114(1), 124(1), 133(1) and 139(1) (emphasised added).

[27] EEA Agreement, Art 6.

by EU neighbourhood law. In that light, mechanisms of organisational interaction in arrangements of EU neighbourhood law can be construed as the point of intersection between the three lines of inquiry of this book. They shed light on how EU neighbourhood regimes calibrate proximity to and distance from the EU's legal order. They are thus illustrative of how different political covenants are expressed through techniques of EU neighbourhood law, which result in varying intensity in the echelons of gravitation around the EU legal order.

The EEA and ECAA Agreements can be identified as the two principal paradigms of organisational interaction between the EU legal order and regimes of EU neighbourhood law. They exemplify two different governance models of the extended EU's legal space. The EEA model rests on a two-pillar structure aimed at safeguarding the formal independence of EEA EFTA states through the establishment of a separate although interrelated institutional and judicial pillar. The de facto preponderance of the EU legal order over the EFTA regime has been already highlighted: it is not only expressed through the substantive extension of EU law, but also through the deference to the CJEU's jurisprudence in the interpretation of the Agreement. Significantly, the EEA envisages the possibility of mobilising the CJEU to give a ruling on the interpretation of extended EU rules in case of the EEA Joint Committee's delays in resolving a dispute concerning the interpretation of extended EU law.[28] This type of institutional *renvoi*, while rather exceptional in the two-pillar system of the EEA, is at the basis of the techniques of extension of EU's legal space in the ECAA-type single-pillar model.

The single-pillar model is predicated upon a greater extraterritorial use of EU institutions in EU neighbourhood law regimes.[29] In the one pillar model, the institutional judicial *renvois* to the CJEU are arguably more far-reaching. Indeed, the role of the CJEU is broader in the one-pillar model: it encompasses also the review of the legality of the extended tasks of the EU institutions under the relevant arrangements, as evident both in the ECAA[30] and TCT case.[31] As a matter of fact, the institutional *renvois* in the one-pillar model also concern the Commission, which is entrusted far-reaching monitoring roles.[32] The extraterritorial reach of the powers of the EU institution in this specific arrangement of EU neighbourhood law can be explained in light of the links between these arrangements with the pre-accession process in view of EU membership. This explains the ECAA and TCT's countries acceptance of far-reaching institutional *renvois* and the pervasive reconfiguration of sovereignty they entail.

[28] This is the option envisaged in EEA Agreement, Art 111(3) but has never been used.

[29] Cécile Rapoport, 'Autonomy of the EU Legal Order and International Agreements Extending the Acquis: Opinion 1/00 (European Common Aviation Area)' in Graham Butler and Ramses A Wessel, *EU External Relations Law: The Cases in Context* (Hart Publishing, 2022).

[30] ECAA Agreement, [2006] OJ L 285/3, Art 15(3).

[31] See Transport Community Treaty (TCT) [2017], OJ L 278/3, Art 19(2).

[32] See inter alia ECAA Agreement, Art 12(4) and TCT, Arts 37(3) and 40.

The single-pillar model characterised by institutional *renvois* to the EU legal order had transmigrated from the ECAA arrangement, (seen as an instrument of the pre-accession strategy and as a driving force of the sectoral development of the ENP) into a broader spectrum of EU's proximity policies. Such a passage corroborates the value of *Wider Europe* as a single analytical concept capturing different legal relations in the EU's neighbourhood. The EU–Ukraine Association Agreement offers an example of far-reaching institutional *renvois* in a context that developed as distinct although not precluding pre-accession.[33] In the said Agreement, the Commission is generally given extensive monitoring powers on the implementation of the extended EU *acquis*.[34] For some of the DCFTA chapters, an elaborated dispute settlement mechanism is in place. In that regard, Article 322 of the EU–Ukraine AA establishes the obligation[35] to refer disputes to the CJEU if these relate to the implementation of extended EU law. It establishes that the arbitration panel 'shall not decide on the question, but request the Court of Justice of the European Union to give a ruling on the question. … The ruling of the Court of Justice shall be binding on the arbitration panel'.[36]

The EU–Ukraine dispute settlement mechanism occupies a special place in the composite spectrum of the enforcement mechanisms of EU neighbourhood law. Indeed, the institutional *renvoi* to the Court of Justice is not mobilised directly by the parties to the dispute,[37] nor by the courts of third countries participating in the extended EU's legal space,[38] as in other arrangements. In the EU–Ukraine dispute settlement of Article 322, the institutional *renvoi* to the CJEU is mediated by the *jointly* established arbitration panel. The ensuing ruling of the CJEU is thus final and binding on the arbitration panel. This may suggest a more tenuous reconfiguration of sovereignty as compared to the instances whereby the ruling of the CJEU is final and binding directly on the parties to the disputes, or theoretically on the courts of third states asking for a preliminary reference on the interpretation of extended EU law. The relevant mechanism could thus be construed as a middle ground between arrangements of EU neighbourhood law with a direct involvement of a court of one of the parties to the Agreement (the EU) and a type of arbitration procedure which is virtually based on the equal (and symmetric) standing of the parties under international law.[39] Yet a closer scrutiny reveals that

[33] *In casu* the Eastern Dimension of the ENP.

[34] See for instance, EU–Ukraine AA, Annex XVII, Art 2.

[35] Note instead that in other arrangements like the EEA Agreement, there is a *possibility* of recourse to the CJEU.

[36] EU–Ukraine AA, Art 322.

[37] See for instance EEA Agreement, Art 111(3); ECAA Agreement, Art 20(3); TCT, Art 37(3). See also EU–Turkey Association Agreement, [1963] OJ L361/29, Art 25 where the Association Council may ask the CJEU to resolve a dispute.

[38] See for instance EEA Agreement, Art 107 and especially Protocol 34; ECAA Agreement Art 16(2); TCT Art 19(2).

[39] More precisely the Vienna Convention on the Law of the Treaties, Art 66 and the rulings of the WTO dispute settlement body. See also the more symmetric dispute settlement arrangements present in the EU–Ukraine AA, Art 320; and EU–Canda CETA [2017] OJ L 11/ 23, ch XXIX. This would be the aspiration of the EU–UK TCA.

a distinctive trait of the EU–Ukraine dispute settlement arrangement that renders the relevant institutional *renvoi* pervasive. It pertains to the *obligation* to recur to the Court of Justice, as opposed to the margin of appreciation granted to the parties to the dispute or the referring courts in other arrangements.[40] In fact, such a margin of appreciation is precluded to the arbitration panel established according to specific rules of the EU–Ukraine DCFTA: the arbitration panel at issue *shall* request the CJEU to give a ruling on a question relating to extended EU law.[41]

The elaborated dispute settlement mechanism of the EU–Ukraine AA has been used in other arrangements of EU neighbourhood law. As a matter of fact, a similar clause is part of the EU–UK WA[42] and it features also in the Draft Institutional Arrangement with Switzerland.[43] It thus appears that the EU considers the clause as a versatile dispute settlement mechanism that can govern both the extension and the retrenchment of the EU's legal space. The clause can certainly be counted among the techniques of EU neighbourhood law, predicated on third country gravitation around the EU's legal order. For the superordination of the EU judicial powers it entails, as will be discussed further, the clause was at the centre of contestation of the EU–Switzerland Draft Institutional Agreement.

Arguably, an additional method of enforcement of extended EU law is the conditionality that has traditionally characterised the development of the EU proximity policies. While the effectiveness of conditionality has been significant in extending the EU *acquis* in the context of the EU enlargement policy,[44] more doubtful is its effectiveness when membership or an advanced integration into the EU internal market is not envisaged. Especially in the European Neighbourhood Policy, conditionality has not been able to bring about the transformative change for which the policy was originally launched. This is particularly evident now when the universality of the EU model is increasingly questioned.[45] The remarks made by the European Court of Auditors on the unsatisfactory results of conditionality in the EU financial support to Morocco are an illustration of the limited results of this enforcement method.[46] The ineffectiveness of EU conditionality is due,

[40] Such a margin of appreciation is also precluded in the relevant mechanism of the EU–UK Withdrawal Agreement, [2019] OJ C 384I/1, Art 174 or under the EU–Switzerland Draft Institutional Agreement, EU–Switzerland draft Institutional Framework Agreement, 'Accord Facilitant Les Relations Bilatérales Entre l'Union Européenne et La Confédération Suisse Dans Les Parties Du Marché Intérieur Auxquelles La Suisse Participe' (Institutional Agreement–Draft Text) (23 November 2018), www.eda.admin.ch/dam/dea/fr/documents/abkommen/Acccord-inst-Projet-de-texte_fr.pdf. Hereinafter 'EU–Switzerland InstA', Art 10(3).

[41] EU–Ukraine AA, Art 322.

[42] EU–UK WA, Art 174.

[43] EU–Switzerland InstA, Art 10(3).

[44] Frank Schimmelfennig and Ulrich Sedelmeier, 'Governance by Conditionality: EU Rule Transfer to the Candidate Countries of Central and Eastern Europe' (2004) 11 *Journal of European Public Policy* 661.

[45] This has been already highlighted in European Commission and HR for the EU CFSP, 'Review of the European Neighbourhood Policy' JOIN (2015) 50 Final.

[46] European Court of Auditors, 'Special Report: EU Support to Morocco – Limited Results so Far, (2019), www.eca.europa.eu/Lists/ECADocuments/SR19_09/SR_Morocco_EN.pdf.

inter alia, to the scarce definition of performance indicators. In the case of Morocco, irrespectively of the conditionality results, the EU's willingness to maintain a 'privileged partnership' can be set against the background of the Kingdom's crucial role in migration control and terrorism prevention. This may explain why variable tranches of EU funding for the implementation of EU funded programmes[47] have been disbursed even when conditions were not met nor verified. Such[48] a circumstance once again points towards the crucial place of diplomatic considerations in enforcement mechanisms. The study of the Moroccan case has further brought to the fore the complexity of patterns of dependence and cross-dependence in the EU's relations with its southern neighbours. In that regard, mechanisms of reversed conditionality operate whereby Morocco weaponises the EU's dependence especially in the migration domain to influence the EU's policy orientations towards Western Sahara.

III. Calibrating Proximity: From Homogeneity to Level Playing Field

The enforcement mechanisms are expression of the political covenant of EU neighbourhood law. Political covenants contribute defining the echelons of gravitation around the EU's legal order (across and within partnerships). They calibrate distance from and proximity to EU law. The covenants are nourished by different objectives, expectations and perceptions of the EU and its neighbouring countries.

Homogeneity is the objective that brings about the most advanced forms of extension of the EU's legal space. In the EEA, it governs the extension of the EU's internal market beyond membership. As an objective and legal principle, homogeneity augments the legal and political proximity to the EU legal order. Pursuing homogeneity goes far beyond substantive *renvois*. Homogeneity carries intimations on the nature of extended EU law that are expressed in the enforcement mechanisms: it requires a strong commitment to interpreting and applying extended EU law as uniformly as possible to EU law proper.[49] Homogeneity thus primarily concerns the effects of extended EU law. Political covenants revolving around homogeneity entail significant reconfigurations of sovereignty. The EEA is an example of that. On the one hand, EEA EFTA countries are rule-taker: they do not participate in the decision-making process of the rules they are ultimately

[47] EU-funded programmes in the framework of the EU–Morocco advanced status include those entailing convergence to EU law.

[48] European Court of Auditors (n 46) 25.

[49] See EEA Agreement, recital 15: 'the objective of the Contracting Parties is to arrive at, and maintain, a uniform interpretation and application of this Agreement and those provisions of [Union] legislation which are substantially reproduced in this agreement and to arrive at an equal treatment of individuals and economic operators as regards the four freedoms and the conditions of competition'. See further EEA Agreement, Arts 58, 102 and 105.

going to adopt. On the other hand, the workings of the EEA bring to the fore the relational advantages of participating into the wider European legal space. In the extended EU internal market, these advantages result in the fact that EEA EFTA states and their juridical persons usually benefit form rights and obligations equal to those at play in EU membership law.[50]

Internal market treatment is not necessarily limited to the specificities of the EEA Agreement: it normally occurs when far-reaching techniques of extension of the EU's legal space are in place. In this respect, Van der Loo identifies three homogeneity-defining benchmarks which result in the uniform interpretation and application of EU law in third countries.[51] These three benchmarks consist in a dynamic procedure to keep pace with the development of EU law, an obligation to align extended EU *acquis* along the interpretative canons of the CJEU, and a judicial mechanism to ensure the uniform interpretation and application of extended EU law.[52] The combination of these three element is not frequent across the variety of institutional arrangements of EU neighbourhood law. Beyond the EEA, the combined presence of the three elements occurs most notably in the ECAA and in some chapters of the DCFTA part of the EU–Ukraine AA envisaging market access conditionality.

The ECAA Agreement expressly aims at establishing a homogeneous legal space on the basis of EU law and uniform rights and obligations.[53] The scope of the substantive *renvoi* is mainly discernible in Articles 1 and 3 of the Agreement. With regard to the three benchmarks, there are provisions for the dynamic adaptation to the evolving EU law,[54] an obligation to align to the canons of interpretation of the CJEU[55] and a judicial mechanism amounting to an institutional *renvoi* to the CJEU.[56] The presence of the three benchmarks can also be found in the trade in services/establishment chapter[57] and, partly, in the procurement chapter[58] of the EU–Ukraine AA. Indeed, these chapters envisage mechanisms of dynamic adaptation to the evolving EU *acquis*,[59] an obligation to align to the canons of

[50] See *inter alia* EEA Agreement, Arts 1, 34, 81, 83, 124 and most notably the ECJ in Case C-431/11, *United Kingdom v Council [EEA]*, EU:C:2013:589; Case C-897/19, PPU *IN v Ruska Federacija* EU:C:2020:262.

[51] He identifies the *condition sine qua non* for integration agreements 'the obligation to apply, implement or incorporate a predetermined selection of the EU *acquis*'. The other three benchmarks, as opposed to 'strict criteria … enable us to detect large variation between the different EU integration agreements and categorise them on a continuous scale that varies from "basic" EU integration agreements to "developed" EU integration agreements' Van der Loo (n 2) 49.

[52] ibid 50.

[53] See for instance EEA Agreement, Art 8.

[54] ibid Art 17.

[55] ibid Art 16(1).

[56] ibid Art 16(2).

[57] EU–Ukraine AA, ch 6 (DCFTA).

[58] ibid ch 8.

[59] EU–Ukraine AA, see Annex XVII, Arts 3–5 (for the trade in services/establishment chapter) and Arts 153(2) and 463(3) of the Agreement (for the public procurement chapter). The adaptation to evolving EU law of the public procurement chapter cannot be defined entirely as dynamic. See further on this Van der Loo (n 2) and his ch12.

interpretation of the CJEU,[60] and an institutional *renvoi* to the CJEU.[61] It may be maintained that a similar homogeneity rationale has informed the conception of the EU–Switzerland Draft Institutional Agreement. The Agreement included a provision governing the adaptation of the EU–Swiss relations to the evolution of EU law,[62] a deference to the interpretative canons of the CJEU,[63] and an institutional *renvoi* to the CJEU for disputes concerning the interpretation of extended EU law.[64]

In the political covenants predicated on homogeneity, a distinctive balance between benefits and obligations is at play. The far-reaching reconfiguration of sovereignty entailed in the high gravitational intensity around the EU's legal is counterbalanced by the advantages of access to the EU internal market at the same conditions as the EU Member States. Institutional arrangements based on homogeneity are illustrative of the hybrid nature of EU neighbourhood law, at the crossroads between international law and EU law. This is somewhat captured in Article 4 of the EU–Switzerland Draft Institutional Agreement. While its first paragraph embeds the Agreement in the principles and canons of international law, the second paragraph acknowledges the 'relevance' of EU law for the bilateral regime with regard to the notions of EU law and the EU legal acts mobilised by the Agreement.

The political covenant premised on the homogeneity objectives also entails commitments on the effects of extended EU law in foreign jurisdictions. Provisions of EU neighbourhood law agreements pursuing homogeneity thus may also indicate the manner in which EU acts should be transposed in the third country domestic legal orders.[65] It is worth stressing that homogeneity does not necessarily result in uniform interpretation. In the EEA case, for instance, the EFTA Court extended to the EEA Agreement rights and obligations that the CJEU derived from EU citizenship primary law. In fact, the extension, however, did not occur through the uniform interpretation of extended EU law: EU citizenship primary law is absent from the EEA Agreement. The extension of rights and obligations occurred by means of a different interpretation of extended EU secondary law.[66] In that light, the third homogeneity benchmark highlighted by Van der Loo[67] needs to be qualified. 'Uniform interpretation *and* application' may not necessarily go hand in hand: uniform application may entail a difference in the interpretation.

Thus, while uniform interpretation is often required in EU neighbourhood law agreements, the demarcation between legal orders may intimate different

[60] EU–Ukraine AA Annex XVII, Art 6 (for the trade in services/establishment chapter) and Art 153(2) of the Agreement (for the public procurement chapter).

[61] EU–Ukraine AA, Art 322.

[62] See EU–Switzerland InstA, Art 5.

[63] ibid Art 4(2).

[64] ibid Art 10(3).

[65] EEA Agreement, Art 7; EU–Ukraine AA, Annex XVII, Art 2; ECAA Agreement, Art 3; in different terms EU–Switzerland InstA, Arts 5 and 13.

[66] See ch 4 of this work, particularly section IV.

[67] Namely the one prescribing a judicial mechanism to ensure a uniform interpretation and application of the incorporated acquis.

interpretation of identically worded provisions. In that regard, Levrat has posited that the CJEU has been never requested to issue a preliminary ruling on a provision of *extended* EU law. On the basis of the *Polydor* doctrine, he contends that the CJEU might eventually interpret the extended EU law provision differently from how it would interpret the same provision in the EU legal order.[68] Certainly, arrangements of EU neighbourhood law are distinct in nature from EU membership law. Nevertheless, pursuing the homogeneity objective contributes to nourishing the political covenant underlying these special EU's proximity relations. As the EEA case shows, third country commitments to homogeneity lead to an evolution of the political covenant that is reflected in the judicial pronouncements both of the EU pillar[69] and the EFTA pillar.[70] This tells us that homogeneity in agreements of EU neighbourhood law defines the nature of these agreements and narrows the gap between the effects of extended EU law and EU membership law.[71]

It is worth stressing that homogeneity is far from being a widely present objective in the arrangements of EU neighbourhood law. Especially when the substantive extension of the EU's legal space is not accompanied by mechanisms of organisational interaction, the extension of the EU's legal space is limited to embedding third countries' legal systems in shallower processes of compatibility with EU law. The mechanisms of organisational interaction are thus crucial for determining the effects of extended EU law and the ensuing patterns of gravitation around the EU's legal order. Different objectives and consequently different political covenants gradate the intensity of third country gravitation around the EU legal order.[72]

The renewed emphasis on the balance between benefits and obligations entailed in the EU's economic and legal relations with its neighbouring countries post-*Brexit* emerged especially in the case of advanced economies. This has been the case of the development of the EU's partnerships with the UK and Switzerland. For the UK, the rethinking of the political covenants of the partnership concluded in the neighbourhood led to a shift of focus and of language: from convergence/homogeneity to the level playing field. These concerns are not specific to the neighbourhood and may in fact signal a recourse to more symmetric forms of international law. While level playing field concerns are at the very centre of EU Free Trade Agreements concluded globally,[73] it is in the proximity that they are more significant as a result of the density of interdependence.

The EU–UK WA is paradigmatic of the shift from patterns of gravitation around the EU's legal order to the attention on level playing field obligations.

[68] He refers particularly to *Opinion 1/91, EEA Draft Agreement*, ECLI:EU:C:1991:490 [51]; C-321/97 *Andersson v Svenska staten*, ECLI:EU:C:1999:307 [26]–[28].

[69] *United Kingdom v Council [EEA]* (n 50); *IN* (n 50).

[70] See for instance Case E-28/15 *Jabbi* [2016] EFTA Ct Rep 575.

[71] For a discussion on direct applicability see Tarjei Bekkedal, 'Understanding the Nature of the EEA Agreement: On the Direct Applicability of Regulations' (2020) 57 *Common Market Law Review* 773.

[72] See Marise Cremona and Alessandro Petti, 'Extending the Internal Market Through Free Trade Agreements' in Robert Schütze and Takis Tridimas (eds), *Oxford Principles of European Union Law*, vol 2 (Oxford University Press, forthcoming).

[73] ibid.

Concerns relating to the level playing field in the EU neighbourhood essentially revolve around the political covenants governing EU relations with neighbours that are unwilling to take part in the extended EU's legal space. In that regard, the balance between benefits and obligations in the partnerships with the EU is essential. As aptly noted by Bartels, level playing field encompasses both normative and economic considerations. On the normative side, it is oriented towards the achieving and maintenance of high standards in labour, environment and human rights, preventing a race to the bottom. On the economic side, it 'is essentially about ensuring that the other side raises costs to your levels'.[74]

The willingness to promote and maintain high standards as well as guaranteeing the fairness of the EU–UK economic relations explains the articulated provisions and enforcement apparatus of the EU–UK TCA. In the TCA, non-regression clauses aim at maintaining a high level of environmental[75] and labour standards.[76] They are combined with a strict regime regarding subsidy control.[77] Provisions of Title XI of the TCA concerning level playing field do not generally fall under the ordinary dispute settlement mechanism of the Agreement.[78] Significantly, however, the level playing field provisions of the TCA may be enforced with retaliation.[79] Rebalancing measures envisaged for the non-regression areas of environmental and labour protection and subsidy control.[80] Unilateral remedial measures can also be taken if one party submits that 'there is evidence that a subsidy of the [other] party causes, or there is a serious risk that it will cause, a significant negative effect on trade or investment between the Parties'.[81]

Moreover, it seems clear that the EU is unwilling to concede mutual recognition to the UK as a basis for future relations thus de facto conditioning the UK's access to the EU market on the maintenance of regulatory convergence.[82] In this respect, it is worth noting that the TCA does not envisage mechanisms for the recognition of certification as was included in the CETA arrangement.[83] As put

[74] UK House of Lords, Select Committee on the European Union, EU internal market sub-committee, 'Oral evidence: The level playing field and state aid', London, 27 February 2020, 2–3, committees.parliament.uk/oralevidence/83/pdf/, Lorand Bartels intervention.

[75] See in particular [2021] OJ L 149/10, Hereinafter 'EU–UK TCA', Title XI, C 7, Art 391.

[76] EU–UK TCA, Title XI, Ch 6, Art 387.

[77] See ibid Title XI, Ch 3.

[78] See ibid Art 735(2)(e) TCA and more specifically the dispute settlement provisions of Title XI (by way of example Arts 357, 375 and 396 TCA).

[79] See on this Steve Peers, 'So Close, Yet So Far: The EU/UK Trade and Cooperation Agreement' (2022) 49, 63.

[80] EU–UK TCA, Art 411.

[81] EU–UK TCA, Art 374(3). Art 374(6) specifies the elements which shall inform the Party's assessment of the existence of a subsidy significantly affecting trade. Note that, pursuant to Art 374(15), it is not possible to apply simultaneously rebalancing measures under Art 411 and remedial measures under Art 374 for the same subsidy.

[82] Paul Craig, 'Brexit a Drama: The Endgame – Part I' (2020) 45 *European Law Review* 163, 182.

[83] See 'Protocol on the mutual acceptance of the results of conformity assessment' CETA, see also Paola Mariani and Giorgio Sacerdoti, 'Trade in Goods and Level Playing Field' in Federico Fabbrini (ed), *The Law & Politics of Brexit: Volume III* (Oxford University Press, 2021).

forward by Leinarte and Barnard, on the one hand, a mutual recognition arrangement would be desirable under the TCA. In fact, at present there is a substantial degree of regulatory alignment between the EU and the UK. This is a valuable premise for concluding an arrangement on mutual recognition to regulate remaining divergence.[84] On the other hand, 'the UK's quest for regulatory divergence may put EU negotiators in the difficult position of dealing with a country that offers no guarantees, perhaps even the opposite, that its technical regulations will remain what they are'.[85]

The EU's emphasis on level playing field provisions and its reluctance to engage in mutual recognition arrangements aims to avoid the UK benefiting from proximity and access to the EU internal market, while also having 'an unfair competitive advantage [obtained] through undercutting of levels of protection'.[86] As has been powerfully captured by Mariani and Sacerdoti, rather exceptionally in the history of trade agreements, in the EU–UK TCA 'provisions elaborated to maximize liberalization of trade are being used to establish and operate a less open regime.'[87]

Compared with agreements of EU neighbourhood law, the EU–UK TCA enforcement techniques pertaining to level playing field provisions are different from those envisaged to guarantee homogeneity in the extended EU's legal space. There is no pre-eminence of the EU legal order and EU institution in the governance of the EU–UK TCA framework. In that light, it can be argued that the passage from homogeneity to level playing field signals a deeper transition from EU neighbourhood law to international law; a transition premised on the wish to maintain the regulatory autonomy of the parties. From the UK's perspective, international law is used to mark the distance from EU (and EU neighbourhood) law. From the EU's side, international law cast in terms of level playing field provisions is used to uphold high standards of protection and fair conditions of competition in its relations with a neighbouring country where interdependences remain high.

IV. Calibrating Distance Through (the Lack of) Direct Effect

The effect of extended EU law in the legal systems of third countries varies in function of the objectives of the different arrangements of EU neighbourhood law and the applicable legal principles. When homogeneity is at stake, the gravitational intensity around the EU's legal order is stronger. This is also due to the relevant

[84] Emilija Leinarte and Catherine Barnard, 'Negotiating Mutual Recognition Agreements: Challenges and Techniques' in Albertina Albors-Llorens, Catherine Barnard and Brigitte Leucht (eds), *Cassis de Dijon: 40 years on* (Hart Publishing, 2021) 229.

[85] ibid 250.

[86] European Commission, 'Answer given by Ms Vestager on Behalf of the European Commission, Parliamentary Question Reference: E-003935/2018' (13 September 2018), www.europarl.europa.eu/doceo/document/E-8-2018-003935-ASW_EN.html.

[87] Mariani and Sacerdoti (n 83) 95.

provisions governing the effects of extended EU law in the legal systems of the non-EU contracting parties. In turn, a looser gravitation in terms of interpretation and application may be achieved by means of provisions precluding direct effect of extended EU law.

The attempt to separate international law regimes from the domestic legal system through the preclusion of direct effect is an emerging feature in EU external relations law.[88] It takes different forms in relation to the kind of relationship the international agreements wish to pursue. In free trade agreements with global partners, the text of the agreements often includes a general clause precluding direct effect.[89] This is the case for Agreements with Canada,[90] Singapore,[91] Colombia, Peru and Ecuador,[92] and the association agreements with Central America.[93] The relevant provision of the EU–Canada CETA reads:

> [N]othing in this Agreement shall be construed as conferring rights or imposing obligations on persons other than those created between the Parties under public international law, nor as permitting this Agreement to be directly invoked in the domestic legal systems of the Parties.'[94]

The clauses are present in the main text of the Agreements. In the Agreements concluded in the neighbourhood, preclusion of direct effect is not usually enshrined in a provision of general application in the text but rather in the relevant Council Decision on the signature of the Agreement. This is the case for Ukraine,[95] Moldova[96] and Georgia.[97] The clause present in the Council Decisions on the signature of the EU–Ukraine AA reads: 'the Agreement shall not be construed as conferring rights or imposing obligations which can be directly invoked before Union or Member State courts or tribunals.'[98] The new generation of Association

[88] Narine Ghazaryan, 'Who Are the "Gatekeepers"?: In Continuation of the Debate on the Direct Applicability and the Direct Effect of EU International Agreements' (2018) 37 *Yearbook of European Law* 27; Aliki Semertzi, 'The Preclusion of Direct Effect in the Recently Concluded EU Free Trade Agreements' (2014) 51 *Common Market Law Review* 1125.

[89] With the notable exception of the EU–Korea FTA that contains the clause in the Council Decision on the conclusion of the Agreement. The exception is probably due to the fact that this was the first new-generations FTAs Agreement and the indication of the preclusion of direct effect in the Council Decision was deemed sufficient. Council Decision on the signing, on behalf of the European Union, and provisional application of the EU– Korea Free Trade Agreement [2011] OJ L 127/1. For a broader discussion see Aliki Semertzi, 'The Preclusion of Direct Effect in the Recently Concluded EU Free Trade Agreements' (2014) 51 *Common Market Law Review* 1125.

[90] See EU–Canada CETA [2017] OJ L 11/23, Art 30.6 CETA.

[91] EU–Singapore FTA [2019] OJ L294/3, Art 16.16 labelled 'no direct effect'.

[92] EU–Colombia and Peru Trade Agreement, [2012] OJ L 354/3, Art 336. Ecuador's access to the Agreement was subsequent, see Protocol of Accession of Ecuador [2016] OJ L 356/3.

[93] EU–Central America Association Agreement [2012] OJ L 346/3, Art 356.

[94] EU–Canada, CETA Art 30.6.

[95] Council Decision 2014/668/EU on the signature of the EU–Ukraine AA, [2014] OJ L 278/1, Art 7; Council Decision 2014/669/EU on the signature of the EU–Ukraine AA [2014] OJ L 278/6, Art 3.

[96] Council Decision 2014/492/EU on the signature and provisional application of the EU–Moldova AA [2014] OJ L 260/1, Art 6.

[97] Council Decision 2014/494/EU on the signature and provisional application of the EU–Georgia AA [2014] OJ L 261/1. Art 6.

[98] See Council Decision 2014/668/EU (n 95), Art 7.

Agreements concluded with Ukraine, Moldova and Georgia also contain clauses precluding direct effect in the text of the agreements, but they are limited to specific sections. In the case of Ukraine, these relate to the DSM provisions of the DCFTA,[99] and to the schedules of commitments in services and investment.[100] In general terms, the rationale of the provisions precluding direct effect rests in the fact that these Agreements deal with domains covered by WTO rules, partly replicating WTO principles and mechanisms. Clauses precluding direct effect may be thus seen as a way to avoid that Court's pronouncements circumvent the lack direct effect of WTO corresponding rules.[101]

The legal value of the preclusion of direct effect enshrined in the Council Decisions adopted in the context conclusion of the Agreement is harder to decipher. Article 17 EU–Ukraine AA establishes the non-discrimination on grounds of nationality for the treatment of workers. It has been noted that should direct effect be precluded for this provision, as required by the relevant Council Decision, this would lead to problematic outcomes within the EU's proximity relations.[102] In fact, the Court has established the direct effect of analogous provisions on treatment of workers in the EMA Agreements[103] and the PCA Agreements[104] in countries enjoying a significantly less developed association than Ukraine.[105] In that light, this would entail that EU–Russia PCA provisions to potentially be granted direct effect while the EU–Ukraine AA would not.[106] Clauses precluding direct effect in the Council Decisions resonate with the willingness of Members States to limit the extensive interpretation of direct effect in association agreements as stemming from the Court of Justice's case law.[107] This is especially the case for provisions on the treatment of workers. Reservations on the legal tenor of provisions precluding direct effect enshrined in the Council Decisions, however, were expressed by AG Saggio.

[99] EU–Ukraine AA, fn 1 of Ch 14 (DSM).

[100] EU–Ukraine AA, provisions on the services schedules Annexes XVI-A-C to Ch 6.

[101] Ghazaryan (n 88) 64. See further Semertzi (n 89) 1133: 'Therefore, the reference to the FTA panel and not creating private rights is directly justifiable through the link to the scope of jurisdiction of the FTA panel over WTO provisions. Were the FTA panel ruling both binding and silent as to its legal effects for private parties, it could have allowed an interpretation, that, since it is explicitly binding, the ruling can be invoked by private parties. However such an outcome, which could create a "back door" for directly applicable WTO rights and obligations, is impeded precisely by the reference to the non-invocability of the FTA panel ruling'.

[102] Van der Loo (n 2), 194 ff.

[103] For Morocco, see Case C-18/90, *Kziber* EU:C:1991:36.

[104] For Russia, see Case C-265/03, *Simutenkov* EU:C:2005:213.

[105] See also Eleanor Sharpston, 'Different but (Almost) Equal – The Development of Free Movement Rights under EU Association, Co-Operation and Accession Agreements' in Mark Hoskins and Robinson William (eds), *A True European: Essays for Judge David Edward* (Hart Publishing, 2003).

[106] See ch 3 of this work. See further Van der Loo (n 2), 194 ff. The EU–Russia PCA [1997] OJ L 327/3 has been dormant for a long time especially after 2014. The EEAS website reads: 'The relations between the European Union (EU) and Russia have been strained since the 2014 illegal annexation of Crimea and the city of Sevastopol by Russia and its destabilising actions in eastern Ukraine. After Russia began its invasion of Ukraine on 24 February, 2022, the remaining political, cultural and scientific cooperation was suspended', www.eeas.europa.eu/russia/european-union-and-russian-federation_en?s=177.

[107] On this see Mario Mendez, *The Legal Effects of EU Agreements* (Oxford University Press, 2013). See also discussion in ch 3, section III.B of this work.

He maintained: 'it need hardly be stated that a unilateral interpretation of the agreement made in the context of an internal adoption procedure cannot – outside the system of reservations – limit the effects of the agreement itself'.[108]

With regard to the degree of proximity calibrated through (the lack of) direct effect, congruence of expectations and practices between the EU and its partner countries cannot be taken for granted. In the EEA itself, the most advanced EU neighbourhood regime pursuing homogeneity, the text of the Agreement sheds light on the effects of extended EU law.[109] Yet, competing understandings have been put forward with regard to (the lack of) direct effect in the context of the EEA.[110] The EFTA Court and the CJEU have developed different stances on the issue. The CJEU construed EU Regulations incorporated into the EEA as directly applicable in the legal orders of the EEA EFTA states. In *UK v Council*, the Court found that Article 7(a) of the EEA Agreement 'expressly provides that such an act is "as such" to be made part of the internal legal order of the Contracting Parties, that is to say, without any implementing measure being required for that purpose.'[111] Similarly, in *Fonnship*, the Court of Justice found that the provisions of an EU Regulation incorporated into the EEA 'are an integral part of the legal order of *all* of the States that are parties to the EEA Agreement by virtue of Article 7(a) of the EEA Agreement and Annex XIII thereto'.[112] These findings have been criticised by EEA law scholars,[113] and portrayed as a 'misunderstanding'.[114] The EFTA Court has subsequently confirmed the lack of direct effect of extended EU law provisions incorporated into the EEA Agreement.[115]

A sound argument, however, has been developed to substantiate the CJEU's stance on direct effect in the EEA context: Bekkedal detaches the issue of direct applicability of incorporated Regulations from the issue of transfer of sovereign powers. He relies instead on the key place of individual rights in the EEA, and on

[108] Case C-149/96 *Portugal v Council*, Opinion AG Saggio, EU:C:1999:92 [20].

[109] EEA Agreement, Art 7 reads: 'Acts referred to or contained in the Annexes to this Agreement or in decisions of the EEA Joint Committee shall be binding upon the Contracting Parties and be, or be made, part of their internal legal order as follows: (a) an act corresponding to an EEC regulation shall as such be made part of the internal legal order of the Contracting Parties; (b) an act corresponding to an EEC directive shall leave to the authorities of the Contracting Parties the choice of form and method of implementation'.

[110] See further the discussion in ch 4 of this work.

[111] *United Kingdom v Council [EEA]* (n 50) [54].

[112] Case C-83/13 *Fonnship* EU:C:2014:2053 [24] (emphasis added).

[113] Marthe Kristine Fjeld Dystland and Ida Sørebø, 'Article 7 [Binding Effect and Implementation of EU Legal Acts]' in Finn Arnesen and others, *Agreement on the European Economic Area: a commentary* (CH Beck-Hart-Nomos, 2018) 252. These authors highlight a difference among EEA EFTA states, while the monistic legal system of Lichtenstein allows for direct effect of EEA law, for 'the dualistic States Iceland and Norway, however, a regulation will not be made part of their respective national legal orders by sole virtue of the amendment of the EEA Agreement'.

[114] Henrik Bull, '"Shall Be Made Part of the Internal Legal Order": The Legislative Approaches' in EFTA Court, *The EEA and the EFTA Court: decentred integration: to mark the 20th anniversary of the EFTA court* (Hart Publishing, 2014) 211 fn 29.

[115] Case E-15/14 EFTA Surveillance Authority v Iceland [2015] EFTA Ct Rep 40 [32]. See more generally Halvard H Fredriksen, 'The European Economic Area' in Robert Schütze and Takis Tridimas (eds) *Oxford Principles of European Union Law*, vol 2 (Oxford University Press, forthcoming).

the essential role of homogeneity and loyalty in the EEA Agreement.[116] Even without embracing Bekkedal's argument of direct effect of extended EU regulations in the EEA before their transposition into the domestic legal order, Franklin and Fredriksen acknowledge that:

> [T]he object and the purpose of the EEA Agreement requires [the absence of primacy and direct effect] to be remedied to the furthest possible extent through the recognition of other EU law principles such as State liability and consistent interpretation of national law.[117]

As a matter of fact, direct effect in the EEA has been often achieved in practice, especially in the domain of state liability.[118] The ensuing close gravitation of the EEA regime to the EU legal order results from the objective of homogeneity, which has been pursued with deference both by the CJEU and the EFTA Courts,[119] as well as the foundations of 'proximity, long-standing common values and European identity'.[120] Yet, the Norwegian legal scholarship usually tends to highlight the resistance against primacy and direct effect in the EEA.[121] In other words, the prevalent approach is that primacy and direct effect are characteristic of the political covenant of EU membership law, a covenant that EEA EFTA states have not subscribed to.

Resistance to direct effect of extended EU law has characterised also the jurisprudence of the Swiss Federal Supreme Court, with the notable exception of the Free Movement of Persons Agreement.[122] The direct effect of the 1972 FTA had been excluded by the Swiss Court in *Adams*.[123] The findings were reiterated in *Bosshard* where the Swiss Federal Court dwelled on the different nature of the then EEC, and its supranational structure, and the EU–Switzerland free trade regime. The Swiss Court stressed that the provisions of the free trade regime are addressed to the Swiss legislature and administration: they could not be interpreted in a manner that would establish rights and obligations directly applicable between private parties.[124] The findings were further developed in *Physiogel* where the Swiss Federal Court decided against the application by analogy of the *Cassis de Dijon*

[116] Bekkedal (n 71).

[117] Christian Franklin and Halvard Haukeland Fredriksen, 'Differentiated Citizenship in the European Economic Area' in Dora Kostakopoulou and Daniel Thym (eds), *Research Handbook on European Union Citizenship Law and Policy* (Edward Elgar Publishing, 2022) 297, 661. See along similar lines, Sven Norberg and Martin Johansson, 'The History of the EEA Agreement and the First Twenty Years of Its Existence' in Carl Baudenbacher, *The Handbook of EEA Law* (Springer, 2016).

[118] Case E-9/97 Erla María Sveinbjörnsdóttir v Iceland [1998] EFTA Ct Rep 95 [62]. See also Christopher Vajda, 'The EU and Beyond: Dispute Resolution in International Economic Agreements' (2018) 29 *European Journal of International Law* 205, 207. For a more nuanced discussion, Halvard Haukeland Fredriksen, 'The EFTA Court and the Principle of State Liability: Protecting the Jewel in the Crown' in EFTA Court, *The EEA and the EFTA Court: Decentred Integration* (Hart Publishing, 2014).

[119] See further ch 4 section IV.B of this work.

[120] *cf* the EEA Agreement preamble.

[121] Bull (n 114) 205. See also Norberg and Johansson (n 114).

[122] Swiss Federal Supreme Court, BGE 129 II 249 S. 251 (17 January 2003).

[123] Swiss Federal Supreme Court, BGE 104 IV 175 (2 May 1978).

[124] Swiss Federal Supreme Court, BGE 105 II 49 (25 January 1979), cons 3.b.

principle to the EU–Swiss FTA regime and precluded the direct effect of Article 13 of the EU–Swiss FTA. It found that Switzerland had not 'entered any (international) obligations, that would mandate the direct applicability of the *Cassis de Dijon* principle, nor there [was] any corresponding obligation in domestic law'.[125] Resistance to direct effect and interpretation by analogy was also expressed by the CJEU in the context of the EU–Switzerland partnership.[126] Differently from the EEA setting, in this case there was a congruence between the expectations of the parties regarding the effects of extended EU law.

As already partly hinted to in the context of the discussions on homogeneity, the issues of direct effect and of uniform interpretation are intimately connected. The link had emerged in the considerations of the Advocate General in the *Polydor* case, especially in light of the submissions of the parties. The Court, however, chose not to dwell on this issue. It limited itself to ruling out the interpretation by analogy of the EEC–Switzerland FTA provisions worded similarly to provisions of EU law. In his perceptive review of the judgment, Klabbers questions the approach of addressing first the analogous interpretation with the relevant provisions of EU law before considering their possible effect in the EU legal order.[127] Indeed, the Advocate General adopted a different approach by considering and excluding the issue of direct effect first. She highlighted that the extension of arrangements regarding free movement of persons in the EU (then EEC) to the EU–Portugal FTA could arguably 'prejudge the outcome of negotiations in progress for Portugal's accession to the EEC'.[128] Policy considerations were thus significant in the reasoning of direct effect.[129]

The relevance of the interrelation between direct effect and interpretation by analogy for the political covenants of EU neighbourhood law has distinctively emerged in the context of the Ankara Agreement.[130] The change of approach by the ECJ from *Soysal and Savatli* to *Demirkan* heralded an increased awareness of the ECJ in migration matters, and signalled a passage from the free movement logic to an increased attention to the policy implications of migration.[131] Indeed, the reflection on the policy aspects of the extension of the EU's legal space has led the ECJ to partly overturn its previous case law on direct effect of some provisions

[125] Swiss Federal Supreme Court, BGE, 2A.593/2005 (6 September 2006) cons 6, (my translation): 'Die Schweiz ist bisher keine (völkerrechtlichen) Verpflichtungen eingegangen, welche die direkte Anwendung des Cassis-de-Dijon-Prinzips gebieten würden, und eine entsprechende gesetzliche Grundlage fehlt im internen Recht.'

[126] Case C-351/08 *Grimme*, EU:C:2009:697; Case T-541/08, *Fokus Invest*, EU:T:2014:628.

[127] Jan Klabbers, 'The Purpose of International Agreements and Their Direct Effect: Polydor.' in Ramses A Wessel and Graham Butler, *EU External Relations Law: The Cases in Context* (Hart Publishing, 2022) 148.

[128] Case 270/80, *Polydor v Harlequin and Simons Records*, Opinion of AG Rozès, EU:C:1981:286 [354].

[129] Klabbers (n 127) 151.

[130] See further on this ch 3, section III B.

[131] Bruno De Witte, 'Visa Requirements for Turkish Citizens: Soysal & Savatli and Demirkan' in Graham Butler and Ramses A Wessel (eds), *EU External Relations Law: The Cases in Context* (Hart Publishing, 2022) 585.

of the Ankara Agreement.[132] It can be argued that the evolution of the case law reflects the evolution of the relevant political covenant of EU neighbourhood with an increased distance between the EU legal order and the Ankara regime.

The expectations of the parties certainly influence the evolution of the political covenants in EU neighbourhood law. For instance, the membership expectations of Ukraine have played a part in calibrating proximity with the EU, also in the absence of corresponding expectations on the part of the EU. As a matter of fact, the Ukrainian Supreme Court has recognised the direct effect of some provisions of the EU–Ukraine AA in its domestic legal system well before the granting to Ukraine of the EU membership candidate status.[133]

On the opposite end of the EU neighbourhood continuum, distance from the EU legal order through avoidance of direct effect has been paramount in the *Brexit* process. In the EU–UK TCA, the priority of the negotiators, especially from the UK side, was that of ensuring distance between the EU legal order and the TCA. Such a distance is achieved with an increased reliance on international law. The TCA establishes that:

> 1. … [N]othing in this Agreement or any supplementing agreement shall be construed as conferring rights or imposing obligations on persons other than those created between the Parties under public international law, nor as permitting this Agreement or any supplementing agreement to be directly invoked in the domestic legal systems of the Parties.
> 2. A Party shall not provide for a right of action under its law against the other Party on the ground that the other Party has acted in breach of this Agreement or any supplementing agreement.[134]

Exceptionally, direct effect is envisaged for individual rights protected by the Protocol on Social Security Coordination.[135] It is also applied, but only with regard to the Union, for law enforcement and judicial cooperation on criminal matters.[136] The fact that the clause prohibiting direct effect was included in the text of the EU–UK TCA instead of the relevant Council Decision appears to signal again

[132] The first case was C-192/89 *Sevince*, EU:C:1990:322 [15]. See further on the line of reasoning of direct effect Case C-37/98 *Savas*, EU:C:2000:224 [46]–[54]. See further discussion in ch 3, section III.B of this work.

[133] Ukrainian Supreme Court judgment of 17 July 2018, No 910/14972/17, particularly regarding Art 198 EU–Ukraine AA on trademarks. On this see Anastasiia Kyrylenko, 'Direct Effect in Ukraine of IPR Provisions from the EU/Ukraine Free Trade Agreement: A Principled Approach to the Zentiva Case' (2019) 14 *Journal of Intellectual Property Law & Practice* 716, and Roman Petrov, 'Challenges of the EU–Ukraine AA's Effective Implementation into the Legal Order of Ukraine' in Stefan Lorenzmeier, Roman Petrov and Christoph Vedder (eds), *EU External Relations Law: Shared Competences and Shared Values in Agreements Between the EU and Its Eastern Neighbourhood* (Springer, 2021).

[134] EU–UK TCA, Art 5 private rights.

[135] ibid Art SSC.67: Protection of individual rights.

[136] ibid Art 5 Private rights (see the exception mentioned regarding Part III). See Adam Łazowski, 'Mind the Fog, Stand Clear of the Cliff! From the Political Declaration to the Post-Brexit EU–UK Legal Framework – Part I' (2021) 5 *European Papers* 1105, 1123–24. He notices: 'This caveat was not in the original draft of the provision in questions, which may suggest that it was added on the initiative of the UK negotiators'.

an intention to differentiate this new regime from the traditional paradigms of EU neighbourhood law, an intention that met the expectations of both parties. It remains to be seen whether such a detachment will ultimately endure in the proximity of the EU. The Protocol on Ireland and Northern Ireland is an example of the fact that, for non-EU countries, it may be difficult to maintain distance from the EU legal order, also in terms of direct effect.[137] In the EU's proximity, the magnetism of the EU legal order remains high. Moreover, with respect to the EU–UK TCA relations, on the EU's side, the TCA was concluded under the legal basis of association (Article 217 TFEU), and not under the legal basis usually employed for trade agreements with EU global partners (Article 207 TFEU). On the UK's side, the EU Future Relationship Act incorporating the TCA into the UK legal system,[138] appears to grant 'some kind of direct effect for the TCA, but also some primacy towards all [UK] domestic law'.[139]

V. Asserting Distance: Contestation of the Legal-political Covenants of EU Neighbourhood Law

The patterns of gravitation around the EU legal order may be contested. Gravitation entails a superordination of the EU legal order that neighbouring countries may wish to eschew in the quest for maintaining their regulatory autonomy. In that regard, the *Brexit* process was thought to bring about a Copernican revolution in the EU's proximity relations: the UK wanted to withdraw from EU membership to gain regulatory autonomy and consequently it would *not* embrace the paradigms of gravitation around the EU legal order entailed in the traditional canons of EU neighbourhood law. The EU reacted to this challenge with a renewed emphasis on the balance between benefits and obligations in the EU's proximity partnerships. As would be clarified by the European Council, 'cherry picking' regarding the participation in the EU internal market would be precluded.[140] The motives underlying both the challenges to the patterns of gravitation around the EU's legal order and the EU's ensuing reaction are not entirely new in EU external relations law.

The EU's stance on the 'indivisibility' of the sections of the internal market forcefully advocated during the *Brexit* negotiations was in fact already discernible in more tenuous tones in the context of EU–Swiss partnerships. Already the original package of 1999 EU–Switzerland Bilaterals advised against an *à la carte* participation in the extended EU's legal space. In case of termination of the

[137] *cf* EU–UK Protocol on Ireland and Northern Ireland [2020] OJ L 29/7; hereinafter 'EU–UK PINI', Art 12(5) and discussion in ch 7 of this work.

[138] European Union (Future Relationship) Act 2020 (UK). See in particular Art 29 'General Implementation of the Agreements'.

[139] Pavlos Eleftheriadis, 'Eleven Types of Post-Brexit EU Law' (Oxford Law Faculty, 8 January 2021), www.law.ox.ac.uk/business-law-blog/blog/2021/01/eleven-types-post-brexit-eu-law.

[140] European Council, European Council, European Council (Art 50) guidelines for Brexit negotiations, Brussels, 29 April 2017, EUCO XT 20004/17.

FMPA, the other agreements concluded within the Bilaterals I would be equally terminated. The termination mechanism operates by virtue of a 'guillotine clause' present in the Agreement.[141] A similar and reinforced guillotine clause features in the Draft Institutional Agreement.[142] Its activation would trigger the denunciation of the EU–Switzerland Agreements related to the access to the EU internal market.[143] Such a reinforced guillotine clause has been criticised by Levrat. He suggested that such clauses 'would render irreversible (because [it would be] too costly [to denounce the Agreement]) the limitation to its sovereignty accepted by Switzerland through the bilateral agreements'. 'Manifestly', he maintains, 'this is not the wish of the Swiss people'.[144] Such a reinforced guillotine clause would be then contrary to the Switzerland's quest for autonomy entailed in its decision not to be part of the EU or the EEA. In other words, this clause would entail a political covenant to which Switzerland is not subscribed.

The motives of contestation animating the debates surrounding the Draft Institutional Framework Agreement in Switzerland and EU–UK relations after *Brexit* have a similar tone. The political debate in Switzerland, as well as in the UK, was informed by a rhetoric of acrimony towards the rationales of the extension of the EU's legal space. The hostility was mainly oriented towards the so-called 'foreign judges' and the mechanisms of compulsory adaptation to EU law. Contestation thus revolves around the patterns of institutional gravitation around the EU's legal order. In Switzerland, a strong condemnation towards the Draft Institutional Arrangement originated from the Swiss People's party (UDC). This party labelled the Agreement as '*un traité classique de soumission – un traité colonial!*'[145] liable to undermine Swiss constitutional fundamentals, democracy and independence. Criticism has also been advanced by Baudenbacher, a former president of the EFTA Court. He qualified the dispute resolution mechanism of the Draft Institutional Agreement, as an 'amateurish bricolage' that does not fit the Swiss legal framework and assigns disproportionate privileges to the European Court of Justice.[146] Along similar lines, Levrat has maintained that the envisaged dispute settlement mechanism would be more constraining for Switzerland than its adherence to the EEA: in the latter, the dispute settlement mechanism does not envisage an obligatory intervention of the CJEU.[147] A more positive reception came from Kaddous, who highlighted

[141] EU–Swiss Free Movement of Persons Agreement, Art 25(4).

[142] See EU–Switzerland InstA, Art 22 of the Entrée en vigueur et dénonciation.

[143] See InstA, Arts 2 and 17(3).

[144] Nicolas Levrat, 'Profiter d'un Contexte Favorable Pour Renégocier Un Nouvel Accord-Cadre Avec FUE' (2021) 33, www.fdfa.admin.ch/europa/en/home/europapolitik/ueberblick/institutionelles-abkommen.html.

[145] Swiss UDC website, Le Journal de l'Union démocratique du centre, www.udc.ch/wp-content/uploads/sites/2/1902-Franc-parler_mini.pdf.

[146] Carl Baudenbacher, '"Britzerland": The Problem of Dispute Resolution Post-Brexit' (LSE Brexit, 29 October 2018), blogs.lse.ac.uk/brexit/2018/10/29/britzerland-the-problem-of-dispute-resolution-post-brexit.

[147] Levrat (n 144) 52.

that the mechanism responded to Swiss concerns for the equal participation of the Confederation's officials in the different stages of the operation of the agreements, including dispute settlement.[148] Replicating the mechanism in place in the EU–Ukraine DCFTA, the DSM of the Draft Institutional Agreement is based on a mutually established arbitration panel. The latter is the ultimate arbiter of the disputes arising from the agreements, even in cases where provisions of (extended) EU law are at issue. In fact, the involvement and pronouncements of the CJEU, although mandatory for matters concerning EU law, operate in an indirect manner as they would be mediated by the arbitration panel. This is different from an earlier draft of the Agreement envisaging the direct involvement of the CJEU.[149] The motives of contestation around the EU–Switzerland Draft Institutional Arrangements are thus strikingly similar to those that have animated the *Brexit* debate.[150]

While *Brexit* and the ensuing retrenchment of the EU's legal space challenges the patterns of *Wider Europe*, the process itself has also reinforced and sharpened some of the techniques of extension of the EU's legal space. The Withdrawal Agreement and the PINI are paradigmatic of how the mechanisms of EU neighbourhood law have been applied to the fullest in the *Brexit* process. The Protocol on Ireland and Northern Ireland is a remarkable example of the extension of the EU's legal space in a third country with pervasive substantive and institutional *renvois* to the EU legal order. In Northern Ireland, EU law will continue to be applied with respect to the free movement of goods and the powers of EU institutions, included those of the CJEU, is extended. Also, the distinctive qualities of EU law, such as primacy and direct effect, is maintained. As it was the case of the EU-UK WA, one could thus not think of a better application of the 'everything but institutions' formula. This explains why in the PINI gravitation around the EU legal order ensuing from EU neighbourhood law operates at full intensity.[151] To be sure, the TCA has certainly produced significant changes in the EU's external relations law. Given that the TCA frees the UK from its gravitation around the EU legal order, *Brexit* has thus certainly produced a shift in the framing of the political covenants of EU neighbourhood law.

[148] Christine Kaddous, 'Switzerland and the EU Current Issues and New Challenges under the Draft Institutional Framework Agreement' in Sieglinde Gstöhl and David Phinnemore, *The proliferation of privileged partnerships between the European Union and its Neighbours* (Routledge, 2019) 77.

[149] See further Christa Tobler, 'The EU–Swiss Sectoral Approach Under Pressure: Not Least Because of Brexit' in Stefan Lorenzmeier, Roman Petrov and Christoph Vedder (eds), *EU External Relations Law: Shared Competences and Shared Values in Agreements Between the EU and Its Eastern Neighbourhood* (Springer, 2021) 113.

[150] See Baudenbacher bolg post on the 'foreign court' argument in the British and Swiss contexts: Carl Baudenbacher, 'The ECJ Used to Be a Neutral Court for the UK – It No Longer Is' *LSE BREXIT* (9 March 2021), blogs.lse.ac.uk/brexit/2021/03/09/the-ecj-didnt-used-to-be-a-foreign-court-it-is-one-now.

[151] Although with some limitations recently introduced with the Windsor Framework. See further ch 7, section III.F of this work.

A. Contesting EU Neighbourhood Law Through 'International Law' Rhetoric

The neighbouring countries' desire to eschew the paradigms of gravitation around the EU legal order is often manifested in a wish to reorient the partnership towards 'international law'. The willingness has characterised the partnerships with Ukraine, Switzerland and the UK. In that regard, reliance on international law is usually grounded on expectations and attempts to undertake more symmetric relations.[152] In Ukraine, the quest to turn to international law in the agitated times of the signature of the association agreement in 2013 was inspired by a conception of world politics whereby, more than international organisations, states remain the principal actors in international law.[153] This stance has been often heralded by the Kremlin with a view to circumventing the EU's regulatory power, whose normative reach influences the regulatory choices of the EU's neighbours.[154] In the case of Switzerland and the UK, the willingness to base the relationship on 'international law' and not on EU neighbourhood law is cast in more elaborated terms. For the Swiss, the emphasis is on the preservation of the constitutional characteristics of its domestic legal systems. In May 2021, in fact, Switzerland decided to end talks on the arrangements on the draft institutional framework.[155] In the words of the Swiss campaign group against the Draft Institutional Arrangement, the agreement was 'one sided. It required us to take on EU law without any mechanism for saying No. It would have been a direct interference in our system of direct democracy and cantons in Switzerland'.[156]

The UK withdrawal and ensuing contestation of EU law and EU neighbourhood law was inspired by similar considerations and by a desire to harness the flexibility of the UK's Westminster legal and political system. The EU–UK TCA refers to the 'Parties' autonomy and sovereignty'.[157] Not by chance, the provision of the Agreement devoted to the interpretative framework is titled 'Public International Law'.[158] *Brexit* originated from a desire to disentangle the UK from the EU institutional and legal relations that were perceived as constraints to the

[152] See for instance the *Brexit* minister insistence on a partnership among 'sovereign equals'. 'David Frost: The EU Must Revisit the Northern Ireland Protocol' *Financial Times* (6 June 2021), www.ft.com/content/eb35a108-6186-42a4-b401-5e1df0e2c64a.

[153] Government of Ukraine, 'Resolution on Suspension of Preparation Process to Conclude Association Agreement with EU' (21 November 2013), old.kmu.gov.ua/kmu/control/en/publish/printable_article?art_id=246867400.

[154] Hiski Haukkala, *The EU–Russia Strategic Partnership: The Limits of Post-Sovereignty in International Relations* (Routledge, 2010). See also ch 6, section II of this work.

[155] Hans von der Bruchard and Florian Eder, 'Switzerland Ends Talks on EU Partnership Treaty' *POLITICO* (26 May 2021), www.politico.eu/article/switzerland-eu-talks-partnership-treaty-end.

[156] Philip Erzinger, head of a Kompass Europe, quoted in Sam Jones and Ben Hall, 'Swiss Prepare for EU Chill after Quitting Market Access Talks' (28 May 2021), www.ft.com/content/10ede16f-0b1e-4f4f-8fd6-4ec6ac090ed0.

[157] EU–UK TCA, Art 1.

[158] ibid Art 4.

exercise of UK sovereignty. The *Brexit* campaign was permeated by rhetoric of 'taking back control' in the conclusion of a fertile but troubled UK membership in the EU. The fruits of the UK's membership came from the contribution that the UK had given to the content of the EU rules, particularly in the domain of the internal market.[159] The troubles came from the uneasiness of the UK in taking part in several areas of EU integration. This was manifested in the variable geometry and differentiation arrangements it secured in order not to participate in some sectors of EU membership law.[160]

In the UK, dissatisfaction with EU membership came to a head in 2016. By that time, David Cameron's Government has secured a 'deal' to be submitted to the *Brexit* referendum. Under the label 'New Settlement for the United Kingdom within the European Union', it 'was adopted as a Decision of the EU Heads of States or Governments meeting within the Council'. It reaffirmed the 'entitlements' of the UK under the Treaties, namely its opt-outs and differentiated integration arrangements.[161] Significantly, a section of the deal labelled 'sovereignty' clarified that the references to 'the ever closer union' were not applicable to the UK.[162] This signalled a detachment from the political covenant of EU membership law. It also shed light on the demarcation of the EU and Member States competences, advising against an 'extensive interpretation' of the former. Further, it reasserted the importance of the principle of subsidiarity.

Arguably, the legal-political events leading to *Brexit* might be construed as a product of the UK's increased disenchantment with the progressive over-constitutionalisation of the EU.[163] While over-constitutionalisation is a contested concept, it helps to understand the significance of law in the EU policies, not least in its external action.[164] As Dieter Grimm puts it, in terms that controversially downplay the role of counter-majoritarian institutions,

> combined with the lack of differentiation between the constitutional law level and the ordinary law level, the constitutionalisation of the treaties immunises the Commission and particularly the ECJ against any attempt by the democratically responsible

[159] David Anderson, 'No-Deal Readiness, Lord Cockfield and the British Ingenuity behind the EU Single Market' *Prospect Magazine* (9 October 2019), www.prospectmagazine.co.uk/economics-and-finance/no-deal-readiness-brexit-lord-cockfield-and-the-british-ingenuity-behind-the-eu-single-market.

[160] For a review see Bruno de Witte, 'Variable Geometry and Differentiation as Structural Features of the EU Legal Order' in Bruno de Witte, Andrea Ott and Ellen Vos, *Between flexibility and disintegration: the trajectory of differentiation in EU law* (Edward Elgar Publishing, 2017).

[161] European Council of 18–19 February 2016, Extract of the conclusions of 'A New Settlement for the United Kingdom within the European Union' [2016] OJ C 69I/1.

[162] For a discussion of the visions of 'ever closer Union' and 'Wider looser union' in the wake of Brexit, see Giacinto della Cananea, 'Differentiated Integration in Europe After Brexit: An Institutional Analysis' in Ingolf Pernice and Ana Maria Guerra Martins (eds), *Brexit and the future of EU politics: a constitutional law perspective* (Nomos, 2019).

[163] Susanne K Schmidt, 'No Match Made in Heaven. Parliamentary Sovereignty, EU over-Constitutionalization and Brexit' (2020) 27 *Journal of European Public Policy* 779.

[164] Bruno de Witte, 'Too Much Constitutional Law in the European Union's Foreign Relations?' in Marise Cremona and Bruno de Witte (eds), *EU foreign relations law: constitutional fundamentals* (Hart Publishing, 2008).

> institutions of the EU to react to the Court's jurisprudence by changing the law of the EU the extensive interpretation approach of the Court of Justice especially with respect to the EU citizenship rights.[165]

In this controversial view, which is arguably cognate to that informing the *Brexit* process, over-constitutionalisation thus limits the role of the Member States as the 'masters of the Treaties' especially in the process of EU Treaties application.[166] The thick constitutional framework of the EU may thus be construed as entailing a significant limitation of majoritarian decision-making at the heart of the UK political tradition.[167]

Even in the post-*Brexit* phase, the UK has attempted to counteract the EU legal power and the asymmetries characterising the EU's neighbourhood relations by relying on a problematic understanding of international law, intended as principally concerned with governing relations among national sovereign states. This approach *mutatis mutandis* is similar to Viktor Yanukovych Government's rigid conception of international law that lead to the deferral of the signature of the EU–Ukraine Association Agreement. According to this stance, the EU's status would be that of a 'mere' international organisation. As a matter of fact, the UK attempted to leverage upon the status of the EU under the 1961 Vienna Convention on Diplomatic Relations. Although the objective of the EU is that of having its ambassador recognised at the same rank as those of states, there is no such obligation under the Convention. Consequently, the EU delegation in London has not been granted diplomatic immunities by the UK in a move that been defined as an 'inimical but probably lawful denial'.[168]

VI. Conclusions

This chapter has shed light on the patterns of gravitation and contestation around the EU legal order. Compiling a definitive *repertoire* of techniques of EU neighbourhood law is challenging: different echelons of gravitational intensity around the EU's legal order can coexist in a single EU neighbourhood partnership, and, as in the case of the EU–Ukraine AA, within the same association agreement. The indeterminate language and character of the convergence clauses add to this complexity. The *scope* and *intensity* of gravitation can be considered as the two key factors for making sense of the constellation of the ways in which the EU's legal space is extended in the EU neighbourhood. In light of the often indeterminate

[165] Dieter Grimm, 'The Democratic Costs of Constitutionalisation: The European Case' (2015) 21 *European Law Journal* 460, 471.
[166] Dieter Grimm, *The Constitution of European Democracy* (Oxford University Press, 2017) 100.
[167] Schmidt (n 163) 780.
[168] Mauro Gatti, 'Diplomats or Fonctionnaires? The Contested Status of the EU's "Embassy" in the UK' *EJIL: Talk!* (1 March 2021), www.ejiltalk.org/diplomats-or-fonctionnaires-the-contested-status-of-the-eus-embassy-in-the-uk.

language and nature of the convergence clauses regarding the scope of extension of the EU's legal space, mechanisms of organisational interaction are crucial in capturing the intensity of gravitation around the EU legal order. Mechanisms of organisational interactions have been construed as representing the intersection of the three lines of inquiry of the book. As techniques of extension of the EU's legal space calibrating proximity with and distance with the EU legal order, they are illustrative of the demarcation and complex relationship between EU membership and EU neighbourhood law. Especially when the extraterritorial use of the EU institutions is envisaged, enforcement mechanisms lead to a remarkable reconfiguration of the way in which sovereignty is exercised in *Wider Europe*. Significantly, moreover, enforcement mechanisms are intimately connected with the legal effects of extended EU law. Provisions on (the lack of) direct effect are included by the EU in arrangements of EU neighbourhood law to calibrate distance between the EU legal order and the relevant external regimes. In turn, third country courts' decisions on whether to grant direct effect to provisions of arrangements of EU neighbourhood law are influenced by their understanding on the proximity of their legal systems with the EU legal order. The perceived proximity increases with membership expectations of third countries.

Political covenants of EU neighbourhood law are thus not set in stone, but are nourished by perceptions and expectations of both parties, as well as the parties' attitudes in the implementations of the agreements. While *Opinion 1/91* focused on the autonomy of the EU legal order from international law regimes, the CJEU's findings in *IN* reflected a strong commitment of both the EU and the EEA EFTA States to the principle and objective of homogeneity with a view to upholding equal rights an obligation in the special relationship linking the EU and Iceland and Norway. Interestingly, however, perceptions and expectations may vary between partners even in the EU neighbourhood arrangements closer to EU law like the EEA. Indeed, although the CJEU has recognised a broader reach of direct effect in EEA law, in the EFTA pillar such a stance is not upheld. Albeit not framing the issue in the language of EU neighbourhood law, EFTA States essentially maintain that primacy and direct effect are proper to the political covenant of EU membership law, a covenant they have not subscribed to. The chapter has also brought to the fore the motives of contestation of EU neighbourhood law by partner countries. Contestation has emerged inter alia in the development of the EU's relations with Ukraine, Switzerland and the UK. Some common threads may be inferred form the motives of contestation, namely the attempt to eschew gravitation around the EU's legal order. Contestation often takes the forms of a (largely rhetoric) quest to recur to more canonical forms of international law premised on formal equality among states and the downplaying of the role of *sui generis* international organisations like the EU. The dialectic contestation of EU neighbourhood law sheds light on its characteristics as a distinctive type of international law reconfiguring the way in which sovereignty is exercised in the extended EU's legal space.

10

Conclusions

This book has turned *Wider Europe* into an analytical concept to capture the old and new legal relations promoted by the EU in its geographical proximity. It has introduced the notion of EU neighbourhood law to account for the interplay between law, diplomacy and geopolitics in the institutional arrangements extending the EU's legal space. It has argued that the dynamics of inclusion and exclusion of *Wider Europe* bring about a *lato sensu* reconfigurations of the Union's borders. EU Neighbourhood law contributes to defining the posture of the EU as a regional legal actor. The nature and the characteristics of the law of the EU's proximity relations have been expounded by pursuing three interrelated lines of inquiry. The first pertains to the demarcation and complex relationship between EU membership law and EU neighbourhood law. The second relates to the techniques of extension of the EU's legal space, including the rather elusive processes of socialisation in *Wider Europe*. Strictly connected to the first two, the third line of inquiry discloses the political covenants underlying the EU's relations with its neighbours. Political covenants represent the interaction between politics, sovereignty and law.

The relationship between EU membership law and EU neighbourhood law is one of extension of the EU's legal space, but at the same time of demarcation among different legal orders. The 'everything but institutions' formula epitomises the dynamics of inclusion and exclusion at play in *Wider Europe*. The EU *acquis* is a vector of inclusion. The EU's *Wider Europe* design was that of stabilising borders by extending its legal space. Trade cooperation was crucial in this respect. It would elicit third countries' gravitation around the EU legal order and promote legislative and regulatory convergence with the EU. The Union therefore conceived access to its internal market as a geopolitical tool for achieving stability at its borders. This is not specific to the European Neighbourhood Policy but characterises several of the EU's proximity policies. Exclusion is mandated by the different facets of the principle of autonomy of EU law. First, exclusion pertains to decision-making process of EU law (and relatedly of extended EU law). As evoked by the 'everything but institutions' formula, countries participating in *Wider Europe* are usually excluded from the Union institutions and consequently from the development of EU law in its pre-normative phase. Third countries are thus precluded from taking part in the EU decision-making process. Secondly, the *Polydor* principle brings to the fore the necessity of a contextual approach for ascertaining the effects of extended EU law. Indeed, the principle requires interpreting and applying provisions similarly or identically worded to EU law in the light of the different contexts of the institutional arrangements extending the EU's legal space. Thirdly, the distinctive features of EU citizenship law (largely absent from EU neighbourhood law – especially in its political dimension) further indicate the special nature of EU membership law as compared to EU neighbourhood law.

The dynamics of inclusion and exclusion inherent in *Wider Europe* inform the semantic and methodological choices of this book. The notions of 'extension of the EU's legal space' and of 'EU neighbourhood law' (often used interchangeably) have been favoured over the categories of 'integration beyond membership' to account for the influence and effects of EU law in its neighbourhood. The language of the 'extension of the EU's legal space' is suggested by institutional documents and particularly by judicial pronouncements on the extension of the EU *acquis* in a larger geographical area than that of EU membership law.[1] The notion of 'legal space' (instead of the more restrictive notion of EU *acquis*) has been juxtaposed to the word 'extension' to account for the more elusive process of third country socialisation in *Wider Europe* including participation in EU programmes and administrative networks of cooperation. Processes of socialisation are characterised by a mixture of hard and soft law instruments and instances of mimetic imitation of EU law.

In turn, the notion of 'EU neighbourhood law' has been introduced to signify its difference from EU membership law. Moreover, this notion brings to the fore the geographical and geopolitical nature of this type of regional law. The ensuing semantic choice thus arises from the necessity to bring to the fore the operation of the dynamics of inclusion and exclusion in *Wider Europe*. Both dynamics contribute to the 'transporting of actual borders beyond the borderline'.[2] In the words of Balibar, this dual phenomenon is an aspect of what he calls a '*would-be "power politics"*' of Europe, following the model of the capacity to `project power' beyond the mere territory of the new superstate, but, in fact, illustrating its incapacity to regulate differences and conflicts *within* its own limits, using the capacities of its domestic institutions and societies'.[3] The exhaustion of the ability to regulate differences and conflicts within membership resulted in what was referred to as 'enlargement fatigue', or exhaustion of the EU's absorption capacity. On the methodological plane, the study of the extension of the EU's legal space requires unravelling the sets of relations connecting different regimes. In this respect, the theoretical corpus of *Santi Romano* has been mobilised to describe the asymmetric relations of dependence linking the EU neighbourhood law regimes with the EU legal order.

Third country gravitation around the EU legal order is governed by techniques of extension of the EU's legal space. The scope of gravitation is determined by substantive *renvois* through which regimes of EU neighbourhood law refer to EU law, by mimetic imitation of EU law, and by processes of third country

[1] See inter alia Case C-452/01 *Ospelt* EU:C:2003:493 [29]; *Opinion 1/00* ECAA, EU:C:2002:231 [3].

[2] Etienne Balibar, 'Europe as Borderland' (2009) 27 *Environment and Planning D: Society and Space* 190, 203.

[3] ibid 203–04 (emphasis in the original).

socialisation in the extended EU's legal space. The intensity of the gravitation is determined by mechanism of organisational interaction between the EU legal order and regimes of EU neighbourhood law. Mechanisms of organisational interactions concern the management and implementation of the EU neighbourhood law agreements. Significantly, these mechanisms may also involve the use of the EU institutions. As the province of enforcement methods of extended EU law, the techniques of organisational interaction offer a better appraisal the different articulations and developments of the EU's neighbourhood partnerships. In fact, the scope of the extension of the EU's legal space alone, which may be defined by shallow best endeavours clauses or by rather elusive processes of socialisation in *Wider Europe*, gives only a partial account of the different echelons of gravitation around the EU legal order.

The EEA and the ECAA models have been characterised as two poles of the EU neighbourhood continuum where the intensity of gravitation around the EU legal order operates at its strongest. While the pre-existing integration of EEA EFTA States has allowed for a two-pillars structure in the EEA Agreement, the absence of pre-existing institutional links among the Western Balkans lead to a single-pillar model in the ECAA. The single-pillar model entails the extraterritorial extension of the powers of the EU institutions. This suggests qualifying the purport of the 'everything but institutions' formula: EU institutions do operate in *Wider Europe*. Yet, and crucially, these institutions are not extended in their composition to non-EU members. The principle of autonomy of EU law mandates that the composition and essential character of the EU institutions remains unaltered. The use of the EU institutions is not a prerogative of the one-pillar model; also, the EEA envisages a possible recourse to the CJEU for interpreting EEA law directly by the EFTA States courts[4] or, in case of failure of solving the dispute by the EEA Joint Committee, by the parties to a dispute.[5] In both the single-pillar and two-pillar arrangements of dispute settlement the substantive *renvois* to EU law and the institutional *renvois* to the CJEU in the context of dispute settlements are mediated by interpretative *renvois* to the case law of the CJEU.[6]

The elaborated techniques of EU neighbourhood law in the EEA Agreement and in the ECAA are governed by the principle and objective of homogeneity. Homogeneity also prescribes the effect of EU law in third countries' legal systems.[7] The ensuing high intensity of gravitation around the EU legal order in these multilateral arrangements locate them at the pole closest to the EU in the EU neighbourhood continuum. Less far-reaching techniques of EU neighbourhood law determine less proximate echelons of gravitational intensity around the EU legal order Union. This is especially the case of bilateral partnership, but also of the multilateral EnCT where, although the scope of gravitation is wide,

[4] EEA Agreement, Art 107 and protocol 34.
[5] EEA Agreement, Art 111; see similarly ECAA Agreement, Art 20(3); TCT, Art 37(3).
[6] EEA Agreement, Art 6; ECAA Agreement, Art 16(2); TCT, Art 19(1).
[7] EEA Agreement, Art 7; ECAA Agreement, Art 7; TCT, Art 3.

the mechanism of organisational interaction and the enforcement mechanisms are tenuous. The study of the EnCT has shown the validity of *Wider Europe* as an analytical framework. Indeed, the joining of Ukraine, Moldova and Georgia in addition to the Western Balkans[8] (well before the membership application of these three Eastern partners of the EU could be envisioned), demonstrates how EU neighbourhood law captures a variety of EU's proximity policies.

In examining the bilateral partnerships with the EU, this book has embraced the comparative turn in the study of the EU's proximity relations elicited by *Brexit*. In doing so, it has revealed an ambivalence in *Wider Europe*. On the one hand, bilateral partnerships show how similar techniques and rationales of extension of the EU's legal space are used with different third countries. It has been pointed out how the specific dispute settlement arrangement applicable to some of the Deep and Comprehensive Free Trade Area of the EU–Ukraine Association Agreement has transmigrated to other institutional arrangements of EU neighbourhood law. It has been employed also in the EU–UK Withdrawal Agreement[9] and in the EU–Switzerland Draft Institutional arrangement.[10] The study of the *Brexit* process has brought to the fore the similarities between the techniques of extension of the EU's legal space characterising *Wider Europe* and the retrenchment of the EU's legal space, which has opened the prospects of a *Narrower Europe*. This further validates the value of *Wider Europe* as an analytical concept capturing the old and new EU's proximity policies. In that regard, the book has argued that one could hardly think of a more accurate application of the 'everything but institutions' formula than in the EU–UK Withdrawal Agreement.

On the other hand, bilateral partnerships show the difficulty of compiling a definite *repertoire* of techniques of extension of the EU's legal space. The echelons of gravitation around the EU legal order remain often difficult to delineate. This is due to the fragmented nature of the bilateral partnerships (the patchwork of the EU–Switzerland Agreements is a case in point); but also to the fact that varying echelons of gravitational intensity feature within a single institutional arrangement (as it is the case with the EU–Ukraine AA). The reflection on the fragmentation of the bilateral arrangements lead to question the EU's rhetoric on the indivisibility of the four freedoms, informing the *Brexit* negotiations. A special place in the EU bilateral partnerships is occupied by Morocco, the first country to be mentioned in Prodi's *Wider Europe* speech. The study of the Moroccan case has brought to the fore how the extension of the EU's legal space occurs not only via legally binding agreements of EU neighbourhood law, but also through more legally elusive processes of socialisation in *Wider Europe*. The Moroccan case is also illustrative of the dynamics of inclusion and exclusion operating primarily through trade and the externalisation of the EU's border controls.

[8] With the Western Balkans already in the pre-accession process.
[9] EU–UK WA, Art 174.
[10] EU–Switzerland InstA, Art 10(3).

The *Brexit* process has led the EU to spell out the political covenants underlying its neighbourhood relations. This was cast in terms of a balance between benefits and obligations that should govern third country participation in *Wider Europe*. In the context of the UK's withdrawal, the EU posited that non-EU members cannot benefit from the same rights enjoyed by EU members. The need for rationalising the balance between benefits and obligations for third countries participating in *Wider Europe* has particularly informed the EU's attempts to overhaul its fragmented bilateral partnership with Switzerland. Political covenants of EU neighbourhood law are characterised by relations of asymmetry and dependence. They reflect and structure the complexties between the EU and third countries participating in *Wider Europe*. The extension of the EU's legal space comes with an extension of the EU's claims to authority beyond the Union's borders. These claims, together with third countries' recognition of the normative and technical qualities of EU law, trigger third country gravitation around the EU's legal order. Crucially, in the extension of the EU's legal space, the distinctive political covenant of EU membership law is not replicated. The reconfiguration of sovereignty exercise entailed in the transfer of legislative and judicial powers to the EU institutions remains specific to EU membership law. Arguably, such a transfer generates a 'sovereignty surplus',[11] enabling the Union to address transnational issues better than the single Member States.

The distinctiveness of this sovereignty reconfiguration is not replicated in *Wider* Europe. For EFTA States generally qualifying for EU membership, the costs of non-membership amount to being largely rule-takers of extended EU law.[12] Indeed, the preservation of sovereignty resulting from the absence of transfer of sovereign powers in the relevant arrangements of EU neighbourhood law as the EEA needs to be read against the background of the patterns of 'independence under hegemony',[13] ensuing from the participation in the extended EU internal market. For countries not qualifying for EU membership, the Commission spelled out the benefits of participation in *Wider Europe*, highlighting how

> with only few regulatory models in a globalised world, the EU model tends to be attractive to partners, reducing the "invention costs" of political and economic costs of reform. Thus, many partners have adopted a broad-ranged approach to convergence with EU policies and regulatory standards.[14]

The choice of the EU as a regulatory model is particularly significant in the EU neighbourhood, where the EU is often regarded as a normative power.[15]

[11] Neil Walker, 'The Sovereignty Surplus' (2020) 18 *International Journal of Constitutional Law* 370.

[12] See Marja-Liisa Öberg, *The Boundaries of the EU Internal Market: Participation without Membership* (Cambridge University Press, 2020).

[13] Erik Oddvar Eriksen and John Erik Fossum, *The European Union's Non-Members: Independence under Hegemony?* (Routledge, 2015).

[14] European Commission, 'Taking stock of the European Neighbourhood Policy', COM(2010), 207 final, 6.

[15] Henrik Larsen, 'The EU as a Normative Power and the Research on External Perceptions: The Missing Link' (2014) 52 *Journal of Common Market Studies* 896, 906.

EU neighbourhood law reconfigures the way in which sovereignty is exercised, although in a different manner form EU membership law. Such a reconfiguration, ensuing from the political covenants of EU neighbourhood law, emerges particularly in enforcement mechanisms envisaging the extension of the powers and tasks of EU institutions beyond membership. In that light, enforcement mechanisms of regimes of EU neighbourhood law can be construed as the point of intersection between the three lines of inquiry of this book. They shed light on how EU neighbourhood regimes calibrate proximity to and distance from the EU's legal order while reconfiguring the exercise of sovereignty in *Wider Europe*.

Several multilateral arrangements of EU neighbourhood law present far-reaching institutional *renvois* to the EU legal order, especially with regard to the dispute settlement mechanisms. The CJEU can be invoked in matters concerning the interpretation of extended EU law by courts of third states[16] for a preliminary reference or by the parties to a dispute not solved by the relevant joint committee.[17] Arguably, in the one-pillar model the judicial *renvois* are more pervasive in light of the fact that the CJEU's prerogatives are extended together with the extraterritorial powers of the other EU institutions in the management of the relevant arrangements.[18] Such a pervasive gravitation of the one-pillar model around the EU legal order (and the ensuing reconfiguration of the way in which sovereignty is exercised) can be explained when one considers the Western Balkans' inclusion in the EU accession process.

Moreover, a major institutional *renvois* to the CJEU is also operated in the EU–Ukraine AA. In the EU–Ukraine DCFTA dispute settlement mechanism, the intensity of gravitation appears tempered by the fact that the decisions of the CJEU are final and binding on the arbitration panel not on the parties to the disputes or the courts of Ukraine. However, the institutional *renvoi* is mandatory when disputes pertain to issues of extended EU law. In these cases, 'the arbitration panel shall not decide the question, but request the Court of Justice of the European Union to give a ruling on the question'.[19] Instead, in the ECAA, as well as in the EEA, there is margin of the appreciation for third country courts and the joint committees established by the Agreements on whether to make recourse to the CJEU to interpret extended EU law. The institutional *renvoi* of the EU–Ukraine Association Agreement thus mandates the recourse to the CJEU for matters of interpretation of extended EU law, while tempering this obligation with the mediation of the arbitration panel. The favour of the EU institutions for this mechanism, which has been employed also in other arrangements of EU neighbourhood law, derives from the fact that it balances the mandatory recourse to the CJEU with a more neutral and independent arbitration panel meditating the gravitation around the EU legal order. In the more

[16] EEA Agreement, Art 107 and especially Protocol 34; ECAA Agreement; Art 16(2); see also TCT, Art 19(2).

[17] EEA Agreement, Art 111(3); ECAA Agreement, Art 20(3); see also TCT Art 37(3).

[18] See inter alia ECAA Agreement, Art 12(4) and TCT, Arts 37(3) and 40.

[19] EU–Ukraine AA, Art 322(2).

developed forms of extension of the EU's legal space, the institutional *renvois* highlight the de facto superordination of the EU legal order over arrangements of EU neighbourhood law.[20] This superordination is at times contested by EU partners seeking more symmetric relations under international law.[21] The study of the special relationship between the EU and Norway and Iceland has also shown how the political covenants of EU neighbourhood law are not set in stone: they evolve over time together with the techniques of extension of the EU's legal space. While at the time of drafting of the EEA the autonomy of the EU legal order was paramount, the commitment of both parties to homogeneity prevailed in the development of the special relationship. This work has further highlighted how the constitutional asymmetry of the EEA Agreement and the EU has led to detach homogeneity from uniformity of interpretation. In order to arrive at a homogeneity of effects of the relevant provisions, the EFTA Court has interpreted secondary provisions on the free movement of persons in the EFTA differently from the canons of interpretation of EU membership law proper to the EU pillar.[22]

In spite of the largely asymmetric relations ensuing from the EU's extended legal space, third countries gravitating around the EU legal order benefit from the networks of cooperation established and nurtured by EU neighbourhood law. Although to a lesser extent than what happens in EU membership law, these networks allow third countries to participate in the relational reconfiguration of sovereignty in *Wider Europe*[23] and benefit from the EU's regulatory capacity. While asymmetrically oriented in favour of the EU, the reconfiguration of sovereignty in *Wider Europe* may be construed as bi-directional: it does not only affect third countries but the Union itself. Hillion has unravelled the additional system of check and balances that the EU special relationship with Norway and Iceland entails for the Union itself, in the context of the rule of law regression of some of the EU Member States.[24] The bi-directional reconfiguration of sovereignty elicits a *lato sensu* reconfiguration of the Union's borders. In a more problematic manner, the bi-directional reconfiguration of sovereignty exercise also occurs in the externalisation of EU's border controls. This is the case of the EU–Morocco cooperative arrangements of migration containment. These legally elusive arrangements are not captured in the existing legal categories and lead to accountability and responsibility gaps. By externalising border controls, EU-led cooperative networks of migration containment elicit a reconfiguration in the sovereignty exercise of the EU and its Member States in the process of externalising sovereign tasks. This enables third

[20] See perceptively in this sense Marise Cremona, 'The "Dynamic and Homogenous" EEA: Byzantine Structures and Variable Geometry' (1994) 19 *European Law Review* 508.

[21] See discussion in ch 9, section V of this work.

[22] See ch 4, section IV.A.

[23] See discussion in ch 3, section VI of this work.

[24] Christophe Hillion, 'The EU External Action as Mandate to Uphold the Rule of Law Outside and inside the Union' (2023) 29 *Columbia Journal of European Law* 228.

countries to confront the EU with a 'reversed conditionality'[25] and to weaponise migration while capitalising on their 'geographical rent'.[26]

The book has been devoted to unravelling the mechanics of the gravitation around the EU's legal order constituting *Wider Europe* with an attention to the geopolitical implications of the extension of the EU's legal space. Law is a major source of the EU power:[27] it ensues from the size of the EU market[28] as well as its regulatory capacity.[29] Gravitation around the EU legal order in *Wider Europe* certainly leads to a degree of satellisation. Yet, the hegemonic understanding of the extension of the EU's legal space should be nuanced. In the context of the *Brussels effect*, Bradford points out that what could be read as 'regulatory imperialism' is revealed, with closer scrutiny, as an 'inadvertent by-product' of the EU's internal goals and preferences.[30] The EU has always been reluctant to overtly acknowledge or project its power. In a similar vein, the EU's policies have been rather ambiguous with regard to territory and borders. The European Neighbourhood Policy is a case in point: it comfortably rests on the indefinite notion of *Europe*. Notwithstanding this territorial ambiguity, the book has argued that by reconfiguring the way in which sovereignty is exercised in *Wider Europe*, the extension of the EU's legal space brings about a *lato sensu* reconfiguration of the Union's borders through law.

While the legal mechanisms of *Wider Europe* have produced articulated framework of interdependences, the material geopolitical achievements of the EU's proximity policies look uncertain at best. Already in 2014, 10 years after the launch of the ENP, a Charlemagne editorial in *The Economist* brought to the fore how the alleged 'ring of friends' (still spanning 'from Morocco to Russia') actually turned out to be 'a ring of fire'. The editorial addressed the convoluted process of signature of the EU–Ukraine Association Agreement signalling how the EU was concerned to 'downplay its neighbours' aspiration'. It perceptively highlighted how 'the Russian took the ENP far more seriously than the Europeans ever did'.[31]

In 2024, the flames of the 'ring of fire' are arguably more worrisome. Migration, especially from the southern shores, continues to be a highly topical and divisive terrain in European politics. After the largely failed attempts following the Arab Springs to engage more with its southern neighbours, the southern dimension

[25] Fanny Tittel-Mosser, 'Reversed Conditionality in EU External Migration Policy: The Case of Morocco' (2018) 14 *Journal of Contemporary European Research* 349.

[26] Katharina Natter, 'The Formation of Morocco's Policy Towards Irregular Migration (2000–2007): Political Rationale and Policy Processes' (2014) 52 *International Migration* 15.

[27] Marise Cremona and Joanne Scott, 'Introduction' in *EU Law Beyond EU Borders: The Extraterritorial Reach of EU Law* (Oxford University Press, 2019).

[28] Chad Damro, 'Market Power Europe' (2012) 19 *Journal of European Public Policy* 682.

[29] Anu Bradford, *The Brussels Effect: How the European Union Rules the World* (Oxford University Press, 2020).

[30] Anu Bradford, 'The Brussels Effect' (2012) 107 *Northwestern University Law Review* 1, 6.

[31] Charlemagne, 'Europe's Ring of Fire' *The Economist* (20 September 2014), www.economist.com/europe/2014/09/20/europes-ring-of-fire.

of the ENP lacks momentum and vision. The development of EU–Moroccan relations have been under strain for years pending new developments of the convoluted politico-judicial saga on the controversial extension of the EU–Morocco Agreements to the territories of *Western Sahara.* Besides, countries like Azerbaijan have been included in the European Political Community while Morocco has not.

On the other side of the 'ring of fire', the 'European choice' of Ukraine will depend on the results on the battlefield. The Russian aggression in Ukraine in 2022 after the annexation of Crimea in 2014 exposes the EU to the harsh and deplorable realities of power politics waged through war. For its geopolitical position and positioning, Ukraine has always been a vanguard point from where to appreciate the political covenants of EU neighbourhood law. This is even more true today when the covenants of *Wider Europe* stand in contrast to the prospects of a *Russkiy mir* established through military force. In that light, the Russian aggression in Ukraine reveals the absence of the EU as a military actor, not least as a deterrent to foreign powers' military threats. Against this background, the geopolitical implications of *Wider Europe* are liable to shift from the inadvertent to the irrelevant in the absence of closer integration on matters of Common Foreign and Security Policy and industrial policy.

Both *Brexit* and Ukraine's membership application have challenged *Wider Europe* in different terms. *Brexit* has challenged not only the idea of an ever-enlarging EU but also that EU neighbourhood relations would be inevitably premised upon gravitation around the EU legal order. The placing of the new EU–UK relations away from the canons of *Wider Europe* was due both to the wish of the UK to flee from the regulatory and institutional/judicial reach of the EU and of *Wider Europe* and the Union's willingness to clearly demarcate the difference between being a Union member and a third country. Notwithstanding that, the realities of interdependences still entangle the UK in the extended EU's legal space. This becomes apparent when considering the regimes regulating the free movement of goods between EU Ireland and Northern Ireland as well as some regimes of AFSJ cooperation. Moreover, the EU's insistence on the level playing field provisions in the TCA are likely to hinder significant divergences of UK law from EU law.

The combined challenges of *Brexit* and Ukraine's membership application have reconfigured the geography of *Wider Europe*, shifting its centre of gravity to the East. Notwithstanding the eastern shift of *Wider Europe*'s centre of gravity, an overhaul of the institutional frameworks of the EU's partnerships in the south would be equally important. Indeed, a disengagement from the southern neighbours would further ignite the *Wider Europe* ring of fire. A new engagement in the south would however require a deeper reflection and on third countries' expectations arising from their participation in *Wider Europe.*

This study has shed light on the *lato sensu* reconfiguration of the Union's borders through the interplay of law and diplomacy. The *Wider Europe* design has been originally informed by geopolitical rationales of security at the new

EU's borders. The ensuing extension of the EU's legal space is predicated on the *de facto* superordination of the EU legal order over EU neighbourhood regimes. There is thus a degree of satellisation for non-EU members participating in *Wider Europe*. EU neighbourhood law is hence certainly asymmetrical. The exclusion of third-country participation in the decision-making process of the law that they ultimately adopt is liable to erode a major source of legitimacy of EU membership law, which pertains to the internalisation of externalities.[32] While this internalisation may arguably occur also through access to the decision-shaping phase, there are additional sources of legitimacy for the extension of the EU's legal space. The gravitation around the EU legal order is not only due to far-reaching techniques of EU Neighbourhood law. In *Wider Europe*, the magnetism of EU law also derives from several legitimacy resources that are primarily expressed by the political covenants of EU neighbourhood law. Political covenants are nourished by the objectives and expectations of the relevant partnerships. They establish a balance of rights and obligations for the participation in the extended EU's legal space, usually entailing a degree of EU market access. They provide for third country socialisation in (extended) EU's regulatory networks, which results beneficial in light of the EU's regulative capacity, the technical qualities of EU law, and the recognition of the EU as a normative power.

Political covenants of EU neighbourhood law offer a political association grounded on shared legal values predicated on openess, individual rights and fundamental freedoms. They are deferent to the constitutional identities of the states, within the limits of EU law and EU neighbourhood law. This stands in contrast to the violence of military aggression frustrating the choices of sovereign states that Ukraine is strenuously facing. EU membership expectations especially characterising the eastern dimension of *Wider Europe* are a key source of legitimacy for the extension of the EU's legal space and cannot be underestimated. The complexity of a possibly lengthy *interregnum* between EU *friendship* and *membership*, urges the EU to better spell out the rights and obligations of being part of *Wider Europe*, not disregarding institutional aspects and enforcement issues. This would be beneficial for candidate countries, for the neighbours not aspiring to EU membership, and crucially also for the credibility of the Union as a regional legal actor.

[32] See Ch 3 of this work, especially text to fn 195–198.

BIBLIOGRAPHY

Aalto, P, *The EU–Russian Energy Dialogue: Europe's Future Energy Security* (Ashgate, 2008).

Abderrahim, T, 'A Tale of Two Agreements: EU Migration Cooperation with Morocco and Tunisia' (2019) 41 *IEMed- EuroMeSCo.*

Adomeit, 'Russia, ENP Competitor' in Erwan Lannon (ed), *The European Neighbourhood Policy challenges. Les défis de la politique européenne de voisinage* (Peter Lang, 2012).

Al-Shammari, N and Willoughby, J, 'Determinants of Political Instability across Arab Spring Countries' (2019) 24 *Mediterranean Politics* 196.

Ambos, K, 'Ukraine and the double standards of the West' (2022) 20 *Journal of International Criminal Justice* 875.

Andenas, M, 'Sovereignty' in Carl Baudenbacher (ed), *The Fundamental Principles of EEA Law: EEA-ities* (Springer, 2017).

Anderson, D, 'No-Deal Readiness, Lord Cockfield and the British Ingenuity behind the EU Single Market' *Prospect Magazine* (9 October 2019).

Armstrong, K, 'Long Read | It's the Autonomy, Stupid – Can the EU and UK Agree the Rules of a Future Relationship?' (LSE BREXIT, 10 February 2020).

Arnesen F et al, 'Introduction: The EFTA States, the EEA and the Different Views on the Legal Integration of Europe' in *Agreement on the European Economic Area: a commentary* (Beck, 2018).

Ashworth, LM, *A History of International Thought : From the Origins of the Modern State to Academic International Relations* (Routledge, 2014).

Azoulai, L, 'The Acquis of the European Union and International Organisations' (2005) 11 *European Law Journal* 196.

——, '"Euro-Bonds" The Ruiz Zambrano Judgment or the Real Invention of EU Citizenship' (2011) 3 *Perspectives on federalism* 31.

——, 'The Many Visions of Europe' in M Cremona and A Thies (eds), *The European Court of Justice and external relations law : constitutional challenges* (Hart Publishing, 2014).

——, 'Appartenir à l'Union européenne' in C Mestre (ed), *Europe(s), droit(s) européen(s): une passion d'universitaire: Liber amicorum en l'honneur du professeur Vlad Constantinesco* (Bruylant, 2015).

——, 'Solitude, Community, and Critique. Motives for a Reshaping of EU Legal Studies' (2015) No 50 *Politique européenne* 82.

——, 'Integration through Law and Us' (2016) 14 *International Journal of Constitutional Law* 449.

——, 'Le droit européen de l'immigration, une analyse existentielle' (2018) 54 *Revue trimestrielle de droit européen* 519.

——, 'Structural Principles in EU Law: Internal and External' in M Cremona (ed), *Structural principles in EU external relations law* (Hart Publishing, 2018).

Azoulai, L, Barbou des Places, S and Pataut, E, *Constructing the Person in EU Law: Rights, Roles, Identities* (Hart Publishing, 2016).

Azoulai, L and Jaeger, E, 'Book Review: The Passage to Europe Trans. from Dutch by L.Waters, by Luuk van Middelaar (New Haven: Yale University Press, 2013)' (2014) 51 *Common Market Law Review* 311

Baczynska, G, 'EU Wants Brexit Britain to Stick to Aid, Environment, Rights Rules – Sources' *Reuters* (8 November 2018).

Balibar, E, 'Europe as Borderland' (2009) 27 *Environment and Planning D: Society and Space* 190.

Bange, O and Niedhart, G, *Helsinki 1975 and the Transformation of Europe* (Berghahn Books, 2008).

Bartels, L, 'A Legal Analysis of The Human Rights Dimension of the Euro-Mediterranean Agreements' (*ECDPM*, 2012).
——, 'The EU's Human Rights Obligations in Relation to Policies with Extraterritorial Effects' (2014) 25 *European Journal of International Law* 1071.
Bartelson, J, 'The Concept of Sovereignty Revisited' (2006) 17 *European Journal of International Law* 463.
Bátora, J, 'Does the European Union Transform the Institution of Diplomacy?' (2005) 12 *Journal of European Public Policy* 44.
Baudenbacher, C, 'The EFTA Court and Court of Justice of the European Union: Coming in Parts But Winning Together' in A Rosas, E Levits and Y Bot, *The Court of Justice and the Construction of Europe: Analyses and Perspectives on Sixty Years of Case-Law – la Cour de Justice et la Construction de l'Europe: Analyses et Perspectives de Soixante Ans de Jurisprudence* (TMC Asser Press, 2012),
——, 'Some Thoughts on the EFTA Court's Phases of Life' in EFTA Court (ed), *Judicial Protection in the European Economic Area International Conference by the EFTA Court on 17 June 2011* (German Law, 2012).
——, (ed) *The Fundamental Principles of EEA Law* (Springer, 2017).
——, '"Britzerland": The Problem of Dispute Resolution Post-Brexit' (*LSE Brexit*, 29 October 2018).
——, 'The ECJ Used to Be a Neutral Court for the UK – It No Longer Is' LSE BREXIT (9 March 2021).
Bekkedal, T, 'Third State Participation in Eu Agencies: Exploring the EEA Precedent' (2019) 56 *Common Market Law Review* 381.
——, 'Understanding the Nature of the EEA Agreement: On the Direct Applicability of Regulations' (2020) 57 *Common Market Law Review* 773.
Bekkedal, T, Hillion, C and Petti, A (eds), 'Fundamental Rights Protection in Europe: shedding light on a system of interrelated regimes' *Maastricht Journal of European and Comparative Law* (forthcoming).
Belguendouz, A, 'Expansion et sous-traitance des logiques d'enfermement de l'Union européenne: l'exemple du Maroc' (2005) *Cultures & conflits* 155.
Benabdallah, K, 'The Position of the European Union on the Western Sahara Conflict' (2009) 17 *Journal of Contemporary European Studies* 417.
Bercero, IG and Nicolaïdis, K, 'The Power Surplus: Brussels Calling, Legal Empathy and the Trade-Regulation Nexus' Technical Report (CEPS 2021).
Bergh, SI, 'Public Sector Governance Reforms and "advanced Regionalization" in Morocco: What Role for the European Union?' (2016) EUI RSCAS 2016/ 56 Working Paper.
Bernardo, V and Fageda, X, 'The Effects of the Morocco-European Union Open Skies Agreement: A Difference-in-Differences Analysis' (2017) 98 *Transportation Research Part E: Logistics and Transportation Review* 24.
Beyer, A, 'Les frontières du « Ciel Unique Européen ».' (2008) n° 71 *Metropolis* – Flux 8.
Björgvinsson, DÞ, 'Fundamental Rights in EEA Law' in Carl Baudenbacher et al, *The EEA and the EFTA Court: decentred integration* (Hart Publishing, 2015).
Blockmans, S and van Vooren, B, 'Revitalizing the European Neighbourhood Economic Community: The Case for Legally Binding Sectoral Multilateralism' (2012) 17 *European Foreign Affairs Review* 577.
Bobin, F, 'Entre la France et le Maroc, des réseaux sur le déclin' *Le Monde* (5 October 2023).
Boček, T, 'Report of the Fact-Finding Mission by Ambassador Tomáš Boček, UN Special Representative of the Secretary General on Migration and Refugees, to Spain' (2018) SG/Inf(2018)25.
Bohmann, K, 'The Ownership and Control Requirement in U.S. and European Union Air Law and U.S. Maritime Law-Policy; Consideration; Comparison' (2001) 66 *Journal of Air Law and Commerce* 689.
Bombay, P and Gergely, M, 'The 2006 ECAA Agreement: Centrepiece of the European Community's Aviation Policy Towards Its Neighbours' (2008) 33 *Air Space & Law* 2014.
Börzel, TA and Risse, T, 'From Europeanisation to Diffusion: Introduction' (2012) 35 *West European Politics* 1.
Bradford, A, 'The Brussels Effect' (2012) 107 *Northwestern University Law Review* 1.
——, *The Brussels Effect: How the European Union Rules the World* (Oxford University Press, 2020).

Brunk, I and Hakimi, M, 'Russia, Ukraine, and the Future World Order' (2022) 116 *American Journal of International Law* 687.
Buchanan, A, *Human Rights, Legitimacy, and the Use of Force* (Oxford University Press, 2010).
Bu-Pasha, S, 'Cross-Border Issues under EU Data Protection Law with Regards to Personal Data Protection' (2017) 26 *Information & Communications Technology Law* 213.
Bull, H, '"Shall Be Made Part of the Internal Legal Order": The Legislative Approaches' in Carl Baudenbacher et al, *The EEA and the EFTA Court : decentred integration* (Hart Publishing, 2014).
Buschle, D, 'The Enforcement of European Energy Law Outside the European Union: Does the Energy Community Live up to the Expectations?' (2016) 6 *European Energy Journal* 26.
Camps, M and Royal Institute of International Affairs, *What Kind of Europe?: The Community since De Gaulle's Veto* (Oxford University Press, 1965).
Cañas, J and Peregil, F, 'Incursions at Spain's North African Exclaves Triple after Moroccan Threats' *El País* (27 February 2017).
Cannizzaro, E, *A Higher Law for Treaties?* (Oxford University Press, 2011).
Cappelletti, M, Seccombem M and Weiler, JH, *Integration through Law: A Political, Legal and Economic Overview* (De Gruyter, 1985).
Carrera, S, *EU–Morocco Cooperation on Readmission, Borders and Protection: A Model to Follow?* (2016).
——, 'The Strasbourg Court Judgement N.D. and N.T. v Spain. A Carte Blanche to Push Backs at EU External Borders?' [2020] EUI RSCAS Working Paper 2020/2021.
Carrera, S, Cassarino, J-P and Lahlo,u M, 'EU-Morocco Cooperation on Readmission, Borders and Protection': (2016) No 87 *CEPS Paper in Liberty and Security in Europe* 21.
Cassarino, J-P, 'Informalising Readmission Agreements in the EU Neighbourhood' (2007) 42 *The International Spectator* 179.
——, 'Readmission Policy in the European Union' (European Parliament, 2010) Technical Report.
——, 'Informalising EU Readmission Policy' in A Ripoll Servent and F Trauner, *The Routledge Handbook of Justice and Home Affairs Research* (Routledge, 2018).
Cassese, A, *International Law* (Oxford University Press, 2005).
Cassese, S, 'Che Tipo Di Potere Pubblico è l'Unione Europea?' (2002) 31 *Quaderni Fiorentini per la storia del pensiero giuridico moderno* 141.
Castillo de la Torre, F, 'Opinion 1/00, *Proposed Agreement on the Establishment of a European Common Aviation Area*' (2002) 39 *Common Market Law Review* 1373.
Chayes, A and Chayes, AH, *The New Sovereignty : Compliance with International Regulatory Agreements* (Harvard University Press, 1995).
Checkel, JT, 'The Constructivist Turn in International Relations Theory' (1998) 50 *World Politics* 324.
——, 'International Institutions and Socialization in Europe: Introduction and Framework' (2005) 59 *International Organization* 801.
Cherti, M and Collyer, M, 'Immigration and Pensée d'Etat: Moroccan Migration Policy Changes as Transformation of "Geopolitical Culture"' (2015) 20 *The Journal of North African Studies* 590.
Coleman, N, *European Readmission Policy: Third Country Interests and Refugee Rights* (Brill Nijhoff, 2009).
Coman-Kund, F, *European Union Agencies as Global Actors: A Legal Study of the European Aviation Safety Agency, Frontex, and Europol* (Routledge, 2018).
——, 'Europol's International Exchanges of Data and Interoperability of AFSJ Databases' (2020) 26 *European Public Law*.
Contartese, C, 'The Autonomy of the EU Legal Order in the ECJ's External Relations Case Law: From the "essential" to the "Specific Characteristics" of the Union and Back Again' (2017) 54 *Common Market Law Review* 1627.
Cooper, R, *The Breaking of Nations : Order and Chaos in the Twenty-First Century* (Atlantic Books, 2003).
Copeland, P, 'EU Enlargement, the Clash of Capitalisms and the European Social Model' (2012) 10 *Comparative European Politics* 476.

Corkin, J, 'Who, Then, in [European] Law, Is My Neighbour? Limiting the Argument from External Effects' in S Bardutzky and E Fahey (eds), *Framing the Subject and Objects of Contemporary EU Law* (Edward Elgar, 2017).

Corrale, F, 'Les Origines de La "Question Du Sahara Occidental" Enjeux Historiques, Défis Politiques' in M Balboni and G Laschi, *The European Union approach towards Western Sahara* (PIE Peter Lang, 2017).

Cowburn, A, 'Free movement of people as a founding principle of Eu is a "total myth" says foreign Secretary Boris Johnson' *The Independent* (15 November 2016).

Craig, P, 'Brexit a Drama: The Endgame – Part I' (2020) 45 *European Law Review* 163.

Cremona, M, 'The "Dynamic and Homogenous" EEA: Byzantine Structures and Variable Geometry' (1994) 19 *European Law Review* 508.

——, 'Flexible Models: External Policy and the European Economic Community' in G de Búrca and J Scott (eds), *Constitutional Change in the EU: From Uniformity to Flexibility?* (Hart Publishing, 2000).

——, 'Accession to the European Union: Membership Conditionality and Accession Criteria' (2002) 25 *Polish Yearbook of International Law* 219.

——, 'The Union as a Global Actor: Roles, Models and Identity' (2004) 41 *Common Market Law Review* 553.

——, 'The European Neighbourhood Policy: More than a Partnership?' in M Cremona, *Developments in EU External Relations Law* (Oxford University Press, 2008).

——, 'Disconnection Clauses in EC Law and Practice' in C Hillion and P Koutrakos (eds), *Mixed agreements revisited: the EU and its member states in the world* (Hart Publishing, 2010).

——, 'A Reticent Court? Policy Objectives and the Court of Justice' in M Cremona and A Thies, *The European Court of Justice and external relations law : constitutional challenges* (Hart Publishing, 2014).

——, 'EU External Relations: Unity and Conferral of Powers' in L Azoulai, *The Question of Competence in the European Union* (Oxford University Press, 2014).

—— (ed), 'The ENP and Multilateralism in Sara Poli' in S Poli, *The European Neighbourhood Policy – Values and Principles* (Routledge, 2016).

——, 'A Quiet Revolution: The Common Commercial Policy Six Years after the Treaty of Lisbon' (2017) Working *Swedish Institute for European Policy Studies*, Paper no 2.

——, 'Structural Principles and Their Role in EU External Relations Law' in M Cremona (ed), *Structural principles in EU external relations law* (Hart Publishing, 2018).

——, 'Extending the Reach of EU Law: The EU as an International Legal Actor' in M Cremona and J Scott, *EU Law Beyond EU Borders: The Extraterritorial Reach of EU Law* (Oxford University Press, 2019).

Cremona M and Hillion C, 'L'Union Fait La Force? Potential and Limitations of the European Neighbourhood Policy as an Integrated EU Foreign and Security Policy' EUI Working Paper LAW No 2006/39.

Cremona, M and Leino, P, 'Is There an Accountability Gap in EU External Relations? Some Initial Conclusions' (2017) 2 *European Papers* 699.

Cremona, M and Petti, A, 'Extending the Internal Market Through Free Trade Agreements' in R Schütze and T Tridimas (eds), *Oxford Principles of European Union Law*, vol 2 (Oxford University Press, forthcoming).

Cremona, M and Scott, J (eds), *EU Law Beyond EU Borders: The Extraterritorial Reach of EU Law* (Oxford University Press 2019).

Curtin, D, 'Challenging Executive Dominance in European Democracy' (2014) 77 *The Modern Law Review* 1.

Damro, C, 'Market Power Europe' (2012) 19 *Journal of European Public Policy* 682.

Dashwood, A, 'EU Acts and Member State Acts in the Negotiation, Conclusion, and Implementation of International Agreements' in M Cremona and C Kilpatrick (eds), *EU Legal Acts: Challenges and Transformations* (Oxford University Press, 2018).

Deb, A, 'Parliamentary Sovereignty and the Protocol Pincer' (2023) 43 *Legal Studies* 47.

de Búrca, G and Scott, J, *Constitutional Change in the EU: From Uniformity to Flexibility?* (Hart Publishing, 2000).
De Búrca, G, 'Sovereignty and the Supremacy Doctrine of the European Court of Justice' in N Walker, *Sovereignty in transition* (Hart, 2003).
De Búrca G, 'EU External Relations: The Governance Mode of Foreign Policy' in B van Vooren, S Blockmans and J Wouters, *The EU's Role in Global Governance: The Legal Dimension* (Oxford University Press, 2013).
De Búrca G, 'The Transformation of Europe Revisited: Civilising Interstatal Relations' in M Poiares Maduro and M Wind, *The transformation of Europe: twenty-five years on* (Cambridge University Press, 2017).
de Elera Á, 'The Frente Polisario Judgments: An Assessment in the Light of the Court of Justice's Case Law on Territorial Disputes' in Czuczai and FNaert (eds), *The EU as a Global Actor – Bridging Legal Theory and Practice, Liber Amicorum in honour of Ricardo Gosalbo Bono* (Brill Nijhoff, 2017).
de Larramendi, MH, 'Las relaciones con Marruecos tras los atentados del 11 de marzo' (2004) *Real Instituto Elcano* 5.
de Micco, P, 'When Choosing Means Losing: The Eastern Partners, the EU and the Eurasian Economic Union' (2015) European Parliament, Directorate-General for External Policies.
de Witte, B, Hanf, D and Vos, E, *The Many Faces of Differentiation in EU Law* (Intersentia, 2001).
de Witte, B, 'Too Much Constitutional Law in the European Union's Foreign Relations?' in M Cremona and B de Witte (eds), *EU foreign relations law: constitutional fundamentals* (Hart, 2008)
——, 'European Union Law: How Autonomous is its Legal Order?' (2010) 65 *Zeitschrift für öffentliches Recht* 141.
——, 'Variable Geometry and Differentiation as Structural Features of the EU Legal Order' in B de Witte, A Ott and Vos, *Between flexibility and disintegration: the trajectory of differentiation in EU law* (Edward Elgar 2017).
—— 'Visa Requirements for Turkish Citizens: Soysal & Savatli and Demirkan' in G Butler and RA Wessel (eds), EU External Relations Law: The Cases in Context (Hart Publishing, 2022).
de Witte, F, 'Interdependence and Contestation in European Integration' (2018) 3 *European Papers* 475.
Del Sarto, R, *Contested State Identities and Regional Security in the Euro-Mediterranean Area* (Palgrave Macmillan, 2006).
——, 'Borderlands: The Middle East and North Africa as the EU's Southern Buffer Zone' in D Bechev and N Kalypso (eds), *Mediterranean Frontiers: Borders, Conflict and Memory in a Transnational World* (IB Tauris, 2010).
Del Sarto, RA and Schumacher, T, 'From EMP to ENP: What's at Stake with the European Neighbourhood Policy towards the Southern Mediterranean?' (2005) 10 *European Foreign Affairs Review* 17.
Delcour, L, 'Does the European Neighbourhood Policy Make a Difference? Policy Patterns and Reception in Ukraine and Russia' (2007) 7 *European Political Economy Review* 118.
della Cananea, G, *L'Unione Europea. Un ordinamento composito* (Laterza, 2003).
——, 'Global Security and Procedural Due Process of Law between the United Nations and the European Union: Yassin Abdullah Kadi & Al Barakaat International Foundation v. Council' (2009) 15 *The Columbia Journal of European Law* 512.
——, 'Differentiated Integration in Europe After Brexit: An Institutional Analysis' in I Pernice and AM Guerra Martins (eds), *Brexit and the future of EU politics: a constitutional law perspective* (Nomos, 2019).
Dicey, AV, *Introduction to the Study of the Law of the Constitution* (Macmillan, 1996).
Dougan, M, 'So Long, Farewell, Auf Wiedersehen, Goodbye: The UK's Withdrawal Package' (2020) 57 *Common Market Law* Review 631.
Draghi, M, 'Dichiarazioni Programmatiche del Presidente Draghi al Senato della Repubblica' (Presidenza del Consiglio dei Ministri, 16 February 2021).
Drozdiak, N and Kranolutska, D 'Ukraine Belongs in the "European Family," EU Chief Says on Kyiv Trip' *Bloomberg.com* (8 April 2022).

Dubuisson, F and Poissonnier, G, 'La Cour de Justice de l'Union européenne et la question du Sahara occidental: cachez cette pratique (illégale) que je ne saurais voir' (2017) 2016 *Revue belge de droit international* 601.

Dunoff, JL and Pollack, MA (eds), 'Constructivism and International Law'in *Interdisciplinary Perspectives on International Law and International Relations: The State of the Art* (Cambridge University Press, 2012).

Editorial Comments, 'Is the Indivisibility of the Four Freedoms a Principle of EU Law?' (2019) 56 *Common Market Law Review* 1189.

——, 'Europe Is Trembling. Looking for a Safe Place in EU Law' (2020) 56 *Common Market Law Review* 1675.

——, 'Unfinished Brexit Business: The Windsor Framework on the Northern Ireland Protocol' (2023) 60 *Common Market Law Review* 1224.

Egeberg, M and Jarle, T, 'National Administrative Sovereignty : Under Pressure' in J Erik Fossum and E Oddvar Eriksen (eds), *The European Union's non-members: independence under hegemony?* (Routledge, 2015).

El Houdaigui, R, 'Le Maroc et La Politique Européenne de Voisinage' in A Morillas and I Blázquez (eds), *La cooperación territorial en el Mediterráneo: La Política Europea de Vecindad* (Universidad International de Andalucía, 2009).

El Qadim, N, *Le gouvernement asymétrique des migrations: Maroc–Union européenne* (Dalloz, 2015).

——, 'The Symbolic Meaning of International Mobility: EU–Morocco Negotiations on Visa Facilitation' (2018) 6 *Migration Studies* 279.

——, 'The Funding Instruments of the EU's Negotiation on External Migration Policy. Incentives for Cooperation?' in S Carrera et al (eds), *The EU External Policies on Migration, Borders and Asylum in an Era of Large Flows: Policy Transfers or Intersecting Policy Universes?* (Brill Nijhoff, 2019).

El Yaakoubi, A, 'Morocco Suspends Contacts with EU over Court Ruling on Farm Trade' *Reuters* (26 February 2016).

Eleftheriadis, P, 'Eleven Types of Post-Brexit EU Law' (Oxford Law Faculty, 8 January 2021).

Elliot, M, 'Reflections on the HS2 Case: A Hierarchy of Domestic Constitutional Norms and the Qualified Primacy of EU Law' (UK Constitutional Law Association, 23 January 2014).

——, 'The United Kingdom Consitution' in R Masterman and R Schütze (eds), *The Cambridge Companion to Comparative Constitutional Law* (Cambridge University Press, 2019).

Elmadmad, K, 'La nouvelle loi marocaine du 11 novembre 2003 relative à l'entrée et au séjour des étrangers au maroc, et à l'émigration et l'immigration irrégulières' (2004) EUI, RSCAS Research Reports.

——, 'La gestion des frontières au Maroc' (2007) EUI, RSCAS.

——, 'Migration irrégulière et migrations illégale: l'example des migrants subsharien aux Maroc' (2008) EUI, RSCAS.

——, 'Le Maroc et la Convention sur la protection des droits de tous les travailleurs migrants et des membres de leur famille' (2009) EUI, RSCAS.

Emerson, M, 'The Strategic Potential of the Emerging Wider European Economic Area' (2018) *CEPS Policy Insights* 26.

Eriksen, EO and Fossum, JE, *The European Union's Non-Members: Independence under Hegemony?* (Routledge, 2015).

'Europe's ring of fire, The European Union's neighbourhood is more troubled than ever' *The Economist* (20 September 2014).

Fassi Fhiri, T, 'The Union for the Mediterranean: An Active Commitment for Ambitious Accomplishments' *IEMed/CIDOB Mediterranean Yearbook* (2009) 27.

Fink, M, *Frontex and Human Rights: Responsibility in 'Multi-Actor Situations' under the ECHR and EU Public Liability Law* (Oxford University Press, 2018).

——, 'The Action for Damages as a Fundamental Rights Remedy: Holding Frontex Liable' (2020) 21 *German Law Journal* 532.

Flory, M, 'Note Sur La Demande d'adhésion Du Maroc à La Communauté Économique Européenne', *Annuaire de l'Afrique du Nord* (Editions du CNRS, 1986).
Fossum, JE, *Representation under Hegemony?: On Norway's Relationship to the EU* in EO Eriksen JE and Fossum, *The European Union's Non-Members: Independence under Hegemony?* (Routledge, 2015).
Foucher, M, 'The Geopolitics of European Frontier' in Eberhard Bort and Malcolm Anderson (eds), *The frontiers of Europe* (Pinter, 1998).
Francq, S, 'The External Dimension of Rome I and Rome II: Neutrality or Schizophrenia?' in M Cremona and HW Micklitz, *Private Law in the External Relations of the EU* (Oxford University Press, 2016).
Franklin, CNK and Fredriksen, HH, 'Differentiated Citizenship in the European Economic Area' in D Kostakopoulou and D Thym (eds), *Research Handbook on European Union Citizenship Law and Policy* (Edward Elgar, 2022).
Fredriksen, HH, 'The EEA and the Case Law of the CJEU: Incorporation without Participation?' in EO Eriksen and JE Fossum, *The European Union's Non-Members : Independence under Hegemony?* (Routledge, 2015).
Fredriksen, HH and Franklin, CNK, 'Of Pragmatism and Principles: The EEA Agreement 20 Years On' (2015) 52 *Common Market Law Review* 629.
Fredriksen, HH and Ø by Johansen S, 'The EEA Agreement as a Jack-in-the-Box in the Relationship Between the CJEU and the European Court of Human Rights?' (2020) 5 *European Papers* 707.
Galvín, C and Ángel, M, 'La zona de libre cambio Unión Europea-Marruecos, ¿un paso decisivo para la conclusión de un acuerdo de libre comercio amplio y profundo?' (2013) 15 *Revista de Estudios Internacionales Mediterráneos* 1.
García Andrade, P, 'The Distribution of Powers Between EU Institutions for Conducting External Affairs through Non-Binding Instruments' (2016) 1 *European Papers* 115.
Garner, O, 'New Irish Protocol Could Lead to Indefinite Jurisdiction of EU Court in the UK' *Scottish Legal News* (31 October 2019).
——, 'Part Three of the EU–UK TCA – From a "Disrupted" Area of Freedom, Security and Justice to "New Old" Intergovernmentalism in Justice and Home Affairs?' (2021) *DCU Brexit Institute.*
Gatti, M, 'Diplomats or Fonctionnaires? The Contested Status of the EU's "Embassy" in the UK' *EJIL: Talk!* (1 March 2021).
Getachew, A, *Worldmaking after Empire: The Rise and Fall of Self-Determination* (Princeton University Press, 2019).
Ghazaryan, N, *The European Neighbourhood Policy and the Democratic Values of the EU: A Legal Analysis* (Hart Publishing, 2014).
——, 'Who Are the "Gatekeepers"?: In Continuation of the Debate on the Direct Applicability and the Direct Effect of EU International Agreements' (2018) 37 *Yearbook of European Law* 27.
Gillis, M, 'Let's Play? An Examination of the "Level Playing Field" in EU Free Trade Agreements', (2021) 55 *Journal of World Trade* 715.
Goodman, R and Jinks, D, 'How to Influence States: Socialization and International Human Rights Law' (2004) 54 *Duke Law Journal* 621.
González, M, 'La carta de Pedro Sánchez a Mohamed VI: "Debemos construir una nueva relación que evite futuras crisis"' *El País* (23 March 2022).
Gorla, G, 'Unificazione « legislativa » e Unificazione « giurisprudenziale ». L'esperienza Del Diritto Comune' (1977) 100 *Il Foro Italiano* 91/92;
—— (ed), 'Il Ricorso Alla Legge Di Un Luogo "Vicino" Nell'ambito Del Diritto Comune Europeo', *Diritto Comparato E Diritto Comune Europeo*, vol 21 (Giuffré, 1981).
——, 'Unificazione "Legislativa" e Unificazione "Giurisprudenziale"', *Diritto Comparato E Diritto Comune Europeo*, vol 21 (Giuffré, 1981).
Goulard, H, 'Switzerland Withdraws Application to Join the EU' *Politico* (15 June 2016).
Graver, HP, 'Mission Impossible: Supranationality and National Legal Autonomy in the EEA Agreement' (2002) 7 *European Foreign Affairs Review* 73.
Graziano, M, *Frontiere* (Il Mulino, 2017).

Graziosi, A, *Guerra e rivoluzione in Europa. 1905–1956* (Il Mulino, 2002).
——, 'Viewing the Twentieth Century through the Prism of Ukraine: Reflections on the Heuristic Potential of Ukrainian History' (2015) 34 *Harvard Ukrainian Studies* 107.
——, *L'Ucraina e Putin tra storia e ideologia* (Laterza, 2022).
Grimm, D, 'The Democratic Costs of Constitutionalisation: The European Case' (2015) 21 *European Law Journal* 460.
——, *The Constitution of European Democracy* (Oxford University Press, 2017).
Gross-Wyrtzen, L and Gazzotti, L, 'Telling Histories of the Present: Postcolonial Perspectives on Morocco's "Radically New" Migration Policy' (2021) 26 *The Journal of North African Studies* 827.
Gstöhl, S, 'A Neighbourhood Economic Community – Finalité Économique for the ENP?' (2008) 3 *EU Diplomacy Papers– College of Europe.*
——, 'Models of External Differentiation in the EU's Neighbourhood: An Expanding Economic Community?' (2015) 22 *Journal of European Public Policy* 854.
——, *Mapping the European Union's Neighbourhood Relations The European Economic Area as a 'Prototype' for the Integration of EU Neighbours?* (Routledge, 2017).
Habermas, J, *Between Facts and Norms: Contributions to a Discourse Theory of Law and Democracy* (Polity Press, 1997).
Hailbronner, K, 'Readmission Agreements and the Obligation on States under Public International Law to Readmit Their Own and Foreign Nationals' (1997) 57 *Zeitschrift für ausländisches öffentliches Recht und Völkerrecht* 31.
——, 'The Stand Still Clauses in the EU–Turkey Association Agreement1 and Their Impact upon Immigration Law in the EU Member States' in D Thym and M Zoeteweij-Turhan, *Rights of Third-Country Nationals under EU Association Agreements: Degrees of Free Movement and Citizenship* (Brill Nijhoff, 2015).
Hanf, D, 'The ENP in the Light of the New "Neighbourhood Clause" (Article 8 TEU)' (2011) *College of Europe Research Paper in Law.*
Harding, C, 'The Identity of European Law: Mapping Out the European Legal Space' (2000) 6 *European Law Journal* 128.
Harpaz, G, 'The Front Polisario Verdict and the Gap Between the EU's Trade Treatment of Western Sahara and Its Treatment of the Occupied Palestinian Territories' (2018) 52 *Journal of World Trade* 619.
Harpaz, G and Rubinson, E, 'The Interface between Trade, Law and Politics and the Erosion of Normative Power Europe: Comment on Brita' (2010) 35 *European Law Review* 551.
Harvey, C, 'The Irish Protocol' in Federico Fabbrini, *The withdrawal agreement* (Oxford University Press, 2020).
Hassner, P, 'Fixed Borders or Moving Borderlands? A New Type of Border for a New Type of Entity' in J Zielonka (ed), *Europe unbound: enlarging and reshaping the boundaries of the European Union* (Routledge, 2002).
Haukkala H, *The EU– Russia Strategic Partnership : The Limits of Post-Sovereignty in International Relations* (Routledge, 2010).
Heard-Lauroté, K, 'Transnational Neetworks, Informal Governance in the European Political Space' in W Kaiser and P Starie, *Transnational European Union: Towards a Common Political Space* (Taylor & Francis, 2005).
Hill, C, 'The Capability-Expectations Gap, or Conceptualizing Europe's International Role' (1993) 31 *Journal of Common Market Studies* 305.
Hillion, C, 'The Evolving System of European Union External Relations as Evidenced in the EU Partnership with Russia and Ukraine' (PhD, University of Leiden, 2005).
——, 'Mapping-Out the New Contractual Relations between the European Union and Its Neighbours; Learning from the EU–Ukraine Enhanced Agreement' (2007) 12 *European Foreign Affairs Review.*
——, 'Case C-265/03, Igor Simutenkov v. Ministerio de Educación y Cultura, Real Federación Española de Fùtbol, [2005] ECR I–2579' (2008) 45 *Common Market Law Review* 169.
——, 'The Requirements of Consistency and Coherence" in C Hillion and P Koutrakos, *Mixed agreements revisited: the EU and its member states in the world* (Hart Publishing, 2010).

——, 'The Neighbourhood Competence under Article 8 TEU' (2013) Notre Europe Policy Paper.
——, 'Anatomy of EU Norm Export towards the Neighbourhood: The Impact of Article 8 TEU' in P Van Elsuwege and R Petrov (eds), *Legislative approximation and application of EU law in the Eastern neighbourhood of the European Union: towards a common regulatory space?* (Routledge, 2014).
——, 'Withdrawal under Article 50 TEU: An Integration-Friendly Process' (2018) 55 *Common Market Law Review* 29.
—— The EU external action as mandate to uphold the rule of law outside and inside the Union (2023), 29 *Columbia Journal of European Law* 228.
Hillion, C and Delhomme, V, 'EU Enlargement, Extra-Territorial Application of EU Law and the International Dimension' in I Govaere and S Garben (eds), *The interface between EU and international law: contemporary reflections* (Hart Publishing, 2019).
Hillion, C and Fredriksen, HH, 'The "Special Relationship" between the EU and the EEA EFTA States – Free Movement of EEA Citizens in an Extended Area of Freedom, Security and Justice: Ruska Federacija v. I.N.' (2021) 58 *Common Market Law Review* 851.
Hix, S, 'Brexit: Where Is the EU–UK Relationship Heading?' (2018) 56 *Journal of Common Market Studies* 11.
Hobbes, T, *Leviathan Or the Matter Form and Power of a Commonwealth, Ecclesiastical and Civil* (George Routledge and Sons, 1886).
Hoffmeister, F, 'Strategic Autonomy in the European Union's External Relations' (2023) 60 *Common Market Law Review* 667.
Hofmann, H, 'General Principles of EU Law and EU Administrative Law' in C Barnard and StJ Peers (eds), *European union law* (Oxford University Press, 2020).
Hofmann, HCH, Rowe, GC and Türk, AH, *General Principles Framing European Union Administrative Law* (Oxford University Press, 2011).
Holdgaard, R, *External Relations Law of the European Community: Legal Reasoning and Legal Discourses* (Kluwer Law, 2008).
Holdgaard, R and Spiermann, O, 'Case C-386/08, Brita GmbH v. Hauptzollamt Hamburg-Hafen, Judgment of the Court of Justice (Fourth Chamber) of 25 February 2010', (2011) 48 *Common Market Law Review* 1667.
Hummelbrunner, S, 'Beyond Extraterritoriality: Towards an EU Obligation to Ensure Human Rights Abroad?' (2019) 2 *CLEER Papers*.
Iglesias, M, 'Conflicto y cooperación entre España y Marruecos (1956–2008)' [2010] Centro de Estudio Andaluces.
Infantino, F, 'La frontière au guichet. Politiques et pratiques des visas Schengen à l'Ambassade et au Consulat d'Italie au Maroc' (2010) VII Champ pénal/Penal field, journals.openedition.org/champ-penal/7864.
Irti, N, *Un diritto incalcolabile* (Giappichelli, 2016).
Jamaï, A, 'Les dessous d'une fâcherie franco–marocaine' *Le Monde diplomatique* (1 October 2023).
Jeandesboz, J, 'European Border Policing: EUROSUR, Knowledge, Calculation' (2017) 18 *Global Crime* 256.
Jennings, R and Watts, A (eds), *Oppenheim's International Law* (Longman, 1992).
Jiménez-Alvarez, MG, Espiñeira, K and Gazzotti, L, 'Migration Policy and International Human Rights Frameworks in Morocco: Tensions and Contradictions' 26 *The Journal of North African Studies* 893.
Joerges, C, '"Deliberative Supranationalism" – Two Defences' (2002) 8 *European Law Journal* 133.
——, '"Brother, Can You Paradigm?"' (2014) 12 *International Journal of Constitutional Law* 769.
Jones, S and Hall, B, 'Swiss Prepare for EU Chill after Quitting Market Access Talks' *Financial Times* (28 May 2021).
Kaddous, C, 'Switzerland and the EU Current Issues and New Challenges under the Draft Institutional Framework Agreement' in S Gstöhl and D Phinnemore, *The proliferation of privileged partnerships between the European Union and its Neighbours* (Routledge, 2019).
Kaminski-Morrow, D, 'Brexit and Aviation: All's Well That Ends. Well, Almost … | CAPA' (*CAPA – Center for Aviation*, January 2021).

——, 'EasyJet Restricts Voting Power of Shares Held by Non-EU Interests' (*CAPA – Center for Aviation*, January 2021).

Karova, R, 'Energy Community for South East Europe: Rationale Behind and Implementation to Date' (2009) EUI RSCAS Working Paper.

——, 'The Energy Community in Its Second Decade: Where Does It Stand and Where Is It Heading ?' in L de Almeida and M Cantero Gamito (eds), *The transformation of economic law: essays in honour of Hans-W. Micklitz* (Hart Publishing, 2019).

Kassoti, E, 'The Empire Strikes Back: The Council Decision Amending Protocols 1 and 4 to the EU–Morocco Association Agreement' (2019) 4 *European Papers* 307.

——, 'The ECJ and the Art of Treaty Interpretation: Western Sahara Campaign UK' (2019) 56 *Common Market Law Review* 209.

Kaveshnikov, N and Potemkina, O, 'EU and Russia in Search of Strategic Partnership', *European Integration Without EU Membership: Models, Experiences, Perspectives* (2009) EUI Working Papers MWP.

Kelley, J, 'New Wine in Old Wineskins: Promoting Political Reforms through the New European Neighbourhood Policy' (2006) 44 *Journal of Common Market Studies* 29.

Khodarkovsky, M, 'Russia's War in Ukraine: How the 19th Century Imperialism and 20th Century Fascism Found Home in the 21st Century Russia' (2022) 35 *The Journal of East Asian Affairs* 95.

Kieninger, S, 'Transformation or Status Quo: The Conflict of Stratagems in Washington over the Meaning and Purpose of the CSCE and MBFR, 1969–1973' in O Bange and G Niedhart, *Helsinki 1975 and the Transformation of Europe* (Berghahn Books, 2008).

'King Muhammad of Morocco Weaponises Migration' *The Economist* (22 May 2021).

Klabbers, J, *The European Union in International Law* (A Pedone, 2012).

——, 'The Purpose of International Agreements and Their Direct Effect: Polydor' in RA Wessel and G Butler, *EU External Relations Law: The Cases in Context* (Hart Publishing, 2022).

Koenig, N, 'Taking the ENP beyond the Conception–Performance Gap' (2016) *Delors Institute*, Policy Paper 160.

Koh, HH, 'Why Do Nations Obey International Law Review Essay' (1996) 106 *Yale Law Journal* 2599.

——, 'Internalization through Socialization' (2005) 54 *Duke Law Journal* 975.

Korkea-aho, E, 'Evolution of the Role of Third Countries in EU Law – towards Full Legal Subjectivity?' in S Bardutzky and E Fahey (eds), *Framing the Subjects and Objects of Contemporary EU Law* (Edward Elgar, 2017).

Kourtelis, C, 'The Agadir Agreement: The Capability Traps of Isomorphic Mimicry' (2001) 20 *World Trade Review* 306.

Kube, V, *EU Human Rights, International Investment Law and Participation: Operationalizing the EU Foreign Policy Objective to Global Human Rights Protection* (Springer, 2019).

Kyrylenko, A, 'Direct Effect in Ukraine of IPR Provisions from the EU/Ukraine Free Trade Agreement: A Principled Approach to the Zentiva Case' (2019) 14 *Journal of Intellectual Property Law & Practice* 716.

Labuda, PI, 'Beyond rhetoric: Interrogating the Eurocentric critique of international criminal law's selectivity in the wake of the 2022 Ukraine invasion' (2023) 36 *Leiden Journal of International Law* 1095.

Lacalle, H, 'Swiss Authorized Representatives for Medical Device Manufacturers' (*Decomplix*, 5 February 2021).

Lahlou, M, 'Morocco's Experience of Migration as a Sending, Transit and Receiving Country' (2015) Istituto Italiano Affari Internazionali, Working Papers.

Lannon, E, 'Instruments, Principes et Méthodologie de La Politique Européenne de Voisinage' in E Lannon, *The European Neighbourhood Policy challenges. Les défis de la politique européenne de voisinage* (PIE Peter Lang, 2012).

——, 'L'Accord Euro-Méditerranéen d'association UE-Maroc et l'Accord de Partenariat Économique UE–Afrique de l'Ouest (CEDEAO–UEMOA): Quelles Synergies En Matière de Libre Échange, de Coopération et d'assistance Technique?' in I Martín, *Le Partenariat Afrique–Europe en quête de sens* (OCP Policy Centre, 2018).

Lannon, E et al, 'Barcelona Plus:Towards a Euro-Mediterranean Community of Democratic States.' [2005] EuroMeSCo.
Larik, J, 'Decision-Making and Dispute Settlement' in F Fabbrini, *The withdrawal agreement* (Oxford University Press, 2020).
Larsen, H, 'The EU as a Normative Power and the Research on External Perceptions: The Missing Link' (2014) 52 *JCMS: Journal of Common Market Studies* 896.
——, 'The Western Balkans between the EU, NATO, Russia and China', *CSS Analyses in Security Policy* (ETH Zurich, 2020).
Lavallée, C, 'The Single European Sky: A Window of Opportunity for EU–NATO Relations' (2017) 26 *European Security* 415.
Lavenex, S, 'EU External Governance in "Wider Europe"' (2004) 11 *Journal of European Public Policy* 680.
——, 'A Governance Perspective on the European Neighbourhood Policy: Integration beyond Conditionality?' (2008) 15 *Journal of European Public Policy* 938.
——, 'Concentric Circles of Flexible "EUropean" Integration: A Typology of EU External Governance Relations' (2011) 9 *Comparative European Politics* 372.
——, 'The External Face of Differentiated Integration: Third Country Participation in EU Sectoral Bodies' (2015) 22 *Journal of European Public Policy* 836.
Łazowski, A, 'Enhanced Multilateralism and Enhanced Bilateralism: Integration without Membership in the European Union' (2008) 45 *Common Market Law Review* 1433.
Łazowski, A and Blockmans, S, 'Between Dream and Reality, Challenges to the Legal Rapprochement of the Western Balkans' in R Petrov and P Van Elsuwege, *Legislative Approximation and Application of EU Law in the Eastern Neighbourhood of the European Union: Towards a Common Regulatory Space?* (Routledge, 2014).
——, 'The End of Chocolate Box-Style Integration? EU–Swiss Relations after the Referendum' (2014) CEPS Policy Paper.
——, 'Mind the Fog, Stand Clear of the Cliff! From the Political Declaration to the Post-Brexit EU–UK Legal Framework – Part I' (2021) 5 *European Papers* 1105.
Leal-Arcas, R and Filis, A, 'The Energy Community and the Energy Charter Treaty: Special Legal Regimes, Their Systemic Relationship to the EU, and Their Dispute Settlement Arrangements' (2014) 12 *Oil, Gas & Energy Law Journal* 1.
Leinarte, E and Barnard, C, 'Negotiating Mutual Recognition Agreements: Challenges and Techniques' in A Albors-Llorens, C Barnard and B Leucht (eds), *Cassis de Dijon: 40 years on* (Hart Publishing, 2021).
Lelieur, I, *Law and Policy of Substantial Ownership and Effective Control of Airlines: Prospects for Change* (Routledge, 2003).
Lenaerts, K, 'The autonomy of European Union Law' (2019) Post ASIDUE, I Sezione 'Convegni annuali e interinali'.
Leuffen, D, Rittberger, B and Schimmelfennig, F, *Differentiated Integration: Explaining Variation in the European Union* (Palgrave MacMillan, 2013).
Levrat, N, 'Governance: Managing Bilateral Relations' *Brexit Institute Working Paper Series, No 10/2021.*
——, 'Profiter d'un Contexte Favorable Pour Renégocier Un Nouvel Accord-Cadre Avec FUE' (2021) Swiss Federal Department of Foreign Affairs.
Lewis, DG, *Russia's New Authoritarianism: Putin and the Politics of Order* (Edinburgh University Press, 2020).
Lewis, J, 'The Janus Face of Brussels: Socialization and Everyday Decision Making in the European Union' (2005) 59 *International Organization* 937.
Lindahl, H, 'Sovereignty and Representation in the European Union' in N Walker (ed), *Sovereignty in Transition* (Hart Publishing, 2003).
Lindahl, HK, 'Finding a Place for Freedom, Security and Justice: The European Union's Claim to Territorial Unity' (2004) 29 *European Law Review* 461.
Linde, F, 'The Civilizational Turn in Russian Political Discourse: From Pan-Europeanism to Civilizational Distinctiveness' (2016) 75 *The Russian Review* 604.

Linzell, S, 'Ownership and Control Restrictions in US Aviation Law' (2010) 35 *Air and Space Law* 379.
Lo, M, 'Relations Maroc-Afrique subsaharienne: quel bilan pour les 15 dernières années ?', (2016) *OCP Policy Center*.
Lobjakas, A, 'New Life For Eastern Neighborhood; EU: Poland, Sweden Breathe New Life Into Eastern Neighborhood' *RadioFreeEurope/RadioLiberty* (26 May 2008).
Loughlin, M, 'Ten Tenets of Sovereignty' in N Walker, *Sovereignty in transition* (Hart Publishing, 2003).
Louw-Vaudran, L, 'The Meaning of Morocco's Return to the African Union' (2018) Institute for Security Studies Africa.
MacCormick, N, 'Sovereignty and After' in H Kalmo and Q Skinner, *Sovereignty in Fragments: The Past, Present and Future of a Contested Concept* (Cambridge University Press, 2010).
Maduro, M, 'Three Claims of Constitutional Pluralism' in M Avbelj and J Komárek, *Constitutional pluralism in the European Union and beyond* (Hart Publishing, 2012).
Magen, A, 'The Shadow of Enlargement: Can the European Neighbourhood Policy Achieve Compliance' (2006) 12 *Columbia Journal of European Law* 383.
——, 'Transformative Engagement through Law: The Acquis Communautaire as an Instrument of EU External Influence' (2007) 9 *European Journal of Law Reform* 361.
Maiani, F, Petrov, R and Mouliarova, E, 'European Integration Without EU Membership: Models, Experiences, Perspectives' (2009) Working Paper.
Majone, G, 'From the Positive to the Regulatory State: Causes and Consequences of Changes in the Mode of Governance' (1997) 17 *Journal of Public Policy* 139.
——, 'European Integration and Its Modes: Function vs. Territory' TARN Working Paper No 2/2016.
Manners, I, 'Normative Power Europe: A Contradiction in Terms?' (2002) 40 *Journal of Common Market Studies* 235.
March, JG and Olsen, JP, 'The Institutional Dynamics of International Political Orders' (1998) 52 *International Organization* 943.
Marchetti, A, 'Of Borders and Boundaries The Neighbourhood as the EU's Buffer Zone' in T Schumacher, A Marchetti and T Demmelhuber, *The Routledge handbook on the European neighbourhood policy* (Routledge, 2018).
Maresceau, M, 'Integration Oriented Elements in Bilateral Agreements Concluded by the EU with Third States: A Few Examples' speech delivered in Nicosia (24 June 2010).
——, 'Turkey: A Candidate State Destined to Join the Union' in N Nic Shuibhne and LW Gormley, *From Single Market to Economic Union: Essays in Memory of John A. Usher* (Oxford University Press, 2012).
——, 'Les Accords d'intégration Dans Les Rélations de Proximité de l'Union Europeénne' in C Blumann, *Les frontières de l'Union européenne* (Bruylant, 2013).
Maresceau, M and Tobler, C, *Switzerland and the EU, a challenging relationship* (Brill Nijhoff, 2023).
Mariani, P and Sacerdoti, G, 'Trade in Goods and Level Playing Field' in F Fabbrini (ed), *The Law & Politics of Brexit: Volume III* (Oxford University Press, 2021).
Mark, K and Vasiliki, P, 'From Brexit to Eternity: The Institutional Landscape under the EU–UK Trade and Cooperation Agreement' (*European Law Blog*, 14 January 2021).
Martín, I, 'The EU Has Strengthened Its Relations with Morocco, but Not to the Extent Required to Bring about Real Change in the Country' (*EUROPP – London School of Economics*, 2014).
Martìnez Escamilla, M and et al, '"Hot Returns": When the State Acts Outside the Law' (2014) IUSMIGRANTE, Legal Report.
Mbengue, MM and Schacherer, S, *Africa and the Rethinking of International Investment Law: About the Elaboration of the Pan-African Investment Code* (Oxford University Press, 2018).
Mearsheimer, JJ, 'The Case for a Ukrainian Nuclear Deterrent' *Foreign Affairs* (1 June 1993).
Medicins Sans Frontières, 'Violence, Vulnerability and Migration: Trapped at the Gates of Europe' (13 March 2013).
Melo Araujo, B, 'An Analysis of the UK Government's Defence of the Northern Ireland Protocol Bill under International Law' (2022) 73 *Northern Ireland Legal Quarterly* 89.
Milano, E, 'The New Fisheries Partnership Agreement between the European Community and Morocco: Fishing Too South?' (2006) *XXII Anuario español de derecho internacional* 413.

Minder, R, 'Spain, Seeking Better Ties With Morocco, Shifts Stance on Western Sahara' *The New York Times* (19 March 2022).

Misa, TJ and Schot, J, 'Inventing Europe: Technology and the Hidden Integration of Europe' (2005) 21 *History and Technology* 1.

Mitrany, D, 'The Prospect of Integration: Federal or Functional' (1965) 4 *Journal of Common Market Studies* 119.

Molina, IF, *Moroccan Foreign Policy Under Mohammed VI, 1999–2014* (Routledge, 2016).

Morandi, V et al, 'EU–US Open Skies Agreement: What Is Changed in the North Transatlantic Skies?' (2014) 53 *Transportation Journal* 305.

Moreno-Lax, V and Costello, C, 'The Extraterritorial Application of the EU Charter of Fundamental Rights: From Territoriality to Facticity, the Effectiveness Model' in S Peers et al (eds), *The EU Charter of Fundamental Rights: A Commentary* (Hart Publishing, 2014).

Moroccan Ministry of Finance, 'Relations Maroc–Afrique L'ambition d'une Nouvelle Frontière' Direction des Etudes et des Prévisions Financières (July 2015).

Morris, M, 'A Level Playing Field for Workers: The Future of Employment Rights Post-Brexit' [2018] Institute for Public Policy Research.

Mrabet, EA, 'Readmission Agreements. The Case of Morocco' (2003) 5 *European Journal of Migration and Law* 379.

Murray, B, 'As West Battles China, a Trade Ally Tries to Keep Both Doors Open' *Bloomberg* (22 June 2023).

Murray, CRG and Robb N, 'From the Protocol to the Windsor Framework' (2023) 74 *Northern Ireland Legal Quarterly* 1.

Natorski, M, 'CIDOB – The Meda Programme in Morocco 12 Years on: Results, Experiences and Trends.' (CIDOB edicion 2008).

Natter K, 'The Formation of Morocco's Policy Towards Irregular Migration (2000–2007): Political Rationale and Policy Processes' (2014) 52 *International Migration* 15.

——, 'Crafting a "Liberal Monarchy": Regime Consolidation and Immigration Policy Reform in Morocco' (2021) *The Journal of North African Studies* 850.

Negri, A, 'Sovereignty between Government, Exception and Governance' in H Kalmo and Q Skinner (eds), *Sovereignty in Fragments: The Past, Present and Future of a Contested Concept* (Cambridge University Press, 2010).

Nell, PG, *Suisse–Communauté européenne – au coeur des négociations sur l'Espace économique européen* (Economica, 2012).

Nicolaidis, K, 'Schroedinger's Backstop' *Verfassungsblog* (4 September 2019).

Nolte, G, 'Case 12/86, Meryem Demirel v. Stadt Schwäbisch Gmünd, Judgment of 30 September 1987' (1988) 25 *Common Market Law Review* 403.

Norberg, S, 'The European Economic Area' in P Oliver and S Enchelmaier, *Oliver on free movement of goods in the European Union* (Hart Publishing, 2010).

Norberg, S and Johansson, M, 'The History of the EEA Agreement and the First Twenty Years of Its Existence' in C Baudenbacher, *The Handbook of EEA Law* (Springer, 2016).

Norman, KP, 'Between Europe and Africa: Morocco as a Country of Immigration' (2016) 7 *The Journal of the Middle East and Africa* 421.

Öberg, M-L, 'Expanding the EU Internal Market without Enlarging the Union: Constitutional Limitations' (Phd Thesis, European University Institute 2015).

——, 'Autonomy of the EU Legal Order: A Concept in Need of Revision?' (2020) 26 *European Public Law* 705.

——, *The Boundaries of the EU Internal Market: Participation without Membership* (Cambridge University Press, 2020).

O'Carrol, L, Elgot, J and Rankin, J, 'UK Says It Wants to Substantially Rewrite Northern Ireland Protocol' *The Guardian* (21 July 2021).

Odermatt, J, 'When a Fence Becomes a Cage: The Principle of Autonomy in EU External Relations Law' (2016) *EUI Working Paper*.

——, 'Council of the European Union v. Front Populaire Pour La Libération de La Saguia-El-Hamra et Du Rio de Oro (Front Polisario)' (2017) 111 *American Journal of International Law* 731.

Okyay, A and Zaragoza-Cristiani, J, 'The Leverage of the Gatekeeper: Power and Interdependence in the Migration Nexus between the EU and Turkey' (2016) 51 *The International Spectator* 51.

Olearchyk, R, 'Moscow Lures Ukraine with Cheap Gas' *Financial Times* (7 April 2011).

Ott, A, 'The EU–Turkey Association and Other EU Parallel Legal Orders in the European Legal Space' (2015) 42 *Legal Issues of Economic Integration* 5.

——, 'Free Movement Rights in an Enlarged European Union' in B de Witte, A Ott and E Vos, *Between flexibility and disintegration: the trajectory of differentiation in EU law* (Edward Elgar, 2017).

——, 'The Building Blocks and Stumbling Stones of Constructing the European Legal Space' in WT Douma et al (eds), *The Evolving Nature of EU External Relations Law* (Springer, 2021).

Pascual, J, 'Paris et Rabat, aux frontières de la discorde' *Le Monde* (6 October 2023).

Passos, R, 'Legal Aspects of the European Union's Approach towards Western Sahara' in M Balboni and G Laschi (eds), *The European Union approach towards Western Sahara* (PIE Peter Lang, 2017).

Pedreschi, L and Scott, J, 'External Differentiated Integration: Legal Feasibility and Constitutional Acceptability' [2020] EUI RCAS 2020/54.

Peers, S, 'Living in Sin: Legal Integration Under the EC–Turkey Customs Union' (1996) 7 *European Journal of International Law* 411.

——, 'The EU's Political Institutions' in S Peers and C Barnard, *European Union Law* (Oxford University Press, 2020).

—— 'EU Law Analysis: The Windsor Framework: Limiting the Scope of EU Law in Northern Ireland in Practice, Though Not in Theory (Part 1)' *EU Law Analysis* (4 March 2023).

—— 'EU Law Analysis: Just Say No? The New "Stormont Brake" in the Windsor Framework (Part 2 of the Analysis of the Framework)' *EU Law Analysis* (5 March 2023).

Pérez Crespo, MJ, 'After Brexit … The Best of Both Worlds? Rebutting the Norwegian and Swiss Models as Long-Term Options for the UK' (2017) 36 *Yearbook of European Law* 94.

Pescatore, P, *The Law of Integration: Emergence of a New Phenomenon in International Relations, Based on the Experience of the European Communities* (Sijthoff, 1974).

——, 'Some Thoughts on the Allocation of Power in the External Relations Field' in A Bleckmann and Universiteit van Amsterdam Europa Instituut, *Division of powers between the European communities and their member states in the field of external relations : colloquium, 30 and 31 May 1980, Amsterdam* (Kluwer, 1981).

——, 'Die Rechtsprechung Des EuGH Zur Innergemeinschaftlichen Wirkung Völkerrechtlicher Abkommen: Festschrift Für Hermann Mosler' in R Bernhardt et al, (1983) *Völkerrecht als Rechtsordnung. Internationale Gerichtsbarkeit. Menschenrechte.*

Petrov, R, 'Energy Community As a Promoter of the European Union's Energy Acquis to Its Neighbourhood' (2012) 39 *Legal issues of Economic Integration* 331.

——, 'Challenges of the EU–Ukraine AA's Effective Implementation into the Legal Order of Ukraine' in S Lorenzmeier, R Petrov and C Vedder (eds), *EU External Relations Law: Shared Competences and Shared Values in Agreements Between the EU and Its Eastern Neighbourhood* (Springer, 2021).

Petrov, R and Hillion, C, 'Guest Editorial: "Accession through War" – Ukraine's Road to the EU' (2022) 59 *Common Market Law Review* 1289.

Petti, A, 'ERTA and Us: Shifting Constitutional Equilibria on the Visions of Europe' (2021) 6 *European Papers* 567.

——, 'The Polisario saga: the principle of good administration and the interface between EU law and international law' in D Fromage (ed), *Jacques Ziller an European Scholar* (EUI Cadmus, 2022).

Phinnemore, D, 'Stabilisation and Association Agreements: Europe Agreements for the Western Balkans?' (2003) 8 *European Foreign Affairs Review* 90.

Piet, E, *EU External Relations Law*, 2nd edn (Oxford University Press, 2011).

Pijnenburg, A, 'Containment Instead of Refoulement: Shifting State Responsibility in the Age of Cooperative Migration Control?' (2020) 20 *Human Rights Law Review* 306.

Pirker, B, 'Switzerland and the EEA', in Arnesen F et al, *Agreement on the European Economic Area* (CH Beck, 2018).
Pomorska, K, 'The Impact of Enlargement: Europeanisation of Polish Foreign Policy? Tracking Adaptation and Change in the Ministry of Foreign Affairs' (2007) 2 *The Hague Journal of Diplomacy* 25.
Post, R, 'Constructing the European Polity: ERTA and the Open Skies Judgments' in Poiares Maduro and L Azoulai, *The past and future of EU law : the classics of EU law revisited on the 50th anniversary of the Rome Treaty* (Hart Publishing, 2010).
Puetter, U, *The European Council and the Council: New Intergovernmentalism and Institutional Change* (Oxford University Press, 2014).
Quaglia, L, De Francesco, F and Radaelli, CM, 'Committee Governance and Socialization in the European Union' (2008) 15 *Journal of European Public Policy* 155.
Radio Sweden, 'Sweden Softens Line on Western Sahara Recognition in Face of Boycott Threat – Radio Sweden' (2 October 2015).
Rapoport, C, *Les partenariats entre l'Union européenne et les États tiers européens: étude de la contribution de l'Union européenne à la structuration juridique de l'espace européen* (Bruylant, 2011).
——, 'Balancing on a Tightrope: Opinion 1/17 and the ECJ's Narrow and Tortuous Path for Compatibility of the EU's Investment Court System (ICS)' (2020) 57 *Common Market Law Review* 1725.
——, 'Autonomy of the EU Legal Order and International Agreements Extending the Acquis: Opinion 1/00 (European Common Aviation Area)' in G Butler and RA Wessel, *EU External Relations Law: The Cases in Context* (Hart Publishing, 2022).
Rasmussen, M, 'Revolutionizing European Law: A History of the Van Gend En Loos Judgment' (2014) 12 *International Journal of Constitutional Law* 136.
Reyes, CL, 'WTO-Compliant Protection of Fundamental Rights: Lessons from the EU Privacy Directive' (2011) 12 *Melbourne Journal of International Law* 141.
Reymond, C, 'Institutions, Decision-Making Procedure and Settlement of Disputes in the European Economic Area' (1993) 30 *Common Market Law Review* 449.
Richefeu, L, 'Le droit pénal face à la migration transfrontière' (Université Panthéon-Sorbonne – Paris I, 2, 2018).
Roberts, A, Is International Law International? (Oxford University Press, 2017).
Roig, A and Huddleston, T, 'EC Readmission Agreements: A Re-Evaluation of the Political Impasse.' (2007) 9 *European Journal of Migration & Law.*
Romano, S, *The Legal Order* (Mariano Croce tr) (Taylor & Francis, 2017).
——, *L'ordinamento Giuridico (1st Edition, 1917–18 Annali Delle Università Toscane)* (Quodlibet, 2018).
Rossi, LS, 'EU Citizenship and the Free Movement of Heads of State: Hungary v. Slovak Republic' (2013) 50 *Common Market Law Review* 1451.
Ruggie, JG, 'What Makes the World Hang Together? Neo-Utilitarianism and the Social Constructivist Challenge' (1998) 52 *International Organization* 855.
Rumelili, B, 'Constructing Identity and Relating to Difference: Understanding the EU's Mode of Differentiation' (2004) 30 *Review of International Studies* 27.
Salem, ZOA, 'Mauritania: A Saharan Frontier-State' (2005) 10 *The Journal of North African Studies* 491.
Sam, J, 'Hundreds Storm Border Fence into Spain's North Africa Enclave of Ceuta' *The Guardian* (26 July 2018).
Sasse, G, 'The European Neighbourhood Policy: Conditionality Revisited for the EU's Eastern Neighbours' (2008) 60 *Europe-Asia Studies* 295.
Schadlow, N, 'The Denuclearization of Ukraine: Consolidating Ukrainian Security' (1996) 20 *Harvard Ukrainian Studies* 271.
Scharpf, FW, 'The Asymmetry of European Integration, or Why the EU Cannot Be a "Social Market Economy"' (2010) 8 *Socio-Economic Review* 211.
Schiavone, A, 'Limes, La Politica Dei Confini Dell'impero Romano' *Frontiere: politiche e mitologie dei confini europei* (Istituto Italiano di Scienze Umane, 2003).

Schimmelfennig, F, 'Transnational Socialization Community-Building in an Integrated Europe' in W Kaiser and P Starie, *Transnational European Union: Towards a Common Political Space* (Taylor & Francis, 2005).

——, 'EU Enlargement and Differentiated Integration: Discrimination or Equal Treatment?' (2014) 21 *Journal of European Public Policy* 681.

Schimmelfennig, F, Leuffen, D and Rittberger, B, 'The European Union as a System of Differentiated Integration: Interdependence, Politicization and Differentiation' (2015) 22 *Journal of European Public Policy* 764.

Schimmelfennig, F and Sedelmeier, U, 'Governance by Conditionality: EU Rule Transfer to the Candidate Countries of Central and Eastern Europe' (2004) 11 *Journal of European Public Policy* 661.

Schimmelfennig, F and Winzen, T, *Ever Looser Union?: Differentiated European Integration* (Oxford University Press, 2020).

Schmidt, SK, 'No Match Made in Heaven. Parliamentary Sovereignty, EU over-Constitutionalization and Brexit' (2020) 27 *Journal of European Public Policy* 779.

Schmitt von Sydow, H, 'Die Paneuropäische Energiegemeinschaft Mit Südosteuropa', *Die Herausforderung von Grenzen – Le défi des frontières – Challenging Boundaries: Festschrift/Mélanges en l'honeur de/Essays in honor of Roland Bieber* (Nomos, 2013).

Schumacher, T, 'Back to the Future: The "New" ENP towards the Southern Neighbourhood and the End of Ambition' (2016) College of Europe Policy Brief.

Schuman, R, 'The Schuman Declaration – 9 May 1950' (European Union), europa.eu/european-union/about-eu/symbols/europe-day/schuman-declaration_en.

Scott, J, 'Extraterritoriality and Territorial Extension in EU Law' (2014) 62 *The American Journal of Comparative Law* 87.

——, 'The New EU "Extraterritoriality"' (2014) 51 *Common Market Law Review* 1343.

——, 'The Global Reach of EU Law' in M Cremona and J Scott, *The Global Reach of EU Law* (Oxford University Press, 2019).

Semertzi, A, 'The Preclusion of Direct Effect in the Recently Concluded EU Free Trade Agreements' (2014) 51 *Common Market Law Review* 1125.

Sergejcev, T, 'What Should Russia Do with Ukraine? – RIA Novosti' *Medium* (11 April 2022).

Shane, PM, 'The Rule of Law and the Inevitability of Discretion' (2013) 36 *Harvard Journal of Law & Public Policy* 21.

Sharpston, E, 'Different but (Almost) Equal – The Development of Free Movement Rights under EU Association, Co-Operation and Accession Agreements' in M Hoskins and R William (eds), *A True European : Essays for Judge David Edward* (Hart Publishing, 2003).

Shyrokykh, K and Rimkutė, D, 'EU Rules Beyond Its Borders: The Policy-Specific Effects of Transgovernmental Networks and EU Agencies in the European Neighbourhood' (2019) 26 *Journal of Common Market Studies* 749.

Slaughter A-M, 'In Memoriam: Abram Chayes' (2001) 114 *Harvard Law Review* 682.

Slot, PJ and Dutheil de la Rochère, J, '(Open Skies Judgments) Judgments of the Full Court of 5 November 2002.' (2003) 40 *Common Market Law Review* 697.

Smith, M, 'The European Union and a Changing Europe: Establishing the Boundaries of Order' (1996) 34 *Journal of Common Market Studies* 5.

Snyder, T, *The Reconstruction of Nations: Poland, Ukraine, Lithuania, Belarus, 1569–1999* Yale University Press, 2004).

——, *Bloodlands: Europe between Hitler and Stalin* (Bodley Head, 2010).

——, *The Road to Unfreedom: Russia, Europe, America* (Tim Duggan Books, 2018).

——, 'Russia's Genocide Handbook' (*Thinking about …*, 8 April 2022).

——, 'The War in Ukraine Is a Colonial War' *The New Yorker* (28 April 2022).

Somek, A, 'The Argument from Transnational Effects I: Representing Outsiders through Freedom of Movement' (2010) 16 *European Law Journal* 315.

Stephan, PB, *Comparative International Law, Foreign Relations Law, and Fragmentation: Can the Center Hold?* (Oxford University Press, 2018).

Stevis-Gridneff, M and Erlanger, S, 'Hungary Blocks Ukraine Aid After E.U. Opens Door to Membership' *The New York Times* (14 December 2023).

Suárez-Collado, Á and Contini, D, 'The European Court of Justice on the EU–Morocco Agricultural and Fisheries Agreements: An Analysis of the Legal Proceedings and Consequences for the Actors Involved' (2021) 26 *The Journal of North African Studies* 1.

Suslov, M, '"Russian World" Concept: Post-Soviet Geopolitical Ideology and the Logic of "Spheres of Influence"' (2018) 23 *Geopolitics* 330.

Takac, K, Nitsovych, R and Pavlenko, O, 'Reforming Ukraine's Energy Sector: Critical Unfinished Business' *Carnegie Europe* (6 February 2018).

Talseth, L-CU, *The Politics of Power EU–Russia Energy Relations in the 21st Century* (Springer, 2017).

Tassinari, F, *Why Europe Fears Its Neighbors* (ABC-CLIO, LLC 2009).

Tatham, AF, 'Diffusing EU Law beyond the Borders of the Union: The Judicialization of the European Trading Area' (2014) 81 *Colombia Internacional* 27.

Tezcan Idriz, N, 'Family Reunification under the Standstill Clauses of EU–Turkey Association Law: *Genc*' (2017) 54 *Common Market Law Review* 263.

Thym, D, 'Foreign Affairs' in von Bogdandy, A and Bast, J, *Principles of European constitutional law* (Hart Publishing, 2010).

Tittel-Mosser, F, 'The Unintended Legal and Policy Relevance of EU Mobility Partnerships: A Comparative Implementation Analysis of Morocco and Cape Verde' (2018) 20 *European Journal of Migration and Law* 314.

——, 'Reversed Conditionality in EU External Migration Policy: The Case of Morocco' (2018) 14 *Journal of Contemporary European Research* 349.

——, 'Mobility Partnerships: A Tool for the Externalisation of EU Migration Policy? A Comparative Study of Morocco and Cape Verde' in S Carrera, J Santos Vara and M Hermina Antonia Strik, *Constitutionalising the External Dimensions of EU Migration Policies in Times of Crisis* (Edward Elgar Publishing, 2019).

Tobler, C, 'A Look at the EEA from Switzerland' in EFTA Court, *The EEA and the EFTA court : decentred integration* (Hart Publishing 2014).

——, 'Context-Related Interpretation of Association Agreements. The Polydor Principle in a Comparative Perspective: Eea Law, Ankara Association Law and Market Access Agreements between Switzerland and the Eu' in D Thym and M Zoeteweij-Turhan, *Rights of Third-Country Nationals under EU Association Agreements: Degrees of Free Movement and Citizenship* (Brill, 2015).

——, 'Free Movement of Persons in the EU v. in the EEA: Of Effect-Related Homogeneity and a Reversed Polydor Principle' (2019) 3 *European Papers* 1429.

——, 'Switzerland–EU: Whereto with the Draft Institutional Agreement?' *EFTA-Studies* (19 February 2020), www.efta-studies.org/post/whereto-with-the-draft-institutional-agreement.

——, 'The EU–Swiss Sectoral Approach Under Pressure: Not Least Because of Brexit' in S Lorenzmeier, R Petrov and C Vedder (eds), *EU External Relations Law: Shared Competences and Shared Values in Agreements Between the EU and Its Eastern Neighbourhood* (Springer, 2021).

Tobler, C, Hardenbol, J and Mellár, B, 'Nternal Market beyond the EU: EEA and Switzerland' (2010) European Parliament, PE 429.993.

Tocci, N, 'Can the EU Promote Democracy and Human Rights Trough the ENP? The Case for Refocusing on the Rule of Law' in M Cremona and G Meloni, *The European Neighbourhood Policy: A Framework for Modernisation?*, European University Institute, No 2007/21.

——, 'Turkey and the European Union, A Journey in the Unknown' (2014) Turkey Project Policy Paper Brookings.

Toal, G, *Near Abroad: Putin, the West and the Contest over Ukraine and the Caucasus* (Oxford University Press, 2017).

Trimarchi, A, 'Foreign Investment in National Air Carriers: Political Background, Legal Constraints, and Recent Developments' (2018) 17 *Issues in aviation law and policy* 237.

Trubek, DM, Cottrell, P and Nance, M, '"Soft Law", "Hard Law" and EU Integration' in G De Búrca and J Scott, *Law and New Governance in the EU and the US* (Hart Publishing, 2006).

Tulmets, E, 'Institution-Building Instruments in the Eastern Partnership: Still Drawing on Enlargement?' (2011) 6 *Eastern Partnership Review* 6.
'United States Recognizes Morocco's Sovereignty Over Western Sahara' (2021) 115 *American Journal of International Law* 318.
Vahl, M and Grolimund, N, *Integration without Membership: Switzerland's Bilateral Agreements with the European Union* (CEPS, 2006).
Vahl, M and van der Loo, G, 'Enhancing the Prospects of the EU's Deep and Comprehensive Free Trade Areas in the Mediterranean: Lessons from the Eastern Partnership' (2015) CEPS Commentary Centre for European Policy Studies.
——, *The EU–Ukraine Association Agreement and Deep and Comprehensive Free Trade Area : A New Legal Instrument for EU Integration without Membership* (Brill Nijhoff, 2016).
——, 'Mapping out the Scope and Contents of the DCFTAs with Tunisia and Morocco' [2016] IEMed–EuroMeSCo.
——, 'The Dilemma of the EU's Future Trade Relations with Western Sahara: Caught between Strategic Interests and International Law?' *Centre for European Policy Studies* (20 April 2018).
van der Vleuten, E and Kaijser, A, 'Networking Europe' (2005) 21 *History & Technology* 21.
van Elsuwege, P and Petrov, R, 'Article 8 TEU: Towards a New Generation of Agreements with the Neighbouring Countries of the European Union?' (2011) 36 *European Law Review* 688.
van Elsuwege, P and Van der Loo, G, 'Continuity and Change in the Legal Relations Between the EU and Its Neighbours: A Result of Path Dependency and Spill-over Effects' in D Bouris and T Schumacher (eds), *The revised European neighbourhood policy: continuity and change in EU foreign policy* (Palgrave Macmillan, 2017).
van Middelaar, L, *The Passage to Europe : How a Continent Became a Union* (Yale University Press, 2013).
——, *Le réveil géopolitique de l'Europe* (Collège de France, 2022).
van Rossem, JW, 'The Autonomy of EU Law: More Is Less?' in RA Wessel and S Blockmans (eds), *Between Autonomy and Dependence: The EU Legal Order under the Influence of International Organisations* (TMC Asser Press, 2013).
Van Vooren, B, *EU External Relations Law and the European Neighbourhood Policy: A Paradigm for Coherence* (Taylor and Francis, 2012).
Vianello, I, 'EU External Action and the Administrative Rule of Law: A Long-Overdue Encounter' (PhD thesis, European University Institute, 2016).
von Bogdandy, A, 'The Idea of European Public Law Today' in A von Bogdandy, PM Huber and S Cassese, *The Max Planck Handbooks in European Public Law* (Oxford University Press, 2017).
von der Bruchard, H and Eder, F, 'Switzerland Ends Talks on EU Partnership Treaty' (*POLITICO*, 26 May 2021).
Walker, N, 'The Sovereignty Surplus' (2020) 18 *International Journal of Constitutional Law* 370.
——, 'Late Sovereignty in the European Union', *Sovereignty in transition* (Hart Publishing, 2003).
Wallace, W, 'Where Does Europe Ends? Dilemmas of Inclusion and Exclusion' in J Zielonka (ed), *Europe unbound: enlarging and reshaping the boundaries of the European Union* (2002).
Warren, ME, 'The All Affected Interests Principle in Democratic Theory and Practice' [2010] Institute for Advanced Studies, Vienna.
Wassenbergh, H, 'The Decision of the ECJ of 5 November 2002 in the "Open Skies" Agreements Cases' (2003) 28 *Air Space Law* 19.
Weatherill, S, 'The Several Internal Markets' (2017) 36 *Yearbook of European Law* 125.
——, 'The Protocol on Ireland/Northern Ireland: Protecting the EU's Internal Market at the Expense of the UK's' (2020) 45 *European Law Review* 222.
Webber, J and Bounds, A, 'New EU Arsenic Rules Catch Northern Ireland between Brussels and London' *Financial Times* (9 March 2023).
Weber, B, 'The European Neighbourhood Policy and Energy' in T Schumacher, A Marchetti and T Demmelhuber (eds), *The Routledge handbook on the European neighbourhood policy* (Routledge, 2018).

Weiler, JH, 'The Transformation of Europe' (1991) 100 *The Yale Law Journal* 2045.
Weiler, JHH, Sarmiento, D and Faull, J, 'An Offer the EU and UK Cannot Refuse' *Verfassungsblog* (22 August 2019).
Werner, W and De Wilde, J, 'The Endurance of Sovereignty' (2001) 7 *European Journal of International Relations* 283.
Wessel, RA, 'Normative Transformations in EU External Relations: The Phenomenon of "Soft" International Agreements' (2021) 44 *West European Politics* 72.
Wilde, R, 'Dilemmas in Promoting Global Economic Justice through Human Rights Law' in N Bhuta (ed), *The Frontiers of Human Rights* (Oxford University Press, 2016).
Wolczuk, K, 'Managing the Flows of Gas and Rules: Ukraine between the EU and Russia' (2016) 57 *Eurasian Geography and Economics* 113.
Wolff, S, 'The Politics of Negotiating EU Readmission Agreements: Insights from Morocco and Turkey' (2014) 16 *European Journal of Migration and Law* 69.
Wrange, P, Bring, O and Mahmoudi, S, 'International Law Allows the Recognition of Western Sahara' (Stockholm Centre for Internation Law and Justice, 7 November 2015).
——, 'Self-Determination, Occupation and the Authority to Exploit Natural Resources: Trajectories from Four European Judgments on Western Sahara' (2019) 52 *Israel Law Review* 3.
——, 'Western Sahara, the European Commission and the Politics of International Legal Argument' in A Duval and E Kassoti, *The legality of economic activities in occupied territories : international, EU law and business and human rights perspectives* (Routledge, 2020).
Wrange, P, Bring, O and Mahmoudi, S, 'International Law Allows the Recognition of Western Sahara' (Stockholm Centre for Internation Law and Justice, 7 November 2015).
Wunderlich, D, 'Differentiation and Policy Convergence against Long Odds: Lessons from Implementing EU Migration Policy in Morocco' (2010) 15 *Mediterranean Politics* 249.
Zielonka, J, *Explaining Euro-Paralysis: Why Europe Is Unable to Act in International Politics* (Springer, 1998).
——, *Europe as Empire* (Oxford University Press, 2006).
Ziller, J, 'Sovereignty in France: Getting Rid of the Mal de Bodin' in N Walker, *Sovereignty in transition* (Hart Publishing, 2003).

INDEX

www.ingramcontent.com/pod-product-compliance
Ingram Content Group UK Ltd.
Pitfield, Milton Keynes, MK11 3LW, UK
UKHW021033041026
15470UKWH00014B/1556

9 781509 966653